PERICLEANS, PLUMBERS AND PRACTITIONERS

About the Authors

Fay Woodhouse is an historian and biographer who aims to capture and bring alive a sense of the people and the times she writes about. She has published widely and has been commissioned to write histories of businesses, universities and community organisations. Fay is also the Victorian researcher for *The Australian Dictionary of Biography* and is an Honorary Research Fellow in the School of Historical and Philosophical Studies at the University of Melbourne. Her recent publications include *The Story Behind the Stripe: The 100 Year History of d'Arenberg Wines* and *Vintage Stories: The 150 Year History of Tahbilk*. She is currently writing the sixty-year history of Melbourne's first yoga school, the Gita School of Yoga.

Peter Yule is a Research Fellow of the School of Historical and Philosophical Studies at the University of Melbourne. He has written widely on Australian economic, business and medical history, with his recent books including biographies of Sir Ian Potter and W.L. Baillieu, and histories of Carlton, the Collins Class submarine project and Australian National Airways. He is currently writing a biography of Air Marshal Sir James Rowland and contributing to a major new multi-volume history of Australia in the First World War.

PERICLEANS, PLUMBERS AND PRACTITIONERS

The First Fifty Years of the Monash Law School

PETER YULE AND FAY WOODHOUSE

MONASH University
Publishing

Monash University Publishing
Building 4, Monash University
Clayton, Victoria 3800, Australia
www.publishing.monash.edu

Monash University Publishing brings to the world publications which advance the best traditions of humane and enlightened thought.

Monash University Publishing titles pass through a rigorous process of independent peer review.

http://www.publishing.monash.edu/books/ppp-9781922235411.html

Series: Law

Design: Les Thomas

Cover image: Professor Gerard Nash being escorted to the Nott. Photographer unknown. Image reproduced courtesy of the Monash University Archives (Monpix image 842).

National Library of Australia Cataloguing-in-Publication entry:

Author:	Yule, Peter, author.
Title:	Pericleans, plumbers and practitioners : the first fifty years of the Monash Law School / Peter Yule and Fay Woodhouse.
ISBN:	9781922235411 (paperback)
Subjects:	Monash University. Faculty of Law--History. Law schools--Victoria--Melbourne--History. Law--Study and teaching (Higher)--Victoria.

Other Authors/Contributors: Woodhouse, Fay, author.
Dewey Number: 340.07119451

Contents

PART THREE: THE TWO BOBS – BOB BAXT AND BOB WILLIAMS, 1980–98

PART FOUR: THE MONASH LAW SCHOOL IN THE 21ST CENTURY

Acknowledgements

Soon after we were commissioned to write the history of the Monash University Faculty of Law, one of us was chatting with a distinguished professor from the University of Cambridge Law School. 'And what do you do?' asked the great man. 'I'm writing a history of the Monash Law School', I stuttered nervously. 'Harrumph', he snorted derisively, 'And how old is this law school?' 'Fifty years' I replied. Again a 'Harrumph' followed by the statement, 'I understand Oxford did a history for their eight hundred and fiftieth anniversary, but we're waiting for our thousandth.'

Monash Law School is indeed young in global terms. The three top-ranked law schools in the QS world rankings for 2013–14 – Harvard, Oxford and Cambridge – have a combined age of about 1800 years. In a sense, this emphasises one of Monash's greatest achievements, because the same rankings place the Monash Law School solidly in the world's top twenty law schools. To have risen from the lowly status of a law school primarily for students who were unable to get into Melbourne Law School to be in the world's top twenty within fifty years is truly remarkable. Equally remarkable was the milestone achieved in the early 2000s when every senior law officer in Victoria – the Chief Justice, Chief Judge of the County Court, Chief Magistrate, Chief Magistrate of the Children's Court, President of VCAT, Solicitor-General and State Coroner – was a Monash alumnus.

Of course, the history of the law school has not been simply a matter of one glorious achievement after another. There have been lows among the highs – recurrent financial crises, personality and policy clashes, poor behaviour (by staff as well as students), and the myriad problems of student life in a large and impersonal university. And through it all has been the endless teaching of Crime, Torts, Property, Contracts and the rest to ever-increasing numbers of students.

We were delighted to be commissioned to write the fiftieth anniversary history of the Monash Law School. It turned out to be more challenging than we expected, but it has been a fascinating and rewarding experience. Although we are responsible for the final product (and of course, all errors and omissions are our fault alone), this history could not have been written without the help of many people. We are grateful to the faculty's history committee – Jeff Goldsworthy, Marilyn Pittard, Simon Smith, Graeme Davison and Greg Taylor – for commissioning us to write the history and for their constant support and encouragement. The faculty's elder statesmen – Louis Waller, Richard Fox, H P Lee and Christie Weeramantry – all shared willingly their vast knowledge of the faculty from its earliest days. In the course of our research we interviewed over 100 past and present staff and students and we thank them all. They were chosen by a mixture of serendipity and totally unscientific selection. A large number were self-selected, with many former students responding to our request for their stories – a special thanks to Denis Liner and Nahum Mushin, who were the first to contact us, and to Harry Reicher for his series of eloquent emails from America.

We are grateful that we were able to speak with all the living deans of the law school – Louis Waller, Gerry Nash, Bob Baxt, Bob Williams, Stephen Parker, Arie Frieberg and Bryan Horrigan – and thank them all for their willingness to discuss the problems they encountered as well as their many successes. We have been made most welcome in the law school by both the academic and professional staff and many people have gone out of their way to assist us. Similarly, Jan Getson and Lynette Maloney in the Monash University Archives helped us in many ways and were generous with both time and expertise. McKinley Valentine edited the manuscript with skill and discretion and we thank her for her fine work. Finally, we are grateful to Nathan Hollier, Kate Hatch and the staff at Monash University Publishing for agreeing to publish the book and their great professionalism in its production.

PART ONE

THE FORMATIVE YEARS

Chapter 1

The Foundation of the Monash University Law School

In 1953, the newly appointed professor of jurisprudence at the University of Melbourne, David Derham, travelled to Britain and the United States to study the teaching of law. He was shocked by the generally poor quality of legal education in Britain. Unusually for a Melbourne law professor, he had not studied at Oxford, and he was surprised at the deficiencies he saw even at that august institution. He was far more impressed with the leading American law schools, admiring their lavish facilities and innovative teaching methods. They formed the benchmark he believed that Australian law schools should aspire to. A decade later, Derham was appointed foundation dean of the Monash University law school, taking on the task of establishing a new law school on a desolate building site in Melbourne's uninspiring outer eastern suburbs. Derham himself feared that he was 'mad' to take on the task, and few expected the new law school to be anything more than an 'overflow' school for the University of Melbourne law school. Yet within 20 years Monash was generally regarded as one of the three best law schools in Australia, and by almost any measure superior to Melbourne. Within 50 years Monash was ranked as the 13th best law school in the world, ahead of all but five of the American law schools that had so impressed David Derham in 1953.[1]

In 1937, another Melbourne law professor, Kenneth Bailey, had also visited Britain and the United States to study the teaching of law. The deeper purpose of his trip was to provide ammunition for a bitter struggle he was having with the Law Institute over the nature and purposes of legal education. For the Law Institute, the function of the law school was to give practical training in the law; for Bailey, the chief focus was on a broad liberal

---

1 http://www.topuniversities.com/university-rankings/university-subject-rankings/2013/law-and-legal-studies, accessed 15 June 2013. In the interests of balance, it should be noted that Melbourne law school ranked fifth in this list, behind only Harvard, Oxford, Cambridge and Yale.

education and 'the inculcation of first principles'.[2] The conflict was of central importance at Melbourne because, in contrast to many British and American law schools, its graduates had the right to practice the law subject only to the completion of articles. This had many advantages, but it also imposed on the law school the obligation to structure its courses around the compulsory subjects laid down by the Council of Legal Education, giving the profession a large influence in the shaping of the law course. But should this influence extend to making the law school into simply a technical training school for lawyers? Or should a university law school aspire to give its students a university education? Are law academics technical school teachers or are they true scholars? The conflict was not fully resolved at Melbourne in the 1930s and it did much to colour David Derham's thinking when he planned the Monash law school. Fundamentally, it is a debate that can never be fully resolved. It has been present in all law schools at all times, sometimes bubbling quietly under the surface, at other times erupting in fierce debate.

Law is the oldest university discipline. The University of Bologna is generally credited as the first university and it was founded in the late eleventh century with the sole purpose of teaching Roman law. Law was similarly the foundation discipline at most, if not all, medieval universities.[3] However, while law has always been a fundamental university discipline, the education of lawyers and the purposes of university law schools have been the subject of debate for many centuries. In European countries with legal systems based on Roman law, university training for lawyers became the norm as early as the 17th century. England, and later the English colonies that inherited the common law, followed a very different path. The universities of Oxford and Cambridge were both founded in the late 13th century and, like their continental counterparts, taught Roman law and canon law from their earliest years. However, there were no university examinations in English law until the late nineteenth century. The training given at Oxford and Cambridge qualified graduates only to practise in the Court of Admiralty and the ecclesiastical courts.[4] Consequently a gaping chasm developed between the law faculties at the English universities and the

---

2 John Waugh, *First Principles: The Melbourne Law School, 1857–2007*, Miegunyah Press, Melbourne, 2007, p. ix.

3 Marcia Colish, *Medieval Foundations of the Western Intellectual Tradition*, Yale University Press, 1997, p.269; and H de Ridder-Symoens (ed.), 'Universities in the Middle Ages', vol. 1 of *A History of the University in Europe*, Cambridge University Press, 1992, pp. 47–55, 388–407.

4 F H Lawson, *The Oxford Law School, 1850–1965*, Oxford University Press, Oxford, 1968, pp. 1–3.

legal profession. For many centuries, the vast majority of lawyers in England did not study contemporary law at university but received their legal training 'on the job', either articled to a solicitor or reading with a barrister.

The teaching of law at English universities was gradually reformed during the second half of the nineteenth century and English law slowly crept into the syllabus.[5] However, law as taught in the universities remained largely irrelevant for practitioners and university education in law was not required for admission to practice. The situation was generally the same in North America, Australia and New Zealand, with apprenticeship and self-education being the primary pathways to a career in the law.

The earliest and most important exception was the colony of Victoria. While the University of Sydney, established in 1851, taught law in a desultory fashion from the late 1850s, it was not until 1890 that a comprehensive law course was established and law graduates received exemption from some admission exams. Even a century later there was no requirement to have a university degree of any sort to become a member of the legal profession in New South Wales.[6] The situation was totally different in Victoria. The University of Melbourne was established in 1853 and the teaching of law began in 1857. From the outset graduates in law were exempted from the Supreme Court's entrance exams, making the law course attractive and relevant for aspiring lawyers.

Melbourne adopted this distinct and seemingly far-sighted position purely because of the personal interests of Justice Redmond Barry. A refugee from the overcrowded Irish Bar, Barry was both a judge of the Supreme Court, which made the admission rules, and the chancellor of the new university, which struggled to attract students in its early years. As chancellor Barry saw that an attractive law course could increase enrolments; as a Supreme Court judge he was in a position to persuade his two fellow judges to amend the admission rules to favour law graduates. For the university the changed rules proved highly advantageous and by the early 1860s law students made up over half the university's enrolments.[7] In 1872 the Supreme Court judges went further and made a Bachelor of Laws (LLB) from Melbourne, or some other university recognised by it, a prerequisite for admission to the bar. University graduates in law or arts were also able to reduce their time under articles from five years to three before becoming solicitors. This emphasis on

---

5 Ibid., p. 37.

6 John and Judy Mackinolty, *A Century Down Town: Sydney University Law School's First Hundred Years*, Sydney, 1991.

7 Waugh, *First Principles*, pp. 5–7.

university training for lawyers in Victoria was unique in the common law world. It was not until 1927 that any American state insisted that candidates for admission attend a law school and even today in England a law degree is not a prerequisite for admission.

But what sort of legal education should be provided at a university? One of the reasons for the lengthy delay in the establishment of a law school at the University of Sydney was an equally lengthy debate about the philosophy of legal education. Should a law school be a trade school for lawyers, concerned only with giving students the practical skills needed for legal practice, or should it strive to give a broad liberal education, with an emphasis on legal philosophy, history and ethics?[8] Was the lawyer, in W L Twining's memorable usage, like a Pericles, or was he just a plumber? On the one hand there is 'the image of the lawyer as Pericles – the law-giver, the enlightened policy maker, the wise judge [possessing] intellectual discipline, detachment, breadth of perspective, an interest in human nature and a capacity for independent and critical thought', developed primarily through an education in the liberal arts.[9] On the other, the lawyer as plumber

> is essentially someone who is master of certain specialised knowledge, "the law," and certain technical skills. What he needs is a no-nonsense specialised training to make him a competent technician. A "liberal" education in law for such a functionary is at best wasteful; at worst it can be dangerous. Imagine the effect, it might be argued, on our drains and central heating systems if our plumbers had been made to study the history and philosophy of plumbing, the aesthetics of drains, housing policy, Roman baths, comparative plumbing, and a special subject in the water supply of the Houses of Parliament.[10]

Sometimes the pendulum has swung toward Pericles, at others towards the plumber. At most law schools a working synthesis is developed, but the tensions between the two visions of legal education are always there, even if the proponents are not fully aware of them.[11]

---

8 Mackinolty, *A Century Down Town*, p. 14.

9 Ibid., p. 398.

10 W L Twining, 'Pericles and the Plumber', *Law Quarterly Review*, vol. 83, no. 3, July 1967, p. 397.

11 The debate exists to a lesser extent in other professional disciplines such as medicine and engineering, but in these there can be less argument about the necessity for graduates to have a high level of practical training. Nonetheless, the requirement in the early medical course at Monash for students to take a non-medical subject in first year

For over one hundred years the University of Melbourne was the only university in Victoria and its law school was the sole provider of legal education. Until the mid-1940s the university was tiny – about 3000 students in the 1930s – and its law school in modern parlance might be described as 'boutique'. Between the wars, the law school had on average about 300 students, who were taught by one or two full-time academics, supplemented by four or five part-timers. From 1893 until his retirement in 1927 Professor William Harrison Moore was the only full-time staff member, complaining occasionally of his teaching load of jurisprudence, Roman law, legal history, constitutional history, constitutional law, administrative law and public and private international law.[12]

The years after the Second World War saw a dramatic expansion in tertiary education in Australia. The visionary post-war Commonwealth Reconstruction Training Scheme allowed thousands of ex-service personnel to enrol at university and provided the funds for staff to teach them. Allied with population growth and a rapidly increasing demand for graduates, the number of students at the University of Melbourne rose to almost 8,000 by 1956. The law school grew apace. With no restrictions on entry beyond the requirement to matriculate and the ability to pay fees, the number of first year students exceeded 400 in the late 1950s and the growth showed no signs of slowing. The small staff and antiquated facilities of the law school struggled to cope. A third chair was established in 1952 and the full and part-time teaching staff increased slowly, but the staff-*to*-student ratio in 1959 was an appalling 1:50. The law school was still housed in the original university building constructed in 1854, with staff offices squeezed into converted attics, and the law library was woefully inadequate.

But the leadership of the Melbourne law school in the 1950s was outstanding. Professor of public law and dean from 1951 was Zelman Cowen, who returned to Melbourne after war service in naval intelligence and a brief but glittering interlude at Oxford. Cowen provided the law school with distinguished academic leadership coupled with a high public profile. When George Paton became vice-chancellor in 1951, the chair of jurisprudence was filled by a young barrister, David Derham. Among the lecturers, Norval Morris is remembered as the founder of the discipline of criminology in Australia, Harold Ford became a towering figure in commercial law, and

---

indicates a concern with a broader education, as does the current emphasis in first year medicine on ethical and even legal topics.

12 Waugh, *First Principles*, p. 107.

the young Louis Waller and Peter Brett began building their reputations in criminal law.

In 1957 the Murray Report prompted the federal government to take on the major responsibility for funding higher education and begin an unprecedented investment in expanding Australian universities.[13] The most pressing arguments for this revolution in tertiary education were the rapid growth of Australia's population and the imminent arrival of the baby boomer generation at university age. Those who were trying to make the case for more spending on education were also greatly aided by the launch of the Russian Sputnik satellite in October 1957. At the time this was seen as 'a startling demonstration of Soviet scientific progress which placed education directly in the context of the East–West power struggle'.[14]

An almost immediate response to the Murray Report was the decision to establish a second university in Melbourne and the *Monash University Act* was passed by the Victorian parliament in April 1958. Concern about serious deficiencies in education in science and technology caused the government to state explicitly that the first courses at the new university would be in applied science and technology, science and engineering, with other courses, including law, to be introduced sometime in the future. The intended emphasis on science and technology was further reflected both in the decision to name the new university after Victoria's most famous engineer, Sir John Monash, and the appointment of engineers Robert Blackwood and Louis Matheson as inaugural chancellor and vice-chancellor respectively.

At its first meeting on 19 June 1958, the new university's interim council resolved that the faculties of engineering, science and medicine would be established first, with faculties of arts, commerce, applied science, education and law to follow. Arts would begin teaching in 1962, commerce and applied science in 1963, education in 1964 and law in 1965.[15] However, the Australian Universities Commission (AUC) quickly began to urge Monash to bring this schedule forward and begin teaching on a wider basis as soon as possible. Thus in March 1961 when the first students arrived at the bleak building site in Clayton that was the new university, teaching began in the

---

13 Committee on Australian Universities, *Report of the Committee on Australian Universities*, (Keith Murray, Chairman), Government Printer, Canberra, 1957.

14 Pauline Tompkins, 'Australian Higher Education and the Murray Report', *Journal of Higher Education*, vol. 29, no. 7, October 1958, p. 361.

15 Minutes of Council Meeting No. 1, 1958, 19 June 1958, p. 2, MON 66, Monash University Archives (hereinafter MUA); Matheson to Cowen, 24 May 1960, MON 1 CF/230/0 Pt 1, MUA.

science, engineering, medicine, arts and economics & politics faculties. But law was still scheduled for 1965.

The university's refusal to bring forward the opening of the law faculty until 1965 was met with widespread dismay amongst Melbourne's legal educators and the legal profession. From early 1960, a campaign began to persuade Monash to commence teaching law as soon as possible. Heading the list of campaigners was Zelman Cowen, dean of the Melbourne law school. Strong representations were also made by the Bar Council, the Law Institute, the Council of Legal Education, influential members of the judiciary, members of Parliament and the Victorian solicitor-general, Sir Henry Winneke.[16]

The most urgent arguments for a new law school came from the University of Melbourne. The Melbourne law school was under great pressure from rapidly increasing enrolments at a time when more students did not necessarily mean more income and the modern competition to attract students did not exist. No thought was given to the possible consequences of supporting the establishment of a competitor, probably because few imagined that Monash would ever be much more than an outpost of Melbourne.

In May 1960 Zelman Cowen wrote a lengthy letter to Louis Matheson setting out the difficulties facing the Melbourne law school and urging the early establishment of a law school at Monash.[17] There were 462 first year students at Melbourne and applications were projected to rise by 15 per cent or more over the next few years. By 1963 there would be more than 600 students seeking places. To prevent numbers becoming unmanageable, the law faculty was seriously considering imposing a quota of only 300 first year students in 1961. Planning a new law school would 'take a good deal of time' so Cowen urged Matheson to appoint a dean at once, suggesting that the foundation dean 'could live here with us for a time so that he would not be isolated from law teachers while he was planning and building up his school'. He concluded by stressing that, 'My main point in writing at this time is to tell you how urgent this problem is. If you are not ready to open the doors of the second law school within a relatively short time we shall be faced with some very grave problems'.

---

16 Professor Zelman Cowen to Dr J A L Matheson, 13 May 1960; Vernon F Wilcox MLA to Matheson, 26 July 1960; Mr Justice Crisp, Supreme Court of Tasmania to Matheson, 11 August 1960; G C Wyatt, President, Law Institute of Victoria to Matheson, 8 November 1960; Matheson to Sir Edmund Herring, 21 November 1960; Henry Winneke, Solicitor-General, to Matheson, 5 December 1960, MON1, CF/230/0, Pt 1, MUA.

17 Cowen to Matheson, 13 May 1960; CF/230/0 Pt 1, MUA.

The force of this message was not lost on Matheson. He had been expecting something of the kind since he had arrived at Monash. He would take the letter to the next council meeting, but advised Cowen to apply a quota to 'bring the urgency of the matter into the open'.[18] Matheson's response proved to be a sound strategic move. While acknowledging the urgent need for more places in legal education, Monash would not be rushed into meeting it.

The Monash council did not see any possibility of making an immediate start on establishing a law faculty, although it did agree, at Cowen's urging, to begin accumulating a law library.[19] Understandably, this did not satisfy those perturbed by the immediate crisis at Melbourne, with politicians and leaders of the legal profession calling on the new university to 'stretch itself to the limit' to open a law school as soon as possible.[20] Louis Matheson responded that he was aware of the problem, but Monash was not able to push plans for 1964–65 forward to 1961–62.[21] The professorial board resolved in November 1960 'that a Faculty of Law be the next faculty to be established... in 1963', finance permitting. But the money could not be found. Under the system of university funding then in place, the AUC allocated money for specific purposes, and individual universities had very little flexibility in altering the allocation of funds.

In the meantime Melbourne had reluctantly imposed a quota of 330 for the 1961 intake, leading to the exclusion of 30 qualified applicants. The following year 182 were refused a place.[22] The legal profession was shocked. That Monash had not immediately set up a law course was unfathomable.

The retiring president of the Law Institute, Hulbert Greening, raised the matter in an unusually impassioned presidential address on 6 March 1962.[23] Greening saw the crisis of legal education as the most important challenge facing the Institute in the year ahead. He acknowledged that the University

---

18 Matheson to Cowen, 24 May 1960; CF/230/0 Pt 1, MUA.

19 Matheson to Cowen, 21 June 1960; CF/230/0 Pt 1, MUA.

20 Vernon F Wilcox MLA to Matheson, 25 July 1960; CF/230/0 Pt 1, MUA; Geoffrey Wyatt (president of the Law Institute) to Matheson, 8 November 1960; CF/230/0 Pt 1, MUA; Sir Edmund Herring, chief justice of the Supreme Court, to Matheson, 10 November 1960; CF/230/0 Pt 1, MUA

21 Matheson to Wyatt; 11 November 1960; Matheson to Herring, 21 November 1960; CF/230/0 Pt 1, MUA.

22 Hulbert A Greening, 'Presidential Address', *Law Institute Journal*, April 1962, p. 148; Peter Trumble, 'The Council of Legal Education Course', *Law Institute Journal*, March 1963, p. 145.

23 Greening, 'Presidential Address', pp. 147–48.

of Melbourne had no alternative to imposing a quota, but that this had led to much 'heart-burning and disappointment felt by applicants (and their parents)' who were unable to secure a university place. In a passage that seems particularly anachronistic today, Greening lamented the impact on families with a long tradition of practising law, and painted an emotional picture of 'the Solicitor-Father who from his Son's cradle days looked forward to the Son following in his footsteps and joining him in practice in years to come'. He made the point that academic success was not necessarily a good predictor of competence in practice: 'You all know of many in our profession whose academic careers and attainments were much less brilliant than their success in active practice.' But, he implored, what was to be done? Should those disappointed parents send the boy (no mention of girls here) back to school for another year to repeat matriculation in the hope of better marks to make the quota? The alternative, he lamented, was to abandon all ideas of law and adopt an alternative career. He feared 'that the establishment of a law school at Monash ...[will not] do very much more than offset the ever increasing population and the ever increasing number of reasonably intelligent scholars from colleges and schools who desire to and are entitled to aspire to the law as a profession'. The matter was so urgent that he firmly believed that the Bar Council and the Law Institute Council 'must *immediately*... institute a system of tuition in law which would entitle young men (and women) to pass examinations to practise, at least as solicitors'.

The legal profession continued its pressure on Monash to hasten the opening of a law school. In his memoirs, Louis Matheson recalled being 'waited upon by a formidable deputation' from the legal profession 'comprising the chairmen of the Bar Council and of the Law Society together with a couple of judges'.[24] The reality, however, was that there was little Monash could do to accelerate the establishment of a faculty of law.

In March 1962 the professorial board considered the request made by the Council of Legal Education for the establishment of a law school at an early date and the Bar Council's offer to provide assistance in professional training in the early stages. The board's response was to recommend the immediate appointment of a dean, whose first task would be to present a detailed plan

---

24 Sir Louis Matheson, draft manuscript of autobiography, 'Still Learning', Rare Books Collection, Matheson Library. The published book is a greatly condensed version of this manuscript: *Matheson, Still Learning*, Macmillan, Melbourne, 1980.

for the establishment of a law school. But the board also reiterated that law students should not be accepted until adequate finance was available.[25]

Monash's inability to bring forward the opening of its law school prompted the legal profession to take immediate action. The Victorian Bar Council put forward a scheme under which members of the bar would provide tuition 'until Monash University will itself take over such tuition ... provided that Monash University was prepared to accelerate the establishment of its Law faculty'.[26] This suggestion, however, was pre-empted when the Council of Legal Education set up its own law course in premises provided by RMIT. Teaching began in April 1962, with 51 of the 182 prospective students rejected by the University of Melbourne enrolling in the new course. Lectures were given by practitioners, with no full-time academics being employed.[27]

The establishment of the Council of Legal Education law course appears to have prompted Monash to push forward with its own law course. In March 1962 when the professorial board determined that additional money could not be secured to begin teaching in 1963, it nonetheless resolved that a dean be appointed as soon as possible.[28] Reflecting on the search for a dean, Matheson wrote:

> The Monash Faculty of Law, if it was to meet the serious aspirations of possible students, would have to be professionally impeccable ... The key to this would be the appointment of a dean who would command the respect of the legal profession and also be able to create from scratch a law school with its own individual style and excellence.[29]

Although the university's submission to the AUC for funds for the 1964–1966 triennium had already been lodged, it was revised to include a request for staff and buildings for a law school.[30]

---

25 Monash University, Report of the Professorial Board to the Council, 28 March 1962, Professorial Board Meeting 3/62, Item 1 Establishment of the Faculty of Law. CF/230/0, MUA.

26 'Legal Education', *Law Institute Journal*, May 1962, p. 178.

27 Trumble, 'The Council of Legal Education Course', pp. 144–5.

28 Professorial Board Minutes, Item 2.1 Establishment of the Faculty of Law, CF/230/0, MUA.

29 Matheson, handwritten manuscript of 'Still Learning', ch. 4: 'Further Academic Developments', p. 2.

30 Revised Triennial Submission, June 1962, Triennial Submission 1980/15 80/15/001, MON 3/6, MUA.

A large and distinguished selection committee was appointed but it had scarcely begun its deliberations when the AUC advised that there would be no money for a law building in the 1964–66 triennium.[31] The committee was divided on whether it should proceed with the selection of a dean or wait until the financial position was clearer. In October 1962, the committee sought advice from Zelman Cowen and David Derham of the Melbourne law school. Their reply did not arrive until December, so the new dean's position was not advertised until early 1963 and it was not until May that the selection committee met to consider the applications.[32] None were considered ideal and no offers were made.[33]

The state government encouraged Monash to move more swiftly. In June 1963, Jim Butchart, the assistant registrar, was asked by the Minister for Education in the Bolte government, John Bloomfield, whether there had been any progress in the selection of a dean. The selection committee had held more than one meeting, Butchart explained, but it was proving difficult to find a dean of the required stature. Bloomfield was eager to know whether the law course would be in operation the following year, but was told that in addition to the difficulties of obtaining a dean, the whole question of a curriculum had to be considered. Further, if the proposed curriculum differed from that of the Melbourne law school, then the agreement of the Council of Legal Education would be needed.[34] At best, the issue was months away from being resolved.

Following Bloomfield's intervention, the selection committee was authorised to offer the deanship to the man of their choice (there was no thought of it being a woman) without prior reference to council. In October Professor David Derham was invited to become Monash's first dean of law.[35] Derham had not been an applicant, but, to the delight and relief of the selection committee, he accepted. Further, he advised the council that,

---

31 Council Minutes, 14 May 1962; Members of the committee were: the vice-chancellor, deputy chancellor M Chamberlin, J A Forrest, P V Feltham, Sir George Paton, Professors S R Davis, J D Legge, D Cochrane, W A G Scott and A K McIntyre, J D Butchart, Assistant Registrar, Memo from F H Johnson, Registrar to Committee, 4 July 1962.

32 Matheson to Cowen, 29 October 1962; Matheson to Derham, 29 October 1962, CF/230/0, MUA.

33 Cowen to Matheson, 19 December 1962; Derham to Matheson, 21 December 1962, CF/230/0, MUA; Report of Selection Committee to Council Meeting, 14 October 1963.

34 Registrar to vice-chancellor, 26 June 1963, CF/230/0, MUA.

35 Council minutes, 8 July 1963; Matheson, manuscript of 'Still Learning', p. 2.

despite his existing commitments at Melbourne, he intended to develop a first-year law course at Monash to commence in 1964. Soon after, Derham wrote to a friend, 'I am probably mad to do it but will have some compensating fun no doubt'.[36]

David Plumley Derham, the inaugural dean of the Monash law school, came from a Melbourne establishment family, whose initial fortune came from the Swallow & Ariell biscuit business, with later generations producing several prominent doctors and lawyers. Derham's father, Alfred Derham, a senior physician at the Children's Hospital, was with the 8th Division at Singapore in 1942 and spent three and a half years as a prisoner of war. His mother, Frances Derham, was a prominent artist and art educator. Alfred's brother, Francis, was a solicitor and company director, being co-founder of the leading Melbourne law firm of Moule Hamilton & Derham (now part of Freehills), and their sister Enid was the first female lecturer in English at the University of Melbourne. Born on 12 May 1920, David Derham (like Zelman Cowen) was educated at Scotch College before coming to the University of Melbourne in 1938. Significantly, given the structure he designed for the Monash law course, his own tertiary education followed what is now known as 'the Melbourne model', only completing his law degree after both an arts degree and four years in the army. He finished a BA Hons in 1941 before enlisting in the AIF as a trooper. Commissioned lieutenant in 1942, he rose to the rank of major by the age of twenty-four. After demobilisation, Derham returned to university to complete a law degree with first class honours and win the Supreme Court Prize in 1947. He then went to the bar, though he maintained a foothold in academia by teaching part-time in the law school, where he quickly gained a reputation as an outstanding teacher. When he returned to take the chair of jurisprudence at Melbourne in 1951, more surprise was expressed that he 'had no association with the Oxford School of Law', than that he 'had no higher degree and no profile in scholarship and publications'.[37]

In the style of the era, Zelman Cowen arranged for David Derham to spend the whole of 1953 overseas obtaining what was regarded as essential experience for a Melbourne law professor.[38] Six months at Oxford, followed by six months visiting Harvard, Yale and other leading American law schools

---

36 Derham to Charles O Gregory, 20 January 1964, 1968.0027, Derham, David Plumley, Sir (1920–1985), general correspondence 1951–64, box 2, file G, UMA.

37 Waugh, *First Principles*, p. 155.

38 Zelman Cowen, *A Public Life: The Memoirs of Zelman Cowen*, Miegunyah Press, Melbourne, 2006, p. 185.

fulfilled this requirement. Over the next decade Derham built up a solid academic reputation in jurisprudence and constitutional law, and as a deep thinker about the nature and purposes of legal education. He took on a large part of the faculty's administrative load, and was highly regarded by students as 'the man to see when graduation and the question of articles drew near'.[39]

Urbane, learned, well-connected, widely liked and with a glowing reputation as an academic and administrator, it is hard to imagine that Monash could have found a more suitable inaugural dean. He had experience in practice to complement his academic credentials. Still only in his early forties, he was clearly marked for higher positions. While an overseas import could possibly have brought a wider scholastic reputation, they could never have matched Derham's intimate connections with Melbourne's academic, legal and commercial communities. In the late Sir Zelman Cowen's words, 'he was the obvious choice for the job'.[40]

---

39 Waugh, *First Principles*, p. 156.

40 Interview with Sir Zelman Cowen, 17 June 2011.

Chapter 2

The Derham Vision

Few people in Australia had thought more deeply about the problems of legal education as David Derham. In the decade between his appointment to the chair of jurisprudence at the University of Melbourne and his move to Monash he wrote extensively on both the theory and practice of legal education. After a year in England and the United States studying the varieties of legal education on offer, he began experimenting with some of the teaching innovations he had seen in America. In the late 1950s and early 1960s, as the legal profession in Victoria pondered the future of legal education in the shadow of the imposition of a quota at Melbourne, Derham's reasoned and considered contributions did much to shape the course of the debate. Finally, in 1964 he summarised his views on legal education in the Martin committee's report on tertiary education.[1]

In May 1954 Derham presented a report on his year abroad. As the first professor of law at Melbourne not to have a degree from an English university, it was thought essential that he spend time at Oxford, but he was not totally enamoured with what he saw: 'Viewed in detail as a system for training lawyers,' he wrote, 'it would be difficult to devise a less satisfactory system than the course for BA in Jurisprudence at Oxford'. However, he conceded that Oxford was not trying to train lawyers, 'but merely to provide a good education for a man who might, after leaving Oxford, decide to become a lawyer'.[2] Oxford had adopted a purely 'Periclean' concept of legal education, and left the 'plumbing' training to others.

Derham looked more favourably on the education provided by the University of London and some of the newer English universities, which had

---

1 Sir Leslie Martin, *Tertiary Education in Australia: Report of the Committee on the Future of Tertiary Education in Australia*, 2 vols, Commonwealth Government Printer, Canberra, 1965.

2 'Report on Overseas Leave by Professor D P Derham, University of Melbourne', 28 May 1954, Philip Ayres (ed.), *David Derham, Talks on Universities, History and the Law*, Oryx Publishing, Melbourne, 2009, p. 24.

both more modern teaching methods and a better marriage of theory and practice in their law courses than Oxford. He was scathing, however, about the non-university legal training provided by the English Council of Legal Education and the Law Society which were 'little better than cram-courses' with examinations which were 'a very exacting test of rote knowledge but little more'. Summing up English legal education, he wrote, 'It must be a matter of constant amazement to foreigners ... that such a system, explicable only in terms of history, can produce such a high standard in the legal profession at large'.[3]

In general, Derham was far more impressed with what he saw of American legal education. Harvard he described simply as 'the best law school in the common-law world.' The leading American law schools were far ahead of English and Australian law schools in facilities, teaching methods and willingness to experiment and innovate. Derham was overwhelmed by the library facilities he saw. He was particularly impressed that 'in a number of United States law libraries I visited there was a better collection of Australian case material and sometimes text material than is obtainable at any one library in Victoria'. A great law library became central to his vision of the ideal law school.

Derham looked favourably on the American system wherein students entered law school only after completing a first degree. Students not only had the benefit of a 'liberal education' but, perhaps more importantly, were more mature and aware 'that life has entered upon the serious part of its business and that play-time is over'. This 'not only makes the students themselves more eager to get on with their law school job but enables the teachers to employ teaching methods with profit which might be difficult to reproduce for an English or Australian undergraduate student body'.[4] He was referring here primarily to the 'Socratic' or 'case book' method of teaching which, in various forms, was widely used in American law schools. The essence of this method was 'the analysis of factual situations and the decisions of the courts, performed by the student himself under a Socratic type of questioning'. Students were required to prepare beforehand from a case book or class materials and to participate in 'stimulated discussion and argument in class'. Although Derham had some doubts about the exclusive use of Socratic teaching even in American postgraduate law schools, he believed that if it was used in Australian undergraduate law schools most

---

3 Ibid., p.26.

4 Ibid., p.27.

Professor David P Derham, early 1967.
Photographer Penelope F B Alexander

students would focus exclusively on the set materials and ignore any further reading of cases, articles or texts. Further, he queried whether it is 'better for the passive members of the class to gain vicariously from a low-level discussion involving student participation [than] a high-level discussion carried on by a lecturer alone'.

In spite of these misgivings, he urged the introduction of case-method teaching in some subjects. He argued that it would 'make for a greater self-reliance in students when called upon to speak in public ... make for a greater confidence in approaching problems which at first sight are unfamiliar [and] make for a more apt introduction to the way a lawyer has to think about problems when he faces them in practice.[5] Subsequently, Derham,

5 Ibid., p. 44.

Zelman Cowen and some of the younger lecturers in the Melbourne law school such as Louis Waller and Peter Brett experimented with case-method teaching. After seeing American teaching methods Cowen had written, 'I am now the sworn foe of the teaching method in which the student can come into class knowing that the worst that can be expected or desired is silent comprehension', although he conceded that debate between student and lecturer needed to be combined with 'analysis and coordination' by the lecturer.[6] Early experiments were hindered by a lack of case books, but by 1962 Australian-produced case books were available on the core subjects of the curriculum and some level of class participation was a feature of most courses at Melbourne.

In other areas Melbourne signally failed to take more than small steps towards emulating the great American law schools. The library acquired more space after the opening of the new university library in 1959, but it was still woefully deficient in many ways. The staff:student ratio remained the worst in the university and the faculty was still housed in small and primitive premises in the university's oldest building. A new law building, made a priority by George Paton in the 1930s, became a reality seventy years later – over 30 years after David Derham had been able to build a law school to his own design at Monash. The inertia of an old law faculty in an old university added greatly to the attraction of starting a new law school unburdened with the baggage of the past.

In August 1963, after he had been invited to become the inaugural dean of the Monash law school, but before he had accepted, Derham published an article on 'Legal Education in Australia', in which he summarised his thoughts after 12 years full-time teaching at Melbourne and as he began contemplating the challenges of starting a new law school at Monash.[7]

Derham's starting point was that 'Lawyers have for long claimed to be not merely members of a profession but of a learned profession' and that the education of its members must therefore be a high priority. He argued further that lawyers should be educated in more than simply the skills, techniques and rules of the law, but should have a broad liberal education to equip them properly for their work in an increasingly complex society. He strongly criticised the common form of legal education, which had

---

6 Cowen to Derham, 21 June 1954 and Report on Leave by Professor Zelman Cowen, 19 April 1955, quoted in Waugh, *First Principles*, p. 178.

7 David Derham, 'Legal Education in Australia', *The Australian University*, vol. 1, no. 1, August 1963.

> Little or no teacher/student contact, little or no supervised work by the students, little or no student work concerned with original materials, and, for the majority of students, a strong temptation to satisfy all requirements by cramming potted information in short periods before examinations. Legal education of that kind was fairly simple and very cheap, but it had very little else to recommend it.[8]

Derham pointed out that Australian university law schools faced conflicting demands and performed dual roles in legal education, namely, to 'pursue University aims and standards', and 'to satisfy professional requirements for admission to practice'. This raised the issue of the extent to which universities should respond to the profession's constant pressure to make the university law courses more 'practical'. Historically, articles were meant to provide practical training, but in many – if not most – cases, the training was haphazard at best. Derham was happy to accept that university law schools should do more to shape their courses 'towards the inculcation of skills as well as towards the acquisition of knowledge', particularly through moot courts and legal aid clinics. While emphasising that 'it is proper that universities should be more concerned with legal scholarship than with legal practice', he pointed out that 'the line between the acquisition of skills and the attainment of knowledge is not a sharp one' and argued that 'the study of legal systems and rules of law, once divorced from an awareness and understanding of the way the systems and rules function in fact, diminishes in value and invites speculation of no validity and of little or no use'.[9] Derham further argued that 'the attempt by Australian law schools to pursue both professional and university aims, in spite of the difficulties created, has been very valuable [because] it has kept the profession continually involved in and concerned with the teaching of law [and] it has prevented the academic lawyers from retreating completely into their "ivory towers"'.[10] With this in mind, he emphasised that 'as many law teachers as possible should have had experience in practice'.

Both postgraduate legal education and legal research were still in their infancy in Australia. Derham thought both must be built up. It was no longer good enough to rely on British and American research: 'We must provide our own legal scholarship, our own postgraduate schools, our own research

8 Ibid., pp. 55–6.

9 Ibid., p. 61.

10 Ibid., p. 67.

libraries, and our own facilities for research'. To achieve these aims would require 'more full-time staff, better accommodation, more scholarships for postgraduate students, and greatly expanded research libraries'.[11] An important function of increased postgraduate education would be 'to provide properly qualified recruits for the teaching side of the profession' because 'the disparity between academic financial rewards and the rewards of practice' meant that 'already it is difficult if not impossible to fill all university posts suitably'.

David Derham's appointment to the Martin Committee, set up by the Menzies government in 1961 to advise on the future development of tertiary education in Australia, indicates that he was widely regarded as a leading authority on legal education. It is not coincidental that the section on legal education in the Martin Report is essentially the same as Derham's article 'Legal Education in Australia' published in 1963.[12]

When Derham accepted the invitation to come to Monash he had clear views on the theory and practice of legal education, but neither he nor the university administration had a blueprint to follow for the establishment of the new law school. Appointed in October 1963 and with the first students to arrive in March 1964, Derham had no time for quiet rumination or reflection – there were no retreats or planning days in the 1960s. The urgent needs were to devise a first year course; hire some teachers; lay claim to some space for teaching, staff studies and a library; and acquire books for the library. As he wrote to a friend in October 1963, 'I propose to start teaching at Monash next year relying mainly on hope and faith that I will be able to get sufficient staff, books and accommodation to carry on thereafter.'[13] It was only when these immediate tasks were (almost miraculously) completed, that he could turn his attention to long-term planning.

The document that formed the basis for planning the Monash law school was circulated in August 1964. Short – only 18 pages – it is a succinct and clear outline of the decisions already made that affected the planning, the nature of the courses to be offered, the ideal size of the law school, the law library, the design of a new building, staffing and faculty governance.

---

11 Ibid., p. 66.

12 Martin, *Tertiary Education in Australia*, vol II.

13 Derham to Prof L A Sheridan, Faculty of Law, Queen's University, Belfast, Northern Ireland, 23 October 1963, DDP, general correspondence 1951–64, folder 21, box 4 UMA.

The plan showed influences from both England and America, with the American predominating.[14]

The background to planning was the rapid growth in demand for tertiary education in general and legal education in particular. The law school began at a time when 'Monash as a whole [was expanding] at a rate so fast that continuous flirtation with the danger of break-downs in detailed plans was inevitable'. Further, 'Monash had no definite plans, and no money, for the provision of proper accommodation designed for law school purposes'.

When asked many years later what thought was uppermost in his mind when he came to Monash, Derham answered, 'to tackle the task of founding a law school 13 miles away from the city which would have the co-operation, support and respect of the profession. *That* was the dominating thought'.[15] For somebody whose working life had been divided between the law courts in William Street and the Melbourne law school in Parkville (a short tram ride apart), Clayton was a remote outpost, and he believed that most legal practitioners would feel the same, with the result that part-time staff would be hard to find. Consequently the Monash law school would have to rely on full-time academics to teach its courses and 'new methods for meeting the need for close contact with actual practice will have to be devised.' Derham's main initiatives in this area were the appointment of distinguished practitioners as 'consultants', to advise the full-time staff on planning, teaching and examining their courses, and the inclusion of distinguished members of the profession on the faculty board.

Derham argued that there was no consensus on the optimal size of a law school, and he thought it best to base it on the optimal size of the teaching staff. It was essential, he believed, that 'all academic lawyers in the faculty can feel that they are part of one professional team engaged in teaching and research' and, from this, argued that 'when the senior staff [lecturers and above] of a law school … grows much beyond forty, then the notion of the team working together becomes an unreal one. At that point it is time to think of a new law school rather than of expanding an existing one.'

From the figure of 40 senior staff, Derham worked back to suggest an optimal number of students. In spite of his misgivings with case-method teaching on his return from America, a decade of experience at Melbourne convinced him of its merits. Consequently, while all subjects would have two

---

14 David Derham, 'A Plan for a New Law School', AD/230/0, part 1, Dean and Sub-Dean, 1964–83, MON 1, MUA.

15 'A Conversation with David Derham', part 2, *Law Institute Journal*, February 1983, p. 1030.

lectures and one tutorial each week, he preferred to call the lectures 'large classes' as it was 'intended to require members of the class to participate in discussion of prepared problems and materials'. The value of class participation diminished rapidly if the classes were too large, so 'the intention is that only in rare cases will lecture classes be conducted with a membership of more than one hundred students.' Further, Derham aimed 'to require all law students to produce written work in all years of their course' and this would increase the number of staff required. He concluded that 'with such methods of teaching', combined with his ideal senior staff size of 40, the number of students should not exceed 1200, with the optimal size being 'in the vicinity of 750–800 full-time undergraduate students'. This was close to the size anticipated by the university at that time. The early planning for the university envisaged an eventual enrolment of 12,000, but initial building plans were made on the assumption of 8,000 students. Projections for the distribution of students between faculties, based on the existing distribution at the University of Melbourne, led the university to plan for a law faculty of 930 students.

In his planning Derham placed great emphasis on the law library, 'the most important part of any law school'. One of his mantras was that 'The lawyer's tools are the books of the law [and] a law school's undergraduate laboratory is its law library'. He emphasised that a law library 'is not merely a collection of books and other writings containing information, reason, argument and opinion … but, more important, it is a repository of living systems of authority as well as of reason – systems which change and grow from day to day'.

Derham's stated view was that there was no good law library in Victoria and he aspired for Monash to create the first. It should have specialist staff headed by 'a lawyer-librarian who has standing as a legal scholar', accommodation for 600 readers, ease of access for students and staff, and more space per student than a regular library. It should build its collection up to at least 40,000 volumes as quickly as possible, with provision for at least 150,000 volumes. Clearly inspired by the University of Chicago law school, he proposed that this ideal law library 'should be so placed as to be the working heart of the law school'.

Derham laid out detailed requirements for the rest of the law school building – staff studies, tutorial rooms and a specialised moot court room. There would be no need for large lecture theatres, and classrooms should be designed 'so that students are grouped around and, so far as may be, are equidistant from their teacher'. Staff studies should be bigger than the standard university study because 'Lawyers tend to collect a larger personal book collection than other academic workers.' Finally, it was essential to provide accommodation for the Law Students' Society. As an appendix to his report, Derham set out detailed tables of the number, layout and size of rooms required and calculated that the law school building should be approximately 100,000 square feet (slightly under a hectare).

Derham drew up a table showing the planned growth in staff and student numbers through to the end of 1971. In 1965, 11 academic staff would teach 6 subjects to 320 students, and by 1971, 64 staff would teach 29 subjects to 1180 students. He conceded that undergraduate law courses did not require such a favourable staff:student ratio as was planned for Monash as a whole (1:10), and thought that 1:14 would be sufficient – a figure that was achieved until the late 1970s. The fact that Melbourne law school had a staff:student ratio of about 1:26 over that period goes a long way to explaining why Monash was able to catch and surpass Melbourne so quickly.

In those simpler times, Derham suggested that the administration of the faculty should be in the hands of a 'senior administrative officer', preferably a law graduate, aided by a small clerical staff to do the typing.

The structure of the law course devised by Derham showed strong influences from his experiences of both Oxford and America. He saw the main aims of the law school as being to provide an education in law to qualify for admission, while also giving students 'the benefits of a general and liberal university undergraduate education'. To achieve this, he proposed 'a first degree, the BJuris, with a core of basic legal studies, which will rank with other first degrees in the humanities and the social sciences', to be followed by an LLB course designed 'to encourage all candidates to take advanced studies in various branches of the law which require high understanding of specialised materials and techniques.' He planned for 'sufficient flexibility in the courses available to enable candidates to combine studies in the law with advanced studies in other disciplines'.

The proposed three-year first degree was clearly inspired by the Oxford BA in jurisprudence, but with a firmer grounding in the practice as well as the theory of the law. The six law subjects essentially followed the structure developed at Melbourne in the 1950s, with a general introductory subject called The Legal System, and Criminal Law as first year subjects, followed by the core common-law subjects, Contracts, Torts, and Property. There was also provision for 'one advanced or theoretical subject which requires a knowledge of various basic areas of the common law'. Students were also required to take five non-legal subjects, of which one, British History, was compulsory, with the other subjects to be chosen from two distinct disciplines.

Derham expected most students to take the BJuris, but from the start there was provision for combined degrees, initially with economics/politics and arts. These were structured so that students largely completed a first degree before taking on the bulk of their law subjects.

The law subjects offered in the BJuris/LLB course were inevitably constrained by the rules for admission to practice laid down by the Council of Legal Education and these largely determined the compulsory subjects. A significant concession to the Periclean vision of legal education was that Jurisprudence was made compulsory. Reflecting back on this decision, Derham thought it was right:

> I say that while being well aware that about 60 per cent of the victims will always resent it, but about half of those at some stage later in their life will be glad that they were required to read something. ... It's a breadth of understanding and interest in reading speculative things, and if you're not made to do some of it, many people will not wake up until too late.[16]

The compulsory subjects set out in the 1964 plan were The Legal System, Criminal Law, Contracts, Torts, Property I and II, Constitutional Law, Conflicts of Laws, Administrative Law, Conveyancing and Drafting, and Jurisprudence.

Monash law school has always prided itself on the breadth of elective subjects available for undergraduate students. Already in 1964 Derham listed twelve electives that would be available for the first cohort of students, namely Comparative Law, International Law, Legal History, Advanced Constitutional Law, Family Law, Evidence, Commercial Law, Creditors' Rights, Industrial Law, Taxation, Wills and the Administration of Estates, and Civil and Criminal Procedure. This compared with just four electives offered by Melbourne at that time. He also planned for the early establishment of honours and postgraduate schools. Although the structure of the honours school was not set out in detail in his 1964 plan, it was to be one of the most distinctive (and in retrospect extraordinary) features of the early years of the Monash law school.

---

16 'A Conversation with David Derham', part one, *Law Institute Journal*, December 1982, p.1029.

The development of the Monash law school in its early years followed very closely the blueprint laid down by David Derham – the size, staff structure, building and course structure were all based on his plans. Inevitably, over time aspects of his vision were modified, forgotten or lapsed, but the fundamental structure he set out remains, from the building based around a magnificent law library to the combination of innovation and conservatism that was at the heart of his approach to the law.

Chapter 3

The First Year of the Monash Law School

By March 1964, when the first eager, fresh-faced law students arrived to begin their studies, Monash University's foundation faculties had been teaching for three years, and there were already nearly 3000 students. Several science, medical and engineering buildings had been completed along the western side of the campus, while the humanities and social sciences building, the union building and the main library were nearing completion. The rest of the campus was a mixture of construction sites and empty fields.

There was no law building. A site for one had been chosen, but no plans had been drawn and no money allocated. There were no university regulations regarding the law course and no published details of subjects available. The Monash law course had not been recognised for admission purposes by the Council of Legal Education. The Faculty of Law did not formally exist and could not be established due to a dispute over the interpretation of the *Monash University Act*.[1] In the interim a small 'advisory committee' was set up in November 1963 to assist David Derham. The staff of the law school consisted of the dean, one senior and two junior academics, an administrative officer and two secretaries. For both students and staff, joining the Monash law school was a leap in the dark.

Teaching began on Monday 9 March. David Derham welcomed the students at the first lecture, which was held in the science building. The lecture left an indelible impression on his students. It was an inspiring, if somewhat scary, introduction to their law course. Rob Capes was transfixed by Derham's elegance, dignity and refinement, but when Derham emphasised that standards would be high in his new law school, he knew that he had to be the best he could in order to shape up.[2] Bob Williams recalls that the dean 'invited us to look to our left and to our right and assured us that next

1 The controversy is analysed in Peter Balmford, 'The Foundation of the Monash Law School', *Monash University Law Review*, vol. 15, nos 3 and 4, 1989, pp. 162–4.

2 Email from Rob Capes to authors, 5 August 2013.

Faculty of Law staff and students, 1964.
Photographer unknown, Monpix 5181

year one of the three of us would be gone'.[3] To Nahum Mushin it really hit home when Derham pointed out that the Monash law school did not have accreditation and so it really was an act of faith for them all to be there.[4]

Who were the first students and where had they come from? Many were the first in their family to attend university. Many knew very little about law but had chosen it because they had the marks they needed to get into Monash law. Whereas their contemporaries at the Melbourne law school were overwhelmingly from elite private schools, the backgrounds of the first Monash students were considerably more diverse, with a far higher proportion from government schools than at Melbourne.

University selection processes in Victoria had not yet adapted to the existence of a second university and for the first few years Monash law school simply piggybacked on the Melbourne selection process. Unless an applicant specifically ruled out one university, the application was treated as being for both law schools.[5] The selection process was based on academic merit judged on matriculation exam results, together with interviews and school reports.[6] Derham took part in the selection of students for both Melbourne and Monash and first offers were issued in February 1964. He was pleased that some of the applicants who had given Monash as their first preference were 'particularly well qualified'.[7]

In 1964 there were 591 applicants for admission to the Monash law school, almost all of whom had also applied for Melbourne. Of this number, 161 were rejected while another 281 applicants withdrew after receiving an offer from Melbourne.[8] Monash then made further offers to fill the places available. In total, 150 students (including one postgraduate student) were enrolled. Of the 149 undergraduates all but five were full-time students. Seventeen (11.4 per cent) were women.[9]

---

3 Bob Williams, 'Some Reflections on Monash', notes to the authors, 10 November 2011, p. 1; also Balmford, 'Foundation of the Monash Law School', p. 174.

4 Interview with Nahum Mushin, 23 March 2011.

5 Law School Advisory Committee minutes, 5 February 1964.

6 Zelman Cowen, 'Selection Processes in the Law School 1963', *Law Institute Journal*, May 1963, pp. 186–7.

7 Law School Advisory Committee minutes, 5 February 1964.

8 Ibid., 14 May 1964; Balmford, 'Foundation of the Monash Law School', p. 139.

9 'Student Enrolment', *Monash University Calendar*, 1966, pp. 621–24. The 17 women were Nancy Johnston, Anne Holland, Penelope Duncan, Barbara Brown, Phillipa Kanihan, Emilia Wienfeld, Ruth Aronson, Carolyn Plotkin, Belinda Pring, Christine Hill, Ruth Worland, Elizabeth Game, Sandra McCallum, Susan Bath, Barbara Perlman, Yetta Samuel and Daniella Rubinstein.

Mark Aronson was one of the few among his cohort to have offers from both Monash and Melbourne, but he wanted to go 'somewhere less structured and reverential' than Melbourne. Although his parents were committed left-wingers, they still wanted him to go to Melbourne in the belief this would be better for his career. They arranged for two judges they knew to talk sense into him. The judges told him that Melbourne was the established place with its reputation and its contacts and it would be foolish to go to a new law school. Mark was unconvinced so his parents took him to see the faculty manager at Melbourne. To his parents' horror, the manager advised their son to go to Monash because 'it would be good to follow Derham and the excellent group of teachers he had taken with him'. Further, 'the library at Melbourne was a disgrace, the lecture theatres were sub-standard and much of the teaching was appalling'. That decided the matter, and Aronson went to Monash.[10]

Chris Chenoweth was offered a place at Melbourne after he had already been accepted by Monash. In retrospect he believes that most people in that situation would have chosen Melbourne, but Chris chose Monash on the advice of a family friend who said that Monash would be good because David Derham was going there. He was also strongly influenced by Ann Lahore, who persuaded him of the advantages of the double-degree structure at Monash.[11] Barry Perry's entry was quite different: he was one of the few successful applicants to transfer from the articled clerks' course run by the Council of Legal Education at RMIT. Nahum Mushin had failed first year law at Melbourne in 1963 due to difficult personal circumstances, so he applied for Monash and got in. He recalls that in the early days, a fair number of the Monash students were Melbourne rejects and to some extent they felt they were second-class citizens.[12] Rob Capes failed to get into medicine at either Melbourne or Monash, so he enrolled at the Melbourne Pharmacy College. After finding dissecting a rat too trying, his decision to accept a place in law at Monash was aided by his eligibility for a Commonwealth Scholarship.

One of the seventeen women in the first intake in 1964 was Ruth Thomas (née Worland). Both her father and brother were lawyers, but her father was against her doing law; he thought nursing or teaching were more appropriate for a girl. In fact, Ruth says she 'drifted into law' at Monash. She had attended Melbourne Church of England Girls Grammar School

---

10 Interview with Mark Aronson, 21 February 2011.

11 Interview with Chris Chenoweth, James Kimpton, Ruth Thomas and Bob Williams, 9 November 2011.

12 Interview with Nahum Mushin, 23 March 2011.

in preparation for matriculation and returned for a second year. When her results were not good enough to get into Melbourne University, Monash Law was Ruth's default position.[13]

Bob Williams was one of the many early students to have attended a government school, Burwood High School. His results

> in year 12 were not sufficient to get a first round offer from Melbourne Law which had been my first choice. I was initially very disappointed, but after attending Monash for an interview with Ann Lahore and learning something of the course and in particular the combined B Juris/LL B program I became more enthusiastic about Monash. In the event I received a late offer of a place at Melbourne a matter of a few days before classes started. By this time, however, I had become settled on the idea of Monash and declined the Melbourne offer.[14]

Like Williams and many others in the first cohort, Dennis Liner was the first in his family to attend university. His father was a painter and Liner went to McKinnon High School, which was then one of the worst performing schools in the state, with only about four of the 1963 year twelve class going to university. His marks were only average but they were good enough to get a Commonwealth Scholarship and get into law at Monash.[15] The early 1960s marked the beginning of the transformation of the university system from being the preserve of a tiny elite to today's position of mass higher education, and this was reflected in the high proportion of early Monash students with no family history of university education.

Graeme Golden was another high school student, having matriculated at Glenroy High School, but in every other way his story was unusual. After leaving school in December 1961 he began work as a clerk in the crown solicitor's office, where his role was to act as instructor to the crown prosecutors. He spent every day in court and enjoyed this so much he decided he wanted to become a lawyer. His superiors would only allow him to study at the Council for Legal Education's course at RMIT (because of its proximity to his work) but this course only accepted students who had been rejected by both Melbourne and Monash, so Graeme had to apply for the university courses, while pleading to be rejected. But Monash accepted him. When he went to Monash to tell David Derham and Ann Lahore that this

---

13 Interview with Ruth Thomas, 21 October 2011.

14 Bob Williams, email to authors, 24 July 2012; also Balmford, 'Foundation of the Monash Law School', p. 174.

15 Interview with Dennis Liner, 23 March 2011.

meant he would not be able to study law, Derham immediately phoned the crown solicitor, who, after some persuasion, agreed to make an exception. Graeme was allowed to do one subject in 1964 and if he succeeded he would be allowed to do more in later years. His superiors made it as difficult as possible for him to do his course and he was sure they anticipated he would fail his first subject and give up. He was allowed to go out to Monash only for lectures and had to return to work immediately.[16]

Given Melbourne's established reputation, it is not surprising that most students who were offered a place in both law schools chose Parkville over Clayton. Consequently, there was a significant disparity in the quality of the students in the two law schools in the 1960s. The best students at Monash were every bit as good as the best students at Melbourne, but Monash had a large 'tail' of weak students. Many of these fell by the wayside during the course as failure and drop-out rates were high. Of the 149 students who enrolled in first year in 1964, only 109 passed the year and only 60 eventually completed an LLB. While 39 members of the first cohort completed their LLBs in 1969, many took substantially longer, with the last of the first intake of students graduating in 1980.

The vast majority of the new students in 1964 enrolled for what became the three-year Bachelor of Jurisprudence (BJuris), to be followed by a further two years of study to qualify for a Bachelor of Laws (LLB). A small number enrolled in the first combined courses, BA/LLB and BEcon/LLB. Under Derham's plan, the BJuris was designed to provide a broad undergraduate education with a core of basic legal studies, while the LLB was designed primarily to satisfy the academic qualifications required for admission to practice.

The BJuris students of 1964 enrolled in four subjects: The Legal System, Criminal Law and History 1C (British constitutional history), plus a subject chosen from either arts or economics and politics. As History 1C was taught by staff from the department of history, for 1964 David Derham had only to find teachers for The Legal System and Criminal Law, though preparations would have to be made to teach second year subjects in 1965.

The first three staff members were all Melbourne graduates, appointed by Derham with the minimum of formality. The first academic appointment was Ann Lahore, a Melbourne honours graduate, and a protégé of Derham, who was supervising her master's thesis. As soon as it was announced that Derham was going to Monash, she decided to go with him. She began

16 Interview with Graeme Golden, 25 June 2012.

work at Monash in December 1963, although her formal appointment only dated from 31 January 1964. Her main task over that first summer was interviewing and selecting students. She was soon joined by the first faculty secretary, Hilary Feltham, who, like Ann, had been a tutor at Melbourne. Between them they interviewed every prospective student, encouraging the best to choose Monash, while trying to weed out the weakest. 'Student selection was a bit hit and miss', Ann recalls. They had instructions from David Derham, but basically it was up to them: 'the main criteria were that students could speak English and came across as intelligent', prerequisites that have long since been abandoned. Lahore and Feltham also had to arrange the timetable and find rooms for lectures and tutorials.[17]

Before teaching began, another teaching fellow (as tutors were called at Monash in the 1960s), Norman Reaburn, was appointed. He was the first tutor in Criminal Law and 'David Derham's eyes nearly popped out of his head when he saw Reaburn in his Carnaby Street style clothes, all black with tight trousers and pointy shoes'.[18] His attire added colour and a contemporary look to the otherwise conservatively dressed staff.

The first senior appointment was surprising but successful. Frank Beasley had recently retired as foundation dean of the University of Western Australia law school, and Derham persuaded him to accept an appointment as 'special lecturer in law'. His primary responsibility was the establishment of the law library, and he also helped teach The Legal System and later constitutional law and legal history. 'I hope that my colleagues here, and all those students who are sharing with us the great adventure of starting a new law school, will in future look back with undiminished exhilaration and satisfaction to the formative years of this school', he declared soon after arriving at Monash.[19]

As the faculty did not yet have a lecturer with expertise in criminal law, Derham arranged for Melbourne lecturers Louis Waller and Peter Brett to teach at Monash in 1964. History 1C was taught by John Morgan of the department of history and Peter Corris, a teaching fellow later more famous as the author of the Cliff Hardy novels, took tutorials in this subject. Three further senior appointments were made during 1964, with David Jackson arriving from England in May, Peter Hocker from Queensland in August and Gerry Nash from Melbourne in December.

---

17 Interview with Ann Lahore, 17 July 2012.

18 Ibid. Reaburn later taught at the universities of Tasmania and New South Wales, before moving to the Commonwealth Attorney-General's Department. In 2000 he became director of the Tasmanian Legal Aid Commission.

19 Quoted in Balmford, 'Foundation of the Monash Law School', p. 168.

For the first year of teaching, the staff of the law school squeezed into a tiny space at one end of the Hargrave Library, where the law library collection was also being established. The dean and his secretary both had little offices, but other staff members were in a large open space, divided by head-high partitions. The only wash-basin for the library staff was in Ann Lahore's 'office' and she often had the librarians coming in to wash their hands. Frank Beasley was next to her, puffing continuously on his pipe. Classes were held in rooms within the Hargrave Library building and in various science and engineering lecture theatres.

In 1964 the university campus was still little more than a large construction site and one of the most striking memories among the first students remains the ubiquitous mud. Monash University was nicknamed 'the farm', following from Melbourne's longstanding 'the shop' and reflecting the semi-rural ambience of Clayton in the 1960s. To Dennis Liner the nickname was apt: Monash was 'out in the country' and you needed gumboots to get around because 'the place was full of mud'. Ruth Thomas' first memory of Monash was that 'the car park was a bog'. Nahum Mushin vividly remembers, 'There were no paths around the campus in those early days and torches and gumboots were essential items of equipment.' When the paths were made 'where everyone had walked', he thought this was 'a very sensible arrangement'.

Getting to Monash was a lengthy journey for many students. A 1963 survey found that only about twenty-five per cent of Monash students came by public transport. The rest travelled by car, either as drivers or as passengers. Many hitchhiked. Ruth Thomas took the bus to Toorak station, a train to Huntingdale and then a bus to Monash, one of many making similar trips every day. In the early years, parking at Monash was plentiful and free, so everyone drove if a car was available. Monash's relative isolation had one advantage. As many former students have said, 'Once you got to Monash you stayed there all day'. This had great advantages because it helped students form strong and enduring friendships, participate fully in extra-curricular activities and generally immerse themselves in university life.

The first law students at Monash dressed conservatively. A photo of the first cohort shows the girls in either a dress or skirt and blouse with cardigan and at least half of the boys wearing ties. There is no hint of long hair or a beard, nor even a Beatles-inspired fringe. Memories of Ruth Thomas in her fashionable Toorak attire of neat skirts, twinsets and pearls stand out for two students.[20] Dress, as well as studying law, appears to have been taken seriously by the students when they arrived in 1964.

The Monash Law Students' Society (LSS) was founded early in the faculty's first year. No records of the early years of the society have been found, but the *Monash Reporter* recorded its foundation, noting that Sir Edmund Herring CJ had accepted an invitation to be patron and 'the students have already invited several eminent practitioners to address them on legal topics'.[21] The society aimed to 'encourage debating and forensic speaking amongst Law students'; there was no talk of beer or barbecues, which only became a feature of LSS activities in the late 1970s.

Soon after its formation, the LSS organized the first moot court, held on 26 June 1964. It was held, the *Monash Reporter* noted,

> in the suitably "judicial atmosphere" of the Council Chamber. The students acquitted themselves admirably, notwithstanding the caustic judicial comment from a Bench of three learned judges, presided over by Jackson CJ [senior lecturer David Jackson]. Not even the unexpected appearance in the Public Gallery of the Vice-Chancellor seemed to shatter the nerves or affect the eloquence of the senior counsel.[22]

The *Reporter* continued that, 'It is hoped that the Moot Court programme will expand in time to enable every student to participate at least once during his course'.

In its first year, the LSS published one issue of a journal called *In Gremio Legis* (In the Bosom of the Law), which also appeared again in 1968–70. The first edition featured an introduction by David Derham, a short historical essay about the founding of the new law school by Frank Beasley, and reflections on the structure and aims of the newly founded Law Students' Society. One of the more intriguing articles was a report on a survey of arts, medicine and science students, who were asked: 'What do you think of the Law Faculty and the Law students' society at Monash University?' Responses to the question included 'Down with Chris Smale' (a committee member), 'I haven't seen any action on the part of Law Students for the entire year', 'They are poor boozers – not as good as the Meds', and 'They haven't been very significant have they?'. One respondent replied flippantly that:

---

20 Interviews with Rob Capes, 18 December 2012, and Carol Bartlett, 14 August 2013.

21 *Monash Reporter*, No. 3, August 1964, p. 6.

22 Ibid.

> The Law Faculty is fair enough in itself, but supersilious [sic] and pusillanimous in its outward expression as exhibited in the smoking lounges and the cafeterias. In the future it may become a real dominant force in the University.

The author concluded that the faculty had 'a long way to go before we become a dominant force' in the university and establish a 'respectful name'.[23]

The Law Library

The law is an historical creation and it is essentially a reading discipline. Particularly in the common-law world with its reliance on case law, a law library is an essential ingredient of a law school. As David Derham and Zelman Cowen repeatedly pointed out, 'a Law Library is to a Law course what a laboratory is to a Science course'.[24] In negotiating his appointment Derham insisted on 'a guaranteed annual grant for a number of years to build up the book stocks to a respectable level'.[25] The library got off to a flying start when he was able to acquire around 3,000 books from the libraries of two former Supreme Court judges, Sir Charles Gavan Duffy and Sir Charles Lowe.[26]

No sooner had Derham's appointment been announced than Ernest Cooke of Russell, Kennedy & Cooke wrote to him recommending a standing order for all new law books with the major publishers and enclosing a list of reports, law reviews, texts, encyclopaedias and statutes, 'that seem to me to be at least the skeleton of a library'. Derham sent the list to the Monash Librarian, Ernest Clark, commenting that:

> The Argus Law Reports are not easy to come by. I happen to know that John Kearney, barrister, Owen Dixon Chambers, 205 William Street, has a complete set which he is prepared to sell for £300. This is a very reasonable price. It would be a good thing if you could have your purchasing officer write to him immediately offering to buy the set for that price.[27]

---

23 'Where do we rate?', *In Gremio Legis*, vol. 1, no. 1, 1964, pp. 6–8.

24 Zelman Cowen to Louis Matheson, 13 May 1960, CB/230/0 Part 1 – Admission to Faculty of Law 1963–70, MUA.

25 Matheson, *Still Learning*, p. 17.

26 Balmford, 'Foundation of the Monash Law School', p. 168; P L Waller, 'The Monash Law School', *Australian Bar Gazette*, no. 1, December 1966, p. 5.

27 MON 806, 1995/24, 1963–67, Dean's subject correspondence files, 1963–1969, 'Law Library maintenance and development', 1995/24, 806, acc no 1995/24, item 1, MUA.

Derham asked Professor Frank Beasley to establish the new library because 'He had contacts with every law library in the world'.[28] Soon after he arrived in Melbourne in February 1964, Beasley wrote to colleagues in Australia and overseas, informing them of his new position at Monash and requesting assistance. Thus when writing to publisher Fred R Rothman of South Hackensack, New Jersey, he asked for copies of law reviews such as 'Harvard, Chicago, Columbia, Michigan, Yale, [the] *Index to Legal Periodicals* and *Law and Contemporary Problems*'.[29] Beasley, Derham and Waller all wrote to colleagues in Australian and international universities to request copies of law journals, statutes and other relevant texts, and they received many positive responses and promises of books. Thanking Professor Daniel Turack of Queen's University, Kingston, Ontario for his offer of assistance 'with respect to Canadian materials for our library', Derham added that 'We are buying heavily now and will reach the Canadian section fairly soon. I shall take up your offer if we run into any difficulties and shall be in touch with you.' He also thanked Mr Justice Smithers of the Supreme Court of Papua and New Guinea for the first part of the Papua and New Guinea Law Reports and G J Davies, the editor of the *Federal Law Review* for a copy of the first issue.[30] Derham made a 'plea for assistance for Monash University's new law school' to Arthur Rylah, the Victorian attorney-general: 'Our needs fall naturally into two parts: past legislative material on the one hand and future material on the other. I am attaching a list of deficiencies on our present holdings so far as the past is concerned'. He added that the New South Wales government had presented the faculty with a complete set of NSW legislation from 1824 to 1957 and asked whether 'the resources of your Department may stretch to a similar act of generosity?' Within a short time, the law library's holdings of Victorian statutes were complete from 1851 to 1962.

Until the new law building was completed, the law library was housed on the first floor of the Hargrave Library near the rest of the faculty's temporary accommodation. The collection grew rapidly and by 1966 the law library had

---

28 E K Braybrooke, 'A Personal Tribute', *Monash University Law Review*, no. 3, vol. 4, 1986, p. 12.

29 Beasley to Fred B Rothman, South Hackensack, NJ, USA, 28 February 1964, MON 806, Dean's subject correspondence files, 1963–1969, item 1, MUA.

30 Derham to Turack, 1 April 1964; Derham to Smithers, 4 June 1964; Davies to Derham, 14 July 1964, MON 806, 1995/24, 1963–67, Dean's subject correspondence files, 1963–69, MUA.

about 10,000 volumes.[31] Beasley resigned his position in October 1966 on being appointed a visiting professor at Singapore, although he returned for a year in 1968.[32]

The first year of teaching law at Monash was an exciting adventure for both students and staff. Mark Aronson recalls that the Monash course was fun for the first cohort of students: 'There was a level of engagement between students and staff you would only get when starting up because the place was so small it could happen easily.' Almost all members of the first cohort of students would agree with the sentiment expressed by Bob Williams that 'there was a strong sense that we were creating the traditions and standards that would be the basis for the future'.[33]

---

31 *Monash University Calendar*, 1966, p. 622.

32 Faculty Board minutes, 29 September 1966 and 24 July 1969.

33 Quoted in Penny Rankin, 'Forty Years On: a legal review', *Monash Magazine*, no. 20, spring/summer 2007, p. 2.

Chapter 4

The Pioneer Staff

David Derham left an indelible mark on the Monash law school. The culture, the approach to teaching and research, the law library and the law building all arose from his vision for the law school. But perhaps the most important legacy he left was the staff he appointed. As foundation dean he was the only dean given the opportunity to bring in a complete cohort of academics, and the people he chose provided the core of the faculty for many years to come.

As with most professional disciplines, where the rewards of practice usually greatly exceed the rewards of academia, it has always been difficult to recruit legal academics. The problem was exacerbated at Monash because it grew far more rapidly than any of its predecessors. After its first hundred years Melbourne had ten full-time staff; Monash passed that number in its second year. With an initial undergraduate intake of 149, and a total enrolment of 752 by 1968, combined with his determination to have a far better staff:student ratio than Melbourne, Derham had to find more legal academics more quickly than had ever been done in Australia. His difficulties were exacerbated by Monash's location, which meant that the new law faculty could not rely largely on part-time teachers from the ranks of practitioners, as the older law schools had always done.

In spite of these challenges, by the time he departed in March 1968 Derham had put together a full-time staff of four professors, two readers, twelve senior lecturers, five lecturers, a moot master and a research scholar, supplemented by about eight full-time and eleven part-time teaching fellows, and thirteen distinguished practitioners who acted as consultants in common law subjects. For a conservative man brought up in White Australia, Derham was colour blind in his search for good staff, and although he could never shake off the habit of a lifetime and always referred to the generic law student or teacher as 'he', he appointed Australia's first woman professor of law.

Of the twenty-six full-time staff of lecturer or above recruited by David Derham, exactly half had undergraduate legal training from the University of Melbourne, five from other Australian universities, six from English universities, one from New Zealand, one from Karachi and one from the Hebrew University in Israel. Only two had Australian postgraduate qualifications, but six had postgraduate training at top American law schools and two had BCLs from Oxford. PhDs were still rare among academic lawyers and Monash was probably unusual among Australian law schools in having even one (Enid Campbell).

In its first year of teaching, the faculty only had to find staff for two subjects, The Legal System and Criminal Law, and the lecturers for the latter were borrowed from Melbourne. In 1965, teaching began in Constitutional Law and the core common law subjects: Torts, Property and Contracts; the following year teachers were needed for a further seven subjects. Recruiting staff occupied much of David Derham's time and he used all his charm, advocacy skills and contacts around the world to entice people to take a step into the unknown and come to Monash.

During 1964 three senior lecturers were appointed. The first to arrive was Englishman David Jackson, who had been educated at Oxford and was teaching at the University of Singapore when approached by Derham to come to Monash. A prolific publisher by the standards of the day, Jackson's primary interest while at Monash was property law, though after his return to England he became a leading authority on maritime law. His *magnum opus*, written while at Monash and published in 1967, was *Principles of Property Law*, a learned treatise which students found 'very dense and almost impossible to translate'.[1] Jackson was a popular teacher, particularly with the better students, as he explored concepts and encouraged students to play with ideas. Bob Williams recalls that 'Intellectual ideas could be given free rein in David's classes without over concern as to what the balance of judicial authority might seem to mandate'. For Ruth Thomas, Jackson's teaching of property law provided a 'light bulb appears in the head moment' when she cottoned on to the importance of what he had been teaching. In late 1964 Jackson became the first 'academic advisor to students', as the post of sub-dean was initially known (the vice-chancellor did not like the title 'sub-dean'), and in 1965 was appointed to the third chair in the faculty ahead of over twenty other applicants.

In August 1964 Peter Hocker arrived to teach contract law. A Queenslander, he had an unusual career path, having joined the navy as a boy (topping his class at Flinders Naval College) and studied engineering at the University of Melbourne before turning to the law.[2] He was a nervous

---

1 Comment by Simon Smith, June 2013.

2 Brisbane *Courier-Mail*, 25 October 1952.

lecturer in his early years and the students would count how many times he said 'Um' during each lecture, but improved rapidly with experience.[3] With Cliff Pannam and Richard McGarvie he wrote (and still writes) *Cases and Materials on Contract*, and he later went on to become a leading expert on Japanese law. He left Monash in 1977 to become the first executive director of the Australia Japan Foundation.[4]

At the end of 1964 Patrick Gerard Nash arrived from Melbourne, where he had been teaching law in the commerce faculty. He was a protégé of David Derham, although their backgrounds could hardly have been more different. Nash came from a poor, working class Catholic family and could only complete his secondary schooling at Christian Brothers College St Kilda with the aid of a scholarship and by working before and after school. He looked to law as a way of escaping poverty and enrolled at Melbourne in 1951, again with the aid of a scholarship.[5]

Gerry Nash thinks he is probably the only person to obtain an honours degree from Melbourne after failing first year. His school days had been a fully structured life of work and study, but his habits changed radically in his first year at university. He sat and thought, drank coffee, and chased girls. A workaholic as a teenager, he began to lie on the grass thinking. Perhaps predictably, he discovered the problems with this lifestyle at the end of the year. His scholarship was suspended and he had to pay fees – a good friend lent him some money to tide him over. His results improved dramatically and he graduated in 1956 with a good honours degree.

In 1956, after Nash had completed articles, David Derham suggested he apply for a vacancy in the University of Tasmania law school and Nash agreed as he had come to see the attractions of the life of an academic lawyer. Appointed to the position, he enjoyed the teaching, the lifestyle and the company of other scholars, but the University of Tasmania was in the throes of the Orr case, which culminated in almost the whole law school resigning, leading Nash to return to the bar in Melbourne.[6] After a couple of years

---

3 Interview with Nahum Mushin, 23 March 2011.

4 *Age*, 30 June 1977.

5 Interview with Gerry Nash, 3 October 2011.

6 For accounts of the Orr case, see W D Joske, 'Orr, Sydney Sparkes (1914?–1966), *Australian Dictionary of Biography*, vol. 15, Melbourne University Press, Melbourne, 2000, pp. 543–544; W H C Eddy, *Orr*, Jacaranda, Brisbane, 1961; Cassandra Pybus, *Seduction and Consent: A Case of Gross Moral Turpitude*, Mandarin, Melbourne, 1994. For the impact on the University of Tasmania law school, see Richard Davis, *100 Years: A Centenary History of the Faculty of Law, University of Tasmania, 1893–1993*, University of Tasmania, Hobart, 1993, pp. 46–52.

he was offered a senior lectureship in the Melbourne faculty of commerce. He accepted it essentially for the security it offered, though he did not find much satisfaction in teaching basic legal principles to would-be accountants. When David Derham asked him to come to Monash, Nash was 'wildly enthusiastic'.

Nash felt that the students at Monash were very conscious of being at a new university and they developed a great sense of tribalism, akin, he thought to the tribalism of Collingwood football supporters, and in strong contrast to the relative lack of camaraderie at Melbourne. Although it was obvious that most of the early students came to Monash because they had not been able to get into Melbourne, in the early years the students were more enthusiastic and the atmosphere much less formal than at Melbourne. There was a real feeling that they were all pioneers and there was much greater staff-student rapport.

In September 1965, Gerry Nash became sub-dean and students enjoyed his sense of humour and ability to see the funny side of almost any situation. However, he did not remain in the position for long, leaving in mid-1966 on being appointed foundation dean of the Papua New Guinea law school, again on David Derham's recommendation. After an adventurous four years he returned to the Henry Bournes Higgins chair at Monash in 1970.

The most notable appointment during 1964 was Louis Waller, another former student and colleague of David Derham, and first in Monash's pantheon of outstanding Jewish legal academics. Born in Siedlce, Poland, in 1935 he and his family escaped the impending Holocaust, arriving in Australia in 1938. He decided on a legal career while a student at University High School, vividly recalling opening a copy of Kenny's *Outline of Criminal Law* and seeing a big heading: 'Murder', which aroused his interest in criminal law. He also took classes at a Hebrew Sunday School from the age of fifteen and realised that he enjoyed teaching. Enrolling at Melbourne in 1952, his four years as a law student were 'years of undiminished pleasure'. Although the full-time staff was tiny, the teaching of the likes of Zelman Cowen and David Derham was exceptional. Patrick Donovan, the professor of commercial law, was the first Waller recalls attempting American-style case-based teaching, but the Melbourne law library only had two copies of most reports and with classes of 150 or more, it was impossible for most students to read the cases.

Waller began to think of an academic career during third year, largely under the influence of Zelman Cowen, David Derham and Norval Morris. Cowen and Derham encouraged their best students to study overseas and

Waller spent two years at Oxford studying for the Bachelor of Civil Law, graduating in 1958 with first class honours.

Even before he sat his BCL exams, 24-year-old Waller was offered a senior lectureship at Melbourne and returned to teach criminal law and introduction to legal method from the start of 1959. He worked closely with Peter Brett in developing case-method teaching for criminal law and together they devised pioneering materials leading to the publication of Australia's first criminal law case book in 1962. Zelman Cowen was keen that all academic lawyers should be professionally qualified so Waller enrolled in the four subjects required for admission to practice and in October 1962 began articles at Corr & Corr. Within a week he became immersed in the frantic efforts to prevent the hanging of Robert Tait, which continued until Tait's dramatic reprieve on 5 November.

When teaching began in the law faculty at Monash in 1964, Waller and Peter Brett both helped teach Criminal Law on a part-time basis in addition to their teaching at Melbourne. During the first two terms Waller taught the honours class, many of whom were extremely able students. He thought the most interesting, because he was the quietest, was Bob Williams, who was 'the outstanding student of his era'.

Early in 1964, the Monash law school advertised a second chair. After initial hesitation, Waller applied, with other applicants including Colin Howard, later dean of the Melbourne law school, and John Feltham, a senior lecturer at Melbourne and brother of Hilary Feltham. Waller was interviewed shortly before going overseas on study leave and was in America when he received a letter from David Derham offering him the chair.

Waller's sabbatical was at the University of Pennsylvania, where he taught a course on advanced criminal law, based on the interest he had developed in the interaction between morality and the law in controversial crimes such as suicide, abortion and homosexual acts. Melbourne was generous in not insisting he return after his sabbatical, and he commenced at Monash in June 1965.

In December 1963, the law school's advisory committee suggested that chairs in the faculty should be named after distinguished jurists rather than a subject. This was prompted by the frequent disjunction at Melbourne between the titles of chairs and the interests of the incumbents, notably one professor of jurisprudence, who had wide interests, but jurisprudence was not one of them.[7] Consequently, Louis Waller became the Sir Leo

7 Waugh, *First Principles*, p. 111.

Cussen professor, in September 1965 David Derham's chair was named for Sir Owen Dixon and David Jackson's new chair was called the Sir John Latham chair.[8]

Louis Waller was without question the most memorable teacher in the Monash law school's first fifty years. Generations of students remember his dramatic opening line in their first Criminal Law lecture, 'Imagine, if you will, that I am Queen Victoria', as he began an exposition of the famous cannibalism case of *R v Dudley and Stephens*. In his early years at Monash he still wore the traditional gown, which added to the theatrical effect of his lectures. Bob Williams recalls that 'He possessed all of the skills of an outstanding academic and scholar, and combined them with a flair for the dramatic and a realization that the skills of the thespian can contribute greatly to effective teaching.' Julian Burnside was impressed by his teaching and still remembers Waller's 'emphasis that the law is embedded in society and it can't be looked at separately from society'.[9]

Louis Waller's lectures were deeply imprinted on the memories of generations of Monash students. Greg Carne, a student in the mid-1980s, recalls that

> every lecture would start – with great gravitas and studied phrasing – 'Ladies and gentlemen, are there any questions?' He appeared genuinely shocked one day when someone did ask him a question. At the beginning of his final lecture for the subject he began with 'Ladies and gentlemen, are there any answers?' He gave poignant eulogies in lecture time of recently deceased legal luminaries associated with Monash law school and the Victorian legal profession – one of these took up almost the entire lecture hour.[10]

Waller was one of the main exponents of case-method teaching in the early years at Monash, and many students recall their fear of his probing questioning in lectures. However, the terror he inspired in those who had not done their reading belied his kind and friendly nature, as most students came to realise. Waller helped Harry Reicher plan his BEcon/LLB course:

---

8 Advisory Committee minutes, 19 December 1963, 5 February 1964; Faculty Board minutes, 28 September 1965.

9 Interview with Julian Burnside, 7 March 2012.

10 Interview with Greg Carne, 21 January 2012. Louis Waller recalls that he spoke at some length following the death of Rupert Cross, the Vinerian Professor at Oxford and author of the famous text on evidence.

> Louis ... started mapping out my program over the next five years, year by year, subject by subject. In 1966, he told me, I would take these courses. And in 1967, I would take those. And so on. When he got to 1970, he paused, drew a deep breath, and sighed: "Oy. We should only live so long!"

Waller also built up a deserved reputation as one of the leading scholars in the Monash law school, with a notable publication record over the fields of criminal law, legal education, evidence, criminology, forensic medicine, the law and medicine, and law reform.

During 1965, three new tenured senior lecturers were appointed along with an influential temporary senior lecturer. In their different ways all left significant marks on the faculty. Barry Connell had taught history at Geelong Grammar School in the 1950s before studying law at Melbourne and working for several years in the Commonwealth attorney-general's department. His main field in his early years at Monash was legal history, but as this faded from the curriculum he began the teaching of international law in the faculty. This remained his main teaching and research interest for the rest of his career, although he also taught civil procedure and constitutional law. He became an expert in the legal complexities facing newly independent nations, taking leave in 1969 to advise the Kingdom of Lesotho, and resigning from the faculty in 1971 to become chief secretary and secretary for external affairs for the Republic of Nauru. Even after he returned to Monash in 1974, he retained close links with Nauru, being a member of several Nauruan boards and commissions and a member of the legal team that successfully ran a case before the International Court of Justice in 1989 to gain compensation for the damage caused to Nauru by phosphate mining.[11] Connell was sub-dean 1967–69 and again in 1970–71 and students found him kindly and helpful. When Harry Reicher published the first Australian case book on international law, *Australian International Law: Cases and Materials*, he eloquently thanked Connell for fanning the flames of his interest in the field and his kindness in granting extensions.[12]

---

11 Obituary of Barry Connell by Helen Bogdan, the *Age*, 2 August 2013. The case for compensation for Nauru was based on the work of an independent commission of inquiry, headed by Christie Weeramantry. See, Mary Nazzal, 'Nauru, an Environment Destroyed and International Law', 2005, http://lawanddevelopment.org/docs/nauru.pdf.

12 Harry Reicher, *Australian International Law: Cases and Materials*, Law Book Co., Sydney, 1995, pp. x–xi.

Barry Connell, an influential lecturer who taught international law and was sub-Dean 1967–69 and 1970–71.
Photographer unknown, Monpix 810

New Zealander Peter Hogg graduated LLB from Victoria University in Wellington in 1961 and practised briefly before winning a scholarship to Harvard, where he completed an LLM in 1963. After a year teaching at Victoria he arrived at Monash at the end of 1965. He taught mainly administrative law and is remembered as an outstanding teacher. Ron McCallum found Hogg 'had the clarity the great teachers have and a talent for showing students where the intellectual fault lines were'; George Golvan considered his lectures extremely clear and well-organised. Hogg is notable as the law faculty's first PhD graduate, completing his thesis 'Liability of the Crown in Australia, New Zealand and the United Kingdom' in 1969. The following year (aged only thirty-one) he was appointed to a chair at Osgoode Hall law school in Toronto, where remained for the rest of his career, becoming recognised as the leading authority on the Canadian constitution.

The stories of Barry Connell and Peter Hogg can be told in conventional terms, but these are largely redundant when relating the unusual career of Abe Harari. It is rare to be able to use adjectives such as fanatical, obsessive or even eccentric to describe legal academics. With Abe Harari they barely begin to scratch the surface of this flawed genius. A survivor of the Holocaust, Harari fought in the Jewish struggle against the British in Palestine before studying law at the Hebrew University in Jerusalem after Israel gained independence. In the late 1950s he enrolled as a PhD student at the Australian National University and his thesis on 'The Place of Negligence in the Law of Torts' became one of the most famous theses in legal history. H L A Hart, the professor of jurisprudence at Oxford, was nominated as an examiner, even though the thesis included strong criticisms of Hart's work. Hart suggested major revisions to the thesis, most of which Harari rejected, and the thesis failed (although it was soon published and is still highly regarded). Harari believed in academic rigour and 'regarded illogical argument as abomination' and he felt that the criticisms of his thesis were deeply flawed. Consequently he felt a flaming sense of injustice and began an obsessive campaign against Hart, writing such biting and lacerating letters that Hart began to fear for his life. The obsession with Hart extended to every aspect of Harari's work. Gerald Dworkin recalls that Harari presented an honours seminar on Hart's *Concept of Law*, which at the time dominated thinking on jurisprudence. Harari,

> with his students, undertook a Talmudic page by page, almost line by line, devastating critique of the work, a fascinating exercise for all involved, even though at times the excessive criticism of almost every sentence made it difficult to separate major and minor issues. [He] then wrote up his analyses and sent regular instalments to other jurisprudence scholars around the world.[13]

---

13 Email from Gerald Dworkin to authors, 26 September 2013.

These analyses became the basis of a lengthy essay attacking Hart's scholarship, with the final version being 96 pages long. The account of Harari's vendetta against Hart occupies six pages in Hart's biography.[14]

Before his controversy with Hart gathered momentum, Harari was appointed to one of the many vacancies in the University of Tasmania law school, where he played a helpful part in resolving the long-running Orr controversy.[15] In 1965 he applied for one of the advertised senior lectureships at Monash, and David Derham was willing to take a risk that his obvious brilliance would outweigh his equally obvious obsessions. Harari arrived in August 1965 and made an immediate impact on students. Mark Aronson recalls that

> Harari taught jurisprudence and was a wonderful teacher. He was able to teach his students to read critically and taught them to 'switch frames' and look at issues from all points of view. This was not a bad achievement for a teacher of undergraduates.

Nahum Mushin remembers Harari as 'a most erudite person' with a thick Jewish accent, while Bob Williams recalls a 'dapper man … presenting in the tradition of the European Jewish intellectual'. He was a stimulating lecturer who challenged the students philosophically and emotionally. 'None of my teachers did more to hone my skills of precise and critical analysis than Abe,' Williams says.

Unfortunately Harari's great intellect became obsessed with achieving perfection and he would rewrite each sentence many times before he was satisfied with it. Consequently he published only two articles while at Monash. One was co-written with Gerald Dworkin, a highly influential temporary lecturer, who came to Monash for two years from mid-1965.[16] Dworkin was reader in law at the London School of Economics and had taken two years' leave from the LSE to teach in Nigeria. When the outbreak

14 Nicola Lacey, *A Life of HLA Hart: The Nightmare and the Noble Dream*, Oxford University Press, Oxford, 2004, pp. 274–7, 289, 292. Jude Wallace, a colleague and friend of Harari, believes that he was obsessed but not bitter, and that Harari felt that the fight was for the maintenance of university standards rather than a personal vendetta. She also points out that Harari's behaviour was affected by the brain tumour that eventually killed him. Interview with Jude Wallace, 15 June 2012.

15 Davis, *100 Years: A Centenary History of the Faculty of Law, University of Tasmania, 1893–1993*, University of Tasmania, Hobart, 1993, p. 58.

16 Gerald Dworkin is unrelated to either Ronald Dworkin, who succeeded H L A Hart as professor of jurisprudence at Oxford, or Gerald Dworkin who teaches at the University of California, Davis.

of civil war made this impossible, David Derham invited him to Monash. Dworkin was an outstanding and inspiring lecturer. Although his primary interest was originally in torts, he initiated the teaching of the law of trusts (then called Property II) which was a fast growing and significant area of law with many doctrinal and practical implications. Members of the first honours class agree they were 'seriously blessed to be taught by him'. His honours seminars dissected the rule against perpetuities, which was 'absurd in its application but presented intellectual challenges that would fascinate a grand master in chess' and worked on drafting legislation to change it. Dworkin was offered a chair at Monash, but chose to return to England, where he had a distinguished career primarily at the University of London, where he held the Herchel Smith chair in intellectual property law.

Jack Fajgenbaum joined the staff in 1965 directly from Yale. He had completed an arts/law degree at Melbourne and, although he had not been an enthusiastic law student, Zelman Cowen encouraged him to sit for the honours exams. He did well and Cowen organised a Commonwealth fellowship to Chicago, where he took the final year of the Chicago JD course. He found Chicago far more rigorous than Melbourne, with the law students being extremely ambitious and working ferociously hard. After Chicago, Fajgenbaum went to Yale, where he completed his LLM in 1965. David Derham phoned him at Yale offering him a lectureship, and he came to Monash to teach constitutional and administrative law and occasionally criminal law. However, while on sabbatical to Cambridge in 1972, he 'realised that [he] was not a real scholar', so on his return he taught for just one more year before leaving for a highly successful career at the bar.[17]

Early in 1966 Justice William Charles became the faculty's first moot master. Educated at the University of Melbourne, Charles was admitted to the bar in 1932. After the Second World War he became a member of His Majesty's Overseas Judiciary, serving as a judge in the Solomon Islands, Hong Kong, Nigeria and Zambia, giving him the material for numerous anecdotes. Early moot courts had been run by the law students' society, but from 1967 they became compulsory, with all students having to participate in at least two moots before graduation. Charles himself donated the prize for the best mooter. He remained moot master until his retirement in 1976. Gerald Dworkin recalls that it was an excellent idea of David Derham to recruit an ex-judge as moot master, and that the moots

17 Interview with Jack Fajgenbaum, 22 February 2012.

were always 'highly organised and professional and provided participants with invaluable experience.'[18]

Another new arrival in 1966 was Bryan Dwyer, who graduated LLB from Melbourne in 1959 and then completed an LLM at Michigan and worked with a leading Wall Street firm before returning to private practice in Melbourne in 1963. After returning to academia, he taught property, equity and trusts. A highly respected teacher, he insisted on high standards and had the ability to get students thinking. For Pam O'Connor, he 'planted the seed' that led to her PhD thesis. On the other hand, some students felt he 'knew too much' about the subjects he taught. 'Bryan Dwyer just loves Trusts too much', one complained, 'I'm sure he dreams at night about discretionary Trusts and has dinner parties with Trustees to talk about the effect of *Hardoon v Belilios*'.[19] Another observed succinctly, 'He's tough but he's damn good' and noted that he was 'renowned for eating lazy students for breakfast'.[20] Ill-prepared students soon learnt not to sit up the back in his classes as he always aimed his most penetrating questions at those in the back row. Although his knowledge of property and trusts was encyclopaedic and always current, he published little, though *Introduction to Property Law*, jointly authored with Gim Teh, became a best-selling textbook.

The pace of recruitment increased during 1967, with the biggest influx of new staff members in the faculty's history. Some, such as Igor Kavass[21] and Harry Smith, stayed only a short time, but others became legendary names in the life of the law school. With the appointment of Francis Trindade, David Derham began a faculty tradition of recruiting staff from those Asian countries which had inherited the British common law. Born in what was then British India when the Raj still ruled, Trindade completed his LLB at Karachi in 1958, studied at Oxford and Strasbourg and was called to the English bar before being appointed to a lectureship at the University of Singapore in 1963. David Derham was an external examiner in constitutional law at Singapore and visited each year to review exam papers and ensure

18 Email from Gerald Dworkin to authors, 26 September 2013.

19 *Counter Faculty Handbook*, 1986, p. 54. In *Hardoon v Belilios*, [1901] AC118, as many readers will recall, it was laid down that an adult beneficiary can be liable to indemnify a trustee in respect of losses on the trust estate.

20 *Counter Faculty Handbook*, 1994, pp. 47–8.

21 Latvian born Igor Kavass left Monash to go to America, where he became director of several major law libraries and the leading authority on America's international treaties. He had studied law at Melbourne in the same year as Louis Waller and Gerry Nash and came to Monash as a 'lawyer-librarian'.

that standards were being maintained. After Derham's appointment to Monash, he offered Trindade a lectureship there, but Trindade was happy in Singapore and did nothing about it. When Derham came back the next year he said 'We sent you an offer last year and you haven't responded' and reiterated that he was very keen to have him. Encouraged by David Jackson, who had also been at Singapore, Trindade accepted. There was some concern that he might have problems getting a visa as the White Australia policy was still in place, but Derham's quiet but effective behind-the-scenes influence ensured there were no difficulties.

When Trindade arrived he taught constitutional and international law, later teaching torts for many years, and this became the main area in which he built up one of the faculty's most outstanding publication records. He recalls that in 1966 Monash was a tiny faculty and had a strong family feeling. Like many of the other staff members, he and his wife Ann (who had a distinguished academic career at Melbourne) had small children and they all socialised together. There was a strongly collegial atmosphere with numerous opportunities for discussion, particularly over morning and afternoon tea. David Derham felt it was easier to sort things out over a cup of coffee than in formal meetings.

The faculty's first family law specialist, Henry Finlay, arrived at Monash in November 1966. The son of a Jewish judge, Finlay was born Günter Freund in Germany in 1923 and never lost his thick German accent, although he and his family escaped to England in 1939. Migrating to Australia after the war, he studied part-time for an LLB at the University of Tasmania, which he completed in 1957. Before coming to Monash, Finlay worked in private practice and in both the Tasmanian and Commonwealth public services. He became a leading family law scholar and published extensively for the era, his books including the definitive work *Family Law in Australia*, first published in 1972, and a widely cited study of the legal implications of sex change. Nahum Mushin was the first Monash graduate to be raised to the bench when he was appointed to the Family Court in 1990, and he thanked Finlay: 'You taught me all I know of family law' – to which Finlay replied, 'I'm surprised you became a judge'.[22]

England was a fertile recruiting ground for Monash law school in its early years. In 1967 Don Greig arrived with a first class honours degree

---

22 This paragraph is based on an obituary of Henry Finlay in *Family Matters*, no. 71, winter 2005, p. 3; Minute of appreciation for Associate Professor HA Finlay, Faculty Board minutes, 6 October 1988; and interview with Nahum Mushin.

from Cambridge. His main research interest was in international law, but he mainly taught contract at Monash, where students were impressed with his sharp mind and acerbic wit. Another Englishman, Stanley Robinson, had graduated from Manchester and had experience in private practice and both the British and Australian public service before coming to Monash to teach property, planning law and drafting. 'A real character with an unusual personality, who was both amusing and knowledgeable', is how George Golvan remembers him. *Counter Faculty Handbook* reviews of his teaching in later years invariably commented on his flamboyant style of dress and novel lecturing style, though not all went as far as the 1979 reviewer who described him as 'mad as a hatter'.[23]

Americans were less frequently seen. Allen Afterman was the first, coming to Monash as a 'senior teaching fellow' in 1967 after teaching at Wellington. He taught company law and with Bob Baxt wrote *Cases and Materials on Corporations and Associations*, which ran into eight editions. For a commercial lawyer, Afterman had a romantic streak, publishing two books of poems (possibly the only Monash law lecturer to do so, at least under his own name) and marrying (for a short while) a fellow staff member. He resigned in 1973 to pursue a career in writing and theatre.

Three further members of the staff intake of 1967 became, in their different ways, legends of the faculty. Ian 'Sam' Spry, the son of Charles Spry the director of ASIO, had graduated from Melbourne in 1961 and was an associate to Sir Owen Dixon before going to the bar. At Monash he taught taxation law and was regarded by his students as an effective lecturer but extremely conservative. He dressed formally, always wearing three-piece suits, and was described by one former colleague as looking 'a bit like an English country version of J. Edgar Hoover'. Spry berated Chris Chenoweth and other students for not maintaining the standards of dress appropriate for law students. One is tempted to think that attempting to maintain dress standards in the late 1960s makes tilting at windmills seem eminently practical. When one of Spry's students was asked a tough question in class and responded with a lengthy rhetorical answer ending with 'Why not?' he was surprised when Spry responded, 'Why not indeed?'.[24]

In 1971 Spry published his highly praised *Principles of Equitable Remedies*, described by Owen Dixon as 'the best legal book to have come out of

---

23 For example, *Counter Faculty Handbook*, 1979, pp. 48, 51.

24 Interview with Simon Smith, 5 April 2011.

Australia', and which is now in its eighth edition. The following year he published his handy guide, *Arrangements for the Avoidance of Taxation*, which was equally popular, though perhaps with a different audience. Spry was promoted to reader in 1973, but soon after decided to return to the bar, where his career and his personal life have had their colourful moments.

The contrast between Spry and the next new appointment of 1967 could not have been greater. With her long, flowing hair, flower power clothes and left-wing views, Jude Wallace came to be seen by her colleagues as by far the most radical member of staff. However, she emphasises that when she came to Monash from private practice with a large firm, she was not radical and 'took a decade to frame a socially conscious view of the law and legal system'. As a graduate of Melbourne law school, she says 'one could hardly be other than a formalist lawyer' and in moving to Monash she was conscious that 'we were setting ourselves against the traditional Melbourne model'. In Wallace's view,

> the merit of the law school in those days lay in its ability to contain and even encourage academics who broke with legal formalism and sought to create new legal ideas and theories. We were not Marxist ... or even radical, but we demanded law (academics, legislators and judges) be socially conscious, even if they pretended social neutrality.[25]

The 1967 intake of students was low, which meant 'a small class and tutorial base' allowing for a remarkable level of staff-student interaction.[26] Wallace taught property law from a perspective that was highly influenced by David Jackson and his 'reconstructed theories on the importance of equity in property law' and many of the more conservative students found this unsettling to their preconceived notions. Those students who sympathised with her views found her an inspiring teacher, but others were startled and confused.[27] Tony Pagone recalls that Wallace inspired students to become politically engaged and encouraged them to join the Tenants' Union. Jude Wallace campaigned strongly for reforms to the residential tenancy laws and the *Residential Tenancies Act* 1992 owed much to her advocacy.

---

25 Email from Jude Wallace to authors, 21 September 2013.

26 Interview with Jude Wallace, 15 June 2012.

27 Interview with Basil Fogarty, 11 January 2012; interview with Jon Faine 7 March 2012; and interview with Jude Wallace, 15 June 2012.

When she was appointed in 1967, Jude Wallace was seen by her colleagues as a very radical staff member, yet it was a decade before she sought to create new legal ideas and theories.
Photographer Richard Crompton, Monpix 847

The most universally liked and admired lecturer in the history of the Monash law school was unquestionably Lawrie McCredie. Born in 1928, McCredie followed family tradition by joining the army and after graduating from Duntroon completed a tour of duty with the British Army of the Rhine. However, his military career was cut short when he was seriously wounded in an accident in March 1952, losing his sight and his right arm. Following an exercise simulating battle conditions, with gunfire, grenades and sticks of gelignite, McCredie was left with three sticks of armed gelignite. Fearing they would become unstable, he decided to detonate them by lighting their fuses and hurling them safely toward vacant ground. The first stick was exploded uneventfully, but after lighting the second fuse, he saw a soldier walking into the danger area. Before he could throw the gelignite down a nearby rabbit hole, it exploded prematurely, leaving him and two other soldiers with appalling injuries.[28] Although McCredie survived, his army career was over. Showing amazing courage and resilience, he enrolled in law at Melbourne, where David Derham was ahead of his time in encouraging disabled students. After graduating with honours in 1960, Derham arranged for him to get articles at Arthur Robinson & Co., and then offered him a job at Monash when the new law school began. However, McCredie was happy at Arthur Robinson's and it was not until November 1966 that he came to Monash as a lecturer. He brought with him his secretary from Arthur Robinson's, Barbara Jones, and together they formed a remarkable team, influencing the lives and careers of numerous Monash law students. There was an 'enormous loyalty and trust' for him amongst the students. Barbara recalls that Lawrie had a sense of humour and that 'he was naughty!' but she stressed that he was an absolute gentleman, and importantly, 'you worked with him, not for him'.[29]

McCredie taught wills, equity, and trusts and estates, and his book *Administration of the Estates of Deceased Persons in Victoria*, first published in 1979, became a standard work. Ray Finkelstein was one of his early students and thought he was 'one of the really great teachers'. Although he taught a dry subject that was very heavily rule based, he made it interesting and inspired Ray to do more work in this subject than almost any other. His students from over three decades recount similar stories. However, it was as the faculty's longest-serving sub-dean that McCredie had his most profound influence. Friendly and approachable, he combined a deep knowledge of the law school and the university with a deep empathy with students. As sub-dean for nearly twenty-five years he had an uncanny ability to give career-defining and even life-changing advice to students. He told Ron McCallum to take Industrial Law, assuring him he would get on with the lecturer, even though he was a bit strange, and this set Ron on the path to becoming a leading authority in that field. When Marilyn Pittard included Family Law in her subjects one year, he strongly advised her against it because as soon as she went to a law firm, she would inevitably be stuck with practising in that area. Many other students tell stories of similarly perceptive advice. He was trusted and liked by the students and they knew that he would help them if a lecturer was not giving them a fair go.[30] As Pam O'Connor observed, he was 'an absolutely crucial person for the success of the faculty'.

---

28 Di Websdale-Morrissey, *Blind Optimism: The Life of Lawrie McCredie*, Arcadia, an imprint of Australian Scholarly Publishing, North Melbourne, 2013, pp. 30–35.

29 Interview with Barbara Jones, 26 October 2011.

30 Ibid.

Basil Fogarty, who had a young family and studied law part-time while working full-time as a clerk of courts, recalls that McCredie was immensely helpful in getting him through his course. Basil decided early on that 'any mark over 50 is wasted' and got 51 for most of his subjects – 'it was all I needed'. After an exam in one of McCredie's subjects, the exam papers went missing, and Lawrie gave every student an oral exam. After the exam, he asked Basil, 'Is that what you wrote in the exam?' to which Basil replied 'Most of it'. He told McCredie he'd be happy to get 51 and, sure enough he got 51. McCredie often said, 'The university is not here to fail people – the real pass rate is determined by what you do after you leave.'

There are more anecdotes about Lawrie McCredie than almost anybody else in the faculty. In 1977, blind lecturer Ron McCallum taught one of the faculty's first Indigenous students, but no one had told Ron and, when the student didn't turn up for his final exam with no excuse, Ron automatically put him down as a fail. Soon Lawrie came storming into his room asking why he failed the faculty's only Indigenous student without giving him a second chance. Ron excused himself, saying 'I didn't know he was Indigenous', to which Lawrie said 'I'm blind too, but I know'.

In 1981 McCredie was made a Commander of the Order of the British Empire (CBE) for services to the disabled and in 2007 he was awarded an AM 'for service to legal education, particularly in the areas of tertiary administration and teaching, and to the community through advocacy roles for people living with a disability'.

In 1967 David Derham gained approval for a fourth chair in the faculty, to be called the Sir Isaac Isaacs chair. The appointment was remarkable and did much to shape the culture of the growing faculty. Enid Campbell was far more than the first female law professor in Australia and the second woman professor at Monash (after Maureen Brunt); she was one of Australia's leading legal scholars and made a massive contribution to establishing Monash law school's academic reputation.

Enid Campbell was born in Launceston, Tasmania, in 1932 and was educated at the Launceston Methodist Ladies' College (where she was dux) and the University of Tasmania. After graduating LLB (Hons)/BEc, she won a scholarship to Duke University where she wrote a highly regarded PhD thesis on the nineteenth century legal philosopher John Austin. Returning to Australia, she taught at Tasmania and Sydney before David Derham invited her to apply for the new chair at Monash. By that time she had published three books and seventeen journal articles – a vast research output for the time – and she continued to publish until her death in 2010.

Enid Campbell was appointed to the Sir Isaac Isaacs Chair of Law, 1967.
Photographer John Hearder, Monpix 09

Campbell's main fields of teaching and research were constitutional and administrative law, legal philosophy and legal history. She always 'stood for uncompromising quality in legal scholarship'[31] and was regarded with awe and admiration by staff and students alike. To Jack Fajgenbaum she was 'a formidable woman and the most able lawyer in the faculty', while Arie Freiberg saw her as 'a towering figure' and rather intimidating to a new academic. Most students were similarly impressed. Victor Perton described

31 Minute of Appreciation to Professor Enid Campbell, Faculty Board minutes, 22 April 1998.

Campbell as 'a legendary teacher' who had a 'huge commanding presence' and 'made administrative law come alive'. Similarly Malcolm McComas found her teaching of administrative law 'sensational – her knowledge and enthusiasm for what was regarded as a boring subject was amazing'. Amanda George also remembers the impact of Enid Campbell's classes in administrative law: 'It was a dry subject but she brought it to life... she engaged you with a fierce intellect ...she was quite terrifying but she had a real presence.'

Her success inspired many female students. Deborah Glass, a student in the 1970s, recalls that sexism was rife at that time and 'it took the likes of Enid Campbell to make it unremarkable for women to do remarkable things'. However, she never became a mentor for younger women and was hostile to feminist lawyers. She was strongly opposed to affirmative action, reasoning that she had made it purely on her own merits and that everyone else should do the same.[32]

When the faculty moved into its new building in 1968, Enid Campbell was allocated a professorial room in the north-east corner of the third floor. Three decades later the walls and ceiling were brown and the air vents clogged with black tar from Enid's chain smoking. Even today, a keen nose can detect the aroma of stale tobacco smoke in room 309.

Enid's mischievous sense of humour had frequently led her into trouble at the Methodist Ladies' College in Launceston and this characteristic changed little over the course of her life. When some artificial greenery was placed around the entrance to the law school in the early 1990s, Enid disapproved. She went to the faculty manager, Eileen Wilson, to tell her she had seen birds nesting in the greenery and warned of the awful legal and reputational consequences 'if a bird pooped on the head of a distinguished visitor'. Greatly perturbed, Eileen went to see the birds' nests, only to return wagging her finger and saying, 'You're a naughty girl, Enid'. To which Enid could only reply, 'Yes, I am'.

Enid Campbell was a member of several government commissions and inquiries, notably the Royal Commission on Australian Government Administration (1974–6), the Pearce committee of inquiry into the discipline of law (1984–6) and the Constitutional Commission (1985–8). In 1979 she was awarded an OBE and in 2005 became a Companion of the Order of Australia (AC), the highest honour in the Australian honours system, 'for service to legal scholarship and education, to raising debate in the field of

---

[32] Interview with Yuri Grbich, 21 March 2012.

constitutional law and to public law reform'. Enid was one of the handful of individuals who 'formulated much of the character' of the faculty.[33]

David Derham's final appointment to the staff was another English lawyer, Patrick Higgins. After war service highlighted by the organisation of mule trains for the Indian Army, Higgins had completed an LLB at the University of London. In 1960 he came to the University of Tasmania as part of the cohort of new staff (including Abe Harari) rapidly assembled following the mass resignations of 1959 (which included Gerry Nash).[34] Appointed as a reader, Higgins taught contract and torts and published highly regarded texts in both fields.[35]

In addition to building up a high quality full-time staff, David Derham was able to enlist the services of a group of Melbourne's leading lawyers as consultants and many promising young lawyers as part-time teaching fellows. The consultants included such eminent silks as William Crockett, Ninian Stephen, William Kaye, Leo Lazarus and Richard McGarvie, while Ron Castan, Ron Meldrum, Alex Chernov, John Coldrey, Neil Brown, Peter Faris, Alan Goldberg and Louis Voumard were among the struggling young barristers happy to earn a few pounds taking tutorials. While the level of interest shown by the consultants varied significantly, most made useful contributions. Gerald Dworkin recalls 'how privileged I was to have Bill Kaye (who later chaired the bridge disaster inquiry and then became a High Court judge) for my Torts course and Ninian Stephen (who later became Governor General of Australia) for my Property course. Both provided lecture input and showed enormous interest in their tasks.'[36]

By the time Derham departed, the Monash law faculty's staff was second to none in Australia. It combined youth and enthusiasm with sound scholarship and a broad range of interests and approaches to the law. The sound and solid foundations he established left the Monash law school well placed to take over the mantle of Australia's leading law school.

---

33 Interview with Jenny Beaton, 12 November 2010.

34 Davis, *100 Years*, pp. 51, 58.

35 P F P Higgins and J G Starke, *Cheshire and Fifoot's Law of Contract*, 2nd Aust. Edn, Butterworths, Sydney, 1969; P F P Higgins, *Elements of Torts in Australia*, Butterworth, Sydney, 1970.

36 Email from Gerald Dworkin to authors, 26 September 2013.

Chapter 5

The Formative Years

During the second half of the 1960s Monash continued to grow at breakneck speed. The total number of students in the university rose from 2,900 in 1964 to 10,000 in 1970. Law student Martin Hudson recalled the campus 'bursting at the seams as the building program tried to keep pace with the growing student numbers'.[1] The number of law students rose sharply with each new intake as, of course, none of the first intake completed their law degrees until the end of 1969. On the other hand, the rise in total numbers was less than one might expect as the failure rate and the drop-out rate were both very high. Thus there were 149 new law students in 1964, 186 in 1965, 150 in 1966 and 246 in 1967, but the total number of students in 1967 was only 567, indicating that 164 students had dropped out or been excluded.[2]

The growth in the faculty demanded a more professional management structure. For the first two years Hilary Feltham had been the only administrator, but in November 1966 Allan York was appointed 'Senior Administrative Officer and Secretary to the Faculty of Law'. A Melbourne BCom graduate, York had previously been administration and finance manager of Chesebrough Ponds International Ltd. He remained with the faculty for twenty-three years and, with Lawrie McCredie as sub-dean, ensured that the administration of the faculty ran smoothly and without incident. York worked well with the faculty's first five deans and inevitably built up a position of great influence, dealing efficiently with administrative matters, maintaining a tight control of the faculty's finances and running the admissions process with great fairness and sensitivity. He recalled that selecting students likely to succeed in law school was as much an art as a science.[3]

---

1 Quoted Rankin, 'Forty Years On', p. 2.

2 It should be noted that these statistics are approximations only as the enrolment figures for the early years could best be described as intelligent guesses.

3 Interview with Allan York, 6 November 2010.

In 1965 the law school moved to new accommodation when a new science building was opened and David Derham was able to obtain some space in it for his faculty. Most of it was open with concrete floors, but the temporary partitions between offices were roof high rather than head high as in the Hargrave Library. Ann Lahore complained to David Derham about the concrete floor, and was pleased when he purchased some carpet, though it was 'the vilest carpet I have ever seen – bright mustard yellow and truly horrible, but better than concrete'. Soon after, with the staff growing rapidly, the law school was allocated some more space in another building and the faculty was split for a while, though everyone met for morning and afternoon tea.

As the faculty grew, it became increasingly difficult to function efficiently in premises designed for other purposes. The worst problems were in the law library, where as early as 1965 there was 'a breakdown in library services which had resulted in a chaotic state in the library in first term this year'.[4] The crisis prompted the advisory committee to call on the university administration to address 'the lack of adequate services in the Law Library'. The root of the problems, however, lay in trying to run a rapidly growing law library without specialised staff in a space designed for a science and engineering library.

The immediate crisis was resolved by the injection of more staff and more money and the library settled down in its temporary premises while preparations began for the move into its permanent home. From the end of 1967 planning was in the capable hands of Ted Glasson, who was acting law librarian from that time until his appointment was made permanent in 1969. Glasson had an unusual pathway to his vocation as Monash law librarian. He completed a law degree at Melbourne in 1957 and then studied for the Methodist ministry, being ordained in 1962. After three years he abandoned the church for librarianship, completing a graduate diploma in librarianship at UNSW before coming to Monash. Glasson was law librarian until 1993 and during his tenure the library's holdings grew from 20,000 volumes to over 120,000. As a trained lawyer he appreciated the special nature of a law library and he worked closely with the academic staff to develop what was clearly the best law library in Victoria and one of the very best in Australia.[5]

---

4 Advisory committee minutes, 8 May 1965.

5 Ted Glasson, minute of appreciation, Faculty Board minutes, 26 April 1993, Australian Law Librarians' Association, 'The Ted Glasson Australian Law Librarian Award', http://www.alla.asn.au/nat/docs/Ted Glasson Australian Law Librarian Award.pdf.

David Derham's contacts in England and America ensured that the new faculty had a steady stream of distinguished visitors. The most notable in the early years were Lord Denning, Master of the Rolls from 1962 to 1982, and Erwin Griswold, the dean of law at Harvard for twenty-one years, who both visited in July 1967. There was some embarrassment about the obvious deficiencies of the faculty's temporary accommodation and before the arrival of the distinguished guests everybody went to great lengths to make the place look as good as possible. Ann Lahore remembers Lord Denning walking into the law school, seeing David Jackson there and saying 'My dear fellow, what a pleasure to see you'. He remembered Jackson from his days in practice in England and told the assembled Monash staff, 'You are so lucky to have this man'.[6]

In the 1960s the students coming to Monash law school differed far more from those going to Melbourne than in any subsequent decade. While still skewed towards private schools, a higher percentage came from government schools. Far fewer students at Monash had previous family ties to the legal profession, with many Monash students being the children of immigrants. Monash also seemed to attract students who were more prepared to question the accepted ways of doing things and looking for new approaches, although this is impossible to quantify.

A major reason for the difference in the student profile was that student preference for Melbourne was stronger in the 1960s than in subsequent decades. Monash's location, its lack of established reputation and its increasingly radical image all meant that the 'best' students, as well as those who were more conservative, tended to choose Melbourne. For those who had the choice, it was something of a gamble to come to Monash. Many, of course, did not have the choice, and a large number of students were at Monash because they could not get into Melbourne. Whether they came from choice or otherwise, anecdotal evidence suggests that few regretted it.

Peter Bartlett's story was common at Monash but would have been rare at Melbourne. He grew up in Warburton where his father was a timber contractor and his mother ran a draper's shop. He went to Upper Yarra High School and very few of his fellow students went to university, but Peter's marks were good enough to get into law so he decided to do law. 'I had at the time never met a lawyer. I really had no idea what law was, but it seemed to be a good degree and I therefore decided to do that.' He had the choice of Monash or Melbourne but chose Monash because it was much easier to get

---

6 Interview with Ann Lahore, 17 July 2012.

to from Warburton. He was the only person from Warburton at Monash and knew nobody when he started first year.[7]

Neither of Mark Weinberg's parents had been to university and he did not know any lawyers while he was growing up, but he wanted to do law from a young age. A Melbourne High School student, he was one of the top students in the state in year twelve in 1965 and was offered a Monash undergraduate scholarship,

> which was what persuaded me to go to Monash law school rather than Melbourne law school. It paid me a very sizeable annual emolument in those days. I've forgotten what it was exactly, but I think it was something like seven hundred dollars a year which was a lot of money in 1966.[8]

Ron McCallum also had the choice of universities and his decision to go to Monash reveals much about David Derham and the ethos of the early Monash law school. Blinded as a baby by retrolental fibroplasia (caused by excessive oxygen in humidicribs), Ron spent his school years at the Royal Victorian Institute for the Blind (where he learnt Braille), Saint Paul's School for the Blind and finally at Saint Bede's Mentone, which 'had very intellectual teachers'. At that time few careers were open to blind people, who either did basket weaving or found some work where ability to read was not essential. Ron decided to be a high school teacher, but his year twelve results were so good he was offered places in law at both Monash and Melbourne. After talking with both law schools as to which to go to, he soon realized that Melbourne with its traditions was not for him, and he would have been lost in its bigger classes. In contrast, David Derham at Monash strongly supported diversity in the law faculty and was happy to take him. Lawrie McCredie was already teaching at Monash and this showed that the interest in diversity was more than just rhetoric.

Ray Finkelstein 'was always going to do law – my father said so'. He went to Elwood High School and chose to go to Monash because some of his close friends did not get into Melbourne and he wanted to stay with them rather than go to Melbourne where he didn't know anybody. Similarly, Julian Burnside chose Monash because an ex-boyfriend of his sister was there and he too didn't know anybody at Melbourne. He wasn't aware that Melbourne

---

7 Interview with Peter Bartlett, 26 April 2012.

8 Interview with Mark Weinberg by Ruth Campbell, 17 April and 4 August 1996; Law in Australian Society Oral History Project, National Library of Australia, TRC 3440.

had greater kudos and Monash had not yet developed the radical image that might have dissuaded a conservative Melbourne Grammar boy from going there.

In contrast to Mark Weinberg, Ron McCallum and Ray Finkelstein, Carol Bartlett (née Simpson) had always thought she would follow a traditional female career in nursing or teaching. However, she went to America as an exchange student halfway through year eleven, and on her return a year later, she decided to go to Taylor's College and sit her year twelve exams. She chose easy subjects because she had missed the first half of the year, and did not bother applying for university because she expected to fail. However, her results were good, but because she had not got the pre-requisites for most courses, the BJuris at Monash was one of the few courses she could get into. She expected to transfer to a different faculty, but found she enjoyed her law subjects and completed her LLB in 1969. She did articles at Gillott, Moir & Winneke, one of Melbourne's oldest law firms, but also one of the most progressive in its attitude towards women lawyers, already having a female partner when Carol began there.[9]

It is a significant feature of the early years of the Monash law school that a high proportion of the most outstanding students and of the students who have gone on to make the biggest mark in the legal profession and in other careers came from government high schools. The Supreme Court Prize winners who began their law studies under David Derham's deanship were Bob Williams (Burwood High School), Mark Aronson (Ballarat College), Kevin Pose (Elwood High School), Mark Weinberg (Melbourne High School), Chris Jessup (Scotch College) and Edward Wallace (Traralgon High School). Former Federal Court judge Ray Finkelstein went to Elwood High School, Monash's first judge, Nahum Mushin, to Melbourne High School, distinguished QC George Golvan to Brighton High School, leading media lawyer Peter Bartlett to Warburton High School and magistrate Graeme Golden to Glenroy High School.

Some students felt there was a deep division between private school and high school students in the early years at Monash. Ray Finkelstein recalls that students had to dress formally for moot courts and he was one of the few students without an old school tie to wear. He also noticed that the politically active law students were almost all from government high schools. Because they came in large numbers from a smaller number of schools, it was rare for private school students to come to Monash without some friends, while

9 Interview with Carol Bartlett, 14 August 2013.

many high school students knew nobody when they arrived. That being said, most found Monash in the early years a friendly and welcoming place, and few experienced the loneliness and isolation of some students in the much larger faculty of later years.

The number of female students in the law school remained very low throughout the 1960s, at less than 15 per cent of enrolments. Of 114 students who graduated BJuris or LLB before 1970, only 14 were women. Nonetheless, women students of that era generally found the law school a welcoming place. Ruth Thomas, for example, did not find it an issue being a woman in the law course. Rather, she felt there was an attitude of equality and she does not remember any instances of discrimination. However, this was not the case when women completed their courses and tried to find articles, with the expectation being that they would leave after a short time to have a family.

There were even fewer students from overseas. The only student from an Asian background in the 1964 cohort was Robert Chan, who completed his BJuris in 1968 and his LLB in 1970. In 1965 the faculty offered several places for sponsored overseas students and this was increased to five places for 1968. The official statistics for 1967 show that the faculty had nine overseas students, all males, representing 1.6 per cent of total enrolments, the lowest proportion of overseas students in the whole university. There were two students from Malaysia and one each from the Gilbert Islands, Hong Kong, India, New Zealand, South Africa, the United States and West Germany. These students have proved hard to trace and their presence left little impact on either their teachers or fellow students.

In the early years, a majority of the lecturers at Monash used Socratic, case-method teaching. For George Golvan, who began in 1965, this was the aspect of the teaching that he most vividly remembers. Students were told to sit in the same places and the lecturer would throw questions round the class. He felt this inspired students to read the cases and think about them. Ray Finkelstein, like many others, would try to sit where he wouldn't be noticed but 'with the small class sizes you really couldn't hide and had to speak on most topics'. Some students thought the Socratic method could be taken too far. Richard Dufty recalls that 'The lectures frequently were not lectures. Students were pinned to the wall by Professor David Jackson whilst he cross-examined them on the idiosyncrasies of property law.'[10] Similarly, Graeme Golden learnt little in Henry Finlay's family law lectures because

10 Quoted in Rankin, 'Forty Years On', p. 2.

the classes consisted solely of Finlay exposing the ignorance of his students through rigorous questioning.

The most prominent exponent of case-method teaching was Louis Waller, whose lecturing style imprinted itself indelibly on the memories of his students. One of them was Harry Reicher:

> Louis cut quite a fearsome figure. He walked into class with his seating chart, and in slow, deliberate, measured terms, proceeded to direct questions to various members of the class ...
>
> In one of his classes, Louis was responsible for what was undoubtedly the most frightening and traumatic event in my whole law school career. He directed a question to a student, who happened to be sitting in an aisle seat in a large, amphitheatre-style lecture room, filled virtually to capacity. It was absolutely clear, from the moment Louis finished the question, that the poor kid didn't have a clue as to the answer. We saw him nervously leafing through his case book, back and forth, as though praying that the answer would somehow leap up out of a page, and hit him between the eyeballs. Of course, it didn't happen. The seconds passed, and seemed like minutes, if not hours. Every one of us in the room intently looked down at our case books, desperate to avoid an eye contact which might provoke a question from Louis. And I think every one of us knew that, there but for the grace of G-d [sic] went every single one of us in that classroom. I also suspect that we all prayed silently that the earth would open up and swallow us. The tension mounted, and then Louis, in his inimitable style, turned the screws even tighter: He slowly, surely and deliberately walked, step by step, one step at a time, up the stairs of the aisle in that classroom. And when he reached the row where the student was sitting, he turned 90 degrees to his right, stared straight at the hapless young fellow, slipped his hands slowly behind his back, and flicked his robe up and down, in a gesture of impatience.[11]

Ann Lahore was in one of Louis Waller's classes in 1959 when he had returned from Oxford determined to teach Socratically, but the students at Melbourne refused to co-operate and his questions were met with stony silence. However, 'everybody used the Socratic teaching method at Monash in the early days' and they found this a much more interesting and effective

---

11 Email from Harry Reicher to authors, 28 February 2012.

way to teach than simply lecturing, though it was also much more demanding. The teacher has to be in complete control of the material and be able to guide the discussion to reach the desired end point. Further, it required skill to encourage the shy and reticent students, while slowing down the brash and over-confident. Overall Ann found that Monash students responded well to the Socratic method and she used it throughout her time at Monash, though eventually it fell victim to increasing class sizes.[12]

Fired with the spirit of innovation that permeated Monash in the 1960s, several lecturers became enthused with the idea of making films on various legal issues to use in classes. In 1966 Barry Connell and William Charles, together with Edward Lloyd, the consultant in criminal law and James Gobbo, who taught evidence at Melbourne, began work on a 'pilot instructional film' on the law of evidence. A committee was set up and, after some debate, the faculty agreed to put some money aside to produce a film.[13]

Lloyd began preparing a script and the committee reached an agreement with Crawford Productions to make the film. In October 1967 the committee reported that arrangements for the pilot teaching film were proceeding satisfactorily and the film would be completed by March 1968. However, there were lengthy delays in completing the script and getting permission from the Bar Council for barristers to appear in the film, and it was not completed until April 1971.

Called *According to the Evidence*, the film focused on the complexity of the rules of evidence and the multiplicity of exceptions to them. By showing students the way in which real questions of life and liberty were daily 'disposed of' by evidentiary rules, it would make students more likely to want to master those rules. In pursuing the aim of authenticity, Lloyd tried to make the script as realistic as possible, with 'no clear-cut solutions' and 'no happy ending'. He wanted the judge to be shown as 'a human figure, not some sort of God-like being'. Counsel were drawn as human too, because they may not always 'make their arguments quite as well as they might, and sometimes they get the arguments wrong'.[14]

The filmed trial was 'a maelstrom of evidentiary problems' in which several distinct questions were explicitly raised and answered and many more questions implied, some of which were also answered. It demonstrated the

---

12 Interview with Ann Lahore, 17 July 2012.

13 Faculty Board minutes, 28 July, 29 September, 24 November 1966.

14 E D Lloyd, 'Aim and Synopsis, Explanatory Note and Script, According to the Evidence', David Hector Monro Collection, 2008/33/17 MON 1214.

"According to the evidence..."

Monash Faculty of Law scored a notable 'first' with the premiere last month of 'According to the Evidence', a half-hour teaching film on the techniques of adducing and testing evidence.

The film has already been enthusiastically acclaimed by other Australian law schools, and it is hoped that copies will be sold in other States and overseas.

Professor David Derham, then dean of the faculty, now Vice-Chancellor of the University of Melbourne, first suggested the film five years ago as an educational research experiment in legal education.

A pilot committee was formed in 1967 to oversee the project. It consisted of Mr H. B. Connell, sub-dean of the faculty (chairman), Mr E.D. Lloyd and Mr J.A. Gobbo, of the Victorian Bar, Mr J.D. Collins of the Law Institute, and Mr W.T. Charles, special lecturer in law. Mr N.P. Williams, senior lecturer, was later co-opted.

Mr Lloyd wrote the script and Crawford Productions was commissioned to produce the film, using a cast of professional actors.

The film - a simple husband-wife altercation resulting in a criminal trial - was completed in December, 1970, at a cost of $8300. It will be shown at the Australasian Universities Law Schools Association Conference next month.

Our picture, taken during production, shows (from left) the producer, Ian Crawford, discussing the script with actors Keith Eden, Nigel Lovell and Tim Elliott.

When a girl turns into a pumpkin

The following question was set at Monash in a recent first year Physics Department examination on relativity.

The department felt it might go some of the way towards meeting student demands for more social relevance in their courses.

(It should be explained that according to Einstein time 'slows down' appreciably for travellers moving near the speed of light (C) relative to the earth.)

Cinderella suffers from the social handicap of turning into a pumpkin if she leaves home at 7 p.m. and does not return before 12 p.m. by HER watch.

Cinderella leaves home at 7 p.m. with a constant velocity V = 4/5 C for a ball on Saturn AT REST a distance X_s = 1 light-hour with respect to the earth.

(a) Till what time, at the latest, by her watch can she remain at the ball and still be sure of not turning into a pumpkin? (She can only travel at a uniform velocity V = 4/5 C with respect to the earth.)

Cinderella leaves Saturn at 11.30 p.m. by her watch (this is 12 p.m. by earth time) to return to earth.

(b) At what time, by an earth clock, does she turn into a pumpkin?

The Prince (there is always a Prince) leaves Saturn 1/12 of an hour (by an earth clock) after Cinderella and chases her with speed V = 8/9 C relative to Saturn frame.

(c) Calculate whether he gets to her before she changes.

Dr. Harry Perlman, senior lecturer in physics, says that the question the department actually would prefer to have asked went like this –

A woman goes off on a rocket trip and on returning two years later by earth time gives birth to a child. What is the minimum speed with which she would have had to travel in order to support a paternity case against a man who stayed on earth?

Dr. Perlman says the department did not ask that one because they thought it had too much social relevance.

And the answers? Ask Dr. Perlman. The Monash number is 544-0811.

BOOKS FOR SALE

The Monash representative on the Women of the University Fund has the following books for sale in aid of the Fund's charities. Anyone interested should telephone Netta McLaren on 25-3424.

Gustafson A. & Z.: The Foundation of Death. A Study of the Drink Question. Pub. H. & S. 1888. $1.50.

Wilkie & Osborn: Almost Human – Reminiscences from the Melbourne Zoo. Pub. Whitcomb & Tombs pre 1918. $1.50.

Blackmore, R. D.: Lorna Doone. Pub. Dent 1911. Leather bound, Gold tooling. $1.20.

Morley, A. C. & Eds.: Australian Manual of Accountancy & Commercial Law, Vicn. Edn, Pub. Elliot, 1912. $1.00.

Crookes, Wm. F. R. S.: Researches in The Phenomena of Spiritualism. Pub. Burns 1874. $1.00.

Educational Course: Rudiments of Zoology illus. with wood engravings. Pub. Chambers 1871. $1.00.

Galsworthy, John: Plays of. Pub. Duckworth 1932. $1.00.

White, James: A Compendium of the Veterinary Art. incl. managements of the stable & structure of the Horse. Illus. 18th Edn. Pub. 1851. $1.00.

Culbertson, Ely: Contract Bridge Complete. Pub. Faber. 80c.

Lin Yutang: Vigil of a Nation. Pub. Heinemann. 1946. 80c.

Feuchtwanger Lion: Jew Suss. 7th Edn. Pub. Secker 1927. 80c.

Gibbons, Stanley: Various stamp catalogues. Prices on application.

What they are saying...

"The function of a law school is to teach basic principles and the ability to think based upon those basic principles. It would be a mistake and no service to students to depart from this basic function." Professor H. Ford, Dean of Law, Melbourne University, at a recent Monash graduation ceremony.

"Pigment protects vital cells from damage by ultra-violet solar radiation; their deficiency in fair-skinned people, to be regarded as a genetic defect in a sunny country such as Australia, often leads to skin cancer. Racial admixture with dark-skinned people could in time help to correct this defect." From an abstract of a paper given at ANZAAS by Professor A.K. McIntyre Professor of Physiology.

"I think there is a mood growing in the Universities and has been growing for some time that they should be outward-looking institutions, looking out to society and seeing how they relate to it.

"I think this has been led to a marked degree by the so-called 'student revolution', but I think there are also academics who feel they want to see their work relating to the outside world and I would like to think that this connection with industry, is one way of doing it. It means that academics, one would hope, would be less narrow, if they are, and would always try and relate their work to the outside world." Dr. John Rushbrooke, an Australian nuclear physicist and Fellow of Downing College, Cambridge University, interviewed on ABC radio.

"Many adults are being denied access to summer schools because of limited resources, facilities and funds . . .

". . . The present Australian programme will be unable to approach a level of achievement comparable to that provided by countries whose economic status is comparable to ours until additional funds and facilities are available." From the press release issued last month after a two-day conference on adult education at Monash.

"To gain a university place a student will struggle very, very hard with whatever he thinks will get him good marks. If Hamlet is set for study, the student will read it ten times rather than study Shakespeare as a whole." Professor S.S. Dunn at his press conference on the first day of his new appointment as Dean of Education.

"Australia's overseas educational aid is misdirected and totally inadequate. It is obvious that the government is not sympathetic to the requests of some of the major subscribers to the Colombo Plan." Ken Newcombe, Education Vice President Australian Union of Students, in a June press release.

SCREEM TEST

SCREEM wants to encourage research projects on university education and will give financial assistance in 1972 for selected projects.

SCREEM is the Steering Committee on Research and Experiment into Education Matters and is part of the Australian Vice-Chancellors' Committee.

In 1972 the committee plans to encourage research into the following fields of undergraduate education: –

1. the possibilities and problems of teaching in groups of different sizes (including teaching in small groups);
2. studies of attitudes, objective, perceptions and skills of university teachers;
3. evaluations of the effectiveness of teaching by TV and by the use of other audio-visual aids within Australian universities;
4. evaluations of the effectiveness of different forms of examinations and of different examining practices;
5. studies of work-loads placed upon undergraduates, including the manner in which they are affected by the requirements of separate departments, or by the introduction of different types of examining practice.

But Note: Preference will be given to projects which have a strong collective interest for all the Australian universities or which involve co-operation or co-ordination between the universities. None of the projects supported in 1971 was in areas (2), (4) or (5) above and the above broad areas will not necessarily be the ones to receive support in 1973.

Members of university staffs are now invited to submit proposals for projects which fall within the areas specified above.

Applications should set out in all necessary detail the objectives of the proposed project, the manner in which it will be carried out, the personnel who will be involved, the estimated length of time required for completion, the estimated cost of the project, and the amount of financial assistance required, together with a statement of the manner in which it is proposed that the results of the experiment will be evaluated.

Applications should be received by mid-August, 1971, be addressed to Dr. K. H. Star, P.O. Box 182, RANDWICK, NSW, 2031, and be forwarded through the Registrar of the applicants' university.

MONASH REPORTER 11 July 9, 1971

The faculty was ahead of its time when it developed a film *According to the Evidence*, as a teaching aid.

The pilot instructional film focused on the complexity of the rules of evidence and the multiplicity of exceptions to them. From 1968 Barry Connell, William Charles, Edward Lloyd and James Gobbo were all involved developing the concept and writing the script. Lengthy delays, including getting permission from the Bar Council for barristers to appear in the film, meant it was not completed until April 1971. It was made by Crawford Productions who produced *Homicide* and *D24* at around the same time.

Photographer unknown, *Monash Reporter*, July 1971, p. 11.

evidentiary rules governing admissibility and why the law excludes much material that might be thought to be logically relevant. The arguments ebbed and flowed and what began as an apparently straightforward case became complex. At the end of the film, 'no-one knows whether the accused is in fact guilty or not' because the film was not interested in the verdict the jury arrived at, examining only the way in which the law treated the evidence.

Although *According to the Evidence* was used in teaching for several years, it did not inspire further movie-making.

The Monash law course structure differed from Melbourne, though not as greatly as many people liked to believe. The faculty always operated within the strait-jacket of the compulsory subjects laid down by the Council of Legal Education. While Monash led Melbourne in the number and variety of elective subjects, the core of the curriculum was essentially fixed. What really distinguished Monash from Melbourne in the early years were the smaller class sizes, the overall higher standard of teaching and the honours program.

However, the ethos of Monash in the early days was in favour of innovation and experimentation and one serious attempt was made to modify the core structure. In June 1967 the faculty board agreed with a proposal for a 'common law' course that would incorporate contracts, torts and criminal law. This began in 1968 with a trial course for about forty students and its fate will be discussed in a later chapter. More commonly innovation took place within individual subjects. The most notable of these in the early years was property, which Mark Aronson recalls as being 'insanely different from the traditional course'. The lecturer, David Jackson, said at the outset, 'You won't understand anything I'm going to tell you for about half a year, but then it will all fit into place.' He did not teach rules but theories and this worked for some students, but for others it was 'a spectacular failure as they did not know what he was talking about'.[15] Graeme Golden remembers his frustration that Jackson 'would say that everything would be in his book, but his book wasn't published'. Further, what Jackson taught was totally different from the Melbourne course, so students who borrowed or bought books or notes from Melbourne students found that they were useless.

One of the major points of difference of the Monash law school in its early years was the honours program. Set up with the intention of demonstrating that the best students at Monash were every bit as good as the best students at

---

15 Interview with Ray Finkelstein, 13 May 2013.

Melbourne, the program was 'unashamedly elitist and highly competitive'.[16] Only members of the honours school could obtain an honours degree, and students joined the honours school only by invitation, usually during first year, but with late bloomers added at any time up to the end of fourth year. Numbers were small. The first honours class had only about ten students, of whom six completed honours degrees.[17]

The honours school was unremittingly demanding on its students. Every subject had an additional honours seminar, extra written work during the year and either an additional exam or additional questions on the pass students' exam. In both fourth and fifth year, honours students took a special honours seminar in lieu of a regular subject. The fifth year seminar aimed at 'presenting an overall view of the legal system by studying the interaction between the various parts of the system, methods of development and principles followed'.[18] Frequently two or even three senior staff members would be involved in teaching the honours seminars, and in some classes there were as many staff as students. Although students had to complete substantial research essays for their honours seminars, there was no requirement to write an honours thesis until 1972.

Standards were extraordinarily high. Early in Ron McCallum's honours contract seminar with Patrick Higgins and Enid Campbell, Enid said his work was like a 'semi-illiterate five year old', although he finished the year with third class honours. He was surprised that this was enough to top the class. There was no presumption that the best student in a class would receive a high distinction. Bob Williams topped most subjects he took, but it was not until fourth year that he received a high distinction. First class honours degrees were rare.

Mark Aronson recalls that in his final year Enid Campbell advised the honours students to apply for scholarships and told them to aim high, for Oxford and Harvard. Her secretary typed the scholarship applications and she shepherded the top students into good postgraduate schools. This level of care was needed because there were no older students to mentor the first class and little information about scholarships and postgraduate programs was available on the campus. With Enid Campbell's guidance, Aronson and Bob Williams both won scholarships to Oxford, where Williams found

---

16 Williams, 'Some Reflections on Monash', p. 2.

17 The six were Bob Williams, Mark Aronson, Chris Chenoweth, Ruth Thomas née Worland, James Kimpton and Barry Perry.

18 Faculty Board minutes, 27 July 1967.

that the Monash honours program had prepared him well for the even more pressured environment of the BCL.

Although the faculty aspired to build up a large and high quality graduate school, during the 1960s this took a back seat to the development of undergraduate teaching. There were few postgraduate students and all but a handful were staff members working for LLMs by thesis. The first three masters' degrees were awarded in 1968 to Ann Lahore, Alan Afterman and Ross Sundberg, all staff members, though Sundberg was already building a distinguished career at the bar.

The first large-scale manifestation of the worldwide student protest movement that swept the world in the 1960s was the Berkeley free speech movement that began in late 1964. Australian student protests followed soon after, prompted by the introduction of conscription in November 1964. Immediately every male student was confronted with the prospect of being conscripted. Nahum Mushin turned 20 in June 1965 about the time of the first ballot for conscription and registered as a conscientious objector. He remembers a ferment of discussion around the campus and 'the great moral issues were talked about all the time'. Monash rapidly gained a reputation as the most radical campus in Australia, with student leaders like Albert Langer and Michael Hyde becoming well-known public figures, and rallies, protests, sit-ins, occupations and demonstrations a weekly, if not daily, occurrence.

To a large extent, however, the unrest of the 1960s passed the law faculty by, and only a small minority of law students became politically engaged. Peter Bartlett's attitude was probably typical of most law students. He was not opposed to conscription and would have gone to Vietnam if his number came up, though he 'took the view that it would be fairer if everyone went rather than the luck of the draw of whether your birthday was drawn out'.

While unrest grew over conscription and the Vietnam War during 1965 and 1966, the event that prompted the first major confrontation between radicals and the university administration was the awarding of an honorary doctorate to the premier, Henry Bolte, at the height of the controversy over the hanging of Ronald Ryan on 3 February 1967. The decision to make the award was taken in December 1966 (though not announced until after the hanging) with the presentation to take place at a graduation ceremony on 25 May 1967. By coincidence, this was also the date for the graduation of the first cohort of BJuris students, and the new graduates were inevitably drawn into the controversy.

In early March 1967, the student newspaper *Lot's Wife* reported that it had information 'from usually reliable sources' that Sir Henry Bolte was to receive an honorary degree from the university.[19] Responding to the report, the president of the Labor Club, David Nadel, said that if the Students' Representative Council did not organise protest demonstrations to coincide with the award ceremony, 'then the Labor Club would'.[20]

The Monash council executive met to discuss the situation and concluded that, despite the controversy that had erupted, 'courtesy prevented Monash University from reversing its decision' to grant an honorary degree to the Premier.[21] However, in early April it was announced that the graduation ceremony would be moved from the Clayton campus to the Melbourne Town Hall.[22] This was explained as being due to the lack of a suitable hall at Clayton, but most believed that it was an attempt to avoid demonstrations. This was admitted by Louis Matheson, who explained to university council member, Anglican Bishop Felix Arnott, that the decision to hold the next graduation ceremony in the Melbourne Town Hall was taken for 'quite a large number of reasons. Among these was, to be frank, the fear of serious student activities which might have prevented the Ceremony from being held at all'. He insisted, he was 'certainly not "frightened of students" but I do not underestimate that, in circumstances that favour their activities, it is all too easy for them to be a serious embarrassment to the University'.[23]

On 7 April a notice was sent to all graduands attending the ceremony to be held on 25 May 1967. The notice contained the surprise announcement that 'Graduands are expected to attend in person to have the degree conferred. Those not able to attend must apply in writing to the Academic Registrar for permission to have the degree conferred in absentia.' This had not been an issue in the past and was seen as an attempt to avoid large numbers of students boycotting the ceremony. Nahum Mushin, who had joined the vigil outside Pentridge Gaol on the morning of the hanging, recalls that 'When the graduation was moved, many students said they wouldn't go, so a rule was quickly brought in tightening up the rules for graduating in absentia.'[24]

---

19 'Sir Henry Bolte', *Lot's Wife*, 7 March 1967, p. 3.

20 'Honorary Monash Degree For Sir Henry Bolte', Warrnambool *Standard*, 11 March 1967.

21 'Monash meeting on Bolte Degree' Melbourne *Herald*, 14 March 1967.

22 'Bar MPs from degrees call', Melbourne *Age*, 16 March 1967; 'Notice to Graduands from J D Butchart', Academic Registrar, 7 April 1967.

23 Matheson to Arnott, 17 April 1967, PW 3/63–8, Graduation Ceremony, MUA.

24 Interview with Nahum Mushin, 23 March 2011.

The move of the graduation to the Melbourne Town Hall succeeded in averting a serious demonstration against the Premier. On campus the Labor Club organised an anti-Bolte award ceremony, where a degree was awarded to 'Sir Henry Pig', which showed its great displeasure by defecating on the rostrum.[25] But at the town hall the first thirty-four graduates of the Faculty of Law received their BJuris degrees in a traditionally decorous atmosphere. A ballot had been held to choose the first BJuris candidate to receive their degree, with John Harvey being the chosen candidate. Bob Williams was awarded the law students' society prize for the top BJuris student, with Ruth Thomas receiving the Flos Greig prize for the top female student.[26]

Nahum Mushin was one of the first thirty-four graduates to receive their BJuris degree at the Melbourne Town Hall on 25 May 1967.

The graduation ceremony was moved from the Clayton campus because Vice-Chancellor Louis Matheson was worried that student protest against Premier Sir Henry Bolte being awarded an honorary doctorate would disrupt the ceremony.

Photographer: Sam Kopai, Monpix 8176

---

25 Graeme Davison and Kate Murphy, *University Unlimited: The Monash Story*, Allen & Unwin, Sydney 2012, p. 124.

26 Harvey has gone on to have a highly successful career in law and accounting, including periods as CEO of Pricewaterhouse Coopers and of the Mt Eliza Business School and as director of several leading companies. The Flos Greig Prize was named for Grata Flos Matilda Greig, who in 1905 was the first woman to be admitted to legal practice in Australia.

Students objected to the awarding of the honorary doctorate to Sir Henry Bolte. The issue featured in *Lot's Wife* in March, April and May 1967.

MU Archives

Chapter 6

The David Derham School of Law

Throughout 1964 and most of 1965 the formal status of the Monash law school was unclear and undefined. The reason for this was a lengthy debate over the correct procedure for setting up new faculties, and it was not until an amendment was made to the *Monash University Act* that the Faculty of Law could be established.[1] Thus, the faculty was not formally established until mid-1965 and the faculty board only met for the first time on 28 September 1965. At about the same time, the Council of Legal Education finally approved Monash courses for admission to practice. Not that the lack of formal recognition impeded the growth of the law school in any way – David Derham and the law school advisory committee had proceeded with the confidence that their actions would not be queried for lack of formal authority. A far greater problem was that even in late 1965 there was still no funding available or timetable in place for the construction of a building for the law school, leaving the faculty in its makeshift accommodation in the engineering and science buildings for the foreseeable future.

It was not in David Derham's nature to sit back and wait for a new law building to be presented to Monash. From the time he became dean he began setting down his ideas for the ideal building for a law school, while at the same time using his great skills at networking and negotiation to speed up approval. By August 1964, he had already had extensive consultations with architects Eggleston, MacDonald & Secomb, and the fundamental design of the building was already set down.

In his 'Plan for a new law school', Derham expressed a clear view of what the new school building should look like. The whole building would be constructed around the law library, which was to be the 'working heart of the law school'.[2] He began with a number of 'assumptions

---

1 The issue of the university's power to establish faculties is discussed fully in Balmford, 'Foundation of the Monash Law School', pp. 162–65.

2 Derham, 'Plan for a New Law School', 7 August 1964, p. 9.

and considerations', most significantly that the faculty would reach its projected maximum number of 1200 students by around 1974. From this he calculated the required number of staff offices, lecture theatres, tutorial rooms, seats in the library, and so on. While his calculations became redundant in later decades, when the faculty was allowed to grow far beyond the size he recommended, overall his plans held up well. The only obvious exception was the inadequate provision for women's lavatories. Derham was not alone in not foreseeing that within forty years women would be a majority of both staff and students.

In terms of academic office space, Derham calculated that a permanent staff member (at lecturer or professorial level) would require 30–40 square feet more than the standard allowance in other faculties because he believed law academics generally had larger personal book collections than their colleagues. They therefore required larger rooms with more bookshelves. The administrative offices also had to be specifically designed for the law school's needs, with a dedicated printing room because 'a modern law school… finds itself committed to the production and distribution of large quantities of printed or roneoed materials'. These claims might have been specious, but Derham knew it is always better to ask for too much than too little.

Derham also argued that law students needed more space in their library than students from other professional faculties. Not only did law students use more books than other students, he estimated that they required about 22.5 square feet as personal working space to allow them to 'make use of large numbers of books at the same time'. Calculating that at least one seat was needed for every two undergraduate students, the library should have 600 seats. Further, the law library should be 'easy of access to students' and near 'to their classrooms and other working areas, and to teaching staff'.

The need for more than the usual allocation of space extended to student society activities such as moot courts and the production of legal literature. He pointed out that 'law students not only supplement the work done in their regular courses, but establish connections with the professional bodies which many of them will someday join. For such reasons it is necessary to provide accommodation for law student organizations and bodies in the law school'.[3] Derham's plan included student committee meeting rooms and a law students' society office, as well as rooms for a law review publication,

---

3 Ibid., p. 10.

and a legal aid office.[4] The need for, and naming of, some of these rooms was later queried by the university buildings committee, but Derham strongly defended them.

Teaching needs also differed from those of other humanities courses, requiring special tutorial and seminar rooms. In particular, a moot court room was needed where students could practise trial work. This room could also serve as a general lecture theatre, but it required a large room designed as a courtroom that could be adapted to other uses.

By the end of 1965 the Australian Universities Commission (AUC) had intimated that money would be made available for a law building at Monash in the 1967–69 triennium. Planning work proceeded rapidly to minimise delays once funding was approved, with the aim of beginning teaching in the new building at the start of the 1968 academic year.

In November 1965 a law school project sub-committee was set up and architects appointed.[5] The architects selected were Eggleston, Macdonald & Secomb, an established Melbourne firm responsible for the design of a number of important buildings in Melbourne in the 1950s including the Beaurepaire Centre at the University of Melbourne (1954–57). The firm's 'house style' used tan brick and exposed concrete in 'a low-key unassuming form of late Brutalism'.[6] At Monash the firm was the university's architect of choice in the mid-1960s, designing the Menzies building, the Rotunda and the Alexander Theatre as well as the law school.

At its first meeting in January 1966, the project committee discussed a suggestion that the law building be attached to the proposed 'T-wing' of the Menzies building. This was sketched as a massive block parallel to the Menzies building and physically linked with it. This was a variant of an idea that had been floating around since the early 1960s – that the most economical way of housing the law school, permanently or temporarily, would be in the Menzies building or an extension to it. However, the committee

---

4 The Victorian legal aid scheme began on 14 April 1964 when the Legal Aid Committee was established. Derham apparently anticipated the establishment of a legal aid clinic in the law building. See *Monash Reporter*, October 1965, p. 9.

5 The members of the building committee were Louis Matheson, Professors Manton, Cochrane, Derham, Waller and Jackson, Mr G Boycott (university buildings officer) and Messrs. MacDonald, Koren and Watson of Eggleston, MacDonald & Secomb.

6 Philip Goad, 'Eggleston, MacDonald & Secomb' in *The Encyclopedia of Australian Architecture*, pp. 120–21. Other University of Melbourne buildings designed and constructed from the 1970s include the Electrical Engineering and Metallurgy (1971–73), McCoy Earth Sciences (1976), Thomas Cherry Building (1984) and Zoology (1986).

quickly agreed that the law building should be free-standing as Derham had always planned. Less dramatic changes to the sketch plans met with ready acceptance, notably provision for the addition of another complete floor if and when required. A 'circular block' incorporating a large lecture theatre – an echo of the Rotunda – was proposed but George Boycott, the university buildings officer, reflected the view of the sub-committee: 'the more I think about the Circular Block the less I like it'. The suggestion was dropped.[7]

In August 1966, the assistant buildings officer wrote to Derham on behalf of the vice-chancellor, expressing his surprise that the building had been designed to take an upper floor at a later date. Derham replied: 'I am surprised at your surprise. This matter has at all stages in the planning for more than two years been brought specifically to your attention'.[8] This apparently satisfied Matheson as there were no more queries about the provision for an upper floor, though debate continued on many other aspects of the building, particularly provision of modern cabling, air conditioning and carpeting, none of which were standard in new university buildings in the 1960s. Derham was interested in new technologies and in the use of audio-visual techniques in law teaching.[9] He suggested providing television monitors in the moot court, classrooms and tutorial rooms, which caused some complications for wiring cables and power but was finally achieved.[10]

By September 1966, the estimated cost of the building, including all fees, electrical and phone wiring, furniture and furnishings, and a reserve, was $1,866,000 leaving 'a shortfall of $176,000 from the amount of $1,690,000 submitted to the AUC'. The project sub-committee recommended that in view of the anticipated cost increase and the depressed state of the building industry (which could favour the university), 'tenders should be called for the project, as designed, to test the market'.[11] The tender was advertised and the lowest tender for the 'whole of works' building came in from A R P Crow, at $1,199,554, well under the estimate.[12]

---

7 Minutes of Law School Project Sub-Committee, 18 January 1966, Attachment p. 1, MON 806, MUA.

8 J L McPhee, assistant buildings officer, to Derham, 1 August 1966; Derham to vice-chancellor, 3 August 1966.

9 *Monash Reporter*, August 1966, p. 9.

10 D Dexter, secretary AUC, to Frank Johnson, 6 April 1966.

11 G W Wildman, acting buildings officer to Derham, 7 September 1966.

12 Eggleston, MacDonald & Secomb to comptroller, Monash University, 7 October 1966.

Construction of the law building began in early 1967, and it attracted an unusual degree of interest. Almost all law students were doing at least one arts or economics subject, with classes in the Menzies Building, from where they could see the construction site. The builders used an innovative construction technique which the students watched with amazement. Peter Bartlett recalls: 'I know nothing about engineering, but to see this building being built where they first of all put all the floors on top of each other and then pumped them up and then built the walls and windows around them was fascinating to watch.' History professor A G L Shaw was on edge for weeks watching the process, as he constantly expected the building to collapse like the house of cards it resembled.[13]

The issue of floor coverings for the new building resurfaced in June 1967 when Derham again put forward arguments for having the staff areas carpeted. The building committee had already agreed to carpet the library, but he argued that staff satisfaction and morale would be significantly affected if carpeting was not provided in the rest of the building. He pointed out that the low building quotes meant that more than enough money was available in the budget to provide for it.[14] University building officer George Boycott rejected Derham's proposal, arguing that hard floor coverings were more economical.[15] Derham was not impressed. He claimed that the university's experience of hard floor coverings showed that they created cleaning problems that had not yet been resolved.[16] In a moment of colourful rhetoric, he claimed that high gloss floors which were not kept 'in a high state of cleanliness and polish', made buildings look like 'tatty milk bars'.[17] The acting vice-chancellor responded with the pious hope that 'all concerned and especially the occupants will never allow our buildings to degenerate to the standard of tatty milk bars'.[18]

---

13 Interview with AGL Shaw, 12 February 2011.

14 Derham 'Report on floor covering for staff rooms', 5 June 1967, p. 3, item 2; Dean's Correspondence, MON 806, MUA.

15 Boycott to Derham, 8 June 1967, p. 3, in ibid.

16 8/8/67 York to Derham re Ristrom; 14/7/67 Derham to Wildman (acting building officer); Derham to Buildings Committee, copies to Acting Vice-Chancellor, Professors Jackson and Waller and Buildings Officer, 21 July 1967, p. 2; items 2 and 3, Dean's Correspondence, MON 806, MUA.

17 Derham to acting vice-chancellor, 31 July 1967, Derham to chairman, buildings committee, 21 July 1967, Dean's Correspondence, MON 806, MUA.

18 R R Andrew, Acting Vice-Chancellor, 28 July 1967 to Derham.

Law building under construction, 1967.
Photographer unknown, Monpix numbers 4038, 4039 and 4040

A view of the first floor of the modern and well stocked centrally located Law library when it opened in 1968.
Photographer unknown, Monpix 064

Discussions on carpeting staff areas came to a head in mid-August 1967.[19] At a meeting of the building sub-committee, Derham pointed out that 'La Trobe University has adopted a policy to carpet all areas other than laboratory areas'.[20] This apparently helped sway the Monash administration, and the buildings committee eventually agreed that Derham could have his building carpeted.

Air-conditioning remained contentious. Derham pushed for the entire building to be air-conditioned but the Australian Universities Commission's policy did not allow this. While conceding that air-conditioning was essential in libraries – for the well-being of the books rather than the users – the AUC did not think it warranted for staff offices or teaching spaces. Consequently, the plans were modified to provide air-conditioning in the library, resulting in slightly lower ceilings to allow for the ducts. This had unfortunate consequences later in the project. When calculating the height of the book shelves, the original ceiling height was used. As a result, when the specially built bookshelves were brought in for installation late in 1967 they were found to be too tall. The bookshelves had to be rebuilt and this delayed the move into the new building until late March 1968.[21]

---

19 Minutes of meetings no. 143 and 144. Acting V-C to Derham re meeting No. 144, 24/7/67.

20 8/8/67 Note: York to Derham.

21 Interview with Louis Waller, 11 July 2011.

The basement lounge with 'comfortable seating for students', 1968.
Photographer unknown, Monpix 8339

Throughout 1967, while the new building was under construction, the faculty was aware that it would lose its foundation dean before it was opened. In November 1966, it was announced that David Derham had been appointed as the next vice-chancellor of the University of Melbourne and he formally tendered his resignation as dean of the Faculty of Law on 12 December 1966. As he would not begin at Melbourne until March 1968, he was able to give long notice, with his resignation from Monash not taking effect until 29 February 1968.[22] David Derham's departure, while not unexpected, was universally regretted by his colleagues. He was an inspiring, innovative and widely liked leader, with the ideal mix of skills needed to found and build up a new law school.

At a special meeting on 28 February 1968, the faculty board placed on record its appreciation of David Derham's services. Motions of thanks and good wishes were moved by Waller, seconded by Jackson and 'carried by acclamation'. The note of appreciation states:

> Professor David Derham was appointed Dean of the Faculty of Law by the Council of Monash University on 14 October 1963. He was charged

22 David Derham Personnel File, Monash University Archives, MON 8.

> with the task of initiating teaching in Law as quickly as possible, and of founding and developing a law school which would be an important and substantial part of the rapidly developing university …
>
> In the four years that Professor Derham has been Dean of the Faculty of Law, his plan for a new Law school has been almost wholly executed, under his imaginative direction and leadership. 1968 sees the introduction of most of the fifth year subjects, and will see the completion by a substantial group of senior students of the whole B.Juris/LL.B programme. This year also sees the opening of the new Law building, in the general and detailed planning of which Professor Derham played a very great part, and its occupation by the law school. It is today a school with more than 700 under-graduate and graduate students, and a body of full-time teachers of Law which numbers 35 …
>
> In spite of the very heavy demands which his office as Dean has imposed upon him since he assumed it, Professor Derham has undertaken large teaching responsibilities, particularly in the first year course, The Legal System. He has pursued his own legal research and strongly encouraged his colleagues in theirs. He has supervised graduate students and has been concerned to stimulate junior members of the full-time staff to pursue studies for higher degrees.

Few buildings at Monash have been named after living people, so it was a rare honour that the new law building was named the David Derham School of Law. The formal opening ceremony was held on 10 July 1968, and on the same day Derham also received the degree of Doctor of Laws *honoris causa* from the university. At the opening ceremony the Chancellor, Sir Robert Blackwood, told of the difficulties faced by the faculty before the building was constructed and Louis Waller spoke about Derham's role in developing the law school. Waller emphasised that Derham did not want law students to be without history or literature, philosophy or economics, 'to be, in Scott's phrase, "mechanics, or mere working masons"'. Rather, he formulated plans which provided for a first degree in law – Bachelor of Jurisprudence with its basic core of legal subjects together with studies in the humanities, economics or the natural sciences'.[23]

In response, Derham stated that he did not believe that 'there is another university in the United Kingdom or in Australasia, perhaps not in the

---

[23] 'Opening of the Law School', *Monash University Gazette*, V. 4, No. 1, 1968, pp. 25–27.

Sir Robert Blackwood opening the David Derham School of Law on 10 July 1968. Professors David Derham and Louis Waller are seated at right.

Photographer unknown, Monpix 383

common law world, which could have done so well in so short a time'. Monash was 'already accustomed to doing things quickly, and with enthusiasm'. To the staff and students he said:

> With the staff of this school and the physical advantages of this building also in mind, I have no hesitation in assuring the graduates of this school that the standards they satisfy here are as high as any in the common law world. They can be as proud to be graduates of Monash University as I am proud to be an honorary graduate of Monash today.[24]

24 Ibid.

PART TWO

THE GOLDEN AGE, 1968–1980

Chapter 7

The Search for Another David Derham

The Deans, 1968–80

The years 1968–80 were a golden age for the Monash Law School. The faculty had room to grow in a brand new, purpose-built building, money was plentiful, staff:student ratios exceptional, and the faculty still small enough to be genuinely collegial. The law school was innovative, progressive and exciting. This period saw the beginnings of the clinical program, continuing professional development, the *Monash University Law Review* and the *Legal Services Bulletin* (now the *Alternative Law Review*), a coursework masters' program, and Australia's first centre for Japanese law. Few argued with Monash's claim to have the best undergraduate teaching, and increasingly Monash was regarded as at least the equal of Melbourne in the eyes both of prospective students and employers.

Yet this golden era also saw the most rapid turnover of deans in the faculty's history, with only one of four deans serving a full term. Whether this shows that deans were irrelevant for the law school's success, or that constant renewal and fresh thinking is critical, is open to debate. The era had two unwilling deans and two who were keener on the role. Relations among the professoriate were generally harmonious with occasional grumblings, but the progress of the faculty continued seemingly unaffected.

The position of dean of a law school is rarely sought after. There is little incentive to exchange the satisfaction of teaching and research for the tedium of administration and endless meetings. It is a largely thankless job in which virtually every decision will make at least some people unhappy, and a build-up of resentments and ill-feeling is almost inevitable. Of Monash law school's nine deans up to 2012, two (Derham and Parker) were outside appointments for whom the deanship was a step on the road to vice-chancellorships, one (Freiberg) returned as a former staff member, and the others have all been internal appointments. Three of the internal appointments (Waller, Campbell and Nash) did not serve full terms; the other three (Allan, Baxt and Williams) all proved, for very different reasons, divisive and controversial.

The greatest difficulty the faculty experienced in finding a new dean came after the departure of David Derham. The three remaining professors, Louis Waller, David Jackson and Enid Campbell, were all averse to taking on the role and there were no strong external candidates. Vice-chancellor Matheson sought Frank Beasley's advice:

> I agree that it is going to be very difficult to find another David Derham; a survey of the present membership of the Australian Universities Law Schools Association leads to the conclusion that unless he is very successfully hiding his light under a bushel he just is not here at present. This conclusion implies a preference for an Australian appointee ... which I think would be wise in view of the present stage of development at Monash ...
>
> More than once ... I have urged Louis Waller to think seriously of himself as David's successor; but he will not hear of it. He is, as you know, a very honest and a very modest man; he once confessed to me that after some months he began to enjoy his administrative duties [as acting dean] but still insisted that (a) he is too young to be permanently appointed as Dean and (b) that for some years he wants to spend more time in teaching and writing than he could do if he were permanent head of school. David Jackson is, I think, an equally able man, much more of an extrovert than Louis, but like him has the itch to write ... Enid Campbell ... has probably never even contemplated her own participation in any rotation scheme that might be adopted; but I think ... she should be given an opportunity to refuse appointment. David Allan [who had arrived as the fourth professor since Derham's departure] is still something of a mystery man ... he declared that he was very glad to shed administrative responsibilities so as to devote more time to Law Asia et al. Very able, and very ambitious; he has toned down quite a lot, and the process may continue before his turn comes; but I still think his conception of the Deanship would be autocratic rather than that of temporary primus inter pares.
>
> On the whole, I would therefore support your [suggestion], "to let the rotation continue until someone has established a clear claim or a good man has appeared from outside".[1]

1 Frank Beasley to Louis Matheson, 6 May 1969, AD/230/0 Part 1, Dean and Sub-Dean, 1964–68, MON 1, MUA.

Louis Waller did not want to be dean as he had 'just clambered on to the professorial steed', was enjoying teaching and had plans for major writing projects. As the time for Derham's departure approached, it was clear that no appointment would be made and the professors agreed to rotate the deanship among themselves until a permanent dean could be found. Waller was first, becoming acting dean on 1 March 1968. At the end of the year, with still no prospect of an external appointment being made, he was confirmed as dean by the university council, on the understanding he would stand down when his next study leave became due.

Having come to the position by default, it is not surprising that Waller had no great plans for changes. He had always been involved in faculty planning and saw his role as continuing on the lines established by David Derham and managing the continued rapid growth of the faculty. He also instituted the first curriculum review, which led to a freeing up of the curriculum to give students many more options, and began summer teaching, when the professional admission subjects were taught in January 1970.

One of the biggest issues Louis Waller faced when still acting dean was the appointment of a professor to fill David Derham's chair. There were three significant candidates: Cliff Pannam, a reader at Melbourne, David Allan, the dean of law at the University of Tasmania, and Abe Harari, then a senior lecturer at Monash. A protégé of Zelman Cowen's, Pannam was clearly brilliant, but his real vocation lay at the bar. The choice between Allan and Harari was difficult, but the selection committee opted for Allan as the safer option. Louis Waller then had the unenviable task of telling the volatile Harari that his application had been unsuccessful. Harari had already made it clear he would resign if he did not receive the chair and he kept his word. However, in the style of Banquo's ghost, he remained at Monash long after his resignation, eventually moving to a position at Dundee in Scotland, where he died of a brain tumour in 1974.

As dean of the law school, Louis Waller was heavily involved with the university administration during 'the troubles' of the late 1960s. He recalls that soon after he became dean, he and Louis Matheson met with representatives of other Victorian universities to grapple with the problems caused by student activism and protest. Waller presided over a steady stream of disciplinary hearings, always insisting on complete transcripts and scrupulous adherence to due process.

Waller was a competent administrator and the faculty ran smoothly and happily during his deanship. However, as foreshadowed, he stepped down to take study leave at the end of 1970. Meanwhile, David Jackson returned to England to a chair at Southampton, leaving Enid Campbell as the senior professor. She reluctantly agreed to act as dean, though again only until her next study leave.

Enid Campbell is notable as the first female dean of an Australian law school, yet it cannot be said that she relished the role. An outstanding scholar and teacher, she disliked administration, although she proved to be quite good at it. Her year as dean was uneventful, illustrated by the fact that the faculty board minutes for 1971 form a significantly slimmer volume than for any other year in the faculty's history. The main focus for the year was on implementing the recommendations of the curriculum review, particularly the introduction of new electives, semesterisation, and the new common law subject. In addition, the rules for the LLM were changed to allow for the introduction of a masters' degree by coursework and minor thesis.[2] Although this proved to be a momentous step which marked the beginning of a dramatic rise in postgraduate education, it took place with little or no fanfare or discussion, and it was left to Enid Campbell's successor to develop a new postgraduate coursework program.

Staffing issues occupied much of Enid Campbell's time as dean. The foundation of the law school at the University of New South Wales tightened an already stretched market for legal academics, and there was a rash of departures from Monash as people gained quick promotions elsewhere. Don Greig and David Jackson both moved to chairs in the United Kingdom, tutors Robert Hayes and Brian Bromberger went to UNSW as lecturers, Peter Hogg left for Canada and Patrick Higgins left for the University of Wales Institute, Cardiff. Replacements were hard to find. Two vacant chairs remained unfilled for almost two years. New Zealander Douglas Whalan actually signed a contract to come to Monash, but was released from it when he decided to stay at the University of Queensland.[3] There were fewer new junior appointments than in any year since the faculty began, primarily because of the difficulty in attracting applications.

When Enid Campbell cheerfully relinquished the deanship in November 1971, her successor, David Allan, was eager to take on the role. Eagerness to become dean was not necessarily a good sign, and Allan's reign saw the first hints of discord in the faculty. Born in Bolton, England, in 1928, David Allan graduated from Cambridge with first class honours in history before being called to the bar at the Middle Temple. He practised for several years on the Northern Circuit, primarily in common law and criminal law, before,

2 Faculty Board minutes, 22 July 1971.

3 Whalan was later dean of law at the ANU.

In 1971 Enid Campbell was appointed the first female Dean of Law in an Australian university but she did not relish the administrative role.
Photographer unknown, Monpix 8342

'being fed up with the cold and sensing an opportunity,' he successfully applied for a senior lectureship at the University of Western Australia. When he arrived he was asked to teach equity and trusts, an area of the law he was unfamiliar with. He immersed himself in it and his research was instrumental in Western Australia being the first jurisdiction in the British Commonwealth to reform the rule against perpetuities (a subject which greatly exercised the minds of the first honours class at Monash).[4]

4 See D E Allan, 'The Rule Against Perpetuities Restated', *University of Western Australia Law Review*, vol. 6, no. 1, 1963; and 'Perpetuities: Who are the Lives in Being?' *Law Quaterly Review*, vol. 81, no. 1, January 1965; also W. Barton Leach, 'London Proposes, Perth Disposes', *University of Western Australia Law Review*, vol. 6, no. 1, 1963; Reginald Hiscock, 'David Allan, 1928–2006', *Bond University Law Review*, vol. 18, no. 1, June 2006, p. 2.

Although dynamic, innovative and a popular teacher, David Allan's term as dean, from 1971–76, was not always harmonious.
Photographer unknown, Monpix 809

In 1963 Allan was appointed to the chair of English and Commercial Law at the Victoria University of Wellington. This led to another total change of direction as he turned his attention to commercial, banking and financial law, which, together with an interest in Asian law, became his research focus for the rest of his career. In 1966 he became dean of the University of Tasmania law school, where he led an ultimately successful campaign for a new law building and law library, before successfully applying for a chair at Monash in 1968.[5]

David Allan had a deserved reputation as an excellent teacher and was popular with most of his students, being particularly generous to students from overseas. He had taught two Monash staff members – Yuri Grbich at

[5] Davis, *100 Years*, pp. 60–63.

Wellington and Janice Luck at Tasmania – and they both speak highly of his teaching abilities. He was a stickler for punctuality and refused to admit students who were a few minutes late for a lecture, telling them off in his deep, broad and booming northern English accent. At Monash, Allan was a committed and productive researcher, focusing on banking and finance law, with an emphasis on comparative studies of South-East Asian countries. He worked closely on his Asian law projects with Mary Hiscock (the first full-time female lecturer in the Melbourne law school), whom he married in 1980.

Allan was a dynamic and innovative dean. He inaugurated Australia's first LLM by coursework, a Centre for Japanese Law, a continuing legal education program and the clinical education program – all this while coping with a 50 per cent growth in the number of staff and students.[6] However, he believed that 'leadership was not always harmonious', [7] and this was certainly the case, as his term as dean was overshadowed by a breakdown in his relations with other senior staff members. An impatient and autocratic man, one of his first actions as dean had been to re-arrange the furniture in the staff common room, in order, so he said, to break up the cliques he had felt were forming among the staff. Many disliked the changes and Enid Campbell, in particular, was furious. Other similarly trivial problems also reflected his frequent failure to consult with his senior colleagues.[8] 'He was not known as Tiger for nothing', one colleague observed. 'Once he made up his mind he never gave up on something and did it his way.' Born and raised as a Jew, Allan later converted to Anglican Christianity. 'This had led to a creative tension in his life – British in manner but Jewish in his restless drive and academic entrepreneurship'.[9] Louis Waller had not known of Allan's Jewish heritage until one day at morning tea the conversation turned to *The Diary of Ann Frank* and Allan had said that 'Otto Frank was my father's cousin'.

The tensions provoked by Allan's style of leadership were largely invisible to the junior staff. He demanded that they 'account for themselves' and they were aware that he disliked disruptions to the teaching program, but many of them also saw his softer side. When Dorothy Kovacs and another tutor became pregnant at the same time, he was upset that the births were not

---

6 Faculty Board minutes, 3 November 1976.

7 Interview with Mary Hiscock, 13 December 2011.

8 Interviews with Mary Hiscock, 13 December 2011, Louis Waller, Bob Baxt, Gerry Nash and Ron McCallum.

9 John Farrar, 'Professor David Allan, AM', *Bond Law Review*, vol. 15, no. 2, 2003, p. 6.

timed to suit the tutorial program, 'but after he thought about it he graciously apologised'.[10] Similarly, Judd Epstein was touched that Allan took the time to meet him at Melbourne Airport when he arrived in Australia for the first time. He could not imagine the dean of any other law school greeting a new staff member at the airport.[11]

After five years in the job, Allan was eager to be reappointed for another term, but faced with the united opposition of his fellow professors, he resigned in November 1976. His successor, Gerry Nash, was a popular and logical choice. He had returned in 1970 from his three years as foundation dean of the Papua New Guinea Law School and served several terms as associate dean under Enid Campbell and David Allan. Charming, genial and everybody's friend, Nash combined administrative ability with the empathy required to manage academics. His interest always lay on the practical side of the law and he was a prime mover in the establishment of the clinical program in the early 1970s. In recruiting staff, he favoured people with experience in practice. 'There were plenty of intellectuals around,' he recalls, 'but I wanted people who could do things'.[12]

The major concern of the first four deans of the Monash law school was the management of rapid growth. It was Nash's misfortune that his appointment coincided with a sharp change in the academic environment, as the economic crisis of the mid-1970s forced a sudden end to the expansion of tertiary education. Money became the overriding concern. Uncertain economic times led to sharp fluctuations in the intake of new students and also the 'articles crisis', as many law graduates found it impossible to get articles. In 1971 the quota for new students was set at 310 and in 1973 it was raised to 340. However, the quota for 1976 was reduced to 280 and it was planned to keep it at that level, with the aim of reducing student numbers to about 1000 by 1981.[13] Before this level was reached, a change in university policy (it suddenly found it had too few students!) together with the closure of the Council of Legal Education law course at RMIT, led the faculty to boost its intake sharply, from 320 in 1978 to 370 in 1979. The vision of a one-thousand student faculty originally espoused by David Derham and endorsed as recently as 1976 was abandoned without discussion. Nonetheless, growth was sluggish at best for the next decade as funding steadily reduced.

---

10 Interview with Dorothy Kovacs, 2 March 2012.

11 Interview with Judd Epstein, 15 February 2012.

12 Interview with Gerry Nash, 3 October 2011.

13 Faculty Board minutes, 5 November 1975.

Financial stringency forced the faculty to adopt a more entrepreneurial stance, a trend that peaked under Nash's successor, Bob Baxt, in the 1980s. The expansion of summer teaching, the introduction of specialised graduate diplomas and the abandonment of the aim of a thousand student faculty were all motivated in part by the faculty's financial position. During Nash's deanship, the faculty also undertook its second major curriculum review, including reviews of the honours and postgraduate programs.

After only three-and-a-half years as dean, Gerry Nash resigned both the deanship and his chair to go to the bar. He decided he wanted to be a lawyer rather than an administrator and felt it best to return to practice before he turned 50. Additionally, he had become frustrated with the university committee system and did not want to stay past his 'use-by date'.[14]

In the twelve years following the departure of David Derham in 1968, the Monash Law School grew to be the largest law school in Australia. The number of undergraduates grew from 752 in 1968 to 1673 in 1980, and the number of full-time staff of lecturer level and above increased from 25 to 52. In spite of this rapid growth, the staff throughout this era was still small enough for a high degree of camaraderie and collegiality. Most staff members look back on this era fondly, recalling many friendships and few divisions among the staff. Even where disagreements existed, they were debated and resolved in a friendly and constructive manner. People differed in their approaches to the law, but this showed up as different 'wings' of the faculty rather than the deep divisions which paralysed some other law schools in this era.

By 1980 Monash had earned a place among Australia's leading law schools.[15] It was the model that all new law schools copied. At the University of New South Wales, for instance, the guiding principle of the founders of the law school was to be like Monash and unlike Sydney.[16] Monash was seen as innovative, exciting and progressive, and yet it could not be dismissed as lightweight or lacking in intellectual rigour. In the 1970s Monash had the strongest record of research and publishing of any Australian law school.

---

14 Interview with Gerry Nash, 3 October 2011.

15 A major review of Australian legal education published in 1987 ranked Monash, ANU and UNSW as the three leading law schools, with Monash ahead on most objective measurements including publications, library facilities and staff:student ratio. Dennis Pearce, Enid Campbell & Don Harding, *Australian Law Schools: A Discipline Assessment for the Commonwealth Tertiary Education Commission*, 3 vols, AGPS, Canberra, 1987.

16 Marion Dixon, *Thirty Up: The Story of the UNSW Law School 1971–2001*, UNSW Law School, Sydney, 2001, p. 15.

When Gerry Nash (dean 1977–80) went on sabbatical in 1973, he was farewelled in style, enjoying an escort to the Notting Hill Hotel ('The Nott').
Photographer unknown, Monpix 841 and 842.

Chapter 8

The Radical Wing

During the late 1960s, Monash was the most radical campus in Australia. Although most law students were conservative and only a small minority became active in radical politics, many younger staff members were swept up in the spirit of the age. During the 1970s they formed a radical wing of the faculty, taking a critical and political approach to the law and setting their stamp on the law school. The progressives were far from being an organised group with shared adherence to a defined philosophy, but there were particular attitudes and beliefs they generally had in common. These included the idea that the law as-it-was tended to serve the interests of the 'ruling class'; that it needed to be reformed in theory and in practice; and that it could become an instrument for the redress of social and economic problems.[1]

On a practical level, the radicals introduced new areas of teaching and research such as poverty law, social security law and indigenous law, pushed for greater faculty democracy, advocated reform of assessment and greater student participation, argued for law reform and were prominent in what became known as the community legal service movement. Support for this general suite of progressive views was widespread in the faculty. Not surprisingly, it was strongest among the younger academics and less so among the senior staff. There were, of course, exceptions – the most reactionary member of staff was the youthful Ian Spry.

The most prominent of the young progressives were Peter Hanks, Terry Carney, Elizabeth Eggleston, Jude Wallace and Bryan Keon-Cohen. Others such as Judd Epstein, Arie Freiberg, Yuri Grbich, Bob Miller and Colin O'Hare gave enthusiastic support to most of their initiatives. Jude Wallace was the first of this group to join the staff, with Elizabeth Eggleston coming

1 Perhaps the most coherent statement of the radicals' views to come out of Monash was Jude Wallace and John Fiocco, 'Recent Criticisms of Formalism in Legal Theory and Legal Education', *Adelaide Law Review*, vol. 7, no. 3, 1980, p. 309.

about the same time as a PhD student. Eggleston was the daughter of Sir Richard Eggleston, for many years the chairman of the Commonwealth Industrial Court, and had been brought up in the liberal legal tradition. Elizabeth Eggleston completed her LLB at Melbourne in 1956 and an LLM at University of California, Berkeley in 1958. On her return to Australia she worked as a solicitor, primarily in industrial law, and studied for an arts degree at Melbourne before being awarded a postgraduate scholarship at Monash, where she became the first non-staff PhD candidate in the law faculty.

While at Berkeley, Eggleston became interested in the situation of Native Americans and this led her to realise how little she, or almost anybody else, knew of Australia's Aboriginal people. She was inspired to write her PhD thesis on Aboriginal Australians and the administration of justice, basing her research on a fifteen-month field trip through Victoria, South Australia and Western Australia. This was truly revolutionary for a PhD student in law. Peter Hanks wrote:

> The aspect of this which really caught my imagination was that a lawyer had actually devised and carried through an intensive empirical study of the impact of our legal system on part of the community: not a piece of theoretical speculation constructed from the buckram-bound volumes of the Law Library, but a mass of hard evidence, gleaned from court files, coaxed out of police officers, magistrates, lawyers and Aborigines. And this research had been encouraged, financially and personally, by Monash Law Faculty: that aspect made the Faculty, and the prospect of working in it, very attractive to me.[2]

Eggleston was the first person in the law school to use computers to analyse data and completed her thesis in 1970. She showed conclusively the extent of 'systemic discrimination against Aborigines in the administration of criminal justice'.[3] An updated and revised version was published in 1976 as *Fear, Favour or Affection: Aborigines and the Criminal Law*. Sadly, most of its findings are still valid today.

In 1969 Eggleston was appointed a lecturer, teaching criminal law and industrial law,[4] and devising and teaching a new course on legal aid, described

2 Peter Hanks, 'Elizabeth Eggleston', *Oracle*, 1977, p. 72.

3 Phillipa Weeks, 'Elizabeth Moulton Eggleston', *Australian Dictionary of Biography*, vol. 14, Melbourne University Press, Melbourne, 1996, p. 84.

4 In 1973 Elizabeth Eggleston co-authored with Harry Glasbeek Australia's first case book on industrial law, *Cases and Materials on Industrial Law in Australia*.

as 'the first law course in an Australian University to confront students with the nature of poverty, deprivation and social injustice, and to show students how social scientists evaluated aspects of our society'.[5] She enthusiastically embraced new ways of teaching and worked with other young lecturers to introduce new subjects in the areas of social welfare and social justice, and also Indigenous law in collaboration with the university's Centre for Research into Aboriginal Affairs, of which she was deputy director from 1971. In 1972 she was a prime mover in setting up the Victorian Aboriginal Legal Service.

Elizabeth Eggleston was one of the most widely liked and admired people in the law faculty. Francis Trindade found she went out of her way to welcome him and his wife and remembers her as 'kind, decent and approachable, with no enemies'. Her biographer wrote that she was 'gentle and unassuming, but was moved to exploit her lawyer's skills by a deep-rooted and burning sense of injustice'.[6] Tragically, she died of cancer in 1976, aged only forty-two. Her memorial service at Monash was a memorable occasion, attended by many of her Aboriginal friends and concluding with an elder of the Yirrkala tribe playing the didgeridoo.[7]

Another vital figure of the radical wing, Peter Hanks studied law at Sydney, beginning a five-year part-time course in 1959 while working in a solicitor's office. It was easy to get into law school in those days, he recalls, but the attrition rate was very high, with about half of his cohort never graduating. After completing his course, Hanks won a scholarship to the University of Pennsylvania, returning with an LLM to teach at Sydney. As a young lecturer teaching classes of 180 to 200 students, he remembers being startled when a student asked a question. The student was Geoffrey Robertson and it was a very thoughtful question, but it was most unusual to have any interaction with students. Practising barristers, some at the peak of the profession, did much of the teaching at Sydney, but few thought deeply about pedagogical issues. However, Hanks had become deeply interested in the ways in which law could be taught and decided that he wanted to go to Monash because it had a modern curriculum, the law school was on campus (unlike Sydney), and the staff:student ratio was excellent. He also knew and admired Enid Campbell and was keen to follow her to Monash as they shared similar teaching and research interests.

---

5 Hanks, 'Elizabeth Eggleston', p. 72.

6 Weeks, 'Elizabeth Moulton Eggleston', p. 84.

7 Obituaries of Elizabeth Eggleston by C D Rowley and Louis Waller were published in the *Monash University Law Review*, vol. 3, no.1, November 1976, pp. 1–7.

Left: Elisabeth Eggleston was a much loved and admired lecturer.

In 1970 her groundbreaking research showed systematic discrimination against Aborigines in the administration of the legal system.

Photographer unknown, Monpix 1519

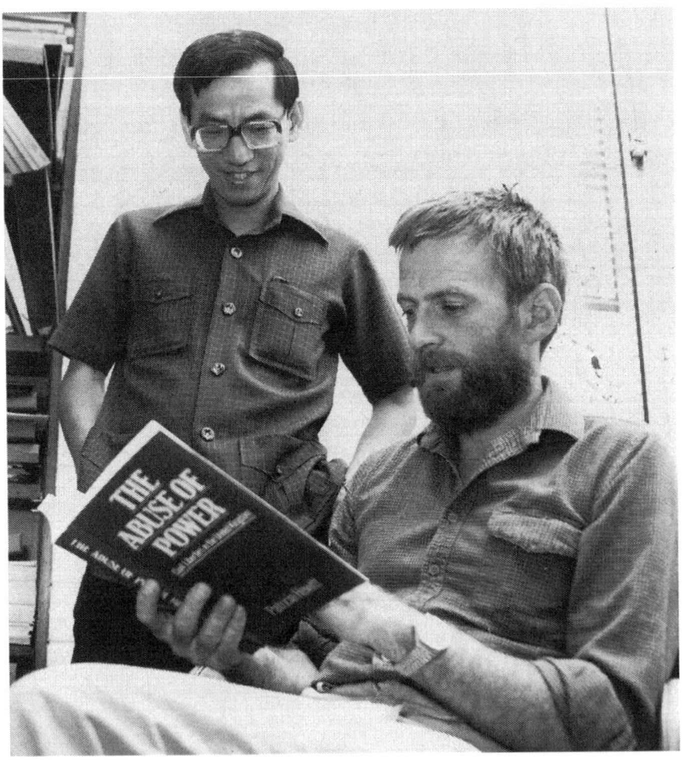

Bottom left: HP Lee and Peter Hanks collaborated on a study of national security.

Photographer Richard Compton, Monpix 997

Arriving in 1969, Hanks began teaching constitutional and administrative law – puffing away at his pipe while he lectured. He was a central figure in all the initiatives put forward by the faculty's young radicals, including the poverty law subject, the law school liaison committee, the clinical education program, the *Legal Services Bulletin*, the *Social Security Reporter* and other 'products of the wave of enthusiasm for socially connected legal practice that swept the law school in the 1970s'.[8]

Terry Carney grew up on the Lachlan River in western New South Wales and was educated by correspondence before he went away to boarding school. His early aspirations were to be a jackaroo or a bank manager, and later he had ideas of being a vet, but when he won a Commonwealth scholarship he chose to enrol in law and criminology at Melbourne, beginning his course 'with starry eyed notions of what law was about'. Having early decided that legal practice was not for him, he was pointed towards an academic career by Elizabeth Eggleston, whom he met while working on his honours thesis. On Eggleston's advice he phoned Louis Waller at Monash to ask whether there were any scholarships or teaching fellowships available. He was nervous about doing this, because while an undergraduate at Melbourne he had only spoken to an academic once, but he found Waller a refreshing contrast from the 'god-people' academics of Melbourne. Carney then went for an interview at Monash, arriving wearing heavy boots and work clothes as he was working in a labouring job after completing university.[9]

In his early years at Monash, Carney was 'lumbered with teaching property law' and this gave him an incentive to develop his own electives. With Peter Hanks, Jude Wallace, Yuri Grbich, Judd Epstein and several others, he devised the Poverty and Social Security Law elective, combining analysis of legislation with a social policy critique. While most members of the academic staff supported the elective, it raised the hackles of some senior representatives of the profession on the faculty board. To retired Supreme Court judge Sir George Lush, the proposal was 'red banners waving'. He argued that the issues could be covered in administrative law and other orthodox subjects and that putting them together as 'poverty law' was overly subjective and left wing. 'What's wrong with the neutral subjects like torts and contracts?' he asked scornfully. However, Lush was out-voted on the faculty board and the subject was approved. The minutes blandly recorded, 'The principal discussion centred around the question whether the course

8 Interview with Peter Hanks, 22 August 2012.

9 Interview with Terry Carney, 23 February 2012.

Terry Carney's courses in poverty law and property law combined analysis of legislation with a social policy critique.
Photographer unknown, Monpix 851

proposed for second semester was of sufficient stature and substance to be included in a Law course and in particular in an undergraduate curriculum.' Significantly, the motion to approve the poverty law course was moved by Enid Campbell, the most rigorous of lawyers.[10] Not all were reconciled to the new course. Richard Fox recalls Ian Spry complaining at morning tea that 'the next thing the faculty will be offering is a subject called "Wealth".'

Almost every progressive staff member wanted to participate in teaching poverty law. As a result it was 'a bit of a rag-bag' with bits of tenancy law, social security law, Marxist theory and other elements of radical iconography. Judd Epstein recalls that they would all assess each submission and there was at least one case where one teacher gave a high distinction and another failed the same piece of work. However, the course evolved quickly, with

10 Faculty Board minutes, 5 March and 30 April 1974.

Peter Hanks and Terry Carney taking it over and developing a more focused curriculum.

Bryan Keon-Cohen originally came to Monash as a medical student in 1964, but his interest in medicine proved short-lived and, after a year jackarooing, he enrolled in arts and law at Melbourne. He found most of the law lecturers at Melbourne didactic and unwilling to engage with students, with one of the rare exceptions being Harry Glasbeek, who soon moved to Monash. On finishing an LLM, Bryan was keen to pursue an academic career and came to Monash as a tutor in 1974, working primarily with Leanna Thomas in the experimental common law course.

A few weeks after arriving at Monash, Keon-Cohen attended a meeting of the Fitzroy Legal Service and found himself editor of the *Fitzroy Legal Service Bulletin*. He produced the first few editions of the journal on the Roneo machine (mimeograph) in the basement of the law school and they were distributed around Monash and Fitzroy. Allan York, the faculty manager, found out about this and was furious, shouting at Bryan: 'You've produced this shabby item with law school paper and ink!' to which Bryan replied, 'I only produced oddments here – most was done elsewhere'. Unsympathetic, York pointed out that it was an inappropriate and wasteful use of faculty resources.

After three issues the *Bulletin* became a properly bound *Legal Services Bulletin*, which Bryan edited with Peter Hanks, Judd Epstein and others. Eventually it developed into an Australia-wide operation, with the Monash radicals co-operating particularly closely with their UNSW colleagues, 'who were also interested in changing how law schools operated'. From the beginning, leading academic and practising lawyers were persuaded to write for the *Bulletin*, including Elizabeth Eggleston on Indigenous justice issues, Henry Finlay on family law, Michael Kirby on privacy and Ron Sackville on property law reform. The *Bulletin* concentrated on the areas of poverty law, legal aid and law reform and by the late 1970s it had around 1500 subscribers. In 1992 the name was changed to the *Alternative Law Journal* (chosen to have the same initials as the *Australian Law Journal*), which is still published out of Monash and is one of the most cited contemporary law journals in Australia.

Bryan Keon-Cohen reflects that the atmosphere of the faculty and its people supported initiatives like the *Legal Service Bulletin*, with a strong belief that 'we're not like Melbourne, we're doing new things'. In 1977, Keon-Cohen took three years' leave to work on Aboriginal customary law for Michael Kirby at the Law Reform Commission. He returned to the faculty in 1981, but left after a year to go to the bar, where he has become well-known for his work on the Mabo case and the 'stolen generations'.[11]

The son of a labourer from Horsham, Bob Miller came to Monash as a lecturer in 1970 with the impeccable credentials of an LLM from Berkeley and seventy games of VFL football for Melbourne. He had worked for several years for the United Nations Human Rights Office in New York and he was strongly committed to what is now called human rights law. His interest in an academic career was eventually subsumed by his interest in radical politics and he resigned on his election as the ALP MLA for Prahran in 1979.

The radical wing of the faculty was boosted in 1973 with the arrival of Judd Epstein. Born in Rochester, New York, and educated at Syracuse and Stanford, he taught at Osgoode Hall in Toronto and Warwick in England before coming to Australia. He had offers from both Melbourne and Monash and chose Monash, partly because Melbourne wanted him to teach mercantile law, in which he had no interest at all, and partly because he heard that Monash was the radical and exciting new law school, while Melbourne was dull and old-fashioned. A natural rebel – if a dean was for it, he was against it – Epstein was aligned with most of the radicals' causes.

Although the radicals had an instinctive ideological sympathy for what became known as the community legal service movement, generally on the 'plumbers v Pericles' debate they were very much on the side of Pericles. They had opted for careers in academia rather than legal practice and in most cases they had little or no experience of private practice and little sympathy for the traditional legal profession. Thus, while they supported legal aid and free legal services, they were ambivalent about clinical legal education as a means of introducing undergraduates to legal practice. The alignment of clinical legal education with the more radical elements in the faculty really only began with the 'second generation' of radicals in the late 1970s and early 1980s.

The radicals gained wide support even among the professors for many of their causes. Louis Waller, for example, had long been deeply concerned about the problems of Aboriginal Australians and the criminal law. He became the first president of the Aboriginal Legal Service, and, after his arrival in 1972, Christie Weeramantry brought a broad humanist and multicultural perspective to his areas of teaching and research. Other professors might have been less sympathetic to radical ideas, but they tended to look on the

11 Interview with Bryan Keon-Cohen, 12 February 2012.

radicals' experiments with amusement rather than horror. Similarly, most of the non-professorial staff members were sufficiently moved by the spirit of the age to let their hair grow just a little bit longer and muffle any scepticism they may have felt towards the new ideas.

A perennial radical cause was the desire for greater democracy within the faculty. Representation of students and junior staff on decision-making bodies was a common catchcry during the 'troubles' of the late 1960s and early 1970s and students and junior staff gained formal representation on the law faculty board from 1968. However, the Monash structure based around powerful appointed deans was barely affected by such token moves and, even as the strength of university radicalism faded during the 1970s, there were still calls in the law faculty for increased democracy. When David Allan resigned in 1976, an 'ad hoc' committee of the full-time staff urged greater faculty say in the choice of his successor, along with measures aimed at curbing autocratic excesses by future deans. The existing power structure, the committee claimed, 'raises the danger that the Faculty might become a bureaucratic institution directed towards attaining one single set of ideas (one paradigm) rather than fulfilling its role as a clearing house for many world views, as a rigorously independent social critic or as a repository for new ideas'.[12] The main authors of the paper were Yuri Grbich and Malcolm Smith (of whom more below) and they received broad support among the staff, with even Professors Nash and Baxt speaking in favour of it. However, once a new dean had been appointed, the agitation faded away with no substantive changes to existing structures. Monash law school never became like Melbourne, where 'village democracy' prevailed, and as one dean put it, 'We decided major and contentious issues by a vote of the staff'.[13]

The failure to extend democracy within the law faculty points to the fact that, while Monash was seen by the wider world as a hotbed of radicalism, in fact its internal structures were more autocratic than Melbourne's and many other universities, and they remained that way throughout the years of student unrest. Monash might have been innovative, new and exciting, but it was emphatically not democratic.

---

12 Report of 'Ad hoc committee of full time staff on promotion and appointments procedures relating to the appointment of deans and professors', Faculty Board minutes, 7 September 1976.

13 Waugh, *First Principles*' pp. 215–7. The quoted dean was Mark Weinberg, the first Monash graduate to become dean of the Melbourne law school.

Chapter 9

David Allan and the Asian Connection

One of the major features of David Allan's term as dean was a strong focus on Asia. In the late 1960s, Allan developed a strong research interest in Asian comparative law and after he came to Monash published widely on aspects of Asian law, particularly relating to contract law and development financing.[1] Through this work he built up contacts with many leading academic lawyers in Asia and this was a major factor in attracting a cohort of outstanding staff members, primarily from Sri Lanka and Singapore. In addition, new Asian-oriented subjects were introduced and a pioneering Centre for Japanese Law established.

Interviewed in 1977, David Allan was asked about the 'spread of nationalities on the staff'. He replied:

> When it became obvious that we were to be the largest law faculty in the whole of Australia, I was concerned that in having so many people working together, it was important that they all did not have the same background. The richness of the law school is going to depend on diversity.[2]

Allan's recruitment certainly added to the diversity of the staff. When he became dean, Francis Trindade had already arrived, and he was followed over the next seven years by Gim Teh, Christie Weeramantry, Wickrema Weerasooria, Lionel de Sousa, HP Lee, Hirokazu Kondo, Kumar Amaresekar and Chin Yen Lee.

The cohort of Sri Lankan academics has been a significant feature of the Monash Law School, beginning with the appointment of Christopher Weeramantry to the Sir Hayden Starke chair in 1972. Born in 1926,

---

1 For example, D E Allan (chief ed.) *Asian Contract Law – A Survey of Current Problems*, Melbourne University Press, 1969; D E Allan (general editor), Mary Hiscock and D Roebuck (co-editors), *Law and Development Finance in Asia*, 8 vols., University of Queensland Press, 1973.

2 *Oracle*, 1977, p. 79.

Christie Weeramantry, the first and most distinguished of the law school's Sri Lankan academics.
Photographer unknown, Monpix 5904

Weeramantry was educated at the Ceylon Law School and also completed external BA and LLB degrees from the University of London. He then combined a successful career at the bar in Colombo with lecturing in Roman law and contracts at the Ceylon Law School. Even after the pressure of work at the bar forced him to resign his lectureship, he always retained academic interests, and in 1967 he published a two-volume treatise on comparative contract law for which he was awarded a doctorate in laws by the University of London.[3] In 1965, aged only 38, he was appointed a Commissioner of Assize of the Supreme Court and two years later he became Sri Lanka's youngest ever Supreme Court judge.

Weeramantry first came to Monash in 1970, when he was invited to be a guest of honour at a Law Council meeting in Melbourne. He had already

---

3 C G Weeramantry, *The Law of Contracts: Being a Treatise on the Law of Contracts as Prevailing in Ceylon and Involving a Comparative Study of the Roman-Dutch, English and Customary Laws Relating to Contracts*, Colombo, 1967.

been in touch with David Allan, who was working on comparative contract law in Asia, and the visit helped prompt his decision to relinquish his assured progress up the judicial ladder in Sri Lanka to take up an academic career. He wrote:

> I had developed an interest in research and writing – not merely on purely legal matters but on the social perspectives associated with legal studies. Life on the bench for the foreseeable future would limit my ability to pursue these avenues. I would of course be able to make a contribution to the development of the law, but this would be largely within the context of Sri Lanka, and Sri Lanka formed a very small part of the legal universe.[4]

In 1971 the law school received permission to advertise a new chair, but when Allan heard that Weeramantry was interested, he invited him to take up the chair. Weeramantry felt some trepidation coming to Australia as 'Australia then had the reputation of still being a white enclave. The White Australia policy was not dead'. He and his wife were relieved to find that 'the resentment and remoteness we had been led to expect from the Australian population were totally absent in our immediate neighbourhood'.[5]

At Monash, Weeramantry taught contract law for about ten years, but increasingly his classes focused on comparative law. He introducing multicultural perspectives to his teaching, arguing that the law in Australia had 'functioned largely within a narrowly Eurocentric, monocultural and formalistic framework of thought'.[6] He began to give lunchtime lectures on different legal systems and was increasingly inspired to write on these things. He expanded his interests to include comparative law, legal philosophy, theories of justice, human rights, bioethical and environmental law and finally international law. He reflects that some in the law school thought that he was ranging too widely and beyond the legitimate topics of academic legal study, but he is firmly of the view that most academics are too narrow in their approach to the law. He is particularly critical of the positivist school of jurisprudence, which, he argues, holds that legal rules can be established

---

4 C G Weeramantry, *Towards One World: The Memoirs of Judge Weeramantry*, vol. 1, Weeramantry International Centre for Peace Education and Research, Colombo, nd, p. 417.

5 Ibid, vol 2, *The Australian Years*, pp. 6, 13.

6 Ibid., vol 1, p. 422.

scientifically and encourages a black letter law approach, while ignoring sociological perspectives.[7]

Christie Weeramantry was greatly concerned with what he saw as a growing gulf between the legal profession and the public, which he addressed in his 1975 book, *The Law in Crisis: Bridges of Understanding*. The book had a remarkable impact, among other things prompting the institution of Law Week, which has become a major annual event bringing together members of the public, lawyers, legal officials and judges. Law Week has been an important Monash contribution towards a better public understanding of the Australian legal system.

Weeramantry always made the subjects he taught as broad as possible. One of his students in Legal Philosophy commented:

> For gentility and erudition Prof Weeramantry is a wonderful mentor. He showed not only his depth of legal scholarship but also his sympathy and concern for universal human rights. During the semester he introduced us to the development of Law from Hammurabi to Julius Stone stopping en route to study Plato, Aristotle, Cicero, St Augustine, Mai Minides [sic], Hobbes, Locke, Rousseau and Bentham. Don't be daunted by having to read the 'Republic' in a week … with the help of Russell's 'History of Western Philosophy' and Prof W's clear and concise lecture notes the beginner can soon lay a firm foundation on which to build.[8]

Weeramantry particularly enjoyed teaching theories of justice with Julius Stone, the famous professor of jurisprudence at Sydney and later UNSW. Stone was one of the world leaders in this area and it was a reflection of Monash's growing reputation that Stone chose to come to Monash every second year. Weeramantry recalls that even though Stone 'scintillated among the stars' he always participated enthusiastically in classes with the students.

When David Allan was looking for a Sri Lankan contribution to his book on Asian contract law, Christie Weeramantry recommended Wickrema Weerasooria, who was working in London for a PhD on banking law. Allan

---

7 An indication of the range of Christie Weeramantry's research interests is given by the books he published in his first twelve years at Monash: *The Law in Crisis: Bridges of Understanding* (1975); *Equality and Freedom: Some Third World Perspectives* (1976); *Apartheid: The Closing Phases* (1980); *An Invitation to the Law* (1982); *Slumbering Sentinels: Law and Human Rights in the Wake of Technology* (1983); *Law: The Threatened Peripheries* (1984); *Human Rights in Japan* (1984).

8 *Counter Faculty Handbook*, 1981, p. 78.

was impressed by Weerasoria's work and in 1973 brought him to the faculty as a senior lecturer. A popular teacher and prolific publisher, Weerasooria's academic career had an unusual, possibly unique, interruption. Returning home for a short holiday during the semester break in 1977, he was unable to come back because, as the faculty board minutes reported, 'of an undertaking given to a Magistrate that he would not leave until the hearing of charges to be brought against him in relation to the publication of a cartoon book containing cartoons critical of the Prime Minister of Sri Lanka had been completed'. He was granted leave without pay and hoped to return after the Sri Lankan elections in July. However, the elections did not lead to his return, but to his resignation from the faculty on being appointed to head the Ministry of Plan Implementation! In 1986 he became Sri Lankan High Commissioner to Australia, only to return to Monash in 1990 as an associate professor.

Another Sri Lankan who had trained in London was Sananda Kumar St Augustine Perera Amaresekara, who came as a PhD candidate and part-time tutor in 1976. On completing his PhD, 'A comparative study of the law of confessions in Sri Lanka and Victoria', Kumar, as he was known, was appointed to a lectureship and taught criminal law and evidence until his untimely death in 2002. Lively and full of fun, he loved social gatherings and dinner parties and always had an energetic social life. He was a popular teacher, particularly for students who liked to be 'spoon fed'. His lectures were 'lucidly structured and eloquently delivered' and 'spiced with witty comments and observations', but his liking for politically incorrect and sexist jokes sometimes led him into trouble. On his death in 2002, Amaresekara left a bequest of $40,000 to the law school for prizes in Criminal Law and Evidence.[9]

The first Indian graduate to join the staff was Lionel de Sousa, who held the degrees of BSc, LLB and LLM from the University of Bombay. He worked as a school teacher and as an executive for a subsidiary of EMI before coming to Monash as a senior teaching fellow in 1972. He taught primarily legal process and contracts, but, as the faculty's minute of appreciation delicately puts it, 'Lionel did not find the pursuit of scholarship easy' and his inability to publish precluded promotion. Nonetheless, he was a popular teacher until his retirement in 1997.[10]

---

9 'Vale KA', *Clayton's Law*, no. 2, 2002, p. 3.

10 Minute of appreciation, Lionel de Sousa, Faculty Board minutes, 24 July 1997.

After Sri Lanka, Singapore and Malaysia were Monash law's most fertile Asian recruiting grounds. The first to arrive was Gim Leung Teh, who came as a tutor in 1970 after completing an LLB with honours at the University of London. Although his master's thesis topic was the limitations of police interrogation, his main teaching and research interest came to be in property law and he co-authored with Bryan Dwyer the popular textbook, *Introduction to Property Law*. In the late 1970s and early 1980s he was also prominent in the movement for tenancy law reform. A well-liked lecturer, he was one of the first to make use of an overhead projector in his lectures and students found he kept his classes alive 'with his inexhaustible supply of surprises and jokes'.[11] Many students remember the aerobics classes he took in the basement and etched in Greg Carne's memory is a picture of Gim Teh 'leaping about the Moot Court'.[12]

Another of David Allan's Asian recruits was Hoong Phun Lee (known universally as HP), who became one of the leading scholars and great characters of the faculty. One of nine children of a grocer from Penang, HP had his primary and secondary schooling at St Xavier's Institution, a Christian Brothers school in Penang, and then studied at the Law School of Singapore, graduating in 1972. There was no family tradition of law but he found he liked research and was attracted to the idea of being a legal academic. After working for a short time as a full-time tutor at the new law school at the University of Malaya, Kuala Lumpur, he was advised to broaden his horizons by working in Australia, so he wrote to David Allan and was offered a teaching fellowship. He took it with the idea of completing a PhD and returning to Malaysia, but ended up staying because he preferred to research and write in English. He found that 'The pursuit of knowledge at Monash was impressive and this made it an ideal environment for an academic'. After a short time, he was promoted to lecturer, and in 1975 began research for his PhD on 'Emergency Powers'. HP's main fields of interest have been in Australian, Malaysian and comparative constitutional law, administrative law and the judiciary, and he has published many highly regarded books in these areas. As a lecturer he has always been popular with students for his deep understanding of his subjects, the clarity of his lectures and his gentle sense of humour.

Another recruit from Singapore, Chin Yen Lee, combined her skills as a lawyer with great talent as a pianist. She studied piano and viola while

---

11 *Counter Faculty Handbook*, 1984, p. 71.

12 Interview with Greg Carne, 21 January 2012.

completing an LLB with first class honours at the University of Singapore and in 1968 was awarded a four-year scholarship by the Associated Board of the Royal Schools of Music to study music in the United Kingdom. She then obtained a University of London PhD writing on Singapore's consumer credit laws, and in 1978 came to Monash to teach banking, consumer credit and other commercial law subjects. Described as 'the daylight express' for the speed and clarity of her lectures, she was a well-liked teacher and prolific publisher before resigning in 1986 to go into private practice.[13] She has now retired and lives in Vancouver, where she plays and tours with the Vancouver Piano Ensemble.

The impact of the influx of academics from Asia could be seen in many ways. It gave the Monash law faculty possibly the most diverse staff of any Australian law school, exposing students to widely differing perspectives of the law. It also boosted the faculty's strength in Asian comparative law, already a key research area through the work of David Allan. Though not all of the staff from Asian backgrounds published work drawing on their countries of origin, HP Lee, Wickrema Weerasooria and Christie Weeramantry did so extensively, and others did also to a lesser extent. However, surprisingly few electives were offered in Asian law, with only East-West Trade Law and Japanese Law being regularly taught.

The apogee of the faculty's Asian orientation during David Allan's deanship came with the establishment of Australia's first Centre of Japanese Law.[14] Allan pointed out that the rapidly growing flow of business between Australia and Japan called for lawyers with knowledge of both legal systems, and he set about creating what was probably the first teaching and research centre in Japanese law in the English speaking world outside the United States. Peter Hocker, whose main area of teaching and research was in contract law, took leave for three years in the early 1970s to work with a Tokyo law firm, and returned fluent in spoken and written Japanese. He was joined in 1974 by Melbourne graduate Malcolm Smith, who had spent a year at a Tokyo law school and was similarly fluent in Japanese. In 2004 Smith reflected that the guiding principle of his teaching career was 'to open Australian Law Schools to a wider vision than training people for the local

---

13 *Counter Faculty Handbook*, 1984, p. 69.

14 The Centre of Japanese Law appears not to have had the formal structures of later centres, but it was often referred to as a centre and operated very much in the style of a modern centre. See, for example, Faculty Board minutes, 3 November 1976.

profession'.[15] Hocker and Smith were joined for a year from July 1974 by Hiokazu Kondo, an attorney from Tokyo with experience in both domestic and international law and these three formed the core of the new centre.[16]

From 1974 the faculty offered an undergraduate elective course on the Japanese legal system and in 1975 a postgraduate subject began. Hocker, Smith and Kondo also presented seminars on Japanese law in collaboration with the Australia/Japan Trade Law Foundation, translated some leading textbooks on Japanese civil and commercial law, and Smith especially published prolifically on Japanese law in both Australian and Japanese journals.

The faculty's early strength in Asian law and the strong connections with Asia built up under David Allan made Monash the clear leader in this field among Australian law schools. It was also important in attracting the first large influx of overseas students in the 1980s, primarily from Malaysia (because Malaysian graduates could practise in Malaysia with a Monash degree). However, for a variety of reasons the faculty did not build on its early lead. The Centre for Japanese Law faded away and Melbourne later took the lead in establishing a new Centre for Asian Law, headed by Malcolm Smith, who had made his name at Monash.

---

15 Justice Kenneth Hayne, quoting Malcolm Smith in a farewell speech on Smith's departure as founding head of the Asian Law Centre at the University of Melbourne, 11 March 2004, http://alc.law.unimelb.edu.au/files/update_june_2004.pdf.

16 'Laying Down the (Japanese) Law', *Monash Reporter*, May 1975, p. 2.

Chapter 10

Bob Baxt and the Rise of Commercial Law

In the 1960s as the economy expanded and became more complex, the demand for well-trained commercial lawyers rose sharply. Yet in the early years of the Monash law school, the most obvious weakness was in commercial law. For some in the faculty it seemed obvious that for Monash to become genuinely competitive with Melbourne, it had to be able to place its best graduates with the leading commercial law firms. To do this it had to build up its expertise in commercial law. This proposition was by no means generally accepted. Enid Campbell never hid her belief that company law and other commercial law areas did not represent 'real law'. She was not alone in looking with disdain on subjects such as company law and taxation, a disdain shared by many of the faculty's radical wing, who saw them as the subjects that most closely tied the law to the capitalist system. Nonetheless, the pressure to develop commercial law was hard to resist, and between 1968 and 1980 the faculty built up a high profile in this area.

The key appointment was made in 1968 when Bob Baxt was lured from Sydney. Baxt's parents were Russian Jews who had fled to China after the revolution in 1917. He was born in Shanghai in 1938, and, after surviving the Japanese occupation, came to Australia with his family in 1947. Dux of Newington College in 1955, Baxt then studied arts and law at the University of Sydney. With New South Wales' curious system of legal education, he completed his articles and was admitted as a solicitor before he had completed his law degree! Among his fellow articled clerks was John Winston Howard, the future prime minister, who Baxt recalls was 'only an average student, who failed several subjects ... but he told me within a month of me being there, "I am going to be prime minister of this country one day".'[1]

Baxt was already attracted to academia, and in 1962 he won a scholarship to Harvard where he completed an LLM by coursework. After some

1 Interview with Bob Baxt, 22 June 2011.

experience in private practice in Boston, he returned to Freehill Hollingdale & Page in Sydney. However, he found practice frustrating, as he wished to explore issues in a scholarly fashion, which did not necessarily suit his clients. So in 1966, he applied for a position in the Faculty of Economics at Sydney: 'I didn't go to the law school because I wanted to work in the area of corporate law and I was very interested in the interaction of economics and law, and accounting and law'.[2]

In 1968 Baxt came to Monash as a senior lecturer. The most dynamic, innovative and energetic member of the academic staff, Baxt taught almost every commercially oriented subject, became the most prolific publisher in the faculty, and was an endless source of new projects and ideas. In his first year at Monash he tutored in taxation and protested long and loud against Ian Spry's insistence on rote learning and a closed book exam. The following year, with Jack Fajgenbaum from law and Maureen Brunt and Gary Purcell of the Faculty of Economics, Baxt set up a multidisciplinary course in competition law, initially as a fourth year honours seminar, and later as part of the masters' program. This course was highly successful and became one of the engines for the reform of Australia's antiquated and ineffective competition laws. Baxt then joined with Harold Ford of the Melbourne law school and Bob Officer of the Faculty of Economics to set up a new course in securities regulation. Graeme Samuel, later to be chairman of the Australian Competition and Consumer Commission, was an early student in this course and later helped to teach it.

Baxt's interest in competition law led him to come up with two important new activities. During the mid-1970s there was much public debate around the regulation of competition, culminating in the *Trade Practices Act 1974*. Baxt thought the time opportune for a journal focusing on competition law and he initiated the *Australian Business Law Review*, which is still the leading competition law journal in Australia. In 1976 he organised a large conference on competition law and the Trade Practices Act. Held at Ballarat under the auspices of the Monash law school, this conference was a great success and led to annual workshops on similar themes. These were the precursor of a rapid growth in continuing legal education and the establishment of the Centre for Commercial Law.

Baxt's ventures were not confined to commercial law. His apparently inexhaustible energy extended to the encouragement of research and publishing for the whole faculty. In 1972 Baxt floated the idea that the

---

2 Ibid.

Monash law school should publish a review and he headed the committee set up to investigate the financial and editorial requirements. By February 1973 the proposed journal had a name, the *Monash University Law Review*, and a business plan for publishing two issues each year, initially with an editorial board composed of staff members, but with an expectation that student editors should take over as soon as possible. As first editor, Baxt led the journal through its teething troubles until it was handed over to student editors in 1979. 'Some two and a half years after it came into existence it was noted by a leading English Law Review as one of the two Australian Law Reviews that it was essential for English Law Schools to obtain,' Baxt proudly claimed.[3]

Another of Baxt's ventures to raise the scholarly standing of the faculty was a monograph series. This had first been mooted in 1972, with Ian Spry appointed as convenor, but following Spry's departure the venture stalled until Baxt took it on several years later. Baxt set up the Monash monograph committee which published 'Monash studies in law', with the aim of encouraging 'research and writing on specific subjects, including those which do not readily come within the scope of text books on traditional legal topics'. At least six titles, primarily chosen from the faculty's best postgraduate theses, were published in the late 1970s and early 1980s, although the economics of the series eventually proved unsustainable and it faded away in the late 1980s.[4]

Baxt's next initiative was the *Annual Survey of Australian Law*. Seeing a need for an annual review of Australian law, he found the resources, a publisher and contributors to produce one. Baxt was co-editor with Gretchen Kewley, a Melbourne Supreme Court Prize winner and the faculty's long-serving research assistant. Many Monash staff members contributed to the survey, giving a useful boost to publication figures. While still a junior lecturer, Marilyn Pittard wrote the section on industrial law for several years and found this to be excellent training in research and writing. The *Annual Survey* continued to be run out of Monash until the early 1990s, when it moved to Adelaide.

---

3 Faculty Board minutes, 5 June 1979.

4 The titles were F H Callaway, *Winding Up on the Just and Equitable Ground*, 1978; Warren Pengilley, *Trade Associations, Fairness and Competition*, 1981; L A Hallett, *Royal Commissions and Boards of Inquiry*, 1982; Enid Campbell et al (eds), *Well and Truly Tried: Essays on Evidence, in Honour of Sir Richard Eggleston*, 1982; S R Derham, *Subrogation in Insurance Law*, 1985; Malcolm Cope, *Duress, Undue Influence and Unconscientious Bargains*, 1985.

Bob Baxt, who served two terms as dean, brought dynamism, innovation and entrepreneurialism to the faculty from 1980–88.
Photographer unknown, Monpix 280

While working at a frenetic pace at Monash, Bob Baxt also read for the bar and worked one day a week as a consultant for Phillips Fox and later Arnold Bloch Leibler. His energy, innovations and scholarship earned him rapid promotion, to associate professor in 1971 and to the Sir John Latham chair the following year. Popular and admired, he was the logical choice to succeed Gerry Nash as dean in 1980.

With Bob Baxt as the catalyst, the commercial law strength of the faculty rapidly built up during the 1970s. Don Doane, an American with an honours law degree from Melbourne, came to Monash in 1969 as a senior tutor and was promoted to lecturer the following year. Doane lectured in company law for many years and students enjoyed his teaching style, although he did not always see eye to eye with Bob Baxt. He resigned in 1983 to go to the bar. Another Melbourne graduate, Michael Pryles, was appointed a senior teaching fellow in 1970 and promoted to lecturer in 1972. His main areas of interest were conflict of laws and private international law, but he had a strong commercial bent and was a member of the commercial law interest group. Pryles published several highly regarded books and was promoted to professor in 1985. He expressed the belief that it was not possible to be an academic without a private income and it was not a great surprise when he left to join Minter Ellison in 1989.[5] He has since gone on to build a stellar reputation as a commercial arbitrator.

Both the commercial law teaching strength of the faculty and the ranks of its radical wing were boosted in 1971 with the appointment of long-haired, bearded Sydney graduate Colin O'Hare. While he taught banking law, his primary interest was in consumer law and in 1972 he introduced the faculty's first subject on consumer protection. An interview he gave to the student journal *Snark* in 1972 gives a feeling for his approach:

> The ethos of our society reflects middle-class values which I personally reject. The legal system reflects policies designed to protect the elitist classes. The education system encourages conformity to the status quo and discourages reasoned criticism. The political system perpetuates all three.[6]

Not surprisingly, such views did not meet with total approval from the profession and his teachings were subject to some criticism in the *Law Institute Journal.*

During the late 1970s and early 1980s, tax avoidance and taxation reform were issues of intense public controversy and the taxation lecturers at Monash played significant parts on both sides of the debate. Yuri Grbich, born in New Zealand of Yugoslav parents, was the senior tax lecturer by this time, having come to Monash in 1971, fresh from completing his PhD at the LSE. Initially, he was unable to teach tax as Ian Spry 'held onto it grimly because he saw me as a radical foreigner and it would be "the thin end of the wedge of the communist conspiracy" if I started teaching tax.'[7] Eventually, David Allan 'managed to slip me into teaching tax through the summer school'. Although he was regarded as a radical, Grbich argues that few issues in law break down to neat left-right divisions. His PhD thesis and

---

5 *Age*, 11 July 1989.

6 *Snark*, vol 2, no 3, October 1972, p. 13.

7 Interview with Yuri Grbich.

many of his subsequent publications were on flexible discretionary trusts, which he approached from an academic point of view, but in the 1970s these became one of the main vehicles for tax avoidance. Much of his research was devoted to arguing the case for tax reform and he wrote extensively on the theories behind consumption taxes, capital gains tax and tax avoidance, culminating in his influential book, *Institutional Renewal in the Australian Taxation System*, published in 1984. Grbich always believed that legal academics should have a strong role in real world change and that academic papers should be a means to an end rather than an end in themselves. One of Grbich's students in the mid-1970s, Tony Pagone, recalls that he was a self-proclaimed 'revenue gatherer' and he taught the tax course from the point of view of political theory, almost going as far as invoking the 'class struggle'. Pagone thinks that politically unaware students frequently did not understand what Grbich was on about, but for those who understood the political dimensions he brought things together in a most impressive way. Grbich left Monash in 1984 to take up a chair at UNSW.

Two other new tax lecturers of this period, Kevin Pose and Harry Reicher, had more orthodox views. They were among the first Monash graduates to lecture in the faculty, and their approach to taxation law shows clearly that the university's early radicalism did not necessarily rub off on law students. Pose, the third Supreme Court Prize winner, completed articles at Grant & Co followed by a BCL at Oxford before being appointed to a lectureship in 1973. Yuri Grbich thought that Pose did not know a lot about tax when he started teaching it, but he was a very quick learner and his students thought highly of his teaching. In 1976 he left full-time teaching for a highly successful career at the bar and then as senior tax partner at Arthur Robinson & Hedderwicks, although he maintained a close connection with the faculty until his death in 2010. Harry Reicher completed his LLB in 1971 and then worked in private practice and completed an LLM at Melbourne before coming back to Monash in 1976.

Pose and Reicher were both active tax practitioners and tended to look at tax from the point of view of their clients, while Grbich took a more academic and policy-oriented approach. Grbich and Reicher both recall that when Harry Reicher became a lecturer he had a bumper sticker on his desk, given to him by a client, saying 'Taxation is Theft'. Yuri walked into his office one day, took one look at the sticker and said, 'No, no, Harry! You've got it all wrong! Private property is theft!' From then on they were good friends. Although they disagreed strongly on many things, they treated their arguments as an opportunity for the law school to participate in a major community debate. Thus, they worked together on a major book, *Modern Trusts and Taxation*, published in 1978, while individually Reicher published articles such as 'What to Do When the Commissioner Attacks: Preserving Your Client's Sanity and Liquidity'[8] and Grbich wrote on themes like 'Problems of Tax Avoidance in Australia'.[9]

Pose, Reicher and Grbich shared a great love of teaching at Monash and their students found their enthusiasm infectious. Grbich 'enjoyed teaching so much I wondered why they were paying me to come to work'. They did much to establish a strong tradition at Monash that tax, traditionally among the driest of subjects, can be taught with flair and excitement.

Industrial law, an area which has undergone a dramatic transformation since the 1970s with the dismantling of the old conciliation and arbitration system, has always been an area of great strength at Monash. It was first taught in 1969 by Harry Glasbeek, a Holocaust survivor who completed an honours law degree at Melbourne and a JD at Chicago before coming to Monash. Seen as something of a left-winger, Glasbeek was an inspiring teacher and a distinguished scholar, publishing not only on industrial law (including occupational health and safety, corporate social responsibility, industrial manslaughter and corporate criminality), but also on torts, evidence, policing and racism, and legal education. He left in 1974 to take up a chair at Osgoode Hall in Toronto.

Glasbeek's successor teaching industrial law was one of his former students, Ron McCallum, who had come to specialise in that area through an accident of timetables. In 1970 McCallum had wanted to organise his timetable so that he could have a day off. The only way he could do this was by taking either Family Law or Industrial Law, and he chose Industrial Law with Harry Glasbeek. In Ron's opinion, some law lecturers teach a set of rules, but others teach with real conviction and Harry was one of these. It took only about two weeks for Ron to decide that industrial law was what he wanted to do and from then on his aim was to be a labour law academic. After completing his LLB, he wanted to go to Chicago like Glasbeek, but Harry advised him that the law school was close to the ghetto and would be too dangerous for a blind man, so he went to Queen's University in Ontario with a British Commonwealth Scholarship.

McCallum was appointed to a tenured lectureship in 1974 at the age of twenty-five. As well as industrial law, he taught administrative law, evidence

---

8 *Tax Strategies for Advisors in 1979*, vol. 1, no. 1, 1979.

9 *Canadian Taxation*, vol. 3, 1982.

and torts. He taught administrative law with Enid Campbell, which 'was very scary' as she knew the subject backwards, and this prompted him to read everything. In his early years of teaching he worked day and night and had no time for relationships. Universally admired as a teacher, Ron also quickly established himself as one of the faculty's most accomplished researchers. From 1979 to 1980 he was seconded to the public service to work in the Fraser government's infamous Industrial Relations Bureau.[10] This was a great experience and it was where he learnt to drink, because 'all the public servants were heavy drinkers'.

One of Ron McCallum's students, Deborah Glass, recalls him as 'an inspirational teacher whose blindness seemed to give him an extra sense – a man of real humanity, not to mention humour'. McCallum

> taught me Evidence and Industrial Law, and I became one of the army of volunteers who used to read to him in his rooms. I was an interested but not particularly industrious student, being much more familiar with the layout of the lawns than the law library, and my comeuppance came one day when Ron decided he needed to check a case reference from an article I was reading him. I had the citation and we headed for the library, where I stood at the top of the stairs, not knowing how to confess I didn't have the foggiest idea where to find it. After a few moments Ron said gently, but with a wicked sparkle, that he thought I would find the volume in the top row of the third stack on the left.[11]

In 1978 the commercial area was strengthened with the appointment of Peter Ellinger to the seventh chair in the faculty, named the Sir John Barry chair. A graduate of both the Hebrew University in Jerusalem and Oxford, Ellinger had previously taught at Singapore and Wellington. He was a leading authority on banking law and students saw him as 'the ultimate academic', but felt he was rather too esoteric for those whose main aim was to pass exams. One student described him as 'a very nervous individual ... [who] seems to be worried about everything except what he wears (Pierre Cardin he isn't)', while also remarking that he was 'one of the most approachable and understanding academics in the faculty'.[12]

---

10 For an account of the Industrial Relations Bureau, see Malcolm Fraser and Margaret Symons, *Malcolm Fraser: The Political Memoirs*, Miegunyah Press, Melbourne, 2011, p. 366.

11 Email from Deborah Glass to authors, 18 April 2011.

12 *Counter Faculty Handbook*, 1981, p. 70.

By the time that Bob Baxt became dean in 1980, the teaching and research strength of the faculty across the broad field of commercial law was the equal of any law school in Australia. During Baxt's deanship in the 1980s, commercial law became the vanguard of his ambitious and visionary attempt to position the faculty to survive and thrive in an era of falling funding and stagnant student numbers.

Chapter 11

New Areas and New People

In the early 1960s few law schools in the world, and none in Australia, offered many optional courses outside the core curriculum. From the start, David Derham encouraged the staff at Monash to explore new courses and offered his support to anybody wanting to develop a new area. The young and enthusiastic staff responded by branching out in many directions. This was reflected in the rapid growth in the number of undergraduate and postgraduate electives. In 1969 undergraduate students had a choice of just thirteen optional subjects and there was no postgraduate coursework program. By 1980 there were fifty-three undergraduate electives and thiry-five postgraduate subjects available for the various masters' and diploma courses. In some cases electives were introduced when new staff members were deliberately recruited to build up particular areas of expertise, but more came about as existing staff were stimulated to explore new areas of research and teaching. Some of the new specialisations already existed at other universities and were standard areas of teaching and research for any large law school, but several were pioneered at Monash.

One area where Monash undoubtedly led the country was intellectual property, or industrial property as it was more commonly known in the 1970s. This came about through the foresight of David Derham, who saw that it would become a vital area of the law and was keen to build it up at Monash. When he became aware that Jim Lahore (husband of Ann, the pioneer Monash staff member) was keen to leave private practice for academia, Derham suggested he specialise in intellectual property. Lahore agreed, and Derham arranged for him to study with a leading intellectual property lawyer at the University of Pennsylvania. On his return in 1970 Lahore was appointed to a senior lectureship at Monash, where he developed Australia's first intellectual property course, as well as becoming the leading researcher in the field. To Yuri Grbich, Jim Lahore was 'without doubt the father of modern intellectual property law in Australia'.

There was some debate as to the most appropriate names for the subjects Lahore taught and even for his area of specialisation. In 1976 he reported to the faculty board on course names:

> We wish to offer these units under the generic title "Legal Protection for Innovation in the Arts, Technology and Trade". We suggest this title because it gives a clearer idea of what the subject is concerned with. The term "Industrial Property" is a misnomer, and it is completely misleading. Some students have stated that they assumed the term "Industrial Property" referred to commercial conveyancing. The term used in Europe, "Intellectual Property", is rather twee.[1]

In the end the handbook entry read: 'Intellectual Property is a generic term ... The subject matter of Intellectual Property is innovation in the arts, technology and trade'. Undergraduate units were taught in Copyright and Designs, Patents for Inventions and Trade Marks, and Commercial Designations, with similar postgraduate units.[2]

In 1973 Lahore took leave to spend three years with the World Intellectual Property Organization in Geneva. He returned in 1976 as a reader, but Monash's failure to promote him to professor led him to accept an offer to become the inaugural Herchel Smith professor of intellectual property law at Queen Mary College, University of London in 1980.

With Lahore's departure, the intellectual property mantle passed to Janice Luck. An honours graduate from the University of Tasmania, Luck was a protégé of David Allan, coming to Monash as a lecturer in 1973. She was asked to teach intellectual property as Jim Lahore was on study leave, and then taught with him after he returned, which was 'a wonderful learning experience and a good example of the benefits of Monash's team teaching approach'. In addition to intellectual property, Janice Luck also taught property for many years, again enjoying team teaching with Gim Teh, Jude Wallace, Terry Carney and Stan Robinson. However, her interest was primarily in intellectual property, and she built up a strong reputation in this area, before leaving to go into private practice in 1987.

Criminal law has always been one of the faculty's great strengths. In Louis Waller, the faculty already had one of Australia's leading criminal law academics, and in the early 1970s three new arrivals helped consolidate what was without doubt the leading criminal law group in Australia, as

---

1 Faculty Board minutes, 7 September 1976.

2 *Faculty of Law 1978 Student Handbook.*

well as building up a new area of expertise in criminology. The first new appointment was Bob Williams, the first Monash graduate to become a lecturer in the faculty. After sharing the Supreme Court Prize with Mark Aronson in the first graduating class in 1969, he tutored in 1970 before going to Oxford where he completed his BCL with first class honours. He returned to Monash as a lecturer in 1972. Williams recalls that 'In terms of staff resourcing and opportunities to follow individual research interests the 70's into the 80's was a wonderful period.' Always an unrelentingly hard worker himself, he was surprised to find that 'By no means, however, were all committed to the hard work and professionalism which I have always believed should characterize both institutions and individual careers'. He observed with disapproval the tennis afternoons and long bridge games indulged in by some staff members.[3] He greatly admired Louis Waller and Enid Campbell, describing them as 'Outstanding academics, they led by example and provided stability and a constant disciplined professionalism at the senior level'. They were the models for his academic career. From the time of his return from England, he produced a steady stream of meticulously researched and argued 'black letter' articles and books on aspects of criminal law and the law of evidence. As a teacher too, he was rigorous and conservative, a style that appealed to many students, though some thought he could be too dismissive in his demolition of arguments based on youthful idealism rather than sound legal reasoning. A student reviewing one of his subjects for the *Counter Faculty Handbook* pointedly commented that 'Mr Williams taught Current Problems in Criminal Law as though there were no problems with the law.'[4]

The second new criminal law appointment was Richard Fox. In common with Louis Waller, Fox comes from a Polish Jewish background, with his parents arriving in Australia shortly before the Second World War. The family name was Fuks and the immigration officer asked Richard's father how that was pronounced. On hearing the answer, the immigration officer said 'You can't call yourself that here, mate' and wrote him down as Fox.

Richard Fox went to Princes Hill Primary School and University High School and originally planned to be a chemist, but a vocational guidance counsellor advised him to study law. He followed this advice and enrolled in law at Melbourne in 1962. Eighteen of the twenty subjects required for the LLB were compulsory and he chose criminology as one of his

---

3 Williams, 'Some Reflections on Monash', p. 8.

4 *Counter Faculty Handbook*, 1985, p. 50.

two optional subjects. He was taught by Norval Morris, a pioneer and leader in criminology who inspired Fox to study after his law course for a postgraduate diploma of criminology in Melbourne's newly created department of criminology.

The theme of Fox's working life has been the interrelationship between the social sciences and the law, and this was seen in his LLM thesis on the law of obscenity. Begun while he was completing his articles, this was the first master's thesis at Melbourne to be awarded first class honours since the 1940s. On the strength of this, Fox then spent several years as a senior research associate at the Centre of Criminology at the University of Toronto, later also teaching in the faculty of law. In 1972, when he wanted to come back to Australia, David Allan offered him a senior lectureship to teach criminal law and establish criminology as a discipline within the Monash law school. Fox always thought criminology was best placed within a law faculty rather than being a separate unit as it was created at Melbourne, because this gives it intellectual involvement in the law and the clout of working with a large faculty. Soon after he arrived Fox successfully applied to the Law Foundation for a grant of $30,000 to build up a criminology library, and this was used to acquire the basis of what became a significant collection. At Monash he found there was far more freedom to do new things and start new electives than there was at Melbourne.

In 1976 the criminology strength of the faculty was reinforced when Arie Freiberg was appointed to a tutorship. His life and career echoed Richard Fox's to a remarkable extent – he even followed Fox in the alphabetical list of the faculty's staff. Freiberg was born in Israel, his parents having survived the Holocaust in Poland. The family came to Australia in 1955 and Arie, like Richard Fox, was educated at Princes Hill Primary School and University High School. From a young age, his ambition was to be a lawyer, an ambition proudly stated in his bar mitzvah speech. Again like Richard Fox he developed a great interest in criminology and by the time he started at the University of Melbourne he was more interested in criminology than 'straight' law, and he enrolled for a combined LLB/diploma of criminology course. The criminology course was 'brilliant' and he put four times more work into his criminology studies than into his law degree. The law course 'didn't inspire me' but he got an honours degree and served on the *Melbourne University Law Review*. He knew from the first day that he would never practise law, although his parents persuaded him to do articles with a small husband and wife firm. Then, in the heady early days of the Whitlam government, he moved to Canberra as a research officer at the new Australian Institute of Criminology, where he 'took the opportunity to write solidly and learn my craft as a criminologist'. His research covered many areas including Aboriginals and criminal justice, and life sentences, and he began a major project on sentencing principles. However, by 1975 he was disillusioned with the leadership at the Institute of Criminology and looking for a move. Richard Fox was regarded as the leading authority on sentencing in Australia, so Arie asked him for a job at Monash and, with the less formal appointment processes of the era, was appointed a full-time tutor from the start of 1976. He tutored for Fox in criminal law, sat in on his classes and worked with him on a project on sentencing in Victoria, learning much about teaching and intellectual rigour.

Monash was a dynamic law school when Arie arrived and he found it a 'stimulating environment'. There was a dynamic group of young academics in the faculty and they made it a congenial place to work. His first year of teaching was in 1976, when he was still not a lot older than the students he taught and he found them 'extraordinarily bright and challenging'. He enjoyed it enormously and found he loved engaging with students. In his first decade at Monash, Freiberg 'worked hard at teaching and publishing', completed an LLM thesis on 'The Civil Offence', and had his first administrative job as tea club secretary – the first step on the way to high office. He was attracted by the outlook of the 'young Turks' including Terry Carney, Yuri Grbich, Peter Hanks and others. Through volunteering in the early years of the Fitzroy Legal Service, he came to believe that solving cases one by one was not the way to achieve social change. He wanted to bring about institutional change and thought the best way to do this was to change the law.

The team of Fox and Freiberg became a formidable combination in both research and teaching, with many jointly authored books and articles, as well as high praise from students. The 1979 *Counter Faculty Handbook* review of their stream in Criminal Law and Procedure commented that 'this course is worth doing purely for the entertainment value of the comical asides which Fox and Freiberg so readily delight in'.

It is a testament to the inspirational teaching of criminal law in the faculty that the next addition to the criminal law strength was, like Bob Williams, a Monash graduate. Francine McNiff completed her LLB in 1971 and was immediately appointed to a tutorship. With a personality strong enough to hold her own in the still strongly male dominated faculty, she built up an expertise in juvenile justice. After completing her masters' in 1977, she became one of the faculty's most prolific publishers, primarily on children and the law, but also writing several pioneering articles on computers and the law.[5] In 1983 McNiff was appointed a magistrate of the Children's Court. This was the first judicial appointment for a woman in Victoria and also the first for a Monash graduate.

In family law, Henry Finlay was already established as one of Australia's leading academics when he was joined in 1969 by Alastair Bissett-Johnson, who was on two years' leave from the University of Leicester. While at Monash Bissett-Johnson was one of the faculty's most active publishers and he went on to a distinguished career highlighted by his successful campaign for greater fairness for women in calculating financial provisions during divorce.[6]

In 1970 Dorothy Kovacs (like Louis Waller, Richard Fox and Arie Freiberg, a graduate of University High School and the University of Melbourne) came to Monash as a part-time tutor, being promoted to lecturer in 1975. In her early years she taught legal process and criminal law, but she soon began to concentrate on family law. In contrast to Henry Finlay, whose research tended to have a high degree of social and historical context, Dorothy Kovacs took more of a black letter law approach, and the two approaches complemented each other well. She was always a student favourite for her comprehensive and well-organised lectures.

The third member of the family law group was Manchester graduate Neville Turner, who came to Monash as a senior lecturer in 1974. A gifted jazz pianist and linguist, Turner was also a sports fanatic, being an accomplished cricket and tennis player as well as a collector of sporting trivia. He frequently digressed at length on sporting matters during his lectures and, while his main academic interest was family law, he also published pioneering work on sport and the law.[7] Neville Turner's versatility earned him high praise in the *Counter Faculty Handbooks* if not necessarily from his colleagues:

> Neville Turner is a living legend. In fact, no Monash law degree is worth having unless you have taken Torts, Contracts or Family with this great man.

---

5 For example, 'Computer Documentation: An Overview of Australian Legislation Facilitating Admissibility', *Journal of Law and Information Science*, vol. 1, no. 1, 1981; and 'The Infancy of Computer Abuse or Awareness? Some Australian Perspectives', *Information Privacy*, 3, 1981.

6 *Edinburgh Herald*, 24 July 2008.

7 Notably J N Turner & C Jenkins (eds), *Sport and the Law*, University of Birmingham Press, 1979.

Neville Turner's lectures were popular with students and are remembered for his historical, literary and sporting insights into legal problems.

A critique in the *Counter Faculty Handbook* praised his invitation to students to share in his appreciation of cultural wealth.

Photographer unknown, Monpix 838

> Why "great"? Simply because in the course of a single Turner lecture, one is liable to be instructed in not only the law, but in such disparate fields as history (usually English), literature (usually English, usually Shakespeare), music (usually English, usually Gilbert and Sullivan) and sport (usually cricket, always English). Neville doesn't merely teach his students, he invites them to share in his store of (English) cultural wealth.
>
> No student should shy from signing up for a Turner class on the grounds of being at a disadvantage to other streams. To the contrary,

> his easy-going, inviting style of lecturing is a viable channel for the passing of legal knowledge, as your attention is rarely diverted from the amiable English squire commanding the lecture rostrum.[8]

The family lawyers had an interesting challenge when the *Family Law Act 1975* totally transformed both their teaching and research. No evidence has been found to support the rumour that one of them continued to teach the old *Matrimonial Causes Act* for several years in the hope that the new law would soon be repealed. It certainly was not Henry Finlay, who had been prominent in campaigning for divorce law reform, played a part in framing the new act and was prominent in its interpretation.[9]

During the late 1960s and early 1970s the faculty recruited a group of new staff members, who, while never aspiring to the heights of academia, made invaluable contributions to the faculty as teachers and colleagues for up to four decades. New Zealander Pat Kilbride taught at the universities of Canterbury and Otago before coming to Monash in 1969. His main teaching areas were criminal law and administrative law, both of which he taught for many years. His interest in administrative law led to the development of several new electives: Urban Legal Problems, Environmental Law and Planning Law. Urban Legal Problems was introduced in 1971 and covered a very broad area, including town planning, sub-division, urban renewal, historic buildings and environmental law. It was an area of rapid growth, with environmental law being the most rapid of all, and by 1977 it justified the establishment of a new course. The *Counter Faculty Handbook* reviewer praised the course as one of the few in the faculty that addressed the social policy issues behind the law and said Kilbride was 'a great guy [who] would fall over backwards to help a student pass'.[10]

Leighton Morris, a Melbourne graduate with a master's degree from the Southern Methodist University in Dallas, came to Monash as a tutor in 1971 and was promoted to lecturer the following year. He taught commercial subjects, with a special interest in air and space law. In 1973 he introduced an undergraduate course on air law and in 1973 an LLM elective on aerospace

---

8 *Counter Faculty Handbook*, 1984, p. 76.

9 Farah Farouque and Peter Freund, 'Champion of Family Laws, a Survivor of Tyranny', obituary of Henry Finlay in the *Age*, 6 August 2005; H A Finlay, 'Reluctant but Inevitable: The Retreat of Matrimonial Fault', *Modern Law Review*, 38, 1975, pp. 153–173; H A Finlay, 'Judicial Discretion in Family and Other Litigation', *Monash University Law Review*, 2, 1976, pp. 221–242; H A Finlay, 'A New Deal for Family Law; the *Australian Family Law Act 1975*', *Rabels Zeitschrift*, 41, 1977, pp. 71–111.

10 *Counter Faculty Handbook*, 1979, p. 50.

law. As the two-airline policy was a central part of his teaching on domestic aviation, it was appropriate that he persuaded TAA to give a prize for the undergraduate subject and Ansett for the postgraduate subject.

Pat Kilbride and Leighton Morris typified the group of lecturers who were not top level researchers and published little, but were dedicated teachers and are remembered with affection by generations of students. Pat Kilbride's door was always open for students and many were grateful for his help. Similarly, Leighton Morris was always a popular teacher and pioneered many teaching innovations. Graham Golden recalls his wise course advice and also his inspirational teaching in postgraduate aerospace law, which was Graham's favourite subject, though he never had the need to use it. As the number of international students rose in the 1990s, Leighton Morris took on the responsibility for advising and mentoring many of them through their courses.

Peter Heffey, like a majority of new lecturers at Monash in the 1970s, was a Melbourne graduate. He completed his articles and tutored at Melbourne before teaching at the University of Chicago in 1966 and then moving on to Oxford where he completed his BCL in 1969. He was appointed a lecturer at Monash in 1970 and for over three decades was one of the mainstays of the faculty's common law teaching. With Peter Hocker he co-wrote the highly regarded *Contract Commentary and Materials*, now in its ninth edition, and his article 'The Duty of Schools and Teachers to Protect Pupils from Injury', has been one of the most influential articles published in the *Monash University Law Review*.[11] A committed and well-liked teacher, Peter Heffey was always approachable and appreciated for his wry sense of humour. One student commented on his 'wonderfully droll accent which doesn't change its rhythm even through the most ludicrous situations. Heffey lets his eyebrows do the exclaiming'.[12] He had the rare honour of being described as 'a delight' in the *Counter Faculty Handbook* for 1984.

Students were more ambivalent about Stanley Robinson, an Englishman who taught property and drafting. Like Neville Turner a Manchester graduate, Robinson joined the staff in 1968 and completed the faculty's fourth PhD thesis in 1973. An active researcher and publisher primarily in the field of property law, Robinson was rapidly promoted to reader, although his teaching style struck many students as unusual. Nahum Mushin found him 'a strange fellow if ever there was one', and Adam Kempton recalls

---

11 *Monash University Law Review*, vol. 11, no. 1, 1985.

12 *Counter Faculty Handbook*, 1986, p. 53.

being taught property law 'by a dishevelled lecturer called Robinson who would physically jump around in class and posed questions in such a way as to make the question itself obscure'. Nonetheless, students appreciated that he was both amusing and knowledgeable.

Queenslander Robin O'Regan, who had worked with Gerry Nash in setting up the law school at the University of Papua New Guinea, came to Monash as a reader in 1972 primarily as library advisor, though his teaching and research interests were in criminal law. He led the continued rapid growth of the law library before leaving in 1975 for a chair at the University of Queensland.

Another of the new arrivals of 1972 also had an unorthodox background for a legal academic. Andrew Farran was a diplomat who had postings to Pakistan, Indonesia and the United Nations before coming to Monash to teach international law. He developed an undergraduate elective on international economic law and a postgraduate course on the law of international political organisations. For the latter course he was able to bring together 'one of the most extensive inter-disciplinary contributions to the Graduate Programme which we have had the good fortune to experience', with participation from Monash and Melbourne law schools, the Monash department of politics and the federal Department of Foreign Affairs.[13] Farran was an active publisher on international and constitutional law as well as defence and foreign policy issues before embarking on a new career as a trade policy advisor in 1984.

New Zealander Graham Taylor is best remembered at Monash – perhaps unfairly – for his unwitting role in the Granville Williams lecture (of which more below), although he was a distinguished administrative law scholar with a Cambridge PhD. Taylor taught at Monash from 1972 to 1977 and his students thought him a well-organised and competent teacher, although he was very intense and a frequent sufferer from migraines. He left Monash for a position as director of research with the newly formed Administrative Law Council in Canberra and later returned to New Zealand, where he worked as legal counsel for the ombudsman before going to the bar.

The early academic staff at Monash had relatively few members with experience in practice, but in 1977, two new arrivals came with experience with large city firms. Monash graduate Carol Bartlett had been an associate partner at Gillott, Moir & Winneke (now part of Minter Ellison) before leaving when her husband went overseas to study. On her return to Australia, she joined the faculty as a tutor, working primarily in the clinical program

---

13 Faculty Board minutes, 2 April 1979.

and also teaching torts and contract. In the early 1980s she became heavily involved in running the continuing legal education program, before leaving in 1987 to become the first director of research at the Law Institute.

A distinctive figure with his wild hair and flowing white beard, Peter Balmford was a favourite with students for his tendency to dance a jig or make a bird call in mid-lecture, and with staff as a 'natural' for Santa Claus at the staff Christmas party. After serving with the RAAF in the Second World War, Balmford had studied law at Melbourne, graduating LLM in 1950. Articled to Whiting & Byrne in 1950, he became a partner in 1952, practising in the areas of company law, commercial revenue, conveyancing, equity and the administration of trusts. He first came to Monash as a visiting lecturer in 1977 before being appointed to a senior lectureship the following year. His academic interests were wide and he taught many subjects over the years.[14] However, his greatest interests were legal history and issues of professional practice. He wrote an erudite history of the foundation of the Monash law school (much used by the present authors) and in the late 1970s he developed and taught (with Guy Powles) a new subject, The Lawyer, designed as an introduction to the role and responsibilities of lawyers, and also to satisfy the Council of Legal Education's requirements for teaching ethics. The *Counter Faculty Handbook* for 1981 described Balmford as:

> A former practitioner, whose comforting eccentricity is certainly more appropriate to the university environment than to busy cut-throat city office life. He is extremely patient and kind, but rather intolerant towards political interpretation of any of the subject matter he teaches ... He veers away from confrontation and will, when challenged on a point, look up wistfully at the far left hand corner of the ceiling, play with his spectacles and pronounce the end of any argument by conceding that everyone is *entitled* to their viewpoint and *that* one is yours, and this one is his and that is all there is to it.[15]

Balmford's collaborator in developing The Lawyer, Guy Powles, also had an unusual academic career. New Zealand born and educated, a defining experience for Powles was the two years he spent as a magistrate in Samoa in his late twenties. He became intrigued with Samoan culture and the way

---

14 The breadth of his interests is indicated in his list of publications, which range from 'Ornithology and the Law', *VORG Notes*, 15, 1979, to 'Changing Patterns in Enrolments at Victorian Law Schools and Their Consequences for the Profession', *Law Institute Journal*, 55, 1981.

15 *Counter Faculty Handbook*, 1981, p. 66.

the society was built on a foundation of customary law, with the legal system combining customary law and the British common law. After his return to practice in Wellington in 1966, he built on his interest with a masters' thesis on customary law in the Pacific. At the same time he worked with some friends to set up a free legal service to provide representation to Maoris and Polynesians, who were severely disadvantaged in their access to justice. Increasingly attracted to academia, in 1974 Powles won a PhD scholarship to the ANU where he continued his work on Pacific law. He wrote his thesis on 'The persistence of chiefly power and its implications for law and political organization in Western Polynesia' while working with a Samoan parliamentary committee on a review of the Land and Chiefly Titles Court. On completion he was offered senior lectureships at UNSW and Monash, eventually choosing Monash because he was promised the chance to pursue his two primary interests, Pacific law and community legal services. Gerry Nash had become interested in Pacific law during his time in New Guinea and he was keen for Powles to build up the faculty's strength in the area. Powles was also excited by what Nash told him of the recently established clinical program, and was keen to be involved.

At Monash Powles taught administrative law and developed new courses in insurance law and Pacific comparative law, which was always his main area of research. With the enthusiastic co-operation of law librarians Ted Glasson and Nicholas Pengelly and their staff, Powles built up a large collection of material on Pacific law that was widely used by practitioners until the onset of the internet age. From the outset Powles was also heavily involved in the clinical program and in 1980 was appointed part-time co-ordinator of clinical legal education. Later in his career, Powles played a leading role in the establishment of a law school at the University of the South Pacific in Vanuatu, where he also taught Customary Law, and he served as an acting judge on the Court of Appeal of the Federated States of Micronesia when the court was dealing with cases based on customary law. After his retirement from teaching, Powles worked with constitutional reviews in Nauru and Tonga and continued his close involvement with supervision of postgraduate students carrying out research on Pacific law issues.[16]

Traditionally law schools in Australia focused primarily on teaching, with research being seen as a slightly eccentric activity undertaken by a minority of legal academics. Frank Beasley's tone was slightly bemused when he commented that Louis Waller had 'the itch to write' as if this was

---

16 Interview with Guy Powles, 19 September 2012.

a distraction from his real work.[17] Given the prevailing attitude it was perhaps slightly surprising that Monash law school developed a culture in which most staff members became enthusiastic researchers. In the late 1960s and early 1970s the faculty had only a handful of regular publishers – in 1971 the research output totalled four articles, all by Enid Campbell! By the end of the decade the situation had changed dramatically. The faculty's research report for 1978 highlighted:

> the present Faculty strengths in the areas of Comparative Law, International Trade Law, Taxation, Company Law, Commercial and Economic Law generally, Family Law, Criminal Law, Procedure and Evidence. Perhaps the most remarkable aspect of the research programme for 1978 is that during the year members of the Faculty, either alone or in collaboration, published a total of 14 books [and 70 articles]. This is a publication record that has not previously been equalled by this Faculty and which must be unique amongst Australian Law Schools. [18]

As the only advantages in publishing were speedier promotion and a sense of personal satisfaction, this was a remarkable achievement. It came about, not through commands from the university or the faculty leadership, but from the development within the faculty of a desire to demonstrate that it was a genuine community of scholars and the resulting peer pressure to publish. Some, of course, were oblivious of this, but by the end of the 1970s, a majority of academics were committed researchers and the faculty's publication record was the best of any Australian law school.

From the earliest days, the Monash law school has attracted many distinguished visitors, some who stayed and taught for a term or a semester, others whose visits might have been restricted to a single lecture. Many visits were associated with the Wilfred Fullagar memorial lecture, the first of several prestigious lecture series held by the Monash law school. An initiative of the Law Students' Society, the first Fullagar lecture was delivered in 1968 by Sir Douglas Menzies. Other lecturers included Professor Harry Street from Manchester, Lord Scarman, Professor Phillip Areeda of Harvard, Sir Harry Gibbs, Gough Whitlam and many other eminent Australian and international lawyers.[19] Displaying great versatility, the seventh Fullagar

---

17 Beasley to Louis Matheson, 6 May 1969, AD/230/0, pt 1, Dean and Sub-Dean, 1964– 83, MON 806, MUA.

18 Quoted in Faculty Board minutes, 2 April 1979.

19 The last Fullagar lecture was given by Gough Whitlam in 1989.

lecturer, Professor David McLean of Sheffield, originally gave his topic as 'Freedom and control in relation to the administration of justice, security and terrorism', but actually lectured on 'The battered baby and the limits of the law'.

Lord Denning was perhaps the most distinguished visitor to the faculty in the 1970s. Denning, who had first visited the faculty in 1967 (on the same day as Enid Campbell arrived at Monash), returned in 1974 to speak at the conference of Australian university law teachers and give the 1974 Fullagar lecture on the subject 'Let justice be done'. Blackwood Hall was full to the rafters, with 2500 people crammed into it. Most were appropriately deferential to the great man, but Ron McCallum, with the brashness of youth, took him to task over his judgement in *Haley's* case,[20] telling Denning that he was glad the judgement had been overturned on appeal. Denning was gracious in his response, without conceding his original judgement might have been wrong.[21]

---

20 *Haley v London Electricity Board*, [1965] AC 778.

21 This story is told in Ron McCallum, 'In Search of Origins: Blindness in History and Law', the 2010 Matt Laffan Lecture in Social Justice, University of Sydney, 27 April 2010, http://sydney.edu.au/law/events/2010/Apr/Matt_Laffan27042010.pdf.

Chapter 12

'A Legal Education Which Was Also a Liberal Education'

Curriculum and Teaching, 1968–80

By 1980, within 16 years of its foundation, the Monash law school had built up a reputation for quality teaching unmatched by any other Australian law school. To a large extent this was a function of the excellent staff:student ratio, which over this period averaged 1:14 at Monash, compared with about 1:26 at Melbourne and most other law schools. But beyond this, Monash was noted for its young and enthusiastic staff, its innovative and exciting teaching, the breadth of the electives on offer and the willingness to explore new forms of assessment.

The most important new development in teaching in this period was the clinical program (of which more in the next chapter), but there were many other significant innovations, including the introduction of Australia's first LLM by coursework and the teaching of Asian and especially Japanese law.

This era of small classes and young, highly motivated staff marked the high point of Socratic teaching in the faculty. During the 1970s, most lecturers rejected the traditional didactic method of doling out information to a passive audience and attempted to involve and enthuse their students through the use of Socratic teaching methods. Encouraging students to participate was always the major challenge with Socratic teaching, and staff and students from the 1970s have differing recollections on the level of participation. Peter Hanks found that the classes at Monash were designed to encourage participation and there was normally a good core of people – perhaps about one-third – who were prepared to participate, while the rest were happy just to coast. Hanks soon learnt how to guide classes –'in the nicest possible way' to get to the pedagogical point he was aiming for. Yuri Grbich, too, found that the Socratic method worked well with Monash's small classes and he was able to use the proper question and answer method in a way that encouraged students to think. Judd Epstein's view was less rosy, having previously taught at Stanford where he

> was used to dealing with absolutely elite students, who were also very eager to impress, so the Socratic teaching method worked really well there. There was no bashfulness on the part of the students. At Monash, however, with the Australian tall poppy syndrome, the best students often kept their heads down and said very little.

He persisted with Socratic teaching, but found it was an uphill battle to involve the students.[1]

Student perspectives also varied. Marilyn Warren recalls there was an attitude that 'only nerds prepared their answers – most people were at university to have fun'. Nonetheless, 'having someone like Louis Waller skewer you with a difficult question was very good training – a toughening up process'.[2] Adam Kempton remembers that the Socratic method of teaching was quite common and 'this was scary early on, particularly if you hadn't done the work, but you soon learned to roll with the punches and wing it'. Kempton later practised in Warrnambool, where he found the Monash training in 'rolling with the punches and winging it' of great help in his career.[3]

Engaging with students through Socratic teaching inevitably led to some humorous moments. Pam O'Connor tells of the time a lecturer directed a question at 'You in the blue jumper'. The student responded instantly by taking off his blue jumper to the applause of the whole lecture theatre. Jack Hammond recalls an even more effective (if not entirely original) response. When Richard Fox asked, 'What are the facts of the case, Mr Smith?' the student replied, 'What is it that you don't remember, Mr Fox?'

Not all students had positive memories of Socratic teaching. The method relied on skilful questioning to lead the class to the desired end point, but a few lecturers found this beyond them and would just ask for the details of cases, without imparting either knowledge or understanding. Worse were those who used it as a form of harassment rather than education. Some lecturers 'picked on students in class and bullied them. They would single one student out and you had to perform, with the lecturer appearing keen to humiliate you.'[4] This appears to have been the exception rather than the

---

1 Interview with Judd Epstein, 15 February 2012.

2 Interview with Marilyn Warren, 9 August 2012.

3 Interview with Adam Kempton, 10 January 2012.

4 Interview with Pam O'Connor, 13 March 2012.

rule, but in the days before lecturers received any formal teacher training or were subject to any form of assessment of their teaching, students felt there was little they could do about it.

Socratic teaching gradually faded away during the 1980s, primarily because the growth in student numbers combined with the deterioration in the university's financial position made it impossible to maintain a high staff:student ratio. Larger class sizes made Socratic teaching much more difficult and many lecturers gave up, though the method persisted in tutorials.

During the era of student radicalism, assessment was the only pedagogical issue to become the subject of student agitation. Traditionally almost all university subjects were assessed solely through closed book exams, but during the late 1960s and early 1970s this was increasingly questioned by both students and staff. The various alternatives – open book exams, 'continuous assessment', marks for class participation and so on – were debated at length and most were introduced in some subjects. By 1975 the faculty agreed that closed book exams should be authorised 'only if cogent reasons are offered'.[5] Few lecturers went as far as Judd Epstein, who allowed students in Modern Civil Law to choose their own mode of assessment from a wide range of options, but by the end of the 1970s no law subject was assessed solely by a closed book exam, and most subjects had a combination of the various new forms of assessment.

Eventually there was a reaction against some of the more radical forms of assessment. In 1978, a meeting of the full-time staff expressed concern about the effects of 'continuous assessment' on a student's overall performance and also questioned the validity of certain types of assignment. Gerry Nash said that he was concerned that continuous assessment led students to concentrate on a limited range of topics rather than on the subject as a whole and also noted that 'there had been doubt at times whether work submitted by a student was entirely the results of his own efforts'.[6]

The structure and content of the undergraduate law course has always been the subject of constant change and modification. In a broad sense the debate ultimately comes down to the fundamental issue of 'Pericles versus the plumber', with most academic lawyers instinctively inclining towards Pericles, while the majority of students and the requirements of the Council of Legal Education leaned heavily towards 'relevance' for practice. Although

---

5 Faculty Board minutes, 7 July 1975.

6 Ibid., 3 April 1978.

the scope for experimentation with the curriculum was limited by the compulsory core laid down by the Council of Legal Education, this did not prevent a determined effort to reshape radically the traditional teaching of the common law. Ever since the development of modern legal education in the nineteenth century, the teaching of common law had been divided into the separate areas of contracts, torts and criminal law. In 1967 the suggestion was first raised that an attempt should be made to encompass all three within one subject, and the faculty agreed to a trial of a new common law subject to be taught over two years of the BJuris course.[7] The arguments in favour were Periclean – to encourage students to understand the history and unity of the common law as opposed to simply learning the required elements of three discrete bodies of knowledge. The new two-year course was first taught on an experimental basis in 1969 and 1970 to a class restricted to 40 students. The experiment was regarded as successful for contracts and torts, but less so for criminal law, so at the end of 1970 the course was reshaped to cover only contracts and torts.[8]

The First Curriculum Review

In 1969 Louis Waller set up the first review of the curriculum since the establishment of the law school. The scope of the review was to consider the content of the BJuris and LLB courses, while accepting the framework of the five-year, two-degree course. There was no thought that students could complete an LLB without a first degree except under exceptional circumstances.[9]

Soon after the review began, Lawrie McCredie, one of the panel members, asked David Derham what he would do differently if he had the opportunity to redesign the Monash curriculum. Derham replied that he 'would put mathematics on the curriculum' on the grounds of the similarity in the logical thinking required for both disciplines.[10] It is not clear whether this idea was seriously considered; the revised curriculum made no recommendations in favour of mathematics, though it made it easier for students to take it if they wished.

The review committee began with two basic conceptions of legal education:

---

7 Faculty Board minutes, 27 July 1967.

8 Ibid., 11 November 1970.

9 Ibid., 30 April 1970.

10 Interview with Lawrie McCredie, 5 October 2011.

> First, that the training of men and women for legal practice is only part of the University law school's function – many of our students will not practise after graduation …
>
> Second, that legal practice … is not a function with a constant or static content.[11]

Consequently, the law school should 'offer the type of broadly based education which will discourage its students from adopting rigid patterns of thought and inflexible attitudes, and will encourage them to adapt to new situations and to meet new problems'. Looking at the existing curriculum, the committee felt that it was 'geared too much towards a narrow professional training'. Even for those graduates planning to go into practice, the law school should not 'be content merely to train skilful mechanics'. Further, 'in the committee's view the law course should be so formed that courses aimed at the effect of law as an instrument of social policy could be introduced, and that there should be encouragement of the investigation of the effect on legal doctrines of economic and social considerations.'[12]

These thoroughly Periclean conceptions were reflected in the practical recommendations of the review committee, limited, as always, by the requirements of the Council for Legal Education. The BJuris was made both more substantial and less legally oriented by increasing the number of subjects from eleven to twelve, while decreasing the number of law subjects from six to five, thus making room for two non-law minors. BJuris students would now do no law subjects in the first year, though the five law subjects of the BJuris – Legal Process (replacing The Legal System), Common Law, Criminal Law and Procedure, Constitutional Law, and Property would all be compulsory in the second and third years. While the legal component of the BJuris was made compulsory, the curriculum review recommended that the LLB be largely freed up, with only two compulsory half-year subjects, Administrative Law and Trusts. This was a reflection of the 'spirit of the times', which favoured freedom of choice, and it was possible because the rapid growth of the faculty meant that many more options were becoming available.[13]

---

11 Peter Hanks, 'A New Law Curriculum', *Law Institute Journal*, vol. 45, no. 11, November 1971, pp. 498–9.

12 Ibid., p. 499.

13 Ibid., p. 501.

The curriculum review committee recommended that the history subject (History 1C, later History 115) become optional, a recommendation that aroused some opposition. When the issue was discussed at the faculty board, David Jackson moved a resolution to reject it, which was defeated by one vote. It is told that Frank Beasley fell asleep during the discussion and when it came to the vote he was confused and accidentally voted the wrong way, thus ending the compulsory study of history in the law school.[14] History 115 had never been overly popular with students and there was no strong push to revive it, but some in the faculty fervently believed that it is impossible to understand the law, and particularly the common law, without some knowledge of history, and they continued to agitate for a compulsory history subject in the law course. Nobody opposed this on philosophical grounds, but Ann Lahore and Gerry Nash both pointed out that it would be difficult to find staff qualified to teach it, and the proposal foundered.[15]

The review committee made no recommendations on whether it should be compulsory for students to participate in a moot court. However, the moot master, William Charles, fought hard for compulsion and, after much debate, he was successful.[16]

Two years after the completion of the first curriculum review, the faculty considered the impact of the changes. Some of the more radical decisions were wound back. From 1974, Legal Process became a first year subject again and the non-law content of the BJuris was reduced from six subjects to five. The non-law subject was replaced by a compulsory year of Administrative Law, restored from an experimental half-year course. There were ambivalent views on the Common Law experiment and it was decided that contracts and torts should again be taught as separate subjects and be offered as an alternative to Common Law I and Common Law II. The experiment with freeing up the LLB was considered a success and the choice of subjects was made completely optional, though in the knowledge that most students would do the 'quasi-compulsory' subjects laid down for admission by the Council of Legal Education.

A complicating factor in the law school's experiments with its curriculum in the 1970s was the university's chronic inability to decide whether to structure the academic year around terms or semesters. In April 1969

---

14 Faculty Board minutes, 11 November 1970, and interview with Francis Trindade, 20 October 2011.

15 Faculty Board minutes, 17 June 1971.

16 Ibid., 29 April and 22 July 1971.

the university decided to introduce a two-semester system from the start of 1970. Consequently, the first resolution arising from the law school's curriculum review was that 'the basic teaching period be the "semester".'[17] New and existing subjects were designed or restructured to fit the semester structure (particularly by the division of year-long subjects into two semester units), and this process was largely completed by 1974, when the university decided to revert to a three-term system. Rather than restructure its courses, the law faculty resolved to retain semesters and work around the terms as best it could in terms of holidays and the like.[18] The university did not fully semesterise until the late 1980s. The faculty's actions were, not for the first time, out of step with, and in this case more forward thinking, than the university's administration.

The Second Curriculum Review

The faculty's second major review of the undergraduate curriculum began in 1978. The members of the review committee were Enid Campbell (chair), Peter Ellinger, Peter Heffey, Pat Kilbride, Malcolm Smith, Jude Wallace and one student representative. The terms of reference were generally predictable with two exceptions: the requests for the committee to advise 'in what ways the desirable requirement of literacy should be achieved' (a task the committee admitted it found beyond it) and to 'investigate the possibility of reforming the present tutorial system into a system of teaching subjects by way of pleadings and practice' (an objective that appears to have been ignored).[19]

The curriculum review committee presented a series of reports during 1979 and 1980, the most important of which were the second report in June 1979 and the third report in April 1980. The second report began with a summary of the evolution of the undergraduate law course since 1964, pointing in particular to the reduction in the compulsory core of subjects, which reflected

> in part a judgement that the requirements for a university degree in law should not be rigidly tied to the requirements prescribed by the regulating bodies for admission to practise law, and in part recognition that the frontiers of legal learning and practice have extended to the point where it is no longer possible or even desirable for university law

---

17 Ibid., 11 November 1970.

18 Ibid., 30 April 1974.

19 Ibid., 3 April and 6 June 1978.

> faculties to attempt to turn out lawyers who are well-furnished in all departments of the law.[20]

The review accepted that the hopes that the BJuris would prove an attractive alternative to degrees like the BA and BEc had not been realised and that the BJuris was no more than a preliminary course for the LLB. Further, the BJuris had become less appealing and a large majority of new students were taking double degrees rather than the BJuris/LLB combination. Rather than abandon the BJuris, however, the review committee recommended that it be restructured to make it more legally oriented. Sceptical of the view that 'somehow schooling in things non-legal will enrich [students'] study of law and make them wiser men and women and better lawyers', the committee argued that there is 'no reason in principle why a faculty of law of the size of the Monash faculty could not provide a legal education which was also a liberal education without, as it were, sub-contracting the provision of the liberalising elements to other departments of the university.'[21] Consequently the committee proposed a reduction in the non-law units, and their replacement with elective law subjects 'and in particular some law subjects in which the study of legal phenomena was approached from a broader perspective than that adopted in the study of particular branches of the law'.

The committee's recommendation to introduce a compulsory 'perspective' subject into the BJuris was greatly influenced by a submission from Christie Weeramantry. 'Are we content to turn out graduates with what is in effect a postgraduate degree in law, who have never at any stage been exposed to an outline of legal concepts or legal theories?' he asked. Very few Monash students ever studied the principal theories of law, the historical evolution of legal concepts, the sources of the law, comparative legal systems, or legal history, and the Monash law school could therefore not legitimately claim to have given them a legal *education*. He concluded that:

> The emphasis on 'bread and butter' subjects which earn marks in the eyes of a prospective employer is now so great that students, given an option, tend to drift away from perspective subjects. They are at the undergraduate stage scarcely equipped to realise the value of such a

20 Curriculum Review Committee, Second Report: Structure of the Bachelor of Jurisprudence and Bachelor of Laws Degree Courses', p. 7, Faculty Board minutes, 27 June 1979.

21 Ibid, pp. 23–24.

> subject as jurisprudence and ... do themselves lasting damage by their uninformed choice.[22]

While the review committee did not support Weeramantry's suggestion that jurisprudence become compulsory, it recommended that BJuris students should have to take at least one half-year subject from within the fields of legal philosophy, legal history, foreign and comparative law. This was a measure of the extent to which the broader conception of legal education championed by the faculty's founders was accepted by their successors.

The review committee largely accepted the structure and content of the 'compulsory core' of both the BJuris and LLB degrees. A questionnaire revealed that many students did not believe that Constitutional Law and Administrative Law should be compulsory, year-long subjects, but the committee (as one would expect of a committee chaired by one of Australia's leading constitutional and administrative lawyers) dismissed the students' opinions as being based on 'little more than ignorance' of the nature and importance of the two subjects.[23]

Of the compulsory subjects, the report noted that there had been lengthy debates and division of opinion among the staff 'in relation to the objects and content of Legal Process [and] Common Law versus Torts and Contracts', and the committee aimed to put into place the consensus which had emerged from these debates. There had been many changes of direction in the way Legal Process was taught during the 1970s, notably a litigation-oriented syllabus taught in 1970 and the 1974 trial in teaching the subject in small groups of less than thirty students. This required up to sixteen groups each year with over half the academic staff involved in teaching. Inevitably this had led to great differences in the way the subject was taught; some streams looked primarily at judicial institutions and litigation, others at sources of the law, case analysis and the use and interpretation of legislation, while a few concentrated on legal history and/or jurisprudence. Many teachers in later year subjects complained that Legal Process had failed to prepare students adequately, with gaps in their knowledge and inadequate training in legal methodology and skills. Consequently, in 1979 Legal Process was reduced to four streams, all with the same objectives and essentially the same content.[24]

The committee looked at the experiment of teaching Common Law I and II as alternatives to Torts and Contracts. There had been great practical

22 Quoted in ibid., p. 25.

23 Ibid., p. 20.

24 Ibid., p. 13.

difficulties in fusing the teaching of the two subjects, including disagreements over the topics to be taught and their sequence, fragmentation of contract law, and continuity over two years. Torts and Contracts were revived as separate subjects in 1973 and enrolments in Common Law steadily declined. By the late 1970s there were only two members of staff both committed to the Common Law concept and willing to teach it, so the committee recommended that it be discontinued. It emphasised that 'in making this recommendation the Committee is not implying any disagreement with the thinking that lies behind the Common Law programme. It is moved simply by pragmatic considerations.'[25]

The curriculum review committee received submissions arguing for certain subjects to be made compulsory in the LLB, most notably Conflicts of Laws, Jurisprudence, Legal Persons and Property II. The committee recognised the importance of these subjects, particularly Conflict of Laws, viewing 'with alarm the prospect of a majority of our graduates entering on the practice of law ... without even being able to recognise the existence of the conflictual aspects of a legal problem or matter'.[26] However, given that, in addition to the 'compulsory core', several elective subjects had become 'quasi-compulsory' due to admission requirements, the committee was reluctant to introduce more compulsion at the expense of the range of electives.

The 1978–80 curriculum review was the first time the electives that had grown up in an ad hoc fashion since the foundation of the faculty were subject to scrutiny. Overall, the committee was satisfied that the existing electives covered a suitably wide spectrum of topics and provided students with 'ample opportunities for both specialisation and for acquisition of generalist legal learning'. The committee also pointed out that maintaining a large range of options had the further benefit of promoting research as 'much legal research is a by-product of teaching'.[27] However, some of the electives listed in the handbook had 'withered on the vine'; some had never been offered and taught, while others had been offered only rarely and attracted tiny enrolments. Consequently, six subjects were discontinued, while various forms of rejuvenation were recommended for others.

Most of the recommendations of the curriculum review committee were accepted and implemented virtually without debate, but several resulted in fierce argument. A significant debate followed the recommendation,

---

[25] Second Report of the Curriculum Review Committee, p. 23.

[26] Ibid., p. 32.

[27] Third Report of the Curriculum Review Committee, p. 31.

approved by the faculty board in May 1979, that BJuris students complete one perspective subject. In May 1980, Terry Carney successfully moved that the requirement be increased to two perspective subjects, with room in the course being made by delaying either Administrative Law or Property I until the LLB. In Carney's view this 'would further the objectives of a liberal education'. Opponents contended that 'it was improper for a decision of the Board to be changed after such a short time' and 'that a student should complete Property I at an early stage as a prerequisite for other subjects'.[28]

Another fiery debate came when Enid Campbell (the chair of the review committee) moved that Legal Philosophy should be compulsory in the LLB, even though this was not a recommendation of the committee. Peter Hanks led the opposition, arguing that 'any special case which could be made for Legal Philosophy could equally be made for other areas of study'. Other faculty members opposed the restriction of options that the resolution would cause and the motion was defeated.[29]

The curriculum review of 1978–80 decided to retain the two-degree structure of the law course, with the BJuris to precede the LLB. The faculty reaffirmed its commitment to allowing students to build their courses around a wide range of options, with the inevitable tendency for them to gravitate towards the subjects required for admission being slightly restricted by the necessity to include two perspective subjects in their courses.

The Honours Program

The honours program went through several major changes during the 1970s. Under the original honours program set up in 1964, about fifteen students were selected at the end of first year to enter the honours program and they underwent as rigorous and demanding an undergraduate legal education as offered by any university in the world. Early honours students 'were effectively separated in their studies, and perhaps to a lesser extent, in their social activities from pass students'.[30] This system was abandoned in 1972, partly because it was too demanding for all but a handful of students, and partly because it required an excessive allocation of resources to the honours program.

---

28 Faculty Board minutes, 5 May 1980.

29 Ibid., 3 June 1980.

30 Honours Committee, 'Special Report to the Faculty Board', Faculty Board minutes, 6 June 1978.

The honours system introduced in 1972 was dramatically different. Instead of honours students being chosen at the end of first year, they were now invited to join the honours program at the end of fourth year, and the completion of a research thesis became the only difference between the courses of pass and honours students. This system was never regarded as wholly satisfactory as thesis supervision and assessment proved difficult, while many lamented the loss of the intellectual stimulation and camaraderie of the early honours classes. In 1977, Malcolm McComas and Chris Dale, the student representatives on the faculty board, successfully moved for a complete review of the honours program.[31]

The report of the review, headed by Christie Weeramantry, noted that an average of fewer than thirteen students had completed honours degrees each year since 1973 and recommended sweeping changes. These included the reintroduction of honours seminars 'to restore the collegial element essential to an Honours school', and the halving of the points value of the research thesis.[32]

The new honours scheme was introduced in 1979, with the first honours seminar on 'Remedies' being conducted by Professors Campbell, Ellinger and Nash. Eight students completed the seminar but only five 'had an overall performance during the year which was sufficiently meritorious to enable them to proceed into the final year of the Honours programme in 1980'.[33] It was quickly apparent that the new system was too demanding for most students and a further review led to the restoration in 1982 of the 1972 scheme, with honours degrees being awarded on the basis of grades received in all law subjects together with a research thesis.[34]

Postgraduate Education

The years 1968–80 saw radical changes in postgraduate legal education at Monash. After originally awarding postgraduate degrees only for the completion of a major PhD or masters' thesis, in the early 1970s Monash became the first law school in Australia to offer an LLM by coursework. The first mention of the possibility of a postgraduate coursework degree was in October 1969 during a discussion of ways in which the faculty could become

---

31 Faculty Board minutes, 3 August 1977.

32 Honours Committee, 'Special Report to the Faculty Board', Faculty Board minutes, 6 June 1978.

33 Faculty Board minutes, 31 March 1980.

34 Ibid., 2 June 1981.

involved in 'vocational legal training', when it was agreed that a coursework masters' might be the optimal method.[35] In 1971 the rules were altered to allow for an LLM by coursework and minor thesis, with candidates required to complete four subjects and a thesis of 25,000 words.[36] It was emphasised that the standard for the LLM by coursework and minor thesis should be comparable to the existing LLM by major thesis, and this aspiration was maintained for many years, though few would argue that it is still the case today.

The first LLM by coursework students enrolled in 1973, with seven optional subjects available: Aerospace Law, Advanced Income Taxation, Advanced Labour Law, Estate Planning, International Economic Law, International Trade and Investment and Problems of Proof. The list expanded further each year, and, after Melbourne had followed Monash's lead and introduced its own postgraduate coursework program in 1974, it became possible for Monash students to enrol in Melbourne subjects and vice versa. By 1980 students had a choice of twenty-nine postgraduate subjects.

The coursework masters proved instantly popular. Five full-time and seventy-three part-time students enrolled in the first year, and numbers rose steadily throughout the 1970s. By 1976 there were 131 coursework students and a graduate students' society was formed. The majority of students were part-timers from the profession, though there was a sizable minority of full-time overseas students from a surprisingly wide range of countries – in 1977 there were fourteen and they came from Uganda, Taiwan, Japan, Papua-New Guinea, Bangladesh, India, Malaysia and Sri Lanka. Among the early students to complete the LLM by coursework were Graeme Golden, Leigh Masel of Phillips Fox & Masel, Phil Opas QC (who took on the course as a retirement project), Graeme Samuel, and Sam Murumba, now a professor at Brooklyn law school in New York.

The major problem with the LLM by coursework in the 1970s was the large number of students who were either very slow to complete their minor thesis, or never completed it at all. In 1975, for example, the graduate studies committee reviewed the academic standing of sixty LLM candidates and found that twenty-five of them had completed all the coursework requirements, but not the thesis. By 1980, several hundred students had enrolled in the LLM by coursework, but only sixty-nine had completed their theses. Frank Vincent QC, later a prominent Supreme Court judge, was one of

35 Ibid., 9 October 1969.

36 Ibid., 22 July 1971.

many LLM candidates who fell at the thesis hurdle. The problem was discussed continually during the 1970s, with frequent suggestions that the thesis be dropped or reduced in length, but a majority of the staff could not countenance a masters' degree without a serious research component.[37]

Partly to give another option for postgraduate students who were wary of the thesis requirement for the LLM, in 1978 the faculty introduced a diploma of commercial law, the first of several graduate diplomas designed 'for practising lawyers seeking certification of specialisation and for the lay professional seeking qualifications in a specialised field of law'.[38] The coursework load for the graduate diplomas was four half-year subjects, half that of the masters', but without any thesis component. Further diploma courses followed in international and comparative law, taxation and family law.

Most staff members enjoyed the expansion of graduate coursework teaching. It gave them the opportunity to develop advanced new optional subjects, frequently closely tied to exciting areas of research, as well as to teach small groups of knowledgeable and motivated students at a time when undergraduate class sizes were inexorably increasing. The new postgraduate subjects also gave greater opportunities for staff to teach in conjunction with leading practitioners and academics from other disciplines. Some of the most notable of the new postgraduate subjects were Trade Practices, taught by the law school's Bob Baxt and Sir Richard Eggleston together with Maureen Brunt, Bob Officer and others from the Faculty of Economics; Christie Weeramantry's Theories of Justice; Graeme Samuel's class on Takeovers; Advanced Taxation of Trusts taught by Yuri Grbich with Mark Leibler; and the Law of International Trade taught by David Allan in conjunction with Mary Hiscock of the University of Melbourne.

In comparison with the excitement of the new postgraduate coursework program in the 1970s, what is now called the HDR (higher degree by research) component of the faculty was a quiet backwater. There was never more than a handful of PhD and LLM by research students, with the majority being staff members. There were so few PhD candidates that the graduate studies committee felt it was unnecessary to enforce the university's strict rules on the length of either candidature or thesis. A research degree was not yet seen as essential for academic staff and by 1980 there had only been eighteen LLM major theses and nineteen PhDs completed in the faculty.

---

37 Ibid., 4 September 1973, 3 March 1975, 2 September 1975, 3 April 1978.

38 Ibid., 6 October 1977.

Chapter 13

'Aflame with a Consuming Passion'

The Early Years of the Clinical Program

One of the dreams of the founders of Monash University was that it would be 'a new *kind* of university', not just more modern and less bound by tradition than the older universities, but 'more experimental, open to the lessons of experience'.[1] This attitude was evident in many of the actions of the early leaders of the law school, from the design of the curriculum to the design of the law school building. While not part of Derham's original plan for the law school, the introduction of clinical legal education, delivered through the professional practice elective, has been one of the major points of difference between Monash and other Australian law schools.

The establishment and sustainability of a clinical program is dependent upon various factors, including the age of the law school, government policy, economic prosperity and social circumstances.[2] As the leader in the field of university-based clinical programs, Monash has been the model adopted by a number of other law schools although not all have been able to sustain the level of commitment or resources required to run a clinical program. Over nearly four decades, Monash has successfully devised and built on a sustainable teaching methodology to become a leader in the field.

Clinical legal education is derived from the widely accepted model of medical education, and is based on the premise that 'people learn best by doing and reflecting'. Jeff Giddings, an early student in the Monash clinical program, who started a similar program at Griffith University in the early 2000s, defines clinical legal education as 'an intensive small group or solo learning experience in which each student takes responsibility for legal and law-related work for a client … in collaboration with a supervisor'.[3] The

---

1 Davison and Murphy, *University Unlimited*, p. 55.

2 Jeff Giddings, *Promoting Justice Through Clinical Legal Education*, Justice Press, South Melbourne, 2013, p. 317.

3 Ibid., p. 14.

students act for real clients in real situations under faculty supervision, and receive credit for their courses.[4]

From the outset the clinical program embraced a theoretical and analytical component, which aimed to encourage students to understand the broader context of the many different problems clients raised with them. Thus, David Allan, dean when the clinical program began, saw clinical legal education in terms of the definition developed in Canada by former Monash academic Peter Hogg as combining the performance by the students of a legal task, with the use of the students' experience as a basis for organised analysis and study.[5] Clinical legal education provides a quite different practical experience from the articles year.

Echoing Sir Owen Dixon's awareness of the 'untidiness of the legislative process', Peter Hanks, one of the founders of the clinical program, focused on one of its main benefits. The program required students to learn 'in a broader and less structured context, to deal with... untidy problems and unsifted facts, to make decisions and to reduce risks'.[6] Another key player in the foundation of the clinics, Gerry Nash, emphasised that the client is 'not merely ... a patient upon whom one can experiment', but a person for whom the student is responsible. 'Without the client, we have merely a skills programme'.[7]

Antecedents

North American universities were decades ahead of Britain or Australia in the introduction of clinical legal education. The first program began at the University of Pennsylvania as early as 1893 when a student volunteer scheme was established, and this was followed by a similar service at the University of Denver in 1907.[8] A 'solid intellectual and pedagogical foundation' for

---

4 Douglas A Blaze, 'Déjà Vu All Over Again: Reflections on Fifty Years of Clinical Education', *Tennessee Law Review*, Vol. 65, 1997, pp. 939–940.

5 This definition is used in the report of the Long Range Academic Policy study group of the Osgoode Hall Law School, known as the Hogg Report and adopted by David Allan in 1974. 'Clinical Legal Education', the text of an address delivered to the 1974 Hobart Conference of the Australian and New Zealand Association of Law Students, CF/230/1.4 Practical Work 1974–88, Clinical Legal Education, Monash University Archives.

6 Peter Hanks, 'Professional Practice', Law Faculty Board Meeting No. 4/74, Agenda Item No. 3.3, Attachment C, Monash University Archives, p. 1.

7 Gerard Nash, 'Skills Course or Clinic?', *The Australian Law Journal*, Vol. 54, September 1980, p. 537.

8 Robert MacCrate 'Educating a Changing Profession: From Clinic to Continuum' in *Tennessee Law Review*, Vol. 64, No. 4, 1997, p. 1099, 1105.

clinical legal education' was developed in the 1920s and 1930s by John S Bradway and Jerome Frank.[9] In 1928 Bradway operated a six-week clinical program at the University of Southern California and he was later involved in the opening of the first in-house clinic that students could complete for academic credit at Duke law school in 1931. News of the University of Southern California clinic was reported in an article in the Melbourne *Herald* in January 1933, probably the first reference in Australia to the clinical teaching of law students.[10]

At Yale law school, leading legal philosopher and liberal judge Jerome Frank called for a clinical 'lawyer-school' in 1933, arguing that 'our law schools must learn from our medical schools.[11] His legacy is the Jerome N Frank Legal Services Organization, encompassing thirteen clinics dealing with different areas of the law. David Derham would undoubtedly have observed the Yale clinical program during his visit in 1953.

In 1936 the Victorian crown solicitor, Frank Menzies, older brother of Sir Robert, called for the establishment of a legal aid clinic staffed by volunteer practitioners and students.[12] No action followed until 1951, when two University of Melbourne lecturers, Norval Morris and Arthur Turner, took the lead in setting up a clinic at the Brotherhood of St Laurence, aided by other staff and student volunteers. However, this clinic closed in 1957 due to the burden on staff, lack of a full-time administrator and lack of commitment from the faculty. As the historian of the Melbourne law school puts it, 'a formal clinical legal education program always eluded the law school'.[13]

In the United States, clinical legal education 'gained greater definition and expanded its foothold in the legal academy' during the 1960s. This was driven principally 'by student demands for relevance', yet in Australia there were no moves to establish clinical programs at any Australian law school.[14] While acknowledging the 'difficulties created by Monash's location' must

9 Blaze, 'Déjà Vu All Over Again', p. 940.

10 Giddings, Chapter One, 'Clinical Legal Education: Learning by Doing and Reflecting', *Promoting Justice Through Clincial Legal Education*, p. 33.

11 Jerome Frank, 'Why Not a Clinical Lawyer-School', *University of Pennsylvania Law Review*, vol. 81, no. 8, June 1933, p. 916.

12 Laurence W Maher, 'Menzies, Frank Gladstone (1892–1978)', *Australian Dictionary of Biography*, vol. 15, Melbourne University Publishing, Carlton 2000, p. 353.

13 Waugh, *First Principles*, p. 190.

14 Margaret Barry, John Dubin and Peter Joy, 'Clinical Education for the Millenium: The Third Wave' (2000) 7, 1, *Clinical Law Review*, 1, 12, quoted in Giddings, 'Influential Factors in the Sustainability of Clinical Legal Education Programs' p. 11.

be overcome by 'perhaps a variety of experiments in the future',[15] Derham's 'Plan for a New Law School' made no specific mention of the possible establishment of a clinical program. How then did Monash come to establish Australia's pioneer clinical education program only eleven years after the foundation of the law school?

Students Learning by Doing and Reflecting

The impetus for a Monash clinical program came from two separate but related activities involving law students. The first was a student initiative to run their own legal referral service. The second was the establishment of an informal telephone referral service attended by law faculty students. Underpinning both of these initiatives was a desire for some form of 'hands on' experience, together with a concern for social justice.

In 1971 Peter Hanks was contacted by Rachel Banchevska, a social worker at the Melbourne Citizens Advice Bureau (CAB) in Russell Street, who suggested that Monash law students might like to help at the CAB. They could not give advice but could listen to people and refer them in the right direction. Hanks raised the matter with the law students' liaison committee and the students responded enthusiastically. Soon they had a roster of about 50 third, fourth and final year students helping out at the CAB.[16]

The following year, the Law Students' Society began its own legal referral service for Monash staff and students located within the faculty. Simon Smith, one of the first volunteers, recalls the earliest days of the Monash service:

> It was on the 3rd floor of the Law School and was called the Monash Student Legal Referral Service. The third floor was half empty then and there were plenty of empty offices. People would ring in with a legal problem and the undergrads would then go and get an expert opinion [from an academic], phone back the caller and refer them to a practitioner. In retrospect it was an innocently audacious venture, as we were effectively giving legal advice with no insurance and no practising certificates.[17]

---

15 David Derham, 'A Plan for a New Law School', 7 August 1964, p. 12.

16 Interview with Peter Hanks, 22 August 2012; Smith, 'Clinical Legal Education', p. 49; Kerry Greenwood, *It Seemed Like a Good Idea at the Time: A History of the Springvale Legal Service 1973–1993*, Faculty of Law, Monash University, 1994, p. 1.

17 Interview with Simon Smith, 5 April 2011.

This limited service gave students practical experience as, assisted by law faculty staff, they could test their knowledge and interact with individuals seeking assistance.

When speculation about the continuation of the service arose late in 1972, Tony Howard, president of the Law Students' Society, assured readers of the *Counter Faculty Handbook* that it would be continuing in 1973.[18] There were legitimate doubts about its viability as a free legal service. Volunteer work by the students was not part of the curriculum, students were given no formal training for their role and the academic advisors were unpaid, unsupervised and uninsured.[19]

Neil Rees, who was one of the service's main protagonists, identifies two important aspects of the experience. He and many other students 'felt that we were not being well prepared for a career as legal practitioners'. And while looking for something more substantial from his course, he saw the students' legal referral service, though supported by the law school, as 'a bit of a "'fob off"'. He also felt some academics were 'condescending in their reference to legal practice'.[20] Nevertheless, the informal, voluntary telephone service run by students, with reference to lecturers and other practitioners, did offer students valuable practical experience.

Students' feelings of remoteness from legal practice, due partly to Monash's location, together with the ethos of the heady Whitlam era 'when we thought we could change the world', led some of them to begin volunteer work with a fledgling free legal service established early in 1972 at the Springvale Community Aid and Citizens Advice Bureau. This service, based on the Russell Street CAB model, was the initiative of the local council, together with Peter Hanks, Rachel Banschevska and Jenny Slade. They had identified the need for accessible legal advice in the largely immigrant, low income suburb. Some of the students who volunteered at Springvale, notably Phil Slade and Neil Rees, were 'continually pushing the envelope', wanting to do more and suggesting that they should bring in real lawyers to work with the students and allow clients to be given legal advice.[21] They were motivated by a combination of the writings of the radical American lawyer Gerald Leftcourt, frustration with the lack of practical training in the law course and a sense of inadequacy about the workings of the referral service

---

18 *Counter Faculty Handbook*, 1972, np. Howard is now a County Court judge.

19 Gerard Nash, 'Clinical Education in Australia – The Monash Experience', *Council on Legal Education for Professional Responsibility, Inc.*, vol. XII, no. 1, October 1979, p. 6.

20 Email from Neil Rees to authors, 7 June 2013.

21 Interview with Peter Hanks, 22 August 2012.

when it was quite clear that 'we could do something useful for people if we could represent them'.[22]

For some students, like Neil Rees, Phil Slade and Simon Smith, the experience they gained through the first forays into staff and student-run free or community legal centres (long before the phrase was coined) whetted their appetite for greater involvement and personal contact with real people and real cases.

Far from exaggerating the situation, the notion of the students' passion providing the impetus to establish a free community-based legal service evocatively captures the spirit of the time. One of the persistent myths of the Monash law school is that Neil Rees and Phil Slade attended the first meeting of the Fitzroy Legal Service and returned to Springvale, 'aflame with a consuming passion for Justice and Power to the People'.[23] While it remains a good story, the reality was different. Rather, Neil Rees recalls that they were already 'quite a long way down the track of getting Springvale off the ground as a fully-fledged legal aid provider' when they heard that a legal centre had started in Fitzroy in December 1972. Slade and Rees visited the Fitzroy Legal Service within a couple of days of its opening and met Peter and Felicity Faris, Phil Molan and John Finlayson, among others. 'Peter was particularly helpful because he gave us a list of lawyers in the eastern suburbs who he thought might be willing to work as volunteers at Springvale.' Neil and Phil began cold-calling people from 'Adrian McKay to David Fogarty to Jonathan Mott and the rest is history'.

The Springvale Legal Service (SLS) officially opened on 27 February 1973 at 5 Osborne Avenue, Springvale. In April 1973, Phil Slade wrote to David Allan telling him of the 'new Free Legal Service at Springvale' and reporting that already it was assisting between thirty and forty people every night.[24] During the first six months of operation, the service handled 727 cases, including 41 court cases and 13 briefs for opinion. The aim of the service was to fill the gap left by the existing legal aid bodies by offering a completely free consultative service and giving aid 'without an arbitrary means test'. It aspired to educate clients while involving them in their own problems and demystifying the legal system at the same time.

---

22 Neil Rees, quoted in email to authors from Simon Smith, 9 May 2013.

23 Greenwood, *It Seemed Like a Good Idea at the Time*, p. 2.

24 Phil Slade to David Allan, attachment to Item 4. Legal Referral Service, Faculty Board minutes 2/73, 7/5/73.

A Subject with Credit

Student pressure grew for time spent with the service at Monash or Springvale to receive credit in the LLB course.[25] Gerry Nash realised that some students were spending a lot of time at Springvale, and was also aware that the legal service might falter once the first flush of enthusiasm faded, if it relied solely on volunteers and if the participating students did not receive any credit for work done.[26] Nash's belief that the Monash staff members involved were 'more concerned at implementing legal aid and in developing a social conscience amongst students' than in the more direct educational benefits of introducing a clinical program was quite accurate.[27] Establishing the free community legal centre was their primary aim; the student experience was a secondary issue.[28]

Planning for a formal clinical program began to take place at all levels in the faculty during 1973 and 1974. In July 1973, the faculty board set up a committee on clinical legal education, chaired by Peter Hanks, to review the operation of the existing informal Monash University legal referral service, consider the relationship between that service and the Springvale free legal service, advise 'on steps that might be taken to improve the quality of the service; and to devise means of giving academic credit for participation in that service.'[29] In September 1973, the Faculty Board adopted the committee's recommendation that a clinical legal education program should be set up based at Springvale, provided staff and finance were available and subject to getting indemnity insurance.[30]

Gerry Nash took on the task of preparing the formal proposal to establish a professional practice subject. A significant consequence of this was that the subject was strongly oriented towards practice rather than theory. Whereas Hanks had intended that the clinical program would have a 'pretty heavy theoretical component [and] be used as an opportunity for the exploration of theoretical issues related to practice', Nash looked to develop 'a course of practical training in which students learned about people, facts and files'. Nash recalls that he became involved because he was concerned that students

---

25 Giddings, 'Influential Factors in the Sustainability of Clinical Legal Education Programs', p. 155.

26 Nash, 'Clinical Education in Australia – The Monash Experience', p. 6.

27 Ibid., p. 6.

28 Interview with Simon Smith, 24 June 2013.

29 Faculty Board minutes, 3 July 1973.

30 Ibid., 4 September 1973.

were being taught 'pure theory, some of it by people who had never been outside the four corners of a university'. However, Nash admitted that he had to stress the academic aspects of the course in order to have it approved by the Faculty Board.[31]

Professor Arthur Berney of Boston College law school, who visited Monash in 1974, suggested that Monash set up a clinical program to which four or five full-time staff would be assigned with one member of staff for three or four students.[32] Although Nash knew this ideal scenario would not be possible, he appreciated Berney's assistance in drafting a proposal for a Monash clinical program, setting out its academic goals:

> The object of the course is to familiarize the student with the way in which the law operates in practice, to enable him to see the reasons for this form of operation and to assist him to assess critically the way in which the law today serves the needs of the community. A student who has completed the course should have a considerable understanding of the practicalities of the day-to-day operation of the law; but it is not intended to be a course of practical training. It is intended to be an academic analysis of the practical operation of the law.[33]

These academically oriented goals and objectives were not popularly received at Springvale, where the overwhelming concern was with social justice and radical law reform. Some of the staff and the passionate student volunteers had serious misgivings about a formal connection with the Monash law school, seeing the faculty's utilisation of the SLS as a 'marriage of convenience', or worse, as a takeover. Simon Smith recalls that he and Neil Rees would have 'resisted the Monash arrangements as a takeover' but they were overseas when the unincorporated committee that was running Springvale agreed to Nash's proposals.[34] A valuable bargaining tool Nash used was the offer of part-time tutorships, which were inevitably appealing to those who had been volunteering their services for several years. Nonetheless, there was continued unrest within the SLS over the ultimate control of the service and its ability to pursue the political objectives that many saw as more important than the educational outcomes desired by the law school.

---

31 Jeff Giddings interviews with Peter Hanks and Gerry Nash, quoted in Giddings, Promoting *Justice Through Clinical Legal Education*, p. 167; Nash, 'Clinical Legal Education in Australia – The Monash Experience', p.7.

32 Giddings, Promoting *Justice Through Clinical Legal Education*, p. 166 fn.

33 Quoted in Nash, 'Clinical Legal Education in Australia – The Monash Experience', p. 7.

34 Email from Simon Smith to authors, 7 October 2013.

Although the new subject, Professional Practice, would be taught over only one semester, the workload for students was heavy, with four hours of clinical work, a two-hour seminar and a one-hour tutorial each week. Consequently, it counted for thirty value units towards the LLB degree, making it the equivalent of full-year optional subjects such as taxation, evidence and civil procedure.[35] Nash agreed to accept responsibility for directing the course and making arrangements with the SLS and the proposed Australian Legal Aid Office (ALAO).[36]

The ALAO had been created in September 1973, with the attorney-general in the Whitlam Government, Lionel Murphy, announcing plans for a large number of 'storefront' offices, which would be staffed by salaried lawyers with a 'social conscience', who were expected to specialise in areas of law adversely affecting the underprivileged. The ALAO expanded briefly and rapidly, with branch offices opening in all state capitals and territories in 1974.[37] Sixty-two new offices were planned for 1975 but they never functioned due to resistance from the legal profession, the collapse in the budgetary position and the change of government in November 1975. The proposed ALAO office in Springvale was one of the casualties of the budget cuts and this prevented any ALAO involvement in the Monash course. Similarly a suggested Legal Aid Commission Victoria office in Springvale did not eventuate, with the result that the SLS remained the only public legal service provider in the Springvale area. This had an immediate impact on the planning for the first professional practice course. The student quota for the first year had been set at thirty, with half the students to be allocated to the ALAO and half to the SLS, but because the ALAO did not open in Springvale as planned, the number was reduced by half, and the first term course was cancelled.[38]

Up and Running

The first professional practice course began in July 1975, supervised by Gerry Nash, with four practitioners, who had been active SLS volunteers – Phil Slade, Peter Rose, Ian Mawson and Don Brookes – as part-time tutors.

---

35 Ibid., 9 September 1974, Item 3.3.1.4, p. 5.

36 Nash to Matheson, 21 November 1974, CF/230/1–4 MON 1, MUA.

37 Stephen Tomsen, 'Professionalism and State Engagement: Lawyers and Legal Aid Policy in Australia in the 1970s and 1980s', *Australia and New Zealand Journal of Sociology*, Vol. 28, No. 3, November 1992, p. 311.

38 Giddings, 'Influential Factors in the Sustainability of Clinical Legal Education Programs', p. 157.

To provide the required academic input, seminars covering topics such as communication with clients, institutional aspects and the lawyer's role in society were conducted over the twelve weeks of the course.

When the first class was completed in October 1975, it was realised that there would be no students available to deal with client queries at SLS over the summer break. Consequently, in his report on the initial course, Nash recommended that the subject should be run three times each year so that students would be attending the Springvale service throughout the year: 'There would appear to be no reason in principle why this subject must be taken during formal term time.'[39] Consequently, Professional Practice was first taught as a summer school elective over the vacation 1976–77.

From the second professional practice program Gerry Nash enlisted extra help in supervising the students, with the first new supervisor being Monash graduate Harry Reicher, who had several years of litigation experience.[40] As the program expanded an increasing number of staff and practitioners were enlisted as supervisors and tutors. In 1978 the staff members involved in the course were Peter Balmford, Carol Bartlett, Barry Connell, Les Glick, Bob Miller, Sara Monester, Yet Bryant, Gerry Nash, Harry Reicher, Leonie Szabo, Joycey Tooher, Guy Powles and Jude Wallace. At this stage, from the point of view of the academic staff involved, the orientation of the professional practice elective was more towards effective practical training than issues of social justice, though both elements were always important.

During the 1970s, despite the setback with the Australian Legal Aid Office, the free legal service movement grew steadily and by 1978 services, including the Aboriginal Legal Service, were operating in seven Melbourne suburbs. The decline in employment opportunities due to the slowdown in the economy after 1974, coupled with the increasing difficulty in getting articles, led many more students to see the benefits of gaining practical experience during their law courses. This, combined with feedback from those who had experienced the reality of working with clients face-to-face in a voluntary legal service, saw a rapid increase in demand for the professional practice elective.

The Springvale Legal Service was initially open on four weekday mornings and four evenings each week. The range of matters included motor accident claims, criminal charges, consumer complaints, matrimonial disputes, small debt claims, landlord and tenant problems, and disputes

---

39 Nash, 'Professional Practice, Report to Executive Committee on the Initial 1975 Course', 13 November 1975, p. 1.

40 Email from Harry Reicher to authors, 19 March 2012.

Neil Rees and David Turnbull facing the camera and talking to clients at Springvale Legal Service, c.1975.
Simon Smith Collection

regarding social welfare payments.[41] Morning tutors were full-time members of the Monash academic staff and evening tutors were full-time practitioners. The extent of the faculty's commitment was demonstrated by the involvement of senior academic staff, including the dean, and by the subject's 'exceptionally high staff-student ratio'.[42]

As the clinical program grew rapidly in its early years, there were inevitable teething problems. Most critical to Springvale was the issue of leadership. Nash had many other responsibilities, Reicher had other teaching duties and a busy career at the bar, and the other staff involved all had other duties and obligations. Once Nash became dean, the leadership problem became instantly more critical as he was unable to give day-to-day leadership, but it also became more soluble. Nash was able to find more staff and resources for the clinical program from within the faculty budget and he also set about finding someone to head the program.[43]

41 Nash, 'Clinical Education in Australia', p. 12.

42 Victor New, 'Clinical Legal Education at Monash', *Law Institute Journal*, vol. 51, no. 8, August 1977, p. 405.

43 Interview with Simon Smith, 5 April 2011.

LEGAL REFERRAL SERVICE.

The following students have intimated that they wish to participate in the Springvale branch of the service. If there are any members of the Service who are not on the following list and who wish to take part in the Springvale part of our operation they are asked to add their names to the list. The Service will continue to operate on Tuesday evenings and one half day per week, to be determined.

Don Brookes
Logan ARMSTRONG
Andrew BARRIE – Wed. Afternoon.
Barry BERGER
Brian CANDLER
Sam CZYZYK
Jim DERUM
Roy FEARNLEY
Gary GLOVER
Ken HANLON
Michael HEAD
Ian HENRY
Tony HOWARD
Terri KEUCHER
Mark MULVANY
Selwyn NEWNHAM
Jill PARROTT
Neil REES
Adrian ROBBINS
Alan ROCHMAN
Geoff SHIFF
Simon SMITH
David TULLOCH
Peter TWINING
Marilyn WARREN
John WISHART

Tom BARRETT
Peter BARTLETT
Chris BUTCHER
Alison CLARKE
Tony D'ALOISIO
Krys ERSKINE
Don FLEMING
Ian GRAY
Jan HANSEN
Celly HENDERSON
Ross HOPKINS
Bruce JOHNSTON
Athol MORRIS
Paul MULVANY
Paul ~~Mark~~ OPAT
Paul PATTISON
Lachlan RICHEY
John ROBINSON
Joycey ROUDA
Phil SLADE
Lawrie TOOHER
Doug TURNBULL
Bill WALLACE
John WILLIAMS

Peter Sim – Wed. afternoon.
Veronica Whittaker
Christine McGowan.

List of volunteers for the Legal Referral Service, c.1972.
Simon Smith Collection

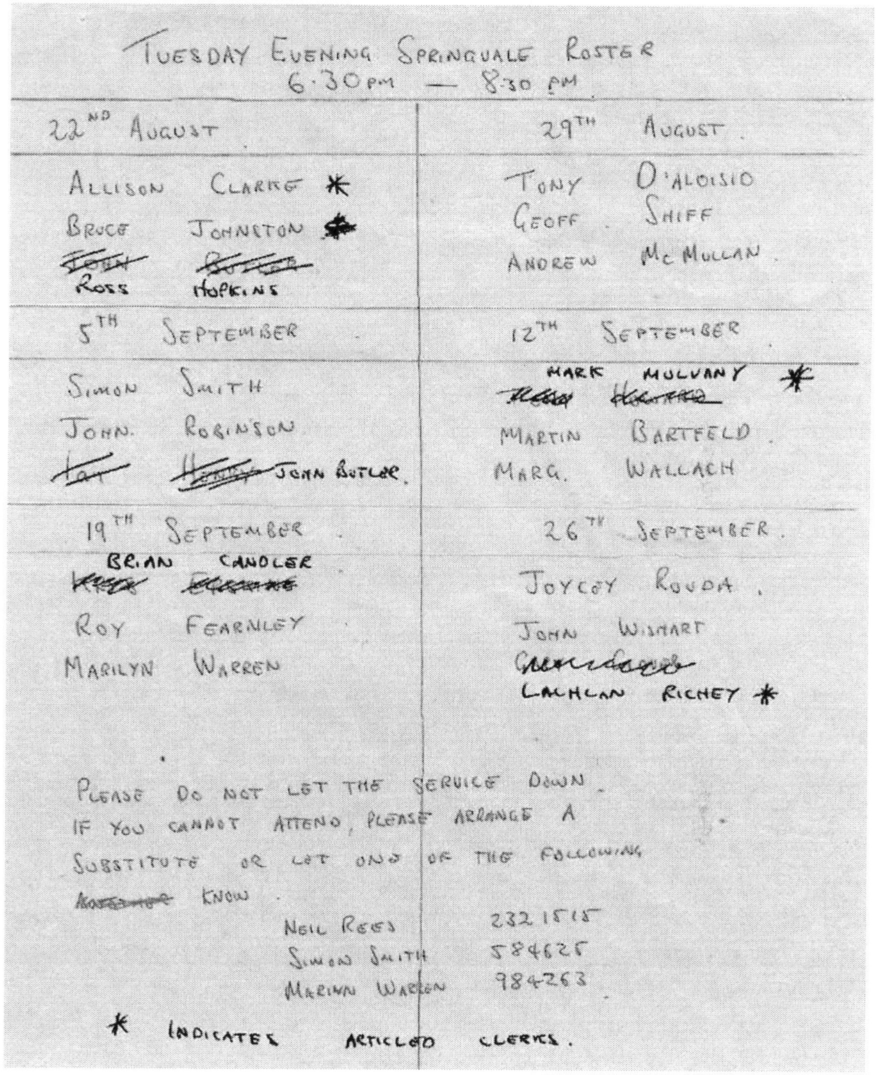

TUESDAY EVENING SPRINGVALE ROSTER
6.30 PM — 8.30 PM

22ND AUGUST	29TH AUGUST
ALLISON CLARKE *	TONY D'ALOISIO
BRUCE JOHNSTON *	GEOFF SHIFF
ROSS HOPKINS	ANDREW McMULLAN
5TH SEPTEMBER	12TH SEPTEMBER
SIMON SMITH	MARK MULVANY *
JOHN ROBINSON	MARTIN BARTFELD
JOHN BUTLER	MARG. WALLACH
19TH SEPTEMBER	26TH SEPTEMBER
BRIAN CANDLER	JOYCOY ROUDA
ROY FEARNLEY	JOHN WISHART
MARILYN WARREN	LACHLAN RICHEY *

PLEASE DO NOT LET THE SERVICE DOWN.
IF YOU CANNOT ATTEND, PLEASE ARRANGE A SUBSTITUTE OR LET ONE OF THE FOLLOWING KNOW.

NEIL REES	232 1515
SIMON SMITH	584625
MARILYN WARREN	984263

* INDICATES ARTICLED CLERKS.

Springvale Legal Service evening roster, c.1973.
Simon Smith Collection

Most importantly, in 1978 he found the funds to employ Guy Powles as co-ordinator of the clinical program. Powles was an experienced New Zealand practitioner with a strong interest in community legal services. His was the first clinical supervision position to be a tenured appointment and was 'a significant foundation stone' in the Monash clinical program.[44] The co-ordinator's responsibilities included staffing arrangements, enrolment and allocation of students, organising the seminar program, approving research project subjects and moderating their assessment, operating the trust accounts for the clinic sites, representing the clinical program in meetings with internal and external groups and working with the clinic sites to obtain outside funding.[45]

A full-time solicitor was also needed at Springvale. It was thought that Phil Slade and Neil Rees would share the role, but when they decided to work with the Aboriginal Legal Service rather than at Springvale, Simon Smith took on the position in January 1978. He recalls that 'I was not approached by Nash, nor did I formally apply' and that taking on the job was seen as 'professional suicide'.[46] The position did not fit the normal academic criteria so it was made under the radar of the university by employing him, initially for six months, as a 'dean's assistant'. Despite the title, he was effectively the co-ordinator of the Springvale Legal Service as well as supervising staff and students in the clinical program. A 1974 Monash graduate, Smith had been involved from the earliest days of the legal referral service and was a volunteer at Springvale, before becoming the first Monash student to do articles in England. He had then worked for a small but 'audaciously run' Melbourne firm that 'cut all the corners' before coming to Springvale.[47]

Simon Smith quickly became the driving force of the Springvale Legal Service. Along with fellow students Phil Slade and Neil Rees, he had been involved from its inception and he was fully committed both to the legal service model and the value of clinical training for law students. He brought a business-like and orderly approach to running the office, setting up a solicitor's trust fund and bringing the chaotic filing system under control.

---

[44] Giddings, 'Influential Factors in the Sustainability of Clinical Legal Education Programs', p. 161.

[45] See ibid., fn 57, p. 162.

[46] Email from Simon Smith to authors, 17 October 2013.

[47] Email from Simon Smith to authors, 17 May 2013.

Tall, thin, 'with a saturnine countenance' and later 'a black pirate's beard', his efforts over more than a decade left 'an irremovable mark' on Springvale.[48]

Five years into the joint relationship with the Monash law school, the SLS chairman reported that

> The university continues to be our major supporter both with personnel and equipment. Despite a fundamental disagreement as to the primary role of the service, our "marriage of convenience" appears to be a sound union. The students vary in their approaches, for some it is a tedious chore, for others it is an invaluable experience in the inter-relationship between law and people.[49]

Gerry Nash's view was that because of the ethos of the SLS, the way in which it began, and the personalities of those who worked there, the educational element was 'perhaps subservient to the legal aid element'.[50] Certainly the legal aid element developed rapidly after the professional practice elective was set up. In the first six months of 1979 there were 3077 client interviews and clients were represented at 300 separate hearings in 20 courts. The most frequent problems dealt with were car accidents, marital disputes, consumer disputes and traffic infringements. Criminal matters and tenancy issues were surprisingly rare.[51]

Neil Rees, who established the clinical legal education program at UNSW and then went on to be foundation dean of the University of Newcastle law school and is now foundation dean of law at the University of the Sunshine Coast, reflects that

> Springvale Legal Service started with no active support from the law school and the more perceptive senior academics such as Gerry Nash and Bob Baxt could see that this was evidence of students rejecting their formal legal education. The great strength of Gerry and Bob was that they recognised this phenomenon and took steps – in the face of some pretty spirited opposition from some colleagues – to bring Springvale within the fold and to make it an essential part of the Faculty. They succeeded and should be congratulated for doing that.[52]

---

48 Greenwood, *It Seemed Like a Good Idea at the Time*, pp. 20–21.

49 Chairman's Report to AGM, 28 June 1978.

50 Nash, 'Clinical Education in Australia', p. 12.

51 Guy Powles 'Professional Practice 1975–1979: The Monash Experience in Clinical Legal Education', September 1979, p. 4.

52 Email from Neil Rees to authors, 7 June 2013.

Largely due to the success of the Springvale Legal Service, in 1976 Gerry Nash was asked if he would expand the Monash clinical program to include the existing volunteer legal service in nearby Doveton. Consequently, in early 1977 the service was 'integrated into the faculty's general clinical programme'.[53] The first professional practice program at Doveton began in July 1977, staffed by Nash and his future wife Gail Owen, a Monash Supreme Court Prize winner and full-time legal practitioner. With the assistance of three students, it initially operated only one night per week. By 1978 it was also opening for one afternoon and became known as the Doveton and District Legal Service.

The clientele at Doveton differed from Springvale; the majority of clients were Australian born and the next largest group were British migrants. Issues of language and poverty were not as prominent as at Springvale, but it seemed to have many unhappy families. The *Family Law Act 1975* made divorce more accessible for many more people; marriage breakdowns were by far the most common problem leading people to seek advice at the centre. In the first six months of 1979, the Doveton service conducted 500 interviews with 245 clients.[54] Unlike the Springvale service, an appointment system was instituted from the outset, differentiating it from the 'community centre ....all-comers must be served' attitude of Springvale. Initially, no more than 15 clients were given appointments on one night because there were only five students on duty, and Nash believed that they should not see more than three clients each per night.[55]

Until 1977 the Monash University Student Union paid a solicitor to operate a legal advice service for students, but in that year the law faculty agreed to manage the service and operate it on the same basis as the Springvale and Doveton services. Initially the service operated in rooms in the law school and was open for five half-days each week. In 1978, when the university acquired the former Marist College in Normanby Road, adjacent to the university, Nash was able to obtain part of the building to house the student legal service. The following year it became a full legal service for university students and staff and also for members of the local community. It was staffed by practitioners who were full-time members of the Monash staff, together with Professional Practice students. The faculty provided a secretary, and

53 Faculty Board minutes, 4 April 1977.

54 Guy Powles, 'Professional Practice 1975–1979: The Monash Experience in Clinical Legal Education', September 1979, p. 4.

55 Nash, 'Clinical Education in Australia', p. 14.

first year student volunteers were rostered as receptionists. The heaviest concentration of work was motor vehicle accidents, followed by matrimonial issues, traffic offences and social welfare disputes. Monash graduate and tutor Carol Bartlett took initial responsibility for the development of the office. She had experience with a major city firm and stamped her emphasis on sound office procedure onto the service. While the official philosophy of the faculty was the same for each centre, the nature of the three operations varied greatly according to the demographics of the clientele and to a certain extent, to the attitudes of the staff and students working there.

Long after the successful establishment of the professional practice course, debate continued within the faculty over whether clinical education really belonged in a university. To placate the doubters, supporters of the program sought to give the program an academic rationale, even if at times it was little more than a veneer. This was true from the earliest days of the program, as Harry Reicher reflects:

> … there were those on the Law Faculty at Monash who felt it was important for a course in the Law Faculty — even a clinical one — to have an 'academic component.' For that reason, the students also had weekly seminars, which I headed, and for which I developed a whole 'academic' program, and curriculum. As part of this, the students had to write papers. My own feeling – and I think Gerry Nash's as well – was that the time spent on 'academic' seminars and papers would have been better spent at Springvale Legal Service, learning the ropes, so to speak, with 'academic' content being left to the many other courses which the students took in the Law Faculty. Be that as it may, given that that was a strongly held view among certain members of the Faculty, the way the program was structured was a good compromise.[56]

In the early years students in the program were assessed on a pass/fail basis. This had been part of the early 1970's radical ethos of Monash, but the phase quickly passed, both in the university as a whole and in the law school. Consequently, a grading system was introduced in the clinical program in 1978. In 1979–80 Guy Powles and Simon Smith, together with Monash Legal Service lawyer, David Sharrock, formulated a more detailed approach to assessment, weighting each component and also introducing a research paper requirement.

---

56 Email from Harry Reicher to authors, 19 March 2012.

Reflecting on the impact the clinical program had on students, Gerry Nash found that in the early years of the clinical program,

> Students who were borderline pass stayed there, but slightly better students might be superb if it inspired them to put in. Third class honours students didn't do better but the best pass students often soared. Kids who did the clinical program often suddenly understood what the law is about, especially procedure and evidence.'[57]

Simon Smith found that 'the students were enthusiastic and you could see them grow as they were confronted with real life problems'. For many students it became a life-changing experience. All but a handful benefited from the clinical training, but for some, particularly for those with a counter-cultural bent, it gave meaning and purpose to their whole law course and often shaped their future careers. Damian Barry was an early professional practice student and recalls that his first client was a heroin addict who didn't know when he was due in court or where. Damian soon found that the 'real practice of law had nothing to do with what they were learning [at Monash]'. This was 'hands on' learning and he loved it.[58] Jon Faine's experience was typical of many. He had not been engaged with his law subjects in the early years of his course but had a 'real lightning bolt moment' when he became involved in legal aid work and the tenants union. He came to see the rules and processes of the law that affect people's lives and suddenly the law was real. He loved it and couldn't get enough of it. From that time he threw himself enthusiastically into his law course and the legal services movement.[59]

Conflicting Academic Views

Writing in 1979, Gerry Nash suggested several reasons why no Australian law school set up a clinical program before 1975. Partly it was due to 'academic conservatism' and the tendency for law schools 'to consider that plumbing is none of their business'. The non-practising academics in the universities believed that students could learn the 'nuts and bolts' of practice during their articled clerkship. A more important argument against a clinical program was simply that of cost. A clinical program was labour intensive and seen as a

---

57 Interview with Gerry Nash, 3 October 2011.

58 Interview with Damian Barry, 23 March 2011.

59 Interview with Jon Faine, 5 March 2012.

costly 'fringe' activity which would detract from the legitimate interests and purpose of a law faculty.[60] However, Monash in its early years was always open to radical innovations, and with more money available than other law schools, the cost was not so strong a barrier.

Two groups of staff members were strongly in favour of a clinical program, though for differing reasons. On the one hand, those who took a plumbing approach to legal education, and believed that the primary role of the law school was to train lawyers for legal practice, saw it as an excellent form of practical training. Gerry Nash was the leading advocate of this view. On the other hand, many of the young radicals, otherwise strongly Periclean in their approach to legal education, supported clinical education as a way to link the university with the free legal service movement and perhaps awaken students to the realities of inequality and injustice in society and in the legal system. Some of them were involved with the new free and voluntary legal services in the Melbourne suburbs in the early 1970s, and began to see the possible advantages a clinical program could provide for both students and the legal services.[61]

The idea of a clinical legal education program was not embraced by all members of the faculty. Arie Freiberg, then a junior academic, was opposed to the clinical program in the 1970s and 1980s because it did not fit his idealistic model of university education. He did not see clinical training as having a place in a university which he believed should be focused on more serious issues of pedagogy and philosophy. He saw clinical training as a distraction and argued that law students could obtain practical training after completing their degrees.[62] Similarly, Bob Williams found Gerry Nash's approach and preconceptions on a number of issues uncomfortable, and in particular did not see eye to eye with Nash's 'plumbing' attitude that law is essentially a trade.[63] On the other hand, Enid Campbell saw clinical education as a good thing and gave her imprimatur to the program.[64]

From its very informal beginnings, by 1978 Monash was involved with three discrete free legal services at Springvale, Doveton and on the Clayton campus. The link with Springvale was critical, as Springvale was a major

---

60 Nash, 'Clinical Education in Australia – The Monash Experience', p. 4.

61 Mary Anne Noone, 'Australian Community Legal Centres – the University Connection' in Jeremy Cooper and Louise G Trubek (eds), *Educating for Justice: Social Values and Legal Education*, Ashgate Dartmouth, Aldershot, 1997, p. 278.

62 Interview with Arie Frieberg 12 April 2012.

63 Correspondence from Bob Williams to authors, November 2011.

64 Interview with Guy Powles, 30 August 2012.

force in the rise of the community legal services movement in the 1970s, and this gave the Monash clinical legal education program both strength and a radical perspective it otherwise would have lacked. For the student, the elective brought together the theory and practice of the law in a different experience to an articles year. Through its involvement with the three free legal services, Monash was at the forefront of establishing community legal centres as well as leading the way in establishing clinical legal education programs in Australian universities. The clinical legal education programs provided at these clinics have enabled over 4000 students (out of about 14,000 Monash law graduates) to experience the realities of legal practice and to see the impact of the law on the lives of ordinary people. For most it was a beneficial educational exercise; for some it was a life-changing experience.

Chapter 14

The High Court Fan Club

Bellbird and Other Fantasies of Student Life, 1968–1980

Generalising about the student experience of university life is inherently hazardous. One overwhelming feature that has emerged from talking to many former students is the uniqueness of each individual's university experience. Sometimes it is hard to believe that two students from the same year are talking about the same universe, let alone the same law course at the same time. What one student remembers as blissful years of camaraderie and intellectual growth were years of misery, loneliness and academic disappointment for another. But most agree that there was never a better time to study law at Monash than in the 1970s. Education was free for almost all, thanks to Commonwealth scholarships and the abolition of fees by the Whitlam government in 1973. The faculty, while growing rapidly, was still small, intimate and friendly, with a young and enthusiastic staff, small classes and innovative teaching and assessment. And campus life was buzzing with excitement in a way never seen before or since!

Within a few years of its establishment, Monash University had earned a justified reputation as Australia's most radical campus. As waves of unrest swept across campuses around the world, triggered by opposition to the Vietnam War and a more general youthful rebelliousness, Monash was at the epicentre of student activism in Australia and student leaders like Albert Langer and Michael Hyde became known well beyond the usually narrow confines of student politics. The peak year for student protest was 1969, when dramatic confrontations between students and administration threatened to close the campus. During the May 1970 Vietnam Moratorium protest, the campus ground to a halt when about half the student population joined the march.[1]

---

1 Michael Hyde, *It is Right to Rebel*, The Diplomat, Canberra, 1972, p. 115.

One small part of the university remained untouched by the Moratorium. In the law school, Ian Spry, attired in his usual pinstripe suit, marched into his taxation class and proceeded (as he had informed the class in advance) to lecture on a central topic of the course which was critical for the exam.[2] Few students were absent. The reality was that a large majority of law students were politically conservative and either uninterested in the radical agitation sweeping the campus or positively disapproving. The radical leaders came from other faculties, primarily arts. Many law students went to the mass meetings on the lawn between the Union and the Menzies building, but most voted against the radicals.

There was a sequel to Spry's notorious tax lecture. One of the few students who missed the lecture to march in the Moratorium was Simon Crean, who complained to the dean, Louis Waller, about Spry's actions. After consulting with his fellow professors, who agreed that Spry's behaviour was unreasonable, Waller spoke with Spry and suggested he should give the lecture again. Somewhat to Waller's surprise, Spry accepted this without argument.[3]

The Vietnam War and conscription made it almost impossible not to become politically aware, even if not active. The war and conscription 'hung over everything' as Ruth Thomas puts it. Almost all the male students faced the possibility of conscription and the massive impact this could have on their lives. Chris Chenoweth was conscripted when he was twenty, but postponed joining up until he finished his course. He then prepared a case for exclusion based on the exceptional hardship provisions, as he did not qualify for conscientious objection. He also persuaded a friendly orthopaedic surgeon to agree that his flat feet precluded his joining up. Eventually, he thinks, the army decided it did not want an argumentative 24-year-old and he was excused from national service.

Within the law school the more politically active students tended to come from government high schools, with private school students largely uninterested. Ray Finkelstein, for example, had been politically active from his days at Elwood High School (where the librarian was the wife of radical Monash academic, Ian Turner) and his group of friends spent all their time talking left-wing politics and taking part in activities like the Ban the Bomb movement. Once at Monash, Finkelstein was one of the founders of the New Left Group (set up in opposition to Albert Langer's Labor Club) and took part in all the demonstrations, marches and sit-ins. There was much friction

---

2 There are many versions of this story, but this appears to be the most accurate.

3 Interview with Louis Waller, 9 July 2013.

between the Maoist Labor Club and the New Left Group. The Labor Club was much more activist and attacked the New Left Group for theorising rather than acting. The ideologically unifying factor was opposition to the Vietnam War and conscription.

Perhaps the most prominent radical among the early law students was former Brighton High School student George Golvan, who was the first president of the Monash Anti-Conscription Society and also secretary of the Labor Club. George recalls that soon after Albert Langer began at university, he asked George about joining the Labor Club. George said the meetings were held at the Notting Hill pub so Langer came along and joined up. Within a very short time, Langer was in charge and began getting rid of people who disagreed with him, including George.

While almost every aspect of university life was dominated by politics in this era, the law school was largely immune. A large majority of law students were essentially conservative. Future Howard government minister Peter Reith was typical of many law students who 'maintained little interest in university affairs, taking no part in the polemic'. He had joined the Young Liberals while still at Brighton Grammar School, but at university felt politically isolated, believing that 'The whole system had shifted to the left. I reckon I must have been the only one there past the mid-point in political views.'[4]

One of the main areas of contention between students and administration in the late 1960s was over the university's discipline statutes (drafted largely by Enid Campbell). It speaks volumes for the detachment of the law school from 'the troubles' that the faculty dissolved its own discipline committee in August 1969, at the height of the unrest. Law students were well-behaved and, in the five years of its existence, the committee had never met.[5] Julian Burnside's three dollar fine for pressing the emergency stop button on the escalators in the Ming Wing marked the limits of rebellion in the law school.

The withdrawal from Vietnam and the end of conscription marked the end of the first wave of student protest at Monash. The second wave of protest was generally milder and involved internal university issues such as car parking, course content and assessment and student representation on decision-making bodies. When Tony Pagone came to Monash in 1972, his mother was unhappy because the university still had a radical reputation, but

---

4 Kevin Summers, 'Looking for Mr Right', written August 1999, http://www.assistnet.info/kev/reith0899.htm, accessed 24 June 2013.

5 Faculty Board minutes, 9 October 1969.

the big issue that motivated students was assessment rather than Vietnam. There was enough radical energy still for the by then traditional storming of the administration building in support of the campaign for continuing assessment rather than exams.

Within the law school, however, the administration had the wisdom to concede most student demands on these issues, often before they were made. On student representation, the rationale was that representation would encourage responsibility and this largely proved the case in practice. Gerry Nash found most student representatives on the faculty board became noticeably more conservative, and putting dissenters on to the executive committee 'always calmed them down'.[6] On matters of assessment and course content, the faculty was generally committed to being innovative and progressive, and the young radical element among the staff pushed harder for reform in these areas than the students.

As early as November 1968, the faculty board agreed that 'a Law student may be permitted to attend meetings of the Law Faculty Board as an observer', and made provision for student representation on most of the faculty's committees.[7] At the same time it set up the law school liaison committee (LSLC) as a conduit for student views within the faculty. Made up of three staff members and three students, the LSLC was headed initially by Peter Hanks, who saw it as a positive gesture towards giving students a voice.[8]

The presence of students on faculty committees quickly became the norm, but whether they accepted their responsibilities was another question. During 1969 the faculty's administrator, Allan York, wrote repeatedly to the LSS president, Jamie Luxton, requesting that student members of committees take up their places and attend meetings.[9] Having conceded representation without a fight, the students, as was anticipated by the wise old heads in the faculty, gradually lost interest, and, far from preaching revolution, had to be coaxed into carrying out their new responsibilities.

Student Publications

The LSLC was largely responsible for creating the second wave of law faculty student magazines, the first magazine, *In Gremio Legis*, having been

6 Interview with Gerry Nash, 3 October 2011.

7 Faculty Board minutes, 9 October 1969.

8 Ibid.; interview with Peter Hanks.

9 13 February 1969, York to J V Luxton, MON 1096, 2003/43/625, Law Faculty, Law students' society 1967–1994, MUA.

published sporadically from 1964 until 1970. In July 1971 the first edition of a new bulletin entitled *Snark* appeared, named for Lewis Carroll's poem 'The Hunting of the Snark'. *Snark* included staff interviews, reports on law conferences and even poetry, with a left-wing inclination that increased with every issue. By 1972 it was criticising the state of legal education, questioning the relevance of exams in the education system and calling for students and academics to develop a broader view of the place of law in society.

Another new journal, *Pobble* (named for the Edward Lear poem), was first published by the LSS in October 1972. Again, it took a surprisingly radical stance, with articles on conservation, consumerism and women's liberation. One article called on readers to 'expose the governments' and 'save the earth' because lawyers are uniquely placed to 'free the people, redistribute the power and squeeze the bureaucrats'.[10]

1973 saw the arrival of a third law students' magazine. *Oracle* was the official magazine of the Monash Law Students' Society and aspired to present a wide spectrum of opinion on the law, the profession and practitioners. It was far less radical than *Snark* or *Pobble* and lasted much longer, informing and entertaining students until the mid-1980s.

The radicalism of both *Snark* and *Pobble* owed much to LSS president and now County Court judge, Tony Howard, who edited both and wrote a substantial percentage of the content. Howard also wrote the LSS contribution to the first *Counter Faculty Handbook*, published in 1972. Whereas later editions concentrated on assessing different subjects and teachers, in his 1972 article Howard simply gave his views on the faculty and the law course. On the positive side, he considered the 1972 curriculum review a good thing for the faculty and for prospective students who, he believed, would be able to design their courses to suit their interests. He applauded the continuance of the legal referral service, proclaimed that the Law Students' Society was actively investigating law reform, and welcomed the new assessment methods being implemented in the faculty. However, he argued that the law student 'will remain a liability to himself and others until he is prepared to look beyond his self-interested endeavour and cynical disregard for the social priorities with which his discipline should be concerned', and lamented what he saw as the 'malaise in the faculty'.[11]

---

10 *Pobble*, October 1972, p. 2.

11 Tony Howard, 'Blind, Bound and Fettered', *Counter Faculty Handbook*, 1972, no page numbers. It is significant that even one of the more radical students still referred to the generic student as 'he'.

Most full-time students found that once they arrived at the Clayton campus they stayed at Monash all day; this meant they had time for sporting and other extra-curricular activities such as this staff and student cricket match in 1973.

Back row from left to right: Basil Lust, Ian McCrossin, Bill Cody, Nolan ?, Tony McCormick, Adrian Robbins, Victor ?, Tony Williams, Simon Smith; Front row: Peter Hitchins, Martin Harrow, Ross Hyams.

Simon Smith Collection

The *Counter Faculty Handbooks* for this era frequently give a highly misleading and one-sided impression of students' views of the law school and its staff. The authors were self-selected from a small minority of radical students and many of them admitted they detested the attitudes of most of their fellow students. The reviewer of Property I in 1978, for example, after lamenting that 'total allegiance to the system of private property was assumed', commented 'I can't stand most of the dead shits doing Law' because most of them 'intend using Law degrees for careers, money, privilege'.[12]

More Apathetic than Rebellious

In the law faculty, apathy was a far greater problem than rebelliousness. In 1972 the faculty organised a program of lectures on the theme of 'Law and

[12] *Counter Faculty Handbook*, 1978, p. 60.

Final year students celebrating 1973.
Left to right: Ross Hopkins; Iain West; Tony McDonough; Tony Williams (on bike graduating BEc); Adrian Robbins; Simon Smith; Laurie Tooher in helmet.
Simon Smith Collection

Social Action'. In April, after only twenty-five students attended a lecture on 'Poverty', the dean, David Allan, wrote to every student on the subject of 'Student Apathy'. He contrasted the general level of apathy with the 'chiding the faculty received in the pages of *Snark*' for its alleged 'lack of interest in important events in the world around us'. The law school, he claimed, had an international reputation 'for energy and imagination in extending the horizons of legal studies', but he was left to think that if the faculty were to offer the student body 'nothing more than basic tuition in the bare minimum number of subjects to qualify for a meal ticket in the legal profession' all but twenty-five students would have no ground for complaint.[13]

The apathy of the large majority of law students was a major reason for the sharp shifts in orientation of the LSS in the 1970s and 1980s, because it allowed a variety of small but enthusiastic groups to take control. The vagaries of student politics meant that at various times the LSS was controlled by left-wingers, notably in the early 1970s and the early 1980s,

---

13 20 April 1972, 'The Dean to Every Law Student', CF/230/0 part 3, Faculty of Law 1969–85, MON 1, MUA.

while at other times it was taken over by groups of conservatives aligned with the university Liberal Club. Only for reasonably short periods was it run by groups reflecting the interests of the majority of law students, which appear to have been beer, barbecues, balls and student services.

In the early 1970s, the dominant group in the LSS were from the moderate left. They had little interest in internal law school affairs but turned the LSS outward to campaign on community, social justice and environmental issues. Their agenda dominated the pages of *Snark* and *Pobble*. This group lost its dynamism following the end of conscription and the Vietnam War but maintained its hold on the LSS by default. A change in the balance of power began when Stephen Stern became the first year representative on the LSS in 1974 'because nobody else wanted to'. The following year, he became the second year rep, again because he was the only candidate, but the LSS that year was 'virtually moribund and financially destitute', having been taken over by a small clique of 'Trotskyites' (a generic term used by many law students for anybody to the left of centre). The president, the vice-president and most of the executive were self-described Marxists, focused on external social and political issues and with no interest in organising functions or providing services to law students. Eventually Stephen and his friends mounted a coup against the radicals, calling a general meeting in mid-1976 at which a motion of no confidence in the executive was passed. New elections saw the moderate Marshall Segan elected president, with like-minded students making up the executive. They quickly began an energetic program of social events, restored the society's financial position and became involved in student-focused activities ranging from moot courts to supporting the establishment of Legibook, a co-operative bookshop.[14] The coup of 1976 marked the beginning of the modern role of the LSS

The Rise of the Right

The takeover of the LSS by a more conservative student cohort also marked the beginning of an era in which law students began to play leading roles in student politics. The left-wing radical leaders of the late 1960s and early 1970s came from arts, economics and politics, but the conservative reaction in the late 1970s was led by law students, many of whom went on to enjoy successful political careers. The most prominent of these was Peter Costello, who enrolled as an arts/law student in 1975, two years after his older brother Tim.

---

14 Interview with Stephen Stern, 12 April 2011.

Life at Monash was a culture shock for the Costello brothers, who had grown up in a middle-class, Baptist family living in Blackburn, where everybody they knew voted Liberal. Having discovered politics as an HSC student at Carey Grammar in 1974, Peter Costello quickly became involved in student politics at Monash. A defining moment was Malcolm Fraser's visit to the campus in August 1976 to open the Krongold Centre. In Costello's words, 'there was a riot' and the prime minister was locked inside a building for several hours while hundreds of student demonstrators overwhelmed security and blockaded the exit, with Costello and Michael Kroger (then president of the Liberal Club) being caught between the protestors and the police.[15]

Costello and his friends were the first group of students to react against what they saw as 'a ubiquitous, uncritical embrace of Marxist ideology on campus'. In 1976 Costello stood for the position of chairman of the Monash Association of Students (MAS), campaigning on a non-aligned platform with the promise to 'moderate the extremism of previous student leaders'.[16] Supported by Christian and Jewish students, the Liberal Club and some of the Labor Club, Costello was elected against the strong opposition of the remnants of the old left wing groups that had long dominated campus politics.[17] From his power base at Monash, Costello turned his attention to national student politics, which was run out of Melbourne where the Australian Union of Students headquarters was located. He successfully fought to change the anti-Israel Australian Union of Students (AUS) policy on the Middle-East and he then led several constituent campuses to secede from the AUS, leading to its eventual collapse.[18] Although Costello's main focus throughout his university days was on student politics, he still completed a third class honours degree in 1979, a notoriously challenging year for honours students.[19]

When the Costello ticket took control of the MAS, the radical feminist editors of *Lot's Wife* were ousted and a law student, Deborah Glass, had the unusual experience of becoming a co-editor in her first year. The editorial policy was to end the paper's role as a mouthpiece for the extreme radicals

---

15 This paragraph is based on Davison and Murphy, *University Unlimited*, pp. 175–76; Peter Costello and Peter Coleman, *The Costello Memoirs: The Age of Prosperity*, MUP, Melbourne, 2008, p. 22 et seq; and Shaun Carney, *Peter Costello: The New Liberal*, Allen & Unwin, Sydney, 2001, p. 42.

16 Davison and Murphy, *University Unlimited*, p. 176.

17 Interview with Victor Perton and Mark Birrell, 22 May 2012.

18 Costello and Coleman, *Costello Memoirs*, p. 26.

19 Faculty Board minutes, 31 March 1980.

and make it representative of all students. Deborah found it a busy and exciting year but her law studies inevitably took a back seat and she only scraped through her first year.[20]

In the late 1970s, the Liberal Club and the Law Students' Society blossomed together and for a considerable cohort of law students the two organisations were central features of their lives at university. Many of these students, such as Adam Kempton, Victor Perton, Peter Costello and Mark Birrell, arrived at university with their political views largely formed through the influence of family and school – virtually all of them went to private schools. Adam Kempton joined the Liberal Club in orientation week and, with the Law Students' Society, it became 'the big feature of his university days.'[21] Similarly, Victor Perton and Mark Birrell joined the Liberal Club and 'cut their teeth' in the political debates in the union. Student politics at the time was 'nuts, bizarre, complete fruit loop stuff'. It was played hard, but it was a time they could take risks and make mistakes, since 'there were no tweets or email to record it for life'. Several members of the Liberal Club moved from student politics to mainstream politics while still at university, with Mark Birrell making the front page of the *Australian* when he moved a motion at a Liberal Party conference that became official party policy – the first time a student motion was successful.[22]

While the more politically active conservative law students spent much of their time fighting their battles in the union building and even beyond the university, others were building the LSS into the most active student organisation on campus. One of their great achievements in the 1970s was the establishment of Legibook, which is still flourishing today.

The Legibook Story

The Legibook story began in May 1976, when the high prices and limited availability of compulsory textbooks at the Monash University bookshop led to student protests. Law students felt particularly discriminated against because the bookshop gave discounts on all textbooks except law books. While many students favoured dramatic action such as sit-ins, some law students were wary of being arrested in case it affected their legal careers. They argued

---

20 Tracey Aubin, *Peter Costello: A Biography*, Harper Collins, Sydney, 1999, p. 38; Interview with Deborah Glass, 12 May 2012. Deborah has had an exotic career in Switzerland, Hong Kong and London, culminating in the award in 2012 of an OBE for her work as deputy chair of the British Independent Police Complaints Commission.

21 Interview with Adam Kempton, 11 January 2012

22 Interview with Mark Birrell and Victor Perton, 22 May 2012.

for 'negotiations rather than demonstrations'.[23] This group, whose leading figures were Stephen Stern, Malcolm McComas and Peter Garrison, came up with the idea of a co-operative bookshop in the law building to cater only for law students.[24] The concept of the venture and the name 'Legibook' were dreamt up by Stern while sitting in a Constitutional Law lecture by Michael Pryles in mid-1976. He began lobbying for the project by meeting with Eve Mahlab, a member of the university council. Malcolm McComas recalls that he was 'given 15 minutes to sell the Legibook idea to the university', and eventually it was endorsed, even though a similar proposal by the Monash Association of Students to take over the university bookshop was rejected.[25]

Legibook was set up as a co-operative, selling shares under the old Co-operatives Act (which McComas recalls they had learnt about in company law) and memberships for a few dollars. Stephen Stern had share number one and McComas share number two. The certificate of incorporation of 'Monash LSS Book Co-operative Limited', incorporated as a trading society under the Co-operatives Act 1958, was dated 15 November 1976. The money raised from shares and memberships, together with a couple of hundred dollars advanced by the LSS, was Legibook's entire working capital, though the venture gained legitimacy when 'sympathetic and switched-on' lecturer Francine McNiff joined the board. The new venture was given a room in the basement with no shelves or counters, so Mal McComas built some. The organising committee spent hundreds of hours over the summer of 1976–77 taking student orders, collecting money, ordering books and finally distributing them. The policy was to sell at cost plus 15 per cent, and they found this margin was enough to gradually build up some capital. Students received a 17.5 per cent discount on their books. Between December 1976 and September 1977, Legibook's sales revenue was $100,000, and students had received discounts of over $15,000. It was 'a real life exercise in commerce, which also helped to pay for beer parties on Friday afternoons'.[26]

As the business built up, Legibook hired a manager, and entered a more formal arrangement with the faculty to pay a modest rental for space in the basement. Over the years it has been successfully passed from one generation of students to the next, although its future is now in doubt with the rise of online publishing.

---

23 Interview with Stephen Stern, 12 April 2011.

24 'Legibook a Co-op Success Story', *Lot's Wife*, 19 September 1977, p. 8.

25 Interview with Malcolm McComas, 27 February 2012.

26 Ibid.

Feminism in the Faculty

In the mid-to-late 1970s, the Clayton campus became increasingly conservative. The leadership of the LSS was increasingly involved with pragmatic activities such as Legibook and organising balls and barbecues. Even so, during this period a significant minority of law students became committed to left wing radical ideals. The sources of this radicalisation were the growth of feminism, the impact of community legal services and clinical programs and the influence of several inspirational radical lecturers.

Life in the law school in the 1960s and 1970s was often tough for female students. Women were outnumbered about ten to one and sexual harassment was a harsh reality for many. One student of the mid-1970s recalls that in her fourth year she was a victim of a lecturer who was notorious for sexual harassment of his female students. She and other victims got no support at all from the faculty or the university – 'there was a feeling of total powerlessness and we felt there was no point in complaining'.[27]

At the start of 1968 Marilyn Warren was terribly excited about going to university and doing law, but she was almost immediately struck by the intimidation of being part of a gender minority. A dominant group in the law school were private school 'jocks' who 'majored in football and rowing'. Women were aware of being leered at and very quickly began to stick together in groups; they would never go anywhere without a girlfriend. If your 'pair' was away, you'd hide in the library all day. It took several years before the sense of intimidation diminished. In 1974 she graduated as one of only thirty-one women in a class of 200.[28]

It is not surprising that a more militant feminism developed among some of the female law students of the 1970s. Bebe Loff clearly remembers becoming politically active in the Women's Liberation Movement when she was sixteen as a result of a talk by Linda Rubinstein from the Working Women's Centre. She attended The Mac.Robertson Girls' High, where in her final year her class insisted on reading *The Feminine Mystique* by Betty Friedan, one of the pivotal texts of the new feminism. Her first year at Monash in 1974 was lonely until the end of the year when she met Julia Pullen and later Bronwyn Naylor. They believed the 'times', particularly the energising effect of the Women's Liberation Movement, influenced everything in the second half of the 1970s.[29] The three feminist lawyers

27 The former student understandably wishes to remain anonymous.

28 Interview with Marilyn Warren, 23 August 2012.

29 Interview with Julia Pullen, Bebe Loff and Bronwyn Naylor, 20 May 2012.

describe the backdrop to their political awareness as President Richard Nixon's impeachment in 1974, the Whitlam government's dismissal in 1975, and the presence of police on campus during the protests against Prime Minister Malcolm Fraser in 1976. Bronwyn Naylor commented how difficult it is to imagine the heady excitement of those days and the feeling that anything was possible.

Julia Pullen quickly realised the law faculty was a 'male club'. She recalls a part-time lecturer producing a pair of women's frilly knickers as a 'hand-up brief'. Only a tiny minority of students was concerned by the sexist overtones of much of Campbell McComas's famous hoax lecture in May 1976, 'When "No" means "Yes": rape, consent and the law'. To some of the female students the reality of rape, the consequences of abortion and the fight for women's rights were burning issues.

In 1976 Bebe Loff attended a *Women in Medicine* conference and this gave her the idea for a similar conference on women in the law. The conference was conceived and organised by Loff and Pullen and it took them six months to plan and co-ordinate. It did not occur to them to ask the faculty for help. Held at Monash on 14 and 15 May 1977, law students, academics and practitioners from every state of Australia, about 200 in all, came to Monash for Australia's first feminist lawyers conference, focusing on women's issues and the law.

The *Women and the Law* conference aimed to give 'a broad perspective of law, women and society' and give women an opportunity 'to look at the law and to get a handle on working in the law'. The session 'women against rape' aimed to 'dramatically present issues' pertaining to rape victims in society. Sue Wynn-Hughes discussed her impressions of Fairlea female prison; Toula Nikolau from the Migrant Workers' Centre spoke on the difficulties migrant women experienced with the law; and Eve Mahlab discussed employment opportunities for women in the law. *Lot's Wife* publicised the conference and printed the program as a supplement. Speakers gave their time at no cost, and the Wholefood restaurant catered for the event. Fittingly, the Women's Electric Band played at the party after the conference. It was an extraordinary achievement for two students to organise such a large and successful conference. After the conference Bebe Loff convened the first meeting of what was to become 'Feminist Lawyers' at Monash. More than fifty female students attended.[30]

---

30 Ibid.

WOMEN AND THE LAW

CONFERENCE
MAY 14 & 15, MONASH

The 'Women and the Law' Conference is designed to critically survey women as penalised and affected by the law, as instruments of the law, and how the law itself embodies and propagates social attitudes and assumptions about women.
This conference will hopefully give a broad perspective of law, women and society, and is therefore no not designed specifically for women lawyers or law students, though it is hoped they will find it relevant to them.
This conference is one of the first of its kind in Australia, and we hope that further activities and discussions will further explore the issues raised.
This is the Lot's Wife supplement of the Women and the Law Conference. It contains articles on many of the issues to be raised at this Conference. However, this supplement is not restricted to only those who will be participating in the Conference or to those students doing Law. It is envisaged that the following articles will be of use to all people as we are all affected and influenced in some way by the laws in this society.
For those attending the Conference, you will find that this supplement will serve the purpose of Conference papers.

Lot's Wife, Monday 9th May, 1977. Page 9

The front page of *Lot's Wife*, advertised the 'Women and the Law Conference', 9 May 1977

MU Archives

Amanda George began her law course at the University of Western Australia but chose to transfer to Monash in 1978 because she found UWA sexist and conservative and was attracted by Monash's radical reputation. She was immediately drawn to the feminist lawyers' group and found it refreshing that 'everybody had a point of view and they were willing to put it out there'. Possibly aided by choosing subjects taught by the more radical lecturers, she found that Monash 'gave you an appreciation of the political economy of law' and that 'law is about politics and not much else. [It's about] who has the power and what they are trying to achieve'.[31]

Felicity Hampel, who enrolled in 1973, became a member of the LSS and remembers 'the good parties and the feminist lawyers'. She enjoyed being part of the feminist lawyers' conference in 1977, though there was some aggressive male resistance to the conference.[32] It was confronting to discover how sexist the law was in those days, and in particular the ways in which the common law treated women differently, but there was a strong feeling that social change was possible, as symbolised by the achievement of equal pay.

The 1970s was the decade in which female students really made their presence felt in the law school. In 1975 Gail Owen was the first female Supreme Court Prize winner, followed in 1978 by Adele Byrne. Since 1978, 20 out of 36 prize winners have been women (the prize was shared on three occasions). In 1969, 112 out of 870 undergraduates were female; by 1980 it was 512 out of 1510 – a rise from 12.8 per cent to 33.9 per cent.[33] In 1978 the use of 'Ms' first appeared in staff lists and the first use of 'she' rather than 'he' when referring to students in general also appears in faculty board minutes.[34]

The rapid rise in the number of female students again drew attention to an issue that had been raised when the law school building was first opened – the shortage of women's toilets. The problem had never been resolved. Rosemary Lee was a student when the new building opened and recalls there was only one toilet for female students, an oversight which led to it being named 'Derham's dunny'.[35] One of Marilyn Warren's memories of her university days was being told off very sternly by Enid Campbell

31 Interview with Amanda George, 9 June 2012.

32 Interview with Felicity Hampel, 8 August 2012.

33 *Monash University Statistics*, 1979, p. 21.

34 Faculty Board minutes, 6 June 1978.

35 Email from Rosemary Lee to authors, 19 June 2012.

for having the temerity to use one of the staff toilets. By the mid-1970s the problem had become critical, with large queues forming during every break between lectures, and many women being late for lectures as a result. It took a determined campaign by the female students before they received permission to use the staff toilets, and, eventually, more toilets were provided.

Reflecting on the 1970s Bob Baxt recalled that the shortage of toilets drew attention to the rising numbers of female law students, but more important was their growing domination of the prize lists: 'Monash, unlike I think some of the other law schools, was dominated by women… the best students at Monash were the women and that I think continues to be the case'.

High School Radicals and the High Court Fan Club

Whereas the conservative student politicians and the new breed of LSS leaders were almost exclusively from private schools, the radical activists of the mid-to-late 1970s were far more likely to have been government high school students. Typical of this group was Jon Faine, who came to Monash from Melbourne High School in 1975. Like many arts/law students he did not feel like a law student in his first two years at university, but a big turning point came when he took Professional Practice and became involved as a volunteer with the Tenants Union. Suddenly he saw the way in which the law affects people's lives and his law studies became immediate and relevant. He increasingly realised that the law is strongly oriented towards seniority and hierarchy. A lunch time talk by Peter Faris, who had recently returned from working in Alice Springs, inspired him to work to open up and democratise the law. He was also inspired by staff members such as Peter Hanks, Terry Carney, Jude Wallace and Bryan Keon-Cohen, who were highly supportive of radical law reform and free legal services.

In fourth and fifth year Faine became heavily involved in many clubs and committees, especially the socialist lawyers, set up by the radicals as an alternative to what they saw as the conservative-controlled 'hooray Henry' LSS. Among the leading members were ALP aristocrats Sue Hawke and Peter Holding, along with Bryce Menzies, Dick Gross and Heather Clark. John Thwaites, one of the few left-wing private school boys, was peripherally involved, but he spent most of his time surfing and was rarely on campus.[36] The socialist lawyers became the most profitable club

---

36 During the 1990s the Victorian Legislative Assembly included a significant number of Monash graduates in both the government and opposition. Liberal MLA Victor Perton once rushed to the chamber to vote on a division and was unsure which side

on campus in the late 1970s. They put on big events and at the biggest, 'the main band never turned up so we didn't have to pay them, but we were still able to keep the money because the rest of the concert had been good and none of the punters seem to realise that the main band hadn't played'.[37] This was a big money-spinner for the socialist lawyers, but the biggest was the High Court Fan Club.

When it was announced that Her Majesty, the Queen, would open the new High Court building in Canberra in May 1980, the socialist lawyers saw an opportunity to highlight the extravagance of the opening against the meagre funding available for community legal centres. To raise money they sold specially designed T-shirts with the slogan 'The High Court of Australia Fan Club'. Originally the main picture was of a snail but this became a donkey after a dispute with the cartoonist. They put an ad for the T-shirts in the *Legal Services Bulletin* and were overwhelmed with orders, with many coming from people high up in the legal profession, including High Court justice Lionel Murphy. They sold hundreds and soon were on a roll with money, notoriety and growing support.

The protesters (subsidised by T-shirt profits) left Melbourne, heading north in a minibus convoy, and were surprised that they were tailed by the police all the way to the NSW border. Again, when they crossed the ACT border, police were waiting and pulled them over. One of them asked, 'which one of you is Faine? I need to have a word with you.' The policeman had only one major concern, 'You're not planning to put dye or detergent in the fountain are you?' Jon replied truthfully that they hadn't even thought of it, though they suddenly wished they had.

The Monash protestors set themselves up as the 'Lawns Legal Service' in a tent outside the High Court. On the day of the opening they made their case through street theatre, most notably a spoof on the musical *Oliver* written by Stephanie Bunbury. Peter Holding donned a judge's wig to play Fagin and sang 'You've got to pick a pocket or two', with references to making a few 'friendly judgements' and sacking 'a Whitlam or two'. Mr Bumbles, the orphanage owner, and a Malcolm Fraser look-alike, made a deal with Fagin promising him, as a monument, a High Court building.

---

he should be voting on. He asked Labor MLA John Thwaites and had complete faith that Thwaites would not try to take political advantage by misdirecting him. Their years as students together at Monash led to a trust and camaraderie that overrode their political differences. Jon Faine, too, recalls that 'the interested, active students naturally congregated in classes, whatever their politics, and they stayed in touch through articles and later as part of the collegiality of the law'.

37 Interview with Jon Faine, 7 March 2012.

Oliver, in gaol, 'found a friend in the underfunded community legal service volunteer', but could not find justice with a happy ending. There were many other groups protesting that day, but the Monash group attracted most attention for the inventiveness of its activities. The Melbourne *Age* described 'the High Court of Australia fan club' as a 'rather amiable group staging street theatre and free donkey rides'. In contrast, other demonstrators were 'rather more aggressive and less witty or inventive'.[38] For their part, the members of the fan club were pleased that their protest had helped publicise the community legal services movement.

A Political Education

Education has long been regarded as one of the keys to overcoming the massive disadvantages facing Aboriginal Australians, and it was starkly symbolic of the scale of the challenge that before 1980 there were fewer than ten Aboriginal university graduates, and only one law graduate in all of Australia. Monash law school was the first Australian law school to have an Indigenous graduate when Mick Dodson completed his BJuris/LLB course in 1978. The son of an Aboriginal woman of the Yawuru people, the traditional owners of land and waters in the southern Kimberley region of Western Australia, and her white husband, Mick was born in Katherine. Orphaned at a young age, he and his brother Patrick were sent as boarders to Monivae College in Hamilton, Victoria. Boarding school 'can be a bloody tough place' that left some boys 'scarred for life', but he survived and did well, being school vice-captain, adjutant of the cadet corps and a top footballer and basketballer. Interviewed by the Melbourne *Herald* in 1970, he said:

> At the beginning I was content to hope that I would get enough education to win an apprenticeship in some trade back home. Then I began to feel that I might be able to do better. Things like algebra and English were Dutch to me but I was spurred on by my brother and the priests.[39]

Motivated to study law by a conversation with Ian Heath, a crown prosecutor he met in Darwin during school holidays, Mick Dodson was one

---

[38] 'Donkey Rides, Fan Club, but No Invasion', Melbourne *Age*, 27 May 1980, p. 2; interview with Jon Faine, 7 March 2012.

[39] Quoted in Kevin O'Keefe, *Paddy's Road: Life Stories of Patrick Dodson*, Aboriginal Studies Press, Canberra, 2003, p. 208.

High Court High Security

"All of the police on duty at the High Court have been drilled to recognise the faces of several people judged by police intelligence as likely to start a disturbance.

"Among these are several individuals whom police believe have played a key role in the organising of demonstrations against the Prime Minister, Mr Fraser, at Monash University in recent months."

So the *Age* reported the security arrangements surrounding the opening of the High Court in Canberra last Monday (May 26) on its front page of the day. Even considering the journalists' strike, the low standard of reporting is surprising.

The people from Monash singled out in this report for special mention were with the **High Court of Australia Fan Club**, a group protesting at the massive amount of money spent on the new building, with community legal services scandalously underfunded.

Despite a number of interviews with various sections of the media, High Court of Australia Fan Club received little coverage. The most glaring example of deliberate exclusion of mention of the Fan Club, rather than a lack of interest, was the report on the Seven Network News on Sunday when the **Lawns' Legal Service** was opened, opposite the $50 million High Court building, with the aid of some street theatre.

After news reader Roger Climpson had introduced the item, and transmission seemed about to cross to the footage taken that afternoon, his desk phone rang. Seconds later Climpson announced that "that item has been taken out". Such a last minute alteration to the telecast would seem to be a fairly top level decision.

The so-called "security" (other words might be more appropriate) around the opening exposed the increasing powers of Australia's police forces, and the extensive use made of paramilitary forces. The same *Age* article detailed the prepared measures such as two riot control squads in special vehicles equipped with several sorts of gas containers and a varied armoury of weapons, one being the armed offenders squad, and the other the anti-terrorist squad. The *Age* neglected to mention the hiring of a private security firm as well.

The Fan Club endeavoured to convey their message through fairly festive activities such as their version of *Oliver*, performed at the opening of the Lawns' Legal Service on Sunday, and again twice for the High Court opening the next day. Donkey-rides were given to interested parties, the donkey being part of the Club's insignia, and something of an image of the High Court.

The club clearly planned no confrontation, explaining to police that the tent for the temporary legal service, the theatre performance, and the donkey-rides were their means of conveying the need for increased funding for legal aid.

Although High Court Fan Club delegates repeatedly negotiated with police, and thought that they had co-operated adequately with the authorities,they were still the target of the above police release to the press, and police scrutiny intimidation.

The Fan Club had already been under surveillance by police, before they had reached Canberra. When the first busload in a commercially hired vehicle arrived in the ACT, it was followed by a marked police car. The bus drove around the city for some time, going down dead-end streets, with the police car following. The police car had to back out, to allow the bus to do likewise, then it continued on its tail.

Pulling up at the Union Building at the Australian National University, a Fan Club organiser went over to talk to police, who asked him to come to the station with them. He asked them to wait until accommodation could be arranged for the interstate visitors: when he returned, he was told that the other bus from Melbourne had arrived in Canberra, although it had not reached the campus.

Because this was not one of the University's buses, and could not be identified as even being from Melbourne as it had Queensland registration plates, it is obvious to organisers that they were under police surveillance before they left Melbourne.

At the demonstration during the actual opening ceremony, many people from Monash, identified through their participation in the street theatre performed there or in the police "drilling", were closely shadowed by uniformed police. Many plain clothes and special officers were also evident.

During Monday's activities, a megaphone from Monash was missing. It was found later away from the legal service and damaged so as to make it unusable. After the demonstration when a Monash person used the second megaphone, a police officer was heard to remark that "they must have found their megaphone".

A security photographer was busy taking more snaps for the ever expanding files and not even posing in the usual role of press photographer or in the secrecy of a nearby window. He/they were conspicuous in the crowd, photographing participants around them.

On top of the nearby building of the Administrative Services department, and the uncompleted National Gallery, there were several police snipers. Frequently, out of uniform police closely watched proceedings at the tent which housed the Lawns' Legal Service, part of the Fan Club demonstration. Many people noticed an unmarked Commonwealth registered Kombi, with a large radio antenna, parked alongside. Other

continued on page 12

Lot's Wife, Monday 2 June 1980, Page 3

The protest held in Canberra by the High Court of Australia Fan Club, featured in *Lot's Wife*, on 2 June 1980, p. 3.

MU Archives.

of many early students who came to Monash because his marks were not good enough to get into Melbourne.[40] When he arrived he found Monash was 'a radicalising place in an academic and political sense' and it 'very quickly politicised you'. The staff and students in the arts faculty, where his lecturers included Ian Turner, Keith Frearson and other leading radicals, helped shape his political outlook, and he went on the Vietnam Moratorium march in his first year. In the law school, Elizabeth Eggleston was protective of Mick and he admired her because she 'helped him a great deal to meet the challenges'. Pat Kilbride 'was also great' and he describes Louis Waller as 'very young and very good'. Although it was not regarded as a sexy subject, he did Landlord and Tenant Law with Jude Wallace, which proved useful in his early work after graduation.

Dodson completed his BJuris/LLB in 1975 and did articles at the Aboriginal Legal Service, where he worked until he went to the bar in 1981. Since then he has had numerous leadership roles in both the Aboriginal community and the law, including counsel assisting the Royal Commission into Aboriginal Deaths in Custody, director of the Northern Lands Council, director of the Indigenous Law Centre at the University of New South Wales and professor of law at the ANU. In 2009 Mick Dodson was named Australian of the Year, and he is currently the director of the National Centre for Indigenous Studies.

The Articles Crisis

Until the recession of the mid-1970s, law graduates in Victoria rarely had difficulty getting articles. There was a shortage of young lawyers and new graduates were in high demand. Harry Reicher was typical of the earliest Monash graduates, recalling:

> It's a reflection of how the world has changed that I didn't start looking for articles until very late in my final year; there was simply no pressure, as jobs were plentiful. I had four interviews, got a great offer from Slonim Velik & Emanuel, and looked no further. I hope it won't reflect ill on me, but of the four people with whom I interviewed, two ended up in prison, and a third was struck off! But I went straight ...[41]

40 Interview with Mick Dodson, 9 January 2013.

41 Email from Harry Reicher to authors, 3 March 2013.

However, the situation changed suddenly with the economic downturn coinciding with the decision of the Arbitration Commission to make an award for articled clerks, raising their pay from a pittance to a living wage, and also the coming on to the market of the first cohorts of Monash graduates. The consequence was an 'articles crisis'. This hit Monash graduates far harder than Melbourne graduates as fewer had contacts in the profession, and employers were both wary of Monash's radical reputation and uncertain of the quality of Monash degrees.

In September 1974 David Allan told the faculty board that

> The Faculty of Law, like other faculties, could not guarantee employment for all its graduates but it was hoped that all Law graduates could be admitted to practise as a barrister and solicitor of the Supreme Court of Victoria. He thought that those newly-admitted to the Faculty should be warned that not all Law graduates will be able to pursue a professional career after graduation.[42]

Monash and Melbourne law schools worked together to establish a course of practical training at the Leo Cussen Institute as an alternative to articles. This began in 1975 and proved able to take almost all students who were unable to get articles. However, the carefree student attitude of the early years of the law school has never returned. Future employment has been an ever-increasing concern of law students and, with the continuing rapid rise in the number of law graduates, this appears unlikely to change. The change in attitude to employment led students to focus increasingly narrowly on subjects that would (they hoped) increase their chances of getting articles.

Pranks and Hoaxes

The ramifications of the increasing concerns with employment might have been the major factor in a generally observed lessening of the 'fun' element of student life and particularly a decline in pranks, practical jokes and large scale stunts, which had all been rife in the 1970s. Some, like the High Court fan club, were a form of protest, others injected humour into educational activities, while many were just for fun.

Fun and legal studies came together in 1973 when students challenged the producers of the popular ABC TV series, *Bellbird*. One episode concerned a QC, Alan Mitchell, who purchased a property in Bellbird and promptly

42 Faculty Board minutes, 29 September 1974.

evicted the local lay-about, Albie Cross, who had squatted there for many years. As the *Monash Reporter* recorded:

> This outraged the sense of fair play and justice of Monash's law students, and they promptly hit the ABC with a 'Supreme Court' writ, claiming that Albie Cross had a right to the land under the law of adverse possession.
>
> The ABC readily agreed that the matter should be further ventilated and the case was set down for hearing in the Moot Court on August 22. And what a hearing! On the bench were Chief Justice Gary Sebo (final year law student), Mr Justice (Professor R) Baxt and Mr Justice Iain Treloar West (student). Counsel for the plaintiff were students Peter Mitchell and Simon Smith, and for the defendant Paul Mulvaney and Andrey McMullan, all members of the Notting Hill Bar.
>
> From the ABC came Ewen Solon (the defendant, Alan Mitchell), John Russell (the plaintiff, Albert Cross), Moira Carleton (Olive Turner), Terry Norris (Joe Turner), and Alan Hopgood (Dr Matthew Reid).
>
> The proceedings were confused, to say the least, but it was apparent from the start that the learned Mr Mitchell, QC, stood little chance against a biased claret-swigging Bench and a noisy, quarrelsome jury, specially rigged from among law students, most of whom bore the same surname – Cross.
>
> But some startling facts came to light – for instance, that Olive Turner ran the local brothel (with Joe living off her earnings) and that Dr Reid was the town's abortionist, with the largest standing order for knitting needles in the district.
>
> It's thought that a case, of sorts, was proved. Anyway, most parties agreed that honor, justice (and thirst) were well satisfied.[43]

By far the most famous student prank in the history of the Monash Law School was the Granville Williams lecture of 5 May 1976.[44] The 'greatest stunt in the history of Monash' had its origins when Jack Hammond and

---

43 *Monash Reporter*, 26 September 1973.

44 This account of the Granville Williams lecture is based primarily on interviews with Jack Hammond and Malcolm McComas, and 'The Case of the Counterfeit Professor', *Monash Reporter*, July 1976, pp. 3–4.

Bellbird vs Monash Students in Moot Court in 1973. Back row, left to right: Students Iain West and Gary Sebo and Bob Baxt; Front row, left to right: ABC _Bellbird_ characters, Olive Turner, Joe Turner (wearing a hat) and Albie Cross; student Paul Mulvany, ABC _Bellbird_ actors Alan Hopgood and Euan Solan.
Photographer unknown, Monpix 840

Campbell McComas began to chat about the unusual teaching styles and idiosyncrasies of many law lecturers and thought it would be funny to do a hoax lecture in which they included all the mannerisms of the various lecturers in one lecture. After some thought, they decided that the original plan might be a bit cruel and ridicule too many lecturers. Then they reflected on the way that most students sit in lectures with their heads down and write without looking up and without thinking about what they were writing. Hammond and McComas came up with the idea of creating a hoax guest lecture, in which they would combine erudite learning and genuine law with absolute fiction. The idea was that a good student might think 'Well, that's right' about the genuine material and therefore would accept the fiction. They based the lecture on sex to create interest and chose the highly topical recent cases of *R v Collins* and *DPP v Morgan* where the central issue was consent.[45] They dreamt up a catchy title, 'When "No" means "Yes": rape, consent and the law' and decided on leading Cambridge criminal law academic Glanville

---

45 *R v Collins*, 1973 QB 100, *DPP v Morgan*, 1975 2 WLR 913; 1976 AC 182.

Williams as the purported lecturer, deliberately misspelling his name as Granville. They were greatly amused to see a diligent law lecturer correcting the spelling on some of the posters advertising the event!

Hammond and McComas then let Marshall Segan, the president of the LSS, into the secret because they wanted help organising and publicising the event. They thought Louis Waller would know the real Glanville Williams, so they went to him and asked him not to reveal the hoax. He sat back and laughed, agreeing the hoax was marvellous because universities had 'become much too serious'. He also agreed to introduce the speaker.

The lecture was widely publicised and when the organisers heard that many people from the University of Melbourne, the bar and the bench would be coming, they moved the lecture to the large theatre in the Rotunda. One Monash lecturer told his class he would not discuss the question of rape and consent since the distinguished visitor would tell them all they needed to know, while another cancelled a planned visit to the courts so that students could attend the lecture. However, at the last minute, the organisers felt obliged to warn the Victorian solicitor-general when it was learned that he planned to cancel a court appearance to come to hear the learned professor.

The theatre was full. Louis Waller gave a masterful introduction in which he skilfully put together the appropriate platitudes, while saying nothing at all about the speaker. McComas, effectively disguised with dyed hair, bushy black eyebrows and horn-rimmed glasses, was already speaking when he realised that his box of props had been left in the law school building. He ad-libbed brilliantly for about ten minutes while his brother Malcolm ran back to retrieve the box. The contents of the box were central to a fabrication around the 'Cambridge Museum of Law' which supposedly held artefacts relating to many of the most famous cases of English legal history, such as the bottle of Stone's ginger beer from *Donoghue v Stevenson* ('the most prized single legal artefact in Christendom'), the socks which were the only item of clothing worn by Mr Collins when he made his ascent of the ladder, and the underpants manufactured by the Australian Knitting Mills that caused such discomfort to Dr Grant.

Although he was an experienced amateur actor, McComas was 'terrified' before the lecture began, but his nervousness soon vanished as he got into his stride and became 'Granville Williams'.

> We'd presumed beforehand that many of the staff, at least, would quickly guess that it was a hoax, but while people were laughing at

> things the "professor" was saying, nobody gave any indication that they didn't believe he was genuine.
>
> There were reactions from the audience that at times had me staggered. When I talked some utter rubbish about a non-existent Danish law that had abolished the crime of rape and a Bulgarian law that outlawed intercourse between married couples as a birth control measure, everybody took me seriously. Then when I quoted some genuine findings by genuine anthropologist Bronislau Malinowski, concerning primitive tribal customs, everybody laughed uproariously.[46]

Peter Haug remembers rolling around laughing at the lecture. He was doing Criminal Law and recalls that he and his Criminal Law classmates came along armed with lecture pads, took notes (for a while anyway) and were completely taken in by the hoax. 'The 'Professor' took questions at the end of his presentation and Arie Freiberg (one of the first to cotton on to the hoax) asked: "What's the difference between an objective and subjective erection?" to which the professor's answer concluded 'The former being in the eyes of the beholder and the latter being one which would stand up in Court!'[47]

While the hoaxers said afterwards that 'there was no intention of using [the lecture] as a means of putting over a message', there were still opportunities to make some subtle points. One lecturer who was notorious for picking on girls to answer embarrassing questions was asked by McComas to give the facts of a case. The lecturer could only mumble shamefacedly before admitting that he hadn't read the case.

Before the lecture, the organisers were concerned that lecturer Graham Taylor, who had done a PhD at Cambridge, would reveal that Williams was an imposter. However, at the end of the lecture Taylor went up to McComas, shook his hand and said, 'You probably don't remember me', to which McComas quickly replied, 'It's young Taylor isn't it – I've heard you're doing good work down here in the antipodes'. It was remarkable that Taylor did not recognise that it was not the real Glanville Williams as Williams and McComas were physically quite different (McComas was tall, while the short, squat Williams was often likened to Friar Tuck), but Taylor admitted later that he had completely convinced himself that it was the real Williams.

---

46 Campbell McComas, interviewed in *Monash Reporter*, July 1976, p. 4.

47 Interview with Peter Haug, 14 June 2011; correspondence with authors 31 July 2013.

Campbell McComas as Professor Granville Williams, May 1976.
This hoax lecture, provocatively titled 'When "No" means "Yes": Rape, Consent and the Law' attracted a huge audience and fooled many students and staff. This hoax launched McComas's career as an impersonator.
Photographer Jon Shiff, Monpix 7807

Following the lecture, the ABC approached the LSS with an invitation for Professor Williams to appear on its 'Guest of Honour' program that evening, but the organisers decided not to push their luck. Initially they planned not to reveal the hoax, but after a few weeks the story was leaked and the subsequent media publicity helped launch Campbell McComas's successful professional career as an actor and impersonator. Professor Granville Williams was the first of 1822 characters McComas developed before his untimely death in 2005.

Immediately after the lecture, the LSS began selling transcripts and tapes of the lecture, with the funds going to buy a change machine for the

Top: Campbell McComas presenting portrait of 'Alternative Professor Granville Williams' to dean of law, Professor Gerry Nash.
Photographer unknown, Monpix 276

Bottom: Emeritus Professor Louis Waller in front of painting by Irene Clark of the 1976 Campbell McComas impersonation of Glanville Williams, 2008.
Photographer Andrew Curtis, Monpix 7469

photocopier, with some left over to have a party. It has long been rumoured that a law lecturer at another institution used the tape for several years in his criminal law classes, apparently believing it was good law. Over the years the Granville Williams lecture has gained an almost mythical stature, with far more people claiming to have been present than could possibly have fitted in the lecture theatre. Jon Faine is one of the few students of the day who admits he was not there, recalling that he thought, 'Why should I go and listen to some old professor when I could be in the caf with my mates?'

PART THREE

THE TWO BOBS – BOB BAXT AND BOB WILLIAMS, 1980–98

Chapter 15

A Bob Each Way

The Eras of Bob Baxt and Bob Williams

For Australian universities, the year 1975 decisively marked the end of the era of abundance they had enjoyed since the late 1950s. For the next twenty years, the Australian economy struggled and the country's poor economic performance meant that the universities were fighting for a share of a shrinking cake. While university funding fell, student numbers virtually ceased to grow and the tertiary sector entered a period described as 'steady state'. Job opportunities for young academics declined steeply and promotion prospects were limited. Students, spurred by rising unemployment, were increasingly job-oriented in their choice of courses and their attitude to university life.

While the tertiary sector was in a state of hiatus, the germs of a new approach were being developed, with the Faculty of Economics at Monash being one of the prime incubators. Always strongly free market even when the university was regarded as a hotbed of radicalism, many Monash economists argued that the Australian tertiary education sector was overly regulated and some campaigned for reduced government spending on universities, the introduction of fees, and other measures to shake up the universities and encourage competition between them.[1] The Canberra bureaucracy was quickly converted to these policies, but they were politically unpalatable and neither the Fraser government nor Susan Ryan, the first Minister for Education in the Hawke government, were willing to adopt them. However, following the 1987 election, John Dawkins took over the education portfolio and almost immediately implemented a radical reform agenda that revolutionised tertiary education. Dawkins abolished the distinction between universities and colleges of advanced education and promoted mergers between them. He restructured the financing of higher education

---

1 For example, M G Porter, 'On the Deregulation of Education', *Australian Economic Papers*, vol. E1, no. 68, October 1981.

to create a mixed public-private funding base, reintroducing fees for the great majority of students through the HECS scheme, and encouraging universities to engage in 'market entrepreneurialism'. He forced universities to place greater emphasis on research and introduced standardised measures of research activity. Finally, Dawkins argued that a great increase in the number of tertiary graduates was needed to boost Australia's economic competitiveness.[2]

During the 'steady state' era in tertiary education, Monash became an increasingly conservative institution, seeing itself more as the last of the old universities rather than the first of the new. In large part this was due to the ageing of the staff as the young academics appointed in the 1960s became encrusted into place and the end of growth meant that opportunities for renewal were few. A higher ratio of senior staff in an era of declining funding led to Monash having the worst staff:student ratio in Australia by the early 1980s (although this was not true of the law school). Coinciding almost exactly with the vice-chancellorship of Ray Martin, the steady state era saw the number of Monash students stabilised at about 13,000, with the number of law students falling slightly from 1143 in 1976 to 1111 in 1986.[3]

Martin's successor, Mal Logan, was a confidante of Dawkins and a leading apostle of his reforms. Under his leadership, Monash enthusiastically embraced the new order and entered upon a decade of frenetic mergers, commercialisation, managerialism and restructuring to emerge a vastly larger, multi-campus university. Simon Marginson argues that 'No university experienced greater change than did Monash University, where the spirit of the times found its most concentrated form'.[4] In just five years the university more than doubled in size.

Coincidentally, the vice-chancellorships of Martin and Logan ran more or less parallel with the terms of Bob Baxt and Bob Williams as deans of the Faculty of Law. Baxt and Williams are two of the outstanding individuals in the history of the Monash law school and both left profound legacies. Since his arrival in 1968, Baxt had transformed commercial law at Monash from a weakness to a strength, and had been the driving force behind many bold ventures, while Williams was one of the original students of 1964, joint

---

2 An excellent concise account of the Dawkins reforms is given in Simon Marginson, *Monash: Remaking the University*, Allen and Unwin, Sydney, 2000, ch. 3.

3 Ibid., and Davison and Murphy, *University Unlimited*, ch. 6. Student numbers are EFTS – effective full-time students.

4 Marginson, *Monash: Remaking the University*, p. xiii.

winner of the first Supreme Court Prize, and the first Monash graduate to become a professor in the faculty.

They could scarcely have been more different. Baxt is gregarious, outgoing, dynamic and entrepreneurial, while Williams is shy, cautious and methodical. Their starkly differing personalities were inevitably reflected in the way they perceived and carried out the role of dean. Both were confronted with far greater external challenges than any of their predecessors, and their response to these challenges was very largely a reflection of their contrasting characters. It was the somewhat strange fate of Monash law school's two deans in the years 1980 to 1998 to be in office during the wrong eras: Baxt attempted to create a dynamic and entrepreneurial law school at a time when Monash was increasingly inward looking and conservative, while Williams' measured and conservative personality found little to like in the university's later policies of frenetic expansion and commercialisation.

When Gerry Nash decided to return to the bar in 1980, Bob Baxt was the obvious internal candidate to succeed him and, although the deanship was advertised, he was appointed for twelve months 'pending decisions in relation to the position as advertised'. No further action was taken regarding advertising the position and in July 1981 Baxt was appointed to a five-year term. Soon after his initial appointment, Baxt outlined his priorities as dean. Typically, he was a decade ahead of the pack in calling for a 'greater positive recognition' for research, proposing the introduction of 'research trimesters' and increased faculty funding for research to be funded from outside earnings. Income would be boosted by building up continuing legal education and raising funds from alumni and the wider community, with the establishment of an alumni association as a key measure. To address the lack of job security for junior staff members he had already begun discussions with the vice-chancellor for more tenured positions, and he was also talking with the Law Institute and other outside bodies to 'tackle the problem of finding positions for law graduates'. Finally, he set up a 'long-term planning committee' to prioritise initiatives given the limitations of the 'steady state' university.[5]

In October 1980 there was a large cut in the faculty's budget for the following year. Baxt's reaction was typical. While fighting hard for the faculty on the university decision-making bodies, he saw this could have at best limited success, and the way of the future would be for the faculty to become increasingly self-sufficient. The option of attracting fee-paying students was

---

5 Faculty Board minutes, 30 July 1980.

not yet available, so Baxt looked to other means to raise funds, while also being forced, much against his instincts, to make savings.

During the mid-1970s, Bob Baxt instigated the faculty's first moves into continuing legal education, with programs aimed at both lawyers and non-lawyers. In the early years the main emphasis was on short courses held over summer, but when these proved highly successful an increasing number of courses, seminars and lectures were held through the year.[6] There was little competition, so fees were high and the program proved to be an increasingly valuable source of income for the faculty.

As dean, Baxt looked for a great expansion of the continuing education program, to boost income and build links with the legal profession and other professional groups such as accountants, engineers and managers. Carol Bartlett became the program's co-ordinator and ran it with energy and enthusiasm. Her report for the first half of 1983, for example, recorded that thirteen seminars had been held, with those on social security law and state taxes attracting over 100 registrations. There had also been lecture series on recent developments in banking, company tax and planning law, and fully booked residential workshops on maritime law and trade practices held in Melbourne, Sydney and Canberra. The report noted that 'The successful core of Monash CLE has to date been the fields of Tax and Company Law', and foreshadowed 'an ever widening range of topics that … reflect the expertise of the Faculty and areas of established and developing professional interest'.[7]

In the first six months of 1984, the continuing legal education program made a profit of $52,000, and this successful result, combined with the ever-decreasing funding from government, led Bob Baxt to propose his most ambitious initiative, the establishment of a Centre of Commercial Law and Applied Legal Research. The aims of the centre were to take over and expand the continuing education program, attract outside funding and research grants, and generally become a conduit for raising money to lessen the faculty's dependence on government funding.

The establishment of the centre aroused heated debate. Opponents argued that it would be 'inimical to the maintenance of academic independence' because 'directed research, closely identified with business, labour or governments, would be compromising and lead to the abandonment of independent, creative, theory-based, intellectual analysis'. Further, there were concerns that the project would not be financially viable and would rely

---

6 Ibid., 7 June 1977.

7 Ibid., 19 July 1983.

on hidden subsidies from the faculty, and that the dean 'might tend to favour persons and matters associated with the centre'. Baxt and his supporters countered that 'non-government support of universities was essential ... university members should be dynamic and self-reliant, and not seek to maintain the status quo', and 'checks and balances' would be set up to ensure academic independence and the maintenance of standards. They agreed that 'scholarly endeavour might be at risk but risk is inherent in the present circumstances [and] the gains would outweigh the possible disadvantages.' The establishment of the centre was approved, but seven faculty board members, including Enid Campbell, Peter Hanks, Terry Carney and Henry Finlay, voted against the proposal.[8]

Bob Baxt envisaged that the Centre for Commercial Law would have a full-time director, a part-time assistant director, a clerical officer and a full-time secretary, with temporary research and clerical staff being appointed as needed. The initial income and expenditure projections appear to have been 'back of the envelope' calculations, based as much on hope as anything else – it was assumed, for example, that the income from continuing legal education would double, and the projected income of $80,000 from memberships was no more than a guess. On these figures, it was estimated that the centre would return a profit of over $90,000 in its first year.[9]

The Centre for Commercial Law was formally opened on 16 August 1985, with Bob Baxt as the inaugural director pending the appointment of a full-time director. Many large law and accounting firms signed up as members, along with a number of listed companies including Mayne Nickless and Rothmans of Pall Mall, although efforts to attract financial support from governments were less successful.

The centre's first annual report presented a rosy picture of bustling and productive activities, but there were several jarring caveats. No suitable applications had been received for the position of director, leaving Baxt carrying that load, and the income from continuing legal education, rather than rising as anticipated, had fallen sharply, primarily because of competition from programs run by the Law Foundation and the Leo Cussen Institute. Most significant in the light of later events was Baxt's conclusion:

> Finally a note of disappointment and warning. The Centre's success in 1985 ... has been due to the hard work of very few people. The

---

8 Ibid., 19 November 1984.

9 Bob Baxt, 'Centre for Commercial Law and Applied Legal Research', Faculty Board minutes, 19 November 1984.

> enthusiasm (or so it appeared) with which the Centre was supported at the time of the Faculty Board meeting in 1984, has not been replicated in the contributions made by a majority of Faculty to the work of the Centre.[10]

In September 1986, Lucio Dana, a Monash graduate and partner in the firm of Macpherson and Kelley, was appointed director of the centre, but he stayed for only six months, forcing Baxt to resume the acting directorship.

While the Centre for Commercial Law occupied a great deal of Bob Baxt's attention, he was a man of vast energy and was forever looking for new ways to raise the profile of the faculty, boost its research output and increase its resources. As he told the faculty board in September 1982, 'I believe that Monash Law School will need to display a "bigger", "brighter" and "better" public image in the future if we are to maintain our standing as the leading Law School in Australia'. He saw an important facet of the role of dean as being the public face of the law school and so he maintained close links with the profession, the business community and government. He also made frequent overseas trips to promote the law school, set up staff exchanges and build links with overseas alumni. He set up the Monash Law Alumni Association, and its branch in Malaysia, marking the first attempts by the faculty to keep in touch with its ever-growing ranks of graduates. To promote research he created research trimesters to give staff the opportunity to have teaching-free periods beyond the normal study leave, established scholarships for tutors to study overseas, and appointed the first director of research. Baxt also set up visiting professorships in commercial law, taxation, banking law and trial advocacy, founded the Tax Forum and the Banking Law Association and oversaw the introduction of the first personal computers for staff use.

Bob Baxt's vision was

> to create the best law school. Monash was always regarded as the second law school in Melbourne. When you looked at the cut off scores for Monash students compared to Melbourne, it was always Melbourne ahead of us, and I became very aggressive and perhaps overly aggressive in promoting the people we had at Monash. I used to put out a newsletter around the faculty a couple of times a week, congratulating people on having articles published, doing papers, whatever, and I remember one

---

10 Interim Director's Report, Centre for Commercial Law and Applied Legal Research, Faculty Board minutes, 3 April 1986.

> instance, I was very cheeky, and we were having a particularly successful period, we had won a couple of grants … and published many articles and books and so on, and I said this clearly is illustrative of Monash being the leading law school in Australia, and I remember getting a letter from Colin Howard [dean of the Melbourne law school] saying 'Bob, we are choking on our coffee reading your crap about Monash being the leading law school in Australia'.[11]

In reality, Baxt had more to boast about than Colin Howard. In 1985 the Commonwealth Tertiary Education Commission began the most detailed review ever conducted of the teaching of law in Australian universities and the findings of the review committee (Dennis Pearce of ANU, Enid Campbell of Monash and Don Harding of UNSW) were published in four large volumes (the Pearce Report) in 1987. The cynical might scoff that the review panel found that the three best law schools were at the reviewers' home universities, but the weight of evidence produced amply confirmed the assessment. The Pearce Report was damning in its assessment of the Melbourne law school, criticising its accommodation as non-functional, its law library as having glaring deficiencies, the commitment of its staff to teaching as poor and its staff:student ratio as the second worst in Australia. Only in research was it ranked on a par with Monash.

Monash, by contrast, fared well on almost every measure. Although the law building was nearing the capacity of its original three storeys, it was still near new and functioning effectively, and the law library rated highly, particularly for its visionary location at the heart of the law building. Monash had the second best staff:student ratio and was commended for its range of electives, the quality of its teaching and the commitment of its teachers, and particularly for the strength of the clinical program. Many of Bob Baxt's innovations, notably 'research trimesters' and the appointment of a research director, were praised, though the review committee was more reserved about the Centre for Commercial Law (which was not surprising as Enid Campbell had voted against its establishment). By any reading the Pearce Report gave strong endorsement to Monash's claim to be, if not the best law school in Australia, then certainly one of the top three.

Nonetheless, while the faculty could bask for a time in the warm glow of the Pearce Report, it was becoming a constant struggle to maintain its position. Baxt's whole period as dean was overshadowed by continued

---

11 Interview with Bob Baxt, 22 June 2011.

funding cuts and the need to find new sources of revenue or cut spending. He was deeply opposed to reducing spending, which he saw as defeatist and pessimistic, but he was forced to make some economies: there was a steady reduction in the quota for new students, from 370 in 1980 to 290 in 1985; the size of the *Monash University Law Review* was reduced and the policy of giving free copies to students was abandoned; vacant positions were left unfilled (Gerry Nash's chair was not filled until 1987); and the number of compulsory moots per student was reduced from two to one. The inability to replace teaching staff meant that by 1988 the faculty was decidedly weak in Baxt's own area of commercial law, as Peter Ellinger, C Y Lee and others left and could not be replaced. An important reason for the problems of the Centre for Commercial Law was the absence of suitable staff to teach its courses and carry out its research.

In 1985 Bob Baxt was appointed to a further five-year term. He had torn his Achilles tendon at about the time he was seeking reappointment and he had a 'terrible argument' with vice-chancellor Ray Martin: 'I was saying, "Why do you have to put me through this whole process of going for interviews again, haven't I done a good enough job? Shouldn't I just get reappointed?'. But Martin insisted that he had to go through the process, so he hobbled to his interviews on crutches. There was no open opposition to Baxt's reappointment, and certainly no alternative internal candidate, but, as so often happens, his second term was far less happy than the first. The dilemma of the dynamic and innovative dean in an era of 'steady state' and shrinking funding weighed heavily on Bob Baxt and he became increasingly resentful of those of his colleagues who he felt were not pulling their weight. His concerns were clearly expressed in his report to the faculty board in April 1986:

> The financial position for 1986 has been made extremely critical as a result of inadequate funding for the Faculty and for the University from Canberra. We are not provided with funds to meet what is known as incremental creep; inflation is not fully met … We have continued to cut our quota to meet the constraints placed on us by reduced Faculty funding [and] we are now at a stage where we have to seriously consider alternatives in the way in which we run the Faculty. We have put off for the last two or three years (due to some careful planning as well as some luck) some of the hard decisions in relation to the number of tutors we can have …; the number of subjects that we can offer; and issues such as whether we should continue with summer teaching; maintain the

> clinical programme at its current level; maintain fractional appointees; etc.
>
> ... The Centre for Commercial Law and Applied Legal Research will provide some funding for specific activities of the Faculty, but cannot be seen as a general reservoir of funds for the Faculty ... The omens from Canberra are very depressing and it is becoming increasingly difficult for me as Dean to find ways of allowing new initiatives to be taken. We have been very lucky that the Faculty has been able to maintain an entrepreneurial and a very flexible approach to development, with the assistance of funds from various organisations, but this is not a complete answer to our difficulties.
>
> I am not a pessimist – I believe we can find the solutions, but I need the help of every member of Faculty ... if these solutions are to be found. Of course we can take the easy way out – cut our losses, reduce the size of the Faculty, and become a much less energetic and innovative Faculty than we have been. I believe that the University, and the general community, will be the loser if that were to be our approach.
>
> I do hope that the pessimism and lack of general initiative that I perceive in so many parts of the University, will quickly dissipate.[12]

However, the other professors in the faculty were increasingly unhappy with the direction in which Baxt was taking the faculty and remained unmoved by his calls to action. The likes of Enid Campbell, Louis Waller and Christie Weeramantry had always had doubts about the commercialisation of the faculty and were concerned about the financial structure of the Centre for Commercial Law. In 1987 the faculty received permission to fill two vacant chairs and Baxt pushed for the appointment of two external candidates, who he hoped would favour his entrepreneurial approach. The selection committees, however, ignored the dean's wishes and chose two internal candidates, Francis Trindade and Bob Williams, who, while eminently worthy in academic terms, were from the conservative side of the faculty. The consequence was that Baxt faced an almost entirely alienated professoriate.

> The last year or so of my deanship was pretty miserable. I didn't believe I got the support of the professors. I told them as much. I said, 'Why aren't you supporting me? Why aren't we doing these things? Why, oh

12 Dean's Report, Faculty Board minutes, 3 April 1986.

> why is it so difficult to get you guys to meet with me and to do these things?' They didn't want to do it.

During 1987 there were raging battles between Baxt and his professors, primarily over financial matters, and it was increasingly difficult to see how the faculty could continue to follow the path the dean had chosen when his chief lieutenants believed he was heading in the wrong direction. It was not surprising that Baxt was attracted by an invitation to become the foundation dean of the new law school at Bond University, and he began negotiations to take leave of absence from Monash. Before the arrangements were finalised, however, he accepted an invitation to become chairman of the Trade Practices Commission. He left Monash in April 1988, initially on three years' leave, but he never returned. The ill-feeling between Baxt and his professors was shown when he was the only dean not to be given a farewell party.

Baxt was a visionary and in many ways a brilliant dean, but the times were unkind for his entrepreneurial style. His deanship kindles a picture of a king leading the charge of his army, but as they advanced his knights were killed, wounded, changed sides or ran away. Eventually he was charging along by himself surrounded by his foes, and like Gustavus Adolphus at the Battle of Lützen or Richard III at Bosworth, he found that it was fatal for a monarch to become separated from his followers.

At first sight Bob Williams' claims to succeed Bob Baxt were little stronger than those of Henry VII to succeed Richard III (unless the right of conquest applies to law school deans). Williams was the most junior of the professors in the faculty and was

> more than a little hesitant about putting myself forward for the Deanship. This was particularly because of the extreme level of conflict between what may broadly be called the Baxt supporters and opponents which existed at the time. At a personal level, as a result of long and hard work I had achieved my ambition of being appointed to a chair … and was attracted to the idea of both enjoying the fruits of that achievement and following scholarly ambitions in what I thought might be the most academically significant period of my career.[13]

Williams favoured Louis Waller becoming the permanent dean, but Waller, after being persuaded to apply for the vice-chancellorship in

13 Williams, 'Some Reflections on Monash', p. 12.

Bob Williams succeeded Bob Baxt as Dean in 1988. He faced a decade of challenges including dealing with the Dawkins reforms of the early 1990s.
Photographer unknown, Monpix 6700

1985 and being (to his great relief) unsuccessful, was determined to avoid administrative entanglements and strongly supported Williams for the deanship. With all the other professors similarly averse to becoming dean, and Williams already being acting dean by virtue of having been appointed associate dean late in 1987, he was the only internal candidate and was confirmed as dean for a five-year term in October 1988. Williams

> assumed the office of dean with two clear ideas. The first was a strong commitment to traditional notions of what a University is and the values and standards that should inform everything we do. The second was an acceptance of the proposition that significant change across the sector had to take place. It was clear that the ways of doing things that had characterised the 70's and early 80's were simply not good enough

> to enable universities to achieve what was necessary for their future and the future well-being of the country. I regarded my major task as dean as being to achieve a proper balance between the competing requirements of necessary adaptation on the one hand, and preservation of the values and traditions of the institution on the other.[14]

Bob Williams began his deanship with the solid support of the professors (except perhaps Michael Pryles, who soon left to join Minter Ellison), and there was a general feeling of relief in the faculty as the bitter divisions of Bob Baxt's last years faded away. No other dean of the Monash law school has faced challenges of the magnitude that confronted Bob Williams over the decade 1988 to 1998. He became dean when the tertiary sector was struggling to understand and adapt to the dramatic changes enforced by the Dawkins' reforms. When Monash chose to embrace these changes and set off on a manic quest for growth by mergers and internal expansion, Williams had to ensure that the law school did not either decline into insignificance in relation to the rest of the university, or compromise its quality by rapid expansion. His efforts were continually compromised by the erratic and unreliable policies of the university's central administration and ever falling government funding. Government policies on overseas students, student fees and other important issues were continually changing and, after the reforming zeal of the Labor government had finally faded, the election of the Howard government in 1996 led to another round of frenetic policy changes and severe budget cutting. In the entire decade there was not a moment free of crisis, and it is not surprising that Bob Williams developed a highly defensive siege mentality. He has been criticised in recent years by those who believed the faculty stagnated under his leadership, but his critics rarely acknowledge the severity of the difficulties he faced.

Within two years of Bob Williams becoming dean, the Centre for Commercial Law had disappeared. Although Williams was convinced that dependence on external money is a 'terrible trap', because reliance on fees, external contracts and grants leads to 'enormous vulnerabilities', the centre was not closed simply to make a statement that the Baxt era was over. One of Williams' earliest actions was to launch a review of the centre headed by Louis Waller. Somewhat surprisingly, given that the centre had made a loss in 1988, the review concluded that 'On its past record the Committee strongly recommended that the Centre should continue'. The

---

14 Williams, 'Some Reflections on Monash', p. 13.

review committee believed that the biggest problem with the centre had been lack of leadership and recommended the appointment of a director with professorial status and salary.[15] The faculty board, after heated debate, agreed with this recommendation and the position of director was advertised. By July 1990, however, no suitable applications had been received and in the absence of a director, the centre's activities declined and eventually it just faded away.

To some extent the money-making role of the Centre of Commercial Law was taken over by the Monash University Law School Foundation, which was set up in mid-1989 to attract donations and grants from alumni, the profession and business. Bob Williams recalls that 'the funds obtained for the foundation were essentially raised by me personally without the assistance of any professional fundraisers or the appointment of any public relations administrators'.[16] The first major donations came from the NAB, the Victorian Bar Council, Westpac and the State Bank of Victoria. Unfortunately the State Bank's promised donation of $100,000 was to be given over five years and the bank ceased to exist well before the five years had elapsed. Nonetheless, the foundation has provided a useful supplement for the faculty's finances, supporting the establishment of research centres, providing scholarships for local and international students and funds to bring leading overseas scholars to Monash.

When vice-chancellor Mal Logan launched Monash's growth surge, which increased the number of students from under 12,000 to nearly 27,000 between 1987 and 1994, the law school also embraced a growth strategy. Although law was less affected by the mergers than most other faculties (because the CAEs swallowed by Monash had not taught law), Bob Williams nonetheless argued that the law school had to expand 'if we were not to become an unacceptably small and potentially vulnerable part of the university.'[17] This fitted the strategy of the university administration and Williams was promised that the university would fund a greatly increased number of students. Consequently the student intake was increased from 300 in 1989 to 450 in 1990, leading to student numbers increasing by more than forty per cent in just four years. Although nine new law schools were established in Australia between 1988 and 1994, Monash grew by nearly

---

15 Faculty Board minutes, 17 April 1989.

16 Ibid., 31 July 1989 and Williams, 'Some Reflections on Monash', pp. 12–13.

17 Williams, 'Some Reflections on Monash', p. 14.

The Law School Foundation was established in 1998.

Left to right: Presentation of cheques to Monash Law Foundation. From left: David Bruce, National Bank; Geoff Kimpton, Westpac; Vice-Chancellor Professor Mal Logan; Dean of Law, Professor Bob Williams; Geoff Mumford, Westpac; Peter Shepard, State Bank.

Photographer Scott Fitzpatrick, Monpix 811

as much as all the new law schools combined.[18] Further, as the University of Melbourne did not embrace the new order with anything like the same fervour as Monash, the numbers in the Melbourne law school remained stable, leading to Monash becoming by far the largest Victorian law school, and second only to Sydney in Australia.[19]

However, no sooner had the law school fully committed to its growth strategy than the university unilaterally introduced a new funding formula which greatly penalised law by giving it a very low weighting for its teaching, with no allowance at all for the clinical program or tutorials, and allocating research-based funding largely on the basis of obtaining grants, many of which the law faculty was not even eligible for.[20] Strong protests failed to

18 Craig McInnis and Simon Marginson, *Australian Law Schools After the 1987 Pearce Report*, AGPS, Canberra, 1994, pp. 16–17.

19 Ibid., p. 17.

20 Faculty Board minutes, 24 October 1991.

alter the position and the faculty was faced with a large deficit for 1992. The result was that the undergraduate intake for 1992 was reduced from 450 to 350, vacant positions were frozen and tutorials were abandoned in most optional subjects and reduced from weekly to fortnightly in compulsory subjects.[21]

The failure of the university to honour its undertakings understandably made Bob Williams wary in his future dealings with the university administration. Richard Fox recalls Williams saying after this episode, 'I'm never going to tell them what I'm going to do; I'll tell them when I've done it.' Williams maintained this defensive attitude for the remainder of his deanship.

When the faculty embarked on its growth strategy, the need for more accommodation became urgent. Initially there was talk of a new building, with Williams telling the faculty board in 1990 that, 'A new building is planned for 1993; this is currently at the top of the University's priority list of major capital works.'[22] During 1991, however, doubts began to be expressed about this proposal, with increasing support for adding a new floor to the existing building – possibly somebody remembered that the original plans for the building had made allowance for an extra storey. By October 1991 it had been decided to proceed with the fourth floor of the law building. Construction began in August 1992 and proceeded rapidly, being completed on schedule in early 1993.

While Bob Williams was able to extract the required building funds from the university, the continually decreasing government funding per student weighed ever more heavily on the faculty. Although the figures are difficult to calculate, it appears that real funding per student halved between 1988 and 1998. The Melbourne law school was subject to many of the same pressures as Monash, but it was able to maintain its financial position, primarily by dramatically increasing its fee-paying postgraduate program. At Monash, however, the early lead in graduate education had faded and fee income fell to an insignificant level during the early 1990s.

The Howard government was elected in March 1996 and its first budget, brought down by Monash law graduate Peter Costello, slashed funding for tertiary education, leading to another heavy reduction for the Monash law school. However, the new government also introduced reforms offering potential for enterprising institutions to improve their financial situation. Most importantly, universities were allowed to enrol Australian students on

---

21 Ibid., 24 October 1991 and 27 April 1992.

22 Ibid., 22 Oct 1990.

a full-fee paying basis, provided they did not exceed twenty-five per cent of the number of government-supported students. Although some universities prevaricated, Monash was quick to approve the admission of fee paying local students, and the law school followed suit. In April 1997 Bob Williams told the faculty board, 'Every year this decade the Faculty has received less funding per student than the year before, and unless steps are taken to seek alternative funding, the quality of programs will be compromised.' Accepting full-fee paying students offered an escape from the funding cutbacks, particularly as the high demand for law degrees meant that there would be many well-qualified students willing to pay.[23]

The introduction of full-fee paying local students was a major factor in finally ending the long period of financial stringency that had overshadowed the deanships of both Bob Baxt and Bob Williams. Williams did not remain dean long enough to enjoy the change:

> As I approached the end of my second term as Dean the new Vice-Chancellor, David Robinson, made it clear that were I to seek a third term he would not be supportive. While David had his own agenda, I fairly quickly came to accept that his conclusion was correct. Within the University I was increasingly working with persons for whom I did not have [high] regard ... Within the Faculty I had adopted a management approach which was becoming increasingly unsustainable. There was none of the widespread delegations to associate deans that is now characteristic of this Faculty and others, and the administrative establishment was extremely lean. The result was that a vast amount of the day to day work was done by me personally, and after 10 years I was approaching exhaustion. Those closest to me were of the view that I had more than done my share for the Faculty. It was also the case that I had both professional and scholarly ambitions remaining that had to a considerable extent been placed on the back burner.[24]

Bob Williams' term as dean finished in April 1998. He left the law school vastly larger than a decade earlier and in a sound financial state. In contrast to the position a decade earlier, relations between the dean and the professoriate were harmonious and friendly, and there had been a high degree of generational renewal among the staff as the first of the original

23 Faculty Board minutes, 23 April 1997.

24 Williams, 'Some reflections on Monash', p. 18.

academics retired and others moved on. Around two-thirds of the academic staff in 1998 had been appointed by Williams.

However, there was a widespread feeling that the Monash law school had fallen behind Melbourne during the 1990s. Melbourne had been stung into action by the damning criticisms of the Pearce Report, while the praise Monash had received had perhaps led to complacency. Financial pressures had ended Monash's long advantage in staff:student ratio, as well as forcing the abandonment of faculty-run moot courts and greatly restricting tutorials. A cohort of outstanding academics left Monash in the early 1990s because they felt the law school was stagnating and there were better opportunities elsewhere.[25] Bob Williams' critics argue that the difficulties of his early years as dean led to him becoming entrenched in a mindset of fiscal conservatism, with the result that he did not take full advantage of the opportunities that presented themselves. It should not be forgotten, however, that he faced far greater challenges than any other dean, and his careful stewardship ensured his successor inherited a budget in better shape than for many years.

---

25 These included Terry Carney, Arie Freiberg, Ron McCallum and Peter Hanks.

Chapter 16

A New Paradigm of Teaching and Research

Throughout the first half of the 1980s the section on 'staff' in the university's annual report began: 'The recruitment of academic staff ... remained at the low level of recent years'. For those who had been at Monash through the 1960s and 1970s it proved difficult to adapt to the shock of the sudden change from rapid growth to steady state. The impact was starkly illustrated in the staff numbers in the law school. After more than doubling from twenty-five to fifty-two in the decade from 1968 to 1978, the number of staff at lecturer level or above actually fell to forty-six by 1987, before stabilising and then rising slowly during the 1990s, reaching fifty-four in 1997. However, the small increase in staff in no way matched the rapid rise in student numbers during the 1990s, leading to the loss of one of the law school's major advantages in its first two decades, its excellent staff:student ratio.

The era 1980–98 saw a major change in the culture of academia across Australia, which was inevitably reflected in the Monash law school. During what older academics still nostalgically look back on as the golden era of university life up to 1975, everybody taught, but research was treated as optional and administration was minimal. In the law school, to a greater extent than the rest of the university, there was also no need to have a higher degree. In 1980 only six of fifty staff members had PhDs, although twenty-seven had masters' degrees and three had Oxford BCLs. The Dawkins' reforms led to a greatly increased emphasis on research in the universities, together with a multiplication of the administration required of academics. Money was tied to research leading to greatly increased pressure to publish.

While the law school always had a solid core of committed researchers, for some academics research was peripheral, with publications intermittent at best. It was not an unusual pattern for a new staff member to have a flurry of publications in the early years after their appointment, only to fade away under the pressures of teaching and family commitments. Others threw all their energies into teaching and never developed a taste for research, while a fair number made full use of the time allowed for private practice. In 1980, thirty-one out of fifty academics published at least one book or article and this was fairly typical of the early 1980s. Over the four years 1980–83 inclusive, all but four of those on the staff for all that time published at least once. While this would be regarded as lamentably inadequate today, by the standards of the time, Monash ranked highly among Australian law schools for its research output.[1]

The first signs of the increased emphasis on research came (as with many other glimpses of the future) in the early years of Bob Baxt's deanship. In 1981, a research committee was set up with Richard Fox as the first chairman and in 1984 Fox became the first director of research. For the first time the faculty's researchers received some sort of organised support and encouragement for their work. Fox compiled a complete list of all the published research carried out in the faculty since its inception, the first in any Australian law school. He wrote a directory of sources of finance available to support research and during his term as director there was a substantial increase in research grants gained by law school staff. However, he had no illusions about the limits of his efforts: 'No Research Director can compel his or her academic colleagues to pursue research, or to apply for grants, or to spend them in a particular way or at a particular rate', he lamented.[2]

The second director of research, Terry Carney, was one of the first in the faculty to recognise the fundamental change that was occurring in the culture of academic research and came to the position with a personal passion to establish strategic policies and programs to foster research. While most of the younger academics responded well to his ideas, he found there was a degree of passive resistance from some among the middle and upper ranks. He felt that the faculty was beginning to lose the dynamism of its early years and that some academics were beginning to go through the motions, claiming that they were researching when they were not. Too much of the faculty's research output, he believed, consisted of the 'plumbing' type of textbook, few of which were truly scholarly. Attempts to define what is 'real' legal research, however, will always be fraught with difficulties.

---

1 Richard Fox, the chairman of the research committee, compiled statistics in 1982 that showed that in the years 1964 to 1981 the Faculty of Law ranked first in the university for the production of books and surprisingly highly in published articles and other research. Faculty Board minutes, 1 June 1982.

2 'Report of the Research Director July 1984–February 1986', Faculty Board minutes, 20 October 1986.

Marilyn Pittard has maintained the law school's tradtional strength in industrial law.
Photographer Richard Crompton, Monpix 836

By the early 1980s, the faculty had a settled and experienced professoriate able to provide academic leadership in most areas. After stepping down as dean in 1976, David Allan maintained a high level of research in international trade and investment law, commercial law and contract law. His interests overlapped to some extent with Peter Ellinger, who published most extensively in banking law, while also having an interest in legal philosophy. Bob Baxt was the driving force of the commercial law side of the faculty, remaining a prolific publisher even after he became dean. On the non-commercial side, Louis Waller, whose age was beginning to match his perpetual image as an elder statesman, and Bob Williams led the leading criminal law group in the country; Christie Weeramantry's interests ranged ever wider across the fields of legal philosophy, jurisprudence and human rights; and Enid Campbell continued to build on her already formidable reputation as one of Australia's leading constitutional and administrative lawyers.

Below the professorial level there was a solid core of productive researchers. Richard Fox and Arie Freiberg were outstanding in criminology, and Michael Pryles, CY Lee, Yuri Grbich, Colin O'Hare and Harry Reicher gave depth to the commercial, banking and taxation areas. Jim Lahore and Janice Luck were highly regarded in intellectual property, as was Ron McCallum in industrial law, where Marilyn Pittard also became an increasingly active publisher. Peter Hanks, Terry Carney and Jude Wallace continued their work on human rights and social justice issues and Hanks also published on constitutional law, where HP Lee made an increasing contribution following the completion of his PhD. International and comparative law were growing strengths of the faculty, with Harry Reicher, Michael Pryles, Malcolm Smith and Andrew Farran being the most active publishers, while Guy Powles was a committed researcher in his speciality of Pacific comparative law. Led by Henry Finlay, the family law group were solid publishers, with Dorothy Kovacs regularly publishing two articles a year and Neville Turner writing more than some of his colleagues recognised. In addition to family law, Turner wrote some memorable articles on law and literature that will last longer than most academic writing.[3] The faculty's most obvious area of weakness was in common law, where, apart from excursions into contract law by some of the commercial lawyers, only Francis Trindade and Peter Heffey were active researchers. Writing on torts, where the principles apply to all common law jurisdictions, Trindade was one of the few in the faculty to publish regularly in leading international journals. Legal history, legal philosophy and jurisprudence were largely ignored, except by Christie Weeramantry.

From the early years of the faculty, informal 'interest groups' were formed of staff members teaching and researching in related areas. In 1971 a committee on faculty government considered whether the faculty should be divided into departments. It recommended against this move but endorsed the formal establishment of the 'interest groups'. Consequently, early in 1972, David Allan set up interest groups in government law; criminal law, procedure and evidence; commercial law; industrial law; property; common

---

3 J N Turner, 'Teaching Law through Literature', *University of Queensland Law Review*, 1985; 'Celebrated, Cultivated but Underrated: W S Gilbert as a Legal Satirist', *University of Tasmania Law Review*, 1987; 'Dostoevesky: The Trial in the Brothers Karamazov', *University of Tasmania Law Review*, 1984.

law; taxation; family law; law and social sciences; and international, foreign and comparative law. The interest groups functioned into the 1990s, often lapsing into a comatose state but reviving during curriculum reviews or in the face of threats or challenges.[4]

The 'government' interest group remained one of the strongest in the faculty throughout this period, with Enid Campbell being generally recognised as the leading scholar in the faculty. As well as publishing a steady stream of clearly written, closely argued and highly influential articles on both constitutional and administrative law, in 1985 she was appointed to the Constitutional Commission (made up of eminent constitutional lawyers and retired politicians), which was set up to assess the constitution in the lead up to the bicentennial of British settlement. The same year she was also asked to join the Pearce committee, charged with investigating Australian law schools at the time of the Dawkins' reforms of higher education.

Until he left to go to the bar in 1993, Peter Hanks worked closely with Enid Campbell in teaching constitutional and administrative law and wrote widely on constitutional law, social security law and human rights. He was also editor of several of the more radical legal journals such as the *Legal Service Bulletin* and the *Social Security Reporter*. In 1982, Hanks and HP Lee received an Australian research award that led to several publications on national security and civil liberties in Australia. Lee also began to write prolifically on Australian and comparative constitutional law and courted controversy with his commentaries on the 'western' versus 'eastern' values debate and threats to the rule of law and the independence of the judiciary in Malaysia.[5]

The most influential new appointment in the government law area was Jeff Goldsworthy in 1984. Goldsworthy recalls that he was 'an argumentative kid and bound to be a lawyer'. He was educated at Adelaide, Illinois and Berkeley, where he completed a PhD on moral scepticism and legal reasoning. He rather blotted his copybook soon after his arrival at Monash by spilling both red wine and port on Baxt's cream carpet when the dean invited him to dinner. In the 1980s, Enid Campbell was the dominant figure in public and constitutional law, and Goldsworthy found her high standards somewhat intimidating, but he soon found that she was more comfortable working

---

4 See discussion of interest groups in the report of the curriculum review committee, Faculty Board minutes, 5 May 1980.

5 For example, 'A Fragile Bastion under Siege: The 1988 Convulsion in the Malaysian Judiciary', *Melbourne University Law Review*, 1989; 'Constitutional Values in Turbulent Asia', *Monash University Law Review*, 1997.

with men than with women, and that if she approved of your work she could be most helpful. In the 1980s and early 1990s much of Goldsworthy's research and writing was in legal philosophy, previously an area of weakness in the faculty, and he published on philosophical subjects in international journals, as well as writing on Australian constitutional law.[6] Since both legal philosophy and constitutional law concern the foundations of law, these interests neatly dovetailed. Goldsworthy has gone on to become Australia's leading constitutional theorist, his work on the history and philosophy of parliamentary sovereignty, and on constitutional interpretation, being influential throughout the common law world.

Another Adelaide graduate to join the staff in the mid-1980s was Susan Kneebone, who came as a senior tutor after a stint lecturing in Hong Kong. In her early years in the faculty she taught mainly administrative law, along with equity and trusts. One of her students thought that 'she seemed to worry a lot about her subject – she was chirpy, chatty and batty', but all students appreciated her well-structured lectures, sense of humour and successful Socratic teaching.[7] As one of the slowly growing number of staff members looking to gain a PhD, she found the faculty was not particularly accommodating of her studies. Bob Baxt was not in favour of women working part-time and she was not allowed to have study leave to work on her thesis. Nonetheless, she published regularly even while working on her thesis. She recalls that she and the other administrative law lecturers wanted to talk more about the philosophical ideas underpinning administrative law, but this met resistance from Enid Campbell, who was perhaps becoming rather set in her ways. In recent years Kneebone's research has focused increasingly on refugee law, migration law, human trafficking and forced migrations.

It was not until 1991 that another serious researcher in the government law area joined the staff. Bruce Dyer was a Monash Supreme Court Prize winner, who went to Cambridge on a Monash tutor's scholarship. His main area of teaching and research was in administrative law and in 1996 he published a highly regarded work, *Judicial Review of Administrative Action*, co-authored with Mark Aronson of UNSW (a member of the first cohort of Monash students). HP Lee recalls that the soft-spoken Dyer was 'highly respected for his principled stand on the various issues which arose in Faculty debates'. Student reviews always commented on his meticulously well-

---

6 For example, 'The Self-Destruction of Legal Positivism', *Oxford Journal of Legal Studies*, 1990; 'God or Mackie: The Dilemma of Secular Moral Philosophy', *American Journal of Jurisprudence*, 1985.

7 Interview with Paul Mishura, 2 July 2012; *Counter Faculty Handbook*, 1996, p. 37.

organised lectures as well as his enthusiastic lecturing style. One student commented that he 'covers about 20 miles around the lectern each lecture [and] also tends to bounce, leap, pirouette and shake that booty.'[8]

The criminal law, procedure and evidence interest group maintained its stellar reputation throughout this period and exercised a strong and direct influence on public policy. Particularly noteworthy was Louis Waller's secondment to serve as Victorian law reform commissioner from 1982 to 1986. During the 1970s and early 1980s, Waller worked closely with the first two law reform commissioners, Tom Smith and John Minogue, and headed the criminal law working group for several years before being appointed commissioner in 1982. Among many achievements during his period as commissioner were a review of the law of homicide and the sentences for murder, which led to the introduction of a maximum sentence as an alternative to the existing mandatory life sentence. Under Waller's leadership, the Law Reform Commission also began a complete review of sentencing policy and practice, leading to a raft of reforms in the late 1980s. In addition to his work on the Law Reform Commission, Louis Waller also chaired the Victorian government's committee on in vitro fertilisation, and this work led to the *Infertility (Medical Procedures) Act 1984* and significant amendments to the *Status of Children Act 1974*. This foreshadowed a growing interest in medicine and the law, which has been Waller's greatest research interest since the 1980s.

Richard Fox and Arie Freiberg formed a dynamic and productive partnership in research and teaching in criminal law and criminology, with their research collaboration continuing after Freiberg's appointment to a chair at Melbourne at the end of 1990. The majority of their work was policy driven and had a significant impact on law reform. One of their collaborative projects was on sentencing, leading to the publication of two highly influential articles and a definitive book on the subject.[9] In the late 1980s they conducted a review of maximum penalties on a taskforce headed by Frank Costigan QC, and were involved in developing the *Sentencing Act 1991*, which still forms the basis of the current law and was emulated by other states and territories. Fox and Freiberg advanced the idea of giving the

---

8 Minute of appreciation for Bruce Dyer, Faculty Board minutes, 28 July 2003; *Counter Faculty Handbook*, 1996, p. 15.

9 'Sentencing Structures and Sanction Hierarchies', *Criminal Law Journal*, vol 10, 1986; 'Sentences Without Conviction: From Status to Contract in Sentencing', *Criminal Law Journal*, vol. 13, 1989; *Sentencing: State and Federal Law in Victoria*, Oxford University Press, Melbourne, 1985.

courts a wider statutory discretion not to record a conviction when imposing a sentence in Victoria, arguing that a conviction is a permanent change in legal status and therefore a sanction in its own right.

While much of the work of Waller, Fox and Freiberg was policy oriented, Bob Williams continued to write solid black letter articles and books on criminal law and evidence. With Mark Weinberg he published in 1977 the leading text on theft offences, republished with substantial new text as *Property Offences* in 1986, and described by Louis Waller as 'still the most comprehensive work on this important segment of the substantive law'.[10] Williams was also the prime author of several editions of *Criminal Law Text and Cases* and in 1995 was the co-ordinating editor and contributing author for the criminal law volume of *Halsbury's Laws of Australia*. In addition to many highly regarded articles in leading journals, he planned and co-authored the leading students' text on evidence. Bob Williams also extended his research into the area of law and psychiatry, being a member of the Mental Health Review Board, and was heavily involved in public debate on the treatment of highly dangerous offenders.

The existing core of committed researchers in criminal law, procedure and evidence was supplemented in the 1980s and 1990s by some outstanding new arrivals. Sue McNicol had an unusual introduction to Monash. A Melbourne graduate, she went to Oxford to read for the BCL. All the students were allocated a numbered library seat and on taking a book from the shelves, they put a marker in the space with their seat number on it. One day a man came along scratching his head and looking for her seat, no. 405. He asked timidly, 'Have you got the Australian edition of *Cross on Evidence*?' It was Bob Williams, in Oxford on sabbatical. They began talking and Bob asked what she was going to do when she finished her BCL. Sue said she was going to return to Melbourne and Bob suggested that she apply for a position at Monash. This had never occurred to her, but she went ahead and applied. She was interviewed in London by a panel of three, who reported to Bob Baxt 'Whatever you want, she's it'.

McNicol was offered a lectureship and started at Monash at the beginning of 1983. She was advised by a member of her interview panel in London not to do a PhD but to write the leading text in her field. Consequently she published *The Law of Privilege* (1992) and, with Monash graduate Debbie Mortimer, *Evidence* (1996), both highly regarded. When McNicol was later

---

10 Louis Waller, 'Professor Bob Williams', *Monash University Law Review*, vol. 24, no. 1, 1998, p.2.

reading for the bar she was unavoidably late for a class on evidence and the lecturer berated her, wisely pointing out that she had no chance of being a successful barrister if she didn't know the law of evidence.

Another outstanding researcher in the areas of crime, procedure and evidence was Adelaide graduate Andrew Goldsmith, who came to Monash in 1987 after completing an LLM in London and an MA in criminology and an SJD in Toronto. His primary research interest was in policing, law enforcement and drug law policy and he published extensively in these areas, notably *Complaints Against the Police: The Trend to External Review* (1991), and (with C Lewis), *Civilian Oversight of Policing: Governance, Democracy and Human Rights* (2000).

An enthusiastic and popular lecturer, Goldsmith was promoted to associate professor in 1994, but left two years later for a chair at Flinders.

In the late 1980s and early 1990s, three Monash graduates, Bronwyn Naylor, Jonathon Clough and Andrew Palmer, with primary teaching and research interests in criminal law, all returned to the faculty after experiencing the real world in a variety of ways. They were joined in 1993 by Melbourne graduate Bernadette McSherry, who has become Australia's most influential researcher on mental health and the law. While the longevity of the mainstays of criminal law and criminology has been remarkable, the new cohort ensured the law school's continued strength in these areas after the departure of Arie Freiberg to a chair at Melbourne at the end of 1991 and, in the following decade, the retirements of Louis Waller and Richard Fox (though both are still involved in teaching at the time of writing).

In contrast to the continued strength in criminal law, procedure and evidence, most areas of commercial law experienced periods of weakness during the 1980s and 1990s, although they partially recovered following intensive recruiting efforts. Teaching and research in taxation law was particularly problematic as it proved increasingly difficult to restrain talented staff from succumbing to the temptations of private practice or accepting promotions to positions in rival law schools. Of the three mainstays of taxation in the 1970s, Yuri Grbich moved to a chair at UNSW in 1984, Kevin Pose left for full-time practice at the bar and Harry Reicher both had a busy practice at the bar and increasingly preferred to teach and research in international law rather than taxation. In 1995 he accepted a position at the University of Pennsylvania, where he has taught primarily in the field of international human rights law as well as pioneering the new field of Holocaust law.

The largest burden of tax teaching from 1984 until 1993 fell on the shoulders of Canadian Rick Krever. A graduate of Osgoode Hall with an LLM from Harvard, the lively and enthusiastic Krever had much in common with Yuri Grbich in both personality and ideology. Like Grbich he approached the tax system with the fervour of a reformer rather than as a barrister fighting the ATO, and in his early papers written at Monash he analysed the tax avoidance boom of the 1970s and put forward proposals for root and branch reform of the tax system.[11] It is perhaps not surprising that Bob Baxt remembers Krever as 'a very, very unusual tax lawyer'. Krever was also one of the first members of the faculty to become computer literate and used to give classes on using PCs. He was promoted rapidly to associate professor, but left in 1993 for a chair at Deakin.

Krever's career in the faculty closely paralleled that of Jeff Waincymer, a Melbourne graduate who joined the staff at Monash in 1983. Although his primary interests were in international trade law and commercial arbitration, Waincymer also taught and published on taxation law. Among his publications before he, like Krever, departed to take up a foundation chair at Deakin law school, was the definitive *Australian Income Tax: Principles and Policy* (Butterworths, 1991). Students appreciated his sense of humour and the fact that he 'doesn't take himself too seriously', though some complained about his 'ghastly habit of setting difficult exam problems'.[12]

Aware of looming problems in maintaining the faculty's expertise in taxation, Bob Baxt looked to groom a promising young Monash graduate, Tony Pagone, to help fill the gap. Encouraged by his interest in politics and Enid Campbell's inspiring teaching, Pagone's main interest lay in constitutional and administrative law, although as an undergraduate he had also been impressed with Yuri Grbich's teaching of tax, which emphasised the political dimensions of taxation law. Pagone tutored in constitutional and administrative law in 1982 and then went to Cambridge on a tutor's scholarship. By this time he was thinking of an academic career and, although he had initially preferred political science to law, he was coming to see law as applied political science (and also realised there were more jobs in law), so on his return from Cambridge he successfully applied for a lectureship in the faculty. The faculty needed a tax lawyer, but Pagone felt he did not have sufficient expertise, so Baxt arranged for him to read at the bar with

---

11 For example, Rick Krever, 'Avoidance, Evasion and Reform: Who Dismantled and Who's Rebuilding the Australian Income Tax System?', *UNSW Law Journal*, vol. 10, no. 2, 1987.

12 *Counter Faculty Handbook*, 1986, p. 54, and 1989, p. 73.

Tony Pagone lectured in tax law before going to the Bar.
Photographer Richard Crompton, Monpix 826

Allan Myers, then the junior with the largest tax practice at the Melbourne bar. Myers had far more work than he could do so he passed work on to Pagone from the start. After he had some early successes, the Commissioner of Taxation started briefing him and he found the work both exciting and rewarding. When he completed his year reading with Allan Myers he had to decide between teaching and practice, and, after some soul-searching, practice won. Although he kept teaching part-time at Monash and later at Melbourne, his main career from this time onward was at the bar. Pagone was appointed to the Supreme Court in 2001, but in the following year was offered a specially created position as special counsel to the Commissioner of Taxation, which he held until 2003. He was reappointed to the Supreme Court in 2007 and in 2013 he moved to the Federal Court.

Tim Pinos had an early interest in computing and legal education.
Photographer Tony Miller, Monpix 846

During the 1980s several other lecturers were appointed with the hope they would fill the void in tax teaching, including Kathleen Lahey, David Payes and Razeen Sappideen, but none stayed for long. There were regular crises and throughout the 1980s and early 1990s it was a struggle to put adequately qualified teachers in front of the taxation classes.[13]

The problems with taxation were only the most obvious signs of a general decline in the faculty's strength in commercial law from about the mid-1980s. This was increasingly serious as the economic boom of the 1980s led to a growing demand from the profession for well-trained commercial lawyers. This obviously led to both a growing demand for education in

13 For example, Faculty Board minutes, 24 July 1991.

commercial law and an increase in the rewards for private practice, so that it became increasingly difficult to retain academic commercial lawyers.

Of the strong commercial group of the early 1980s, not one remained in 1988. In October 1986 Bob Baxt reported that the rash of departures 'would gravely affect the Faculty's capacity to teach in the areas of Banking and Commercial Law' and he was endeavouring to fill the professorial vacancies left by Ellinger and Allan.[14] However, this was easier said than done due to financial constraints and a shortage of quality academic commercial lawyers; the chairs were eventually filled by the decidedly non-commercial Francis Trindade and Bob Williams. It was not until the early 2000s that the faculty again had three commercially oriented professors and even at a junior level, strength was only slowly rebuilt.

During the 1980s many early career lecturers were recruited in the commercial law area, including Tim Pinos, Paul von Nessen, Phillip Clarke, Sally Sievers and Mark Sneddon. All made useful contributions, but none stayed for long enough to fill the increasing void in senior staff in the commercial area. Tim Pinos is particularly remembered for his early interest in computing and legal education. Bob Baxt recalled that he was the first lecturer in the law school to perceive the possibilities of the internet at a time when few people had even heard of it.

The obvious weakness in commercial law at Monash in the late 1980s and much of the 1990s is sometimes ascribed to Bob Williams' lack of interest in the area. In fact, the decline was evident before he became dean and was exacerbated by the departure of Bob Baxt, Australia's foremost scholar in the field. Williams was well aware of the faculty's deficiency in commercial law and worked hard to overcome it. The problem was simply a dearth of academic commercial lawyers. Nonetheless, the situation, particularly in taxation and banking, was critical and increasingly law students with a commercial orientation took commercial law subjects in the Faculty of Economics and Business.

The situation was somewhat relieved in 1990 and 1991 when the commercial law strength of the law school received its greatest boost since the arrival of Bob Baxt. The greatest coup was the recruitment of Tony Duggan, who came from Melbourne to fill the Henry Bournes Higgins Chair in 1990. A Melbourne graduate with a masters' degree from Osgoode Hall, Duggan was a highly regarded teacher and researcher with a growing

---

14 Ibid., 20 October 1986.

Wickrema Weerasooria added his expertise in banking law to the school in 1990.
Photographer Scott Fitzpatrick, Monpix 845

international reputation, particularly in the fields of consumer credit and consumer protection.

In the same year, two more Melbourne graduates, John Duns and John Glover, were recruited to add strength to the commercial law area. Softly spoken and modest, Duns has taught and published over the fields of insolvency, competition and corporate law, and has written standard texts on corporate law, competition law, insolvency and bankruptcy. John Glover's main teaching areas were equity and trusts, and he also taught in the areas of commercial fraud, taxation and insolvency. He was widely admired by students for his 'thoroughness, clarity and his off-beat brand of humour.'[15] A productive researcher, Glover was a co-author of Ford & Lee's *Principles of the Law of Trusts*, and author of the monographs *Equity, Restitution & Fraud* and *Commercial Equity: Fiduciary Relationships*. He left for a chair at RMIT in 2009.

Also in 1990, Wickrema Weerasooria, after his excursion into Sri Lankan politics and a period as Sri Lankan High Commissioner to Australia, returned to the faculty, bringing much needed expertise in banking law. He became the first director of the Banking Law Centre set up in 1998.

The commercial law group was further strengthened as Bruce Dyer responded to market forces by largely abandoning his early interest in administrative law in favour of commercial law. However, Dyer apparently never envisaged a permanent career in academia, famously responding to the question on a staff assessment, 'Where do you see yourself in five years?' with the pointed answer, 'Not here'. It was not a surprise when he left to work at Blake Dawson Waldron in 2000.

The final commercial law appointment of 1990–91 aroused controversy because the appointee, while undoubtedly distinguished, was first and foremost an intellectual property specialist rather than a company lawyer. In April 1990, Bob Williams presented a plan to establish a chair in company law, with about half the costs to be met by seven large law firms and the remainder by the faculty. 'Company Law is a major area of teaching and research ... and a field of crucial and growing importance', he argued, assuring the donors that a chair would 'help ensure that the Faculty's scholarly reputation continues to be maintained and enhanced'.[16] Named for High Court Justice Sir Keith Aickin, the chair was advertised in mid-1990, but it proved impossible to attract applicants of the desired calibre. Eventually, with the fear that the worsening economic downturn might lead the large law firms to withdraw their funding, the selection committee invited Sam Ricketson to apply. The son of famous stockbroker Staniforth Ricketson of JB Were, Ricketson was a reader at Melbourne and as an internationally recognised expert in intellectual property was clearly ready for a professorial appointment. But he was not a company lawyer. When he accepted the chair, 'Ricketson undertook an obligation to develop an expertise in Company Law, to participate in the teaching of Company Law on a regular basis and to provide overall direction and academic leadership in

---

15 *Counter Faculty Handbook*, 1994, p. 52.

16 Faculty Board minutes, 5 April 1990.

relation to curriculum development and the mentoring of younger members of staff in the field'.[17] At Monash he continued his outstanding work in intellectual property, maintaining the law school's eminence in that field, and contributing in many other ways to the faculty. Students enjoyed both his erudition and his deadpan sense of humour – one student recounted that in one lecture 'in the middle of delineating the capacity required of partners, the legal age threshold of Hobbits [33 years] was slipped in, and left to make its own way in the world'.[18] However, the anomaly of a non-company lawyer holding the chair in company law remained, and in 1996 the designation was formally altered to 'commercial law' on the grounds that 'It would seem appropriate that the description of the Chair should be sufficiently wide to cover the major scholarly interest of its holder'.[19]

After the burst of commercial law recruitment in 1990 and 1991, there was a distinct slowing, with only two significant appointments in the remaining years of Bob Williams' deanship. It is noteworthy that in an area traditionally dominated by men, the two new commercial lawyers were both women, Elizabeth Lanyon and Jacqui Lipton. Whereas many commercial lawyers were unable to resist the rewards of private practice, Elizabeth Lanyon had enjoyed those rewards as a partner at Corrs before retiring from the partnership when she had her second child. After coming to Monash, she taught undergraduate courses in equity and trusts, started a new postgraduate unit in the rapidly growing area of superannuation and also pushed through the establishment of the Master of the Digital Economy degree. Her main area of work at Corrs had been in consumer credit and she continued her research in this field at Monash, culminating in the publication in 2001 of the authoritative text *Consumer Credit Law*, jointly authored with Tony Duggan. She was greatly liked by students and not just for her habit of handing out Easter eggs.

In 1996 Jacqui Lipton, like Elizabeth Lanyon a Melbourne graduate, was recruited to bolster the faculty's teaching and research in banking law. A productive researcher, Lipton briefly followed Wickrema Weerasooria as director of the Banking Law Centre, before leaving in 2001 for a chair at Case Western Reserve University in Cleveland, Ohio.

The early 1980s was a high point for intellectual property at Monash, with Jim Lahore, Janice Luck and Ann Dufty all enjoying accolades for

---

17 Ibid., 24 April 1996.

18 *Counter Faculty Handbook*, 1994, p. 62.

19 Faculty Board minutes, 24 April 1996.

Left: Ann Dufty taught intellectual property in the 1980s.
Photographer Richard Crompton, Monpix 848

Bottom: Ron McCallum, Arie Freiberg, Hisao Ishikawa, Malcolm Smith and Bob Baxt, 1981.
Photographer Richard Crompton, Monpix 834

their teaching and research in that area. This was recognised in 1982 when the Industrial Property Advisory Committee asked the faculty to carry out a large part of the research needed for a review of patent law.[20] However, in the general malaise of commercial law in the late 1980s, even intellectual property suffered a decline following the departures of Jim Lahore in 1980, Ann Dufty in 1984 and Janice Luck in 1987. Consequently, the recruitment of Sam Ricketson, while controversial as a company law appointment, was central to restoring the law school's pre-eminence in intellectual property. An internationally renowned scholar himself, he also attracted and mentored a cohort of young academics, including Mark Davison and Ann Monotti, who have gone on to become leaders in the field.

Industrial law has always been another strength for the Monash Law School, with Harry Glasbeek, Ron McCallum and Marilyn Pittard all being in the forefront of academic researchers in the field. The legal framework of industrial relations has undergone enormous changes since the 1980s and consequently it has been a challenging area to teach and a fertile area of research. The undergraduate subjects have been the subject of constant development and revision, and there is now a workplace and employment law specialisation at masters level. The LLM unit Electronic Workplace Law, developed by Marilyn Pittard, explores the legal developments and implications of the technological revolution in the workplace and it is still the only unit of its type in any Australian university. Pittard has written extensively on the transformative changes in industrial relations law, as well as on specific areas such as unfair dismissal laws, public service employment, sanctions on industrial relations and the legal framework for home-based work.

During the 1970s the young radicals helped the law school build up a reputation for teaching and research in the broad areas of human rights and social justice. Like commercial law, these areas faced great challenges in the 1980s, though for very different reasons. While commercial law struggled through the inability to recruit and retain sufficient high-calibre staff in a time of rising demand for its offerings, courses related to human rights and social justice were becoming less attractive to the increasingly conservative student body. Peter Hanks and Terry Carney taught Poverty and Social Security Law – the most radical of the new courses of the early 1970s – with good numbers for about ten years, but student interest steadily fell during the 1980s and the subject was taught for the last time in 1990.

---

20 Faculty Board minutes, 5 April 1982.

In spite of the decline in student interest, the academic interest in human rights and social justice issues not only survived, but was reinforced during the 1980s with powerful new voices emerging and highly influential research being published. The ranks of the original radicals of the 1970s had been thinned through the death of Elizabeth Eggleston and the departure of Bryan Keon-Cohen, but Jude Wallace, Terry Carney and Peter Hanks continued to bring a radical perspective to their teaching and research.

Before her departure in 1986 to become a full-time commissioner of the Law Reform Commission, Jude Wallace taught property from her left-wing perspective and maintained her campaign for the reform of Victoria's tenancy laws. She also published several articles critical of traditional legal philosophy and, with Tony Pagone, wrote an influential book *Rights and Freedoms in Australia*.[21]

Terry Carney was a member of a committee of inquiry into the Guardianship Board, which developed a new model that was the basis of legislation in Victoria in 1986, quickly followed by other states and territories. This led to him working with ethicist Peter Singer on a study for the Australian Human Rights Commission on adult guardianship, which resulted in a highly cited monograph *Ethical and Legal Issues in Guardianship: Options for Intellectually Disadvantaged People*, published in 1986. Between 1982 and 1984 Carney also headed a government inquiry into children and the law which both led to substantial reforms of the juvenile justice system and inspired his teaching. It led to the establishment of a course on juvenile justice which he taught with Henry Finlay, who also had an interest in children and the law. Another of Carney's interests was drug law reform, which was the subject of his PhD thesis, and he published several articles and a book on this issue, though without, as yet, the same impact on government policy as his work on juvenile justice and guardianship.

Terry Carney's departure for a chair at Sydney in 1991, and Peter Hanks' decision to go to the bar soon after, marked the final break-up of the radical group of the 1970s, but the commitment to human rights and social justice was carried on by a new cohort of academics. Prominent among them was Greta Bird, who carried out pioneering research on the related themes of

---

21 Jude Wallace and Tony Pagone, *Rights and Freedoms in Australia*, Federation Press, Sydney, 1990; J Wallace and J Fiocco, 'Recent Criticisms of Formalism in Legal Theory and Legal Education', *Adelaide Law Review*, 1980; J Wallace and Y Grbich, 'A Judge's Guide to Legal Change in Property: Mere Equities Critically Examined', *UNSW Law Journal*, 1979.

Greta Bird talking to Justic Gobbo at the launch of her book, *The Process of Law in Australia*, in 1988.
Photographer John Clark, Monpix 813

Aboriginal land rights and law and multiculturalism.[22] Together with Sue Campbell and several others in the mid-1980s she carried out a ground-breaking project on developing a multicultural law curriculum, although the realities of implementing the project's recommendations proved daunting. In 1988 she became the inaugural director of the National Centre for Crosscultural Studies in Law, a role she retained after moving to Southern Cross University in 1992.

---

22 For example, Greta Bird and P. O'Malley, 'Koori Cultural Heritage: Reclaiming the Past?', *Social Justice*, 1989; Greta Bird, *Law in a multicultural Australia*, National Centre for Crosscultural Studies in Law, 1991; Greta Bird, *Ivory Scales: Black Australia and the Law*, UNSW Press, 1987; Greta Bird, 'Race, Ethnicity, Class and Gender: Integral Issues for a Law Curriculum?' *Crosscultural Communication and Professional Education*, 1990; G Bird, S Campbell, M Barbaryannis, H Smith, 'Preparing Lawyers for a Multi-Cultural Society', *Journal of Professional Legal Education*, 1986.

Another prominent advocate for human rights and social justice in this period was the law school's first African lecturer, Sam Murumba. Born and educated in Uganda, Murumba came to Monash in the late 1970s where he completed an LLM and a PhD under the supervision of Christie Weeramantry. His main interests were in intellectual property and international human rights, and he was a popular lecturer until he moved to Brooklyn Law School in New York in 1992.

Although the Monash law school was always a relatively welcoming place for women, there was clearly a glass ceiling. After the pioneering appointment of Enid Campbell in 1967, no woman was appointed to a chair for nearly a quarter of a century and only a handful even made associate professor level. However, the period of 1980–98 saw a transformation in the structure of the staff and large steps taken towards greater equality of the sexes. Whereas in 1979, there were only seventeen women in a staff of sixty-two and nine of those were tutors, by 1997 over half the staff were women (thirty-four out of sixty-five) and five out of nine associate professors were women. Until 1991, Enid Campbell was the only female professor and, for all her many strengths, she did little to ease the paths of younger female academics. She had made it in a man's world and saw no reason why other women should not do the same. She viewed with disdain the rise of a more radically feminist group in the late 1980s and early 1990s. However, not even the disdain of the formidable Enid slowed the development of a critical feminist approach to the law among a growing group within the faculty.

The most prominent academics to bring an overtly feminist orientation to their work were Beth Gaze and Marcia Neave. After completing a double degree in law and science at Monash, Gaze went to Berkeley on a Monash tutor's scholarship before returning to a lectureship in 1987. Strongly committed to equality of gender, race and access to health care, her work greatly influenced not only the faculty, but the university. Her scientific background encouraged her to pioneer teaching in several cross-disciplinary areas such as bioethics and the teaching of legal issues in the medical faculty, and she also taught multidisciplinary courses on feminist legal studies. Gaze's courses on civil liberties and discrimination attracted large enrolments and her textbook *Law, Liberty and Australian Democracy* written with Melinda Jones was widely used across Australia. In addition to anti-discrimination law and feminist legal thought, she wrote on topics as diverse as copyright protection of computer programs, law and medicine, and the development of the law relating to privacy. She moved to the University of Melbourne in 2005.

The recruitment of Marcia Neave in 1991 was a great coup for Monash. One of Australia's leading legal academics, Neave had been one of Louis Waller's 'star pupils' in his last days at Melbourne, where she won the Supreme Court Prize in 1965. When interviewed for articles, she was always asked if she could type and she decided not to learn because she realised that if she could she would end up doing secretarial duties. After she completed her articles, Zelman Cowen asked her to come back to Melbourne to tutor and this led her into an academic career. In the early 1970s she encountered much hostility when she wanted to set up a social security law course at Melbourne and after speaking about it with Terry Carney and Peter Hanks she could see that at Monash there was much more openness about doing things in different ways.

After working with the New South Wales Law Reform Commission in 1982–83 and heading a Victorian government inquiry into prostitution, in 1986 Neave became Australia's third female law professor when she moved to Adelaide as professor and dean. When she wanted to return to live in Melbourne, Bob Williams encouraged her to apply for a chair at Monash and she received the first personal chair in the law school early in 1991.

Most of Neave's early publications were doctrinal black letter law and this gave her credibility in the eyes of the Melbourne law school hierarchy. However, she gradually became less interested in how the law was written than in how it affected people's lives. By the time she came to Monash, her interests ranged widely across property law, family law, human rights, law reform and gender and the law. Few legal academics have published in a wider range of journals and her work had a direct impact on public policy in many areas. At Monash she quickly became a highly respected and admired leader. Most would have been happy for her to succeed Bob Williams as dean, but she did not see her future as being in administration and in 2000 she left to take up the chair of the Victorian Law Reform Commission, before being appointed to the Court of Appeal in 2006.

In the last twenty years there has been a growing interest in international human rights law and Monash has been in the forefront in this area particularly through the work of the Castan Centre for Human Rights Law. The pioneering voice in this field in the faculty was Christie Weeramantry, who, after arriving at Monash as a teacher of contract law, during the 1970s and 1980s wrote several pioneering books in the broad field of international human rights. His interest in this area played a large part in his appointment to the International Court of Justice in 1990, a unique achievement for an academic from an Australian law school.[23] Most judges have come from large and wealthy countries and his appointment was testimony to his scholarship and international reputation, as well as his astute lobbying. Following his departure, the faculty's strength in the field of international human rights waned for several years before the appointments of Sarah Joseph, Alison Duxbury, Julie Debeljak, Jenny Schultz and Melissa Castan in the mid-1990s.

The more general field of international law remained a strength throughout this period. During the 1980s Jeff Waincymer and Harry Reicher increasingly preferred to teach and research in international law rather than taxation and, following their departures in the early 1990s, new recruits Martin Davies and Richard Garnett maintained the faculty's reputation in this area. Davies was a popular lecturer whose main field of research was maritime law. In 1990 he published *Shipping Law*, which soon came to be regarded as the leading text in the field. He moved to a chair at Melbourne in 1995. Richard Garnett came to Monash in 1994 with an LLM from Harvard and experience in commercial litigation and arbitration with Linklaters in London. His major research interests were in the areas of conflict of laws and international dispute resolution. Remembered as an 'engaging and energetic' lecturer, Garnett followed Martin Davies to Melbourne in 2000.[24]

After the departures of David Jackson in 1970 and Stanley Robinson in 1979, the faculty's property law specialists, notably Gim Teh and Jude Wallace, tended to approach the subject from a radical perspective. This was largely maintained when a new generation of property law academics joined the faculty in the 1980s and early 1990s, notably Marcia Neave, Joycey Tooher and Pam O'Connor. Marcia Neave always went back to the basics and discussed the origins and ethics of private property ownership, and the arguments for and against private property. The statement 'Property is theft' left many conservative law students perplexed, though some were able to jump outside the paradigms and discuss the philosophical issues. Radical ideological underpinnings, however, did not preclude these academics publishing black letter research on issues in property law.

Rapid changes in society, the economy and technology have been responsible for the growth of many new areas of legal research and Monash

---

23 Sir Percy Spender was the only other Australian appointment to the International Court of Justice.

24 *Counter Faculty Handbook*, 1996, p. 49.

academics have been at the forefront in many of them. Notable in this respect during the era 1980–98 were Louis Waller's work on in vitro fertilisation, Moira Paterson's research on freedom of information and privacy and Sharon Rodrick's pioneering articles on the law and new forms of media. Tim Pinos, Rick Krever, Mark Davison, Melissa de Zwart and Beth Gaze were among early researchers on aspects of the legal implications of computers and the internet.

The deanships of Bob Baxt and Bob Williams lasted a total of eighteen years and saw dramatic changes in academic life with new demands in terms of accountability, administration, and perhaps most of all in research. Symbolic of the changes in the eyes of many Monash law academics was the gradual demise of the faculty traditions of morning and afternoon tea, which had been a wonderful stimulus for collegiality and conviviality. When Bronwyn Naylor first joined the staff in 1989, almost everybody still went to morning tea. At that time there was a long table with seats all around it in the staff room and 'you came in and sat down and talked to whoever was there'. She found it particularly comforting to find other junior staff members with similar problems and concerns and it was a wonderful forum for getting ideas. The afternoon tea ritual was the first to fade away, with numbers declining until only Enid Campbell regularly attended, and then, as the pressures of research and administration grew, numbers began falling for morning tea until it too disappeared, in spite of occasional attempts to revive it.

A major change for the senior staff was the introduction of salary packaging in the early 1990s. At a lunch to welcome Sam Ricketson in December 1991, the suggestion was made that professors with higher doctorates should be provided with cars as part of their packages. Richard Fox followed this up and reported to the other professors, 'I have dealt directly with the Vice-Chancellor who has authorised me to say that he is willing to approve of cars being made available to professors on a smaller scale than previously requested'. The professors excitedly took delivery of their vehicles only to find they were Matchbox models. Sam Ricketson immediately demanded that his vehicle be exchanged for 'a black Porsche (full-size)' and Tony Duggan wrote to Richard Fox, 'This is to acknowledge delivery of my vehicle … I note that the vehicle is a Mercedes and I assume that you intend to proceed with your plan to abolish the graduate program in order to pay for it … My secretary will shortly be in touch with yours concerning arrangements for payment of my petrol and vehicle maintenance allowances'. He was somewhat perturbed when an oily rag arrived in the internal mail with the note that it was his fuel allowance for the next five years, while Ricketson was warned of the dangers to the structural integrity of the law building if he persisted in parking his vehicle in his office. The most scathing memorandum was reserved for Enid Campbell, who received this missive, purportedly signed by the vice-chancellor:

> I am very disappointed at your inability to handle your responsibilities. What is the point of making an allowance of a special vehicle to professors holding Higher Doctorates, when they cannot even find the key? I have also given instruction that vehicles allocated to professors are not to be parked in their rooms. Please remove yours. I would have expected something better from a Senior Professor of the University.[25]

---

25 Our thanks to Richard Fox who has retained copies of these intriguing exchanges.

Chapter 17

'The Faculty's First Obligation Is to Prepare Students for the Practice of the Law'

Curriculum and Teaching, 1980–98

Curriculum

Andrew Goldsmith, who taught at Monash from 1987 to 1996, had a deep interest in the philosophy of legal education. Highly critical of the direction legal education was taking in the 1980s and 1990s, he published several articles pleading for Pericles against what he saw as an overwhelming tide of plumbing vocationalism. Goldsmith lamented that 'the trend to mass university education has been linked to the increased emphasis given to vocational and professional higher education by government and the marketplace' and pointed out that 'inevitably the value of liberal-arts style higher education is diminished by this shift, as it does not obviously translate into market-related competencies or employment prospects'.[1] He called for a debate on

> such crucial questions as the mission of the law school within the university (the academic legal degree and legal scholarship), the distinction between an academic legal education and practical training (vocationalism), the compatibility of an academic education with preparation for professional practice (professionalism), and the contribution of legal scholarship to the profession (practice-related

1 Andrew Goldsmith, 'Standing at the Crossroads: Law Schools, Universities, Markets and the Future of Legal Scholarship' in Fiona Cownie (ed.), *The Law School – Global Issues, Local Questions*, Ashgate, Brookfield, 1999, p. 68. See also A Goldsmith, 'Heroes or Technicians? The Moral Capacities of Tomorrow's Lawyers', *Journal of Professional Legal Education*, 1996, and C Parker and A Goldsmith, 'Failed Sociologists in the Market Place: Law Schools in Australia', *Journal of Law and Society*, 1998.

> research), the wider community (law reform), and the economy (competitiveness).'[2]

This call was received with approving nods in the staff room, but in an era of financial stringency and high unemployment, the debate was muted at best. Students demanded training that would get them jobs and it would have been remarkable if the law school had resisted this pressure and insisted that its role was to provide a broad liberal education. Responding to market pressures, Bob Williams made it clear in 1990 that 'The Faculty's first obligation is to prepare students for the practice of the law'.[3]

The primary theme in the changes to both undergraduate and postgraduate curriculum and teaching in the period 1980–98 was that the elements that had differentiated Monash from other law schools (and Melbourne in particular) were gradually lost. By 1998, the clinical program was the only remaining significant point of difference, with the advantages of a better staff:student ratio and the reputation for being new and exciting gradually fading away. As the universities entered into a new era of competition, the most important selling points became 'outputs' such as the number of graduates getting articles with the large firms, while 'inputs' such as teaching quality became motherhood statements rather than real contrasts between the law schools.

The other element making for uniformity in legal education was the ever-present straitjacket imposed by the subjects required for admission to practice. The rules meant that theoretically optional subjects such as Civil Procedure, Evidence and Company Law became quasi-compulsory because a large majority of students understandably preferred to take them as part of their LLB rather than as extras before admission. Consequently, there was no real flexibility in the structure of the law course and little scope to experiment with the curriculum.

During the early 1980s, the faculty successfully implemented most of the recommendations of the curriculum review of 1978–79 and the revised undergraduate course structure remained in place throughout the 1980s. One of the few challenges to the structure came, perhaps surprisingly, from the dean, Bob Baxt. In February 1984 he wrote to Enid Campbell, who was chair of the faculty's curriculum and legislation committee, arguing that both jurisprudence and legal history should be made compulsory undergraduate

---

2 Goldsmith, 'Standing at the Crossroads', p. 63.

3 Quoted in Cathy Laird, 'Legal Education: Theory or Practice?', *Law Institute Journal*, November 1996, p. 7.

subjects. He asked that the committee consider this proposal and suggest ways to implement it.[4] While one would have thought that Enid Campbell would have been fully in agreement with this suggestion, it appears to have disappeared without trace. Enrolments in jurisprudence remained, in Baxt's words 'shamefully small', and legal history was rarely taught.

The following year a list was compiled of optional subjects that were rarely offered or attracted only tiny enrolments, with a view to disestablishing some of them. High on the list was Roman Law, but Christie Weeramantry launched a Quixotic campaign to retain it on the grounds that 'its retention added prestige to the Law curriculum and prevented narrowness'. Enid Campbell pointed out that 'the subject had never been offered and it was a misrepresentation to retain it in the range of available options', but the faculty agreed to retain it when Weeramantry 'expressed readiness to teach it at the first available opportunity'. However, it was offered only once and was disestablished in 1992.

During the 1980s Monash offered the largest number of electives of any Australian law school. However, only a handful of new optional undergraduate subjects were added as increasing financial stringency forced the faculty to husband its resources, and the decision was made to concentrate on the graduate program. One of the most popular new options was Trial Practice and Advocacy, introduced on the initiative of Tim Pinos, who correctly anticipated 'overwhelming student demand'. Another option that was more popular than might have been expected was Law and Social Theory, introduced by Andrew Goldsmith in 1988. This was the first attempt to introduce into the curriculum a study of the theoretical critiques of the law that had been made in the 1960s and 1970s, offering students the opportunity to look at such things as Marxist approaches to the law and the critical legal studies movement. These had implicitly formed part of the curriculum in such subjects as Poverty and Social Security Law, but this was the first time they were considered from a theoretical point of view.[5]

While the compulsory core remained essentially untouched following the failed attempt to replace Torts and Contracts with a single common law subject, some major innovations were made to the teaching of Legal Process. In the mid-1980s Greta Bird carried out a research project on the introduction of a multicultural perspective into the law curriculum and her report led to an attempt 'to incorporate in Legal Process materials which

4 Bob Baxt to Enid Campbell, 23 February 1984, Faculty Board minutes, 28 March 1984.

5 See Law and Social Theory course description, Faculty Board minutes, 26 October 1987.

exposed students to the needs of the Aboriginal communities'.[6] In fact, the concept was broader than this, with students being introduced to Indigenous concepts of law in a way designed to make them question the assumption that law began with British colonisation in 1788. Richard Fox recalls that some students resisted the teaching of Indigenous law 'because they saw no relevance to making money in the city'. One method used by Joycey Tooher and others to circumvent this objection was to set a moot court problem for students based on Aboriginal issues and force the recalcitrant students to defend Aboriginal clients as a way of opening their eyes to the issues.

The Monash law course fared well in the 1987 Pearce Report. Both the curriculum and teaching were highly rated and suggested changes were in the nature of fine tuning rather than root and branch reform. The report did, however, suggest there were gaps in the curriculum in the areas of theoretical dimensions of the law, legislation, remedies, drafting, interpersonal skills, negotiation and mediation and computerised legal research.[7] Subsequently, Bob Baxt asked the curriculum and legislation committee chaired by Peter Hanks to look at these and other areas that the report suggested required attention, and also to begin preparations for a full-scale curriculum review. Hanks was less sanguine about the state of the curriculum than the Pearce committee, pointing to the '"unbalanced" legal education received by the bulk of our students', and what he saw as serious gaps in the curriculum.[8] Going back to basics, Hanks attempted to articulate the aims of a law school education:

> What are the educational aims of the Faculty? Two broad goals compete for endorsement – the humane, liberal or critical goal which many would identify with university learning; and the technocratic, work or skills-oriented goal. There is a considerable variety in the expression of each of these goals; when articulating the first goal, some would emphasise interdisciplinary factors, others would stress the cultivation of a legal perspective; and the second goal can be expressed so as to stress either the immediate demands of solicitor-employers or the demands of economic planners. The reconciliation of these goals is both difficult and continuous.[9]

---

6 Faculty Board minutes, 3 April 1986.

7 'Proposal for Review of the Curriculum', Faculty Board minutes, 26 October 1987.

8 Ibid.

9 'A Discussion Paper on Review Outcomes', Faculty Board minutes, 6 April 1988.

Hanks then considered the possibility of approaching the question of educational aims by considering the competing interests served by the faculty ('stakeholders' in modern jargon). Academics would generally choose to teach in their areas of research and would perhaps accept larger classes if this gave more time for research. The corporate and government sectors were calling for more emphasis on areas such as tax planning and policy, international investment, information technology and intellectual property, while 'non-commercial consumers of legal services' wanted to retain the '1970s emphasis' on how the law could aid groups with little economic power such as migrants, Aboriginal people, the poor and the intellectually disabled. The profession was looking for graduates 'who could step into a lawyer's office and earn their keep almost immediately', while the government was beginning to look at the export potential of education and would therefore support the law school in developing courses that would be readily marketable overseas. Finally, surveys indicated that the direct consumers, the students, had the not necessarily compatible aims of wanting a shorter, easier law course that would gain them prestigious articles, together with small group teaching, flexible assessment and a vague desire for more theoretical and interdisciplinary content.[10]

Hanks analysed ways in which these conflicting interests might be reconciled in the construction of the ideal law curriculum and began planning for a complete revamp of the curriculum. The most important reform he had in mind was the semesterisation of many subjects, including the large compulsory subjects, to make more room for optional subjects. However, when he took the proposal to a staff meeting, it was 'destroyed by senior people who had kept quiet during the consultation process', but then strongly resisted any encroachments on their territory.[11] Consideration of the curriculum then came to a screeching halt in the turmoil surrounding Bob Baxt's departure.

It was not until the early 1990s that the faculty again looked at the curriculum. A curriculum review committee was set up in mid-1992, chaired by Marcia Neave. Over the next three years it produced comprehensive reports on every aspect of the undergraduate and postgraduate curricula. These were discussed exhaustively at staff meetings and within the various interest groups (some of which had to be revived for the purpose) before the final report was presented in 1995. Consequently the interim reports

---

10 Ibid.

11 Interview with Peter Hanks, 22 August 2012.

contained many more far-reaching suggestions than the final report, as radical reforms were knocked out in the consultation process. For example, the fourth report of the committee in 1994 included a strong attack on the existing curriculum. It saw the first year program as 'incoherent' and argued that there was a lack of integration between compulsory subjects. Throughout the curriculum there was 'an excessive emphasis on teaching black letter rules, rather than on enabling students to acquire a broader understanding of "core" legal concepts', and there was 'relatively little discussion of theoretical and critical approaches to law within compulsory subjects', with 'an excessive emphasis on students acquiring knowledge about the substantive content of particular areas of law, rather than on the acquisition by students of the skills of legal analysis, reasoning, research and oral and written communication.'[12] This scathing critique indicates that the review committee was looking at fundamental reforms to the curriculum and had plans to reshape the whole undergraduate program. However, when the members of the committee attempted to make the case for their proposals, they came up against the power of the faculty's 'satrapies'. The faculty's long-serving professors inevitably had built up strong positions in their fields and by the 1990s these had become firmly entrenched, most notably criminal law with Waller, Williams and Fox, government law with Enid Campbell and HP Lee, and torts with Francis Trindade. The rulers of the satrapies were in a position to reject any major changes that impacted on their areas. The most effective opposition came from Enid Campbell, who in her later years became somewhat pedantic and, with her encyclopaedic knowledge of all university and faculty regulations, was able to stonewall proposals she did not like. Consequently, the proposals for root and branch reform were abandoned and the recommendations in the final report were more cosmetic than substantial.

The tone of the committee's reports was strongly in favour of a liberal education over preparation for practice. There was a strong emphasis on introducing students 'to theories about the nature of law … and the relationship between law and other social institutions' and encouraging students 'to analyse the law critically and to take an interest in the development of legal and social policy'.[13] In spite of this rhetoric, the committee recommended that the BJuris be phased out and that it no longer be a requirement for law

---

12 Curriculum Review Committee, 'Report to Faculty Board', Faculty Board minutes, 18 April 1994.

13 Curriculum Review Committee, 'Report to Faculty Board', 1995, p. 5.

students to have either a non-law degree or enrol for a combined degree. The BJuris had been introduced with high ideals of a broad-based liberal education, but by the 1980s the vast majority of law students chose to do other combined degrees and the BJuris was rapidly fading away. Although the committee's recommendation would allow students to do a straight four-year LLB course, it expected that few would do so, and it also insisted that they study two non-law subjects in first year.

With regard to the compulsory subjects in the curriculum, the review committee called for a more 'coherent introduction to the study of law' by insisting that all first year law students should take Criminal Law in addition to Legal Process. It also recommended the order in which other compulsory subjects should normally be taken: Torts in second year; Contract and Property in third year; Constitutional Law in fourth year; and Administrative Law in fifth year.

With regard to undergraduate elective subjects, the review committee for the first time attempted to bring some sort of philosophical coherence into a system that had grown haphazardly from a mixture of the interests of staff, the demands of students and passing intellectual fads. Many subjects that had not been taught for many years were disestablished, with suggestions being made for new subjects in areas not covered in the curriculum. These included Aborigines and the law, alternative dispute resolution, welfare law, information technology law and, once again, legal history.

Further changes were suggested to the honours degree. In 1991 the faculty had adopted a strange hybrid scheme under which there were two honours lists, one for those who did a thesis and one for those who had not; only students completing a thesis were eligible for a first class honours degree. The consequences of this scheme had been that very few first class honours degrees were awarded (only four in both 1993 and 1994) and a significant number of the faculty's best students were precluded because they had chosen not to do a thesis. The committee recommended that honours degrees be given purely on marks, with students being encouraged to do a thesis by a twenty per cent bonus on their mark and a reduction in the length of the thesis from a maximum of 20,000 words to a maximum of 15,000.

Another contentious issue was Monash's notorious 'hard marking', which led to Monash students on average receiving significantly lower grades than law students at other universities. While the percentage of students receiving honours degrees at Monash had risen greatly since the 1991 changes, at thirty-two per cent in 1993 it was still well below the forty-six per cent at Melbourne. The committee suggested a new scale of presumptive marks under which the number of honours degrees would rise further and, in particular, many more first class honours degrees would be awarded. Students of recent years proud of their straight high distinctions and first class honours degrees are probably unaware that in the 1980s they would have been lucky to get a H2B degree.

The curriculum review committee's aspirations for a major restructure of the compulsory core of the law course were rejected well before the final report was drafted. The less contentious recommendations to end the BJuris, rearrange the first year curriculum, set a preferred order for the compulsory subjects, revise the structure of combined degrees, reform the honours program and set a new scale of presumptive marks were all adopted.

One of the cornerstones of the Monash law degree, compulsory moot courts, were abandoned in 1997, a casualty of financial stringency. While few disputed the educational value of moot courts, they were expensive to run, with a salary cost of over $100,000 per annum in 1996. In mid-1997 the faculty was told that its budget for 1998 would be reduced by eight per cent and this prompted the decision to discontinue the position of moot master and disestablish the subject Moot Court. The decision met with little opposition, with antidisestablishmentarianism being restricted to a small minority. The end of compulsory mooting led to the retirement of moot master Peter Balmford, one of the law faculty's great characters, whose manner had done much to persuade students they were appearing before a real court.

Teaching

During the 1980s and 1990s, financial pressures and the ever worsening staff:student ratio led to growing lecture and tutorial sizes. Nonetheless this era also saw an increasing emphasis on the quality of teaching, with the beginnings of teaching evaluations, teacher training and teaching awards. The Monash law school had always prided itself on its high quality teaching, even though the quality of the teachers was as much a matter of luck as good management. New academics were put in front of a class with no training at all and there was no evaluation of their success or failure. Some were brilliant, most were adequate, some were disastrous, but even those in the latter category usually kept teaching. Tenure was easily gained and could be easily abused as nothing short of gross dereliction of duty could lead to dismissal.

From 1975 highly impressionistic and occasionally libellous evaluations of lecturers were published each year in the *Counter Faculty Handbooks*. Most of the comments reflected favourably on the faculty's teaching, although some were absolutely damning. An interesting aspect of the evaluations comes from the widely differing attitudes of their authors: many judged lecturers purely on how easy they made the subject, while others looked for intellectual challenge and mocked lecturers who 'spoon fed' their classes. Similarly, while some evaluations praised lecturers who encouraged class participation, others reacted with horror to the use of Socratic teaching methods and saw their use as reason enough to condemn a subject. Disorganisation, poorly structured lectures and 'unapproachability' were universally condemned.

From the mid-1980s accountability for staff performance steadily increased. In 1986 the faculty adopted a policy on 'academic freedom, tenure and standards for academic performance' that for the first time set out minimum standards of performance, stating that 'the Faculty is entitled to expect from its members serious, innovative and rigorous teaching'.[14] In the same year, Tim Pinos proposed the introduction of compulsory teaching evaluations, arguing that:

> The quality and effectiveness of teaching in the faculty is a responsibility not just of the individual teachers, but of the faculty as a whole.
>
> The faculty's role in ensuring adequate quality and effectiveness of teaching is not discharged by being limited to "crisis management" – reacting to student petitions, rumour, innuendo and the like. It is the responsibility of the faculty to actively take steps to assist all members of staff in the improvement of teaching.
>
> An essential prerequisite to the achievement of good teaching is for the teacher to receive feedback respecting his or her performance in the classroom on a continuing basis.[15]

His arguments were accepted and in 1987 law became the first faculty at Monash to introduce student evaluation of staff.

Several years later when the vice-chancellor's teaching awards began, Richard Fox persuaded the faculty that it would be good for the law school's image to win them. He gained support to 'run them like an election

---

14 Faculty Board minutes, 20 October 1986.

15 'Proposal regarding teaching evaluations', Ibid.

campaign – choosing a good teacher and then giving them the support and resources to win a prize'.[16] This proved highly successful and the faculty won more than its share of teaching prizes in the 1990s, with early winners being Joycey Tooher in 1992, Sue Campbell in 1993 and Richard Fox and Sue McNicol in 1994.

When the faculty was forced to succumb to the odd penchant for 'mission statements' that came into vogue in the early 1990s, the chosen platitudes included 'teaching of the highest quality across the discipline of law'. While few got excited about the mission statement (if they ever read it), the commitment to teaching was genuinely strong in this period. A review of the faculty's teaching in 1993 praised the 'highly imaginative' teaching programmes and methods. Some examples chosen for special mention were the Moot Court (although this did not save it from being abolished within a few years), a negotiation skills exercise in Torts, a Family Law simulation exercise and a project in Legal Process in which groups of students learned about the process of translating policy into law by developing a legislative solution to a problem.[17] However, the Moot Court excepted, these teaching ideas were all relatively cheap to implement. During the 1990s, all the faculty's activities were carried out in the shadow of declining income and this inevitably impacted on teaching. As the curriculum review committee commented in 1996,

> Monash Law Faculty, along with other Law Schools and the tertiary sector generally, has experienced a substantial reduction in resources over the past decade. Around 88% of Faculty budget is devoted to salaries, and the inevitable effect of budget cuts has been to worsen student/staff ratios. This has led to larger lecture classes, a reduction of tutorials in the compulsory subjects from weekly to fortnightly and the removal of such tutorial support as had been available in large enrolment elective subjects.[18]

Tutorials had been seen as a potential area of savings from as early as 1982, when they were dropped from some optional subjects. Over the next decade tutorial sizes steadily increased – tutorials of less than a dozen students, common in the early years, were but a distant memory by 1990.

---

16 Interview with Richard Fox, 26 September 2011.

17 'Examples of Excellent Outcomes in Teaching, Research and Community Service', Faculty Board minutes, 28 October 1993.

18 Curriculum Review Committee Report Part IV, 'The Undergraduate Elective Programme', p. 16.

In 1992 tutorials were abandoned in almost all elective subjects and made fortnightly in the compulsory subjects. Although the LSS filled the gap to some extent with its own tutorial program, the contact between staff and students and the ability to deliver quality teaching were greatly curtailed.

Larger classes also made it much more difficult to use the Socratic teaching method. Almost universal in the 1970s, by the 1990s only a minority of teachers persisted with it. The 1995 edition of the *Counter Faculty Handbook* gave the most comprehensive coverage of the law course of any edition, and students referred to Socratic teaching (either by name or description) being used by only six lecturers, Mark Sneddon in Constitutional Law, Bernadette McSherry in Criminal Law, Pam O'Connor in Legal Process, Joycey Tooher in Property and David McLean and Susan Kneebone in Equity and Trusts. In many of the smaller electives, the *Counter Faculty Handbooks* comment approvingly on lecturers who encouraged class participation, provided that the lecturers were not overly harsh on those who could not answer questions. But unrelenting Socratic questioning? As one student wrote of Philip Clarke's teaching of Restrictive Trade Practices in 1988, 'I was so overpowered by his socratic [sic] method … that I dropped out of the subject'.[19]

Postgraduate Education

In the fifteen years following the establishment of graduate coursework at Monash in 1973 the program continually expanded both in number of students and the range of offerings. The first graduate diplomas were introduced in 1978 and specialist masters' courses in taxation began in 1989. Major new fields of study were opened in the graduate program, including advanced taxation, international trade, South East Asian and Pacific legal systems, law and economics, trade practices and intellectual property. The graduate program attracted high calibre students, with many LLM students of the 1980s going on to distinguished careers in the law (including Marilyn Warren CJ, Michael Watt J, Clyde Croft J, senior counsel David Grace, Richard Maidment, Timothy Margetts and many others); politics, notably Howard government ministers Richard Alston and Kevin Andrews; and many other areas. The graduate program also attracted the first substantial cohort of overseas students to the law school; in 1981, twenty-one out of twenty-four full-time graduate students were from overseas.

---

19 *Counter Faculty Handbook*, 1989, p. 72.

Harry Reicher found teaching in the graduate program in the 1980s both enjoyable and intellectually stimulating. In particular, he appreciated teaching the graduate diploma courses, where many of the students were not lawyers but had 'all sorts of interesting qualifications and backgrounds'. In his taxation classes he had many outstanding tax accountants, including partners in the largest accounting firms and officers of the Australian Taxation Office. Reicher, who was renowned at the bar for his vigorous advocacy on behalf of taxpayers in conflict with the ATO, recalled that in one course

> I had an unusually high concentration of students from the Australian Taxation Office, and they all managed to congregate in the front row, and every single one of them had a tape recorder in full view. Class was like a Presidential press conference! I had to laugh, when I envisioned the scene in the Deputy Commissioner's office the morning after each class, with the Deputy Commissioner of Taxation himself sitting around his conference room table, together with my students, listening to what was discussed in class, and what I said, especially on 'hot-button' topics.

A course that Harry Reicher developed for the graduate tax program was Current Problems in Taxation, which he designed drawing heavily on his experience as a practising tax barrister. The course revolved around the analysis of the latest legislation and court decisions in taxation. He had some particularly memorable classes following the enactment of the *Taxation (Unpaid Company Tax) Act 1982*:

> The legislation went back ten years, to 1972, and made taxable receipts which, under a famous decision of the High Court, in the case of Slutzkin, were held to be capital receipts. It was the most glaring example of retrospective tax legislation in Australia's history. Not surprisingly, the legislation was challenged in the High Court, on the grounds that it was unconstitutional. Two separate cases, along these lines, albeit based on different lines of constitutional argument, went to the High Court, and were decided against the taxpayers. My course in Current Problems in Taxation started on a Monday evening, soon after the two cases were decided, and the following Thursday I was scheduled to argue the third case, in the Supreme Court of Victoria. It was a collections case, in which the Deputy Commissioner of Taxation had issued a Summons for Final Judgment, to enable him to collect

> the tax summarily, without going to full trial. In the Monday class, we dealt at length with the first two cases, which of course was also excellent preparation for my case on the Thursday.
>
> When Thursday came, I argued the case before Mr Justice Clive Tadgell, and I argued it solely on the basis of the retrospectivity of the legislation, the argument being that retrospective tax legislation was a 'taking of property' under the Commonwealth Constitution, and was therefore not valid unless accompanied by 'just compensation' …
>
> The following Monday, I taught my own case in my course. I copied my outline of argument, which I had submitted and used in court, and I obtained permission from my opponent, Michael Black QC (who not long after was appointed as Chief Justice of the Federal Court of Australia), who graciously agreed to my copying his own outline of argument, and distributing it to the students. It was a marvellous pedagogical experience! And it meant that the students were really up-to-the-minute on important developments in tax law. The result went against my clients, in a decision which was subsequently reported, and in which Tadgell J generously commented: 'The defendant's argument… was presented with vigour and ability'.[20]

Exciting and imaginative teaching helped build the reputation of the Monash graduate coursework program. In 1988, when Queenslander Mark Davison decided he wanted to study for a masters' degree, he looked around Australia and chose Monash because it was regarded as the best masters' degree in the country. Jeff Giddings was another aspiring academic who chose to do an LLM by coursework at Monash in the late 1980s. He remembers particularly the informal seminar style teaching, the multidisciplinary character of many of the courses and the high quality of the teaching, singling out Yet Bryant, Tony Duggan, Ron McCallum, Richard Fox and Simon Begg from Corrs, one of many outside experts who taught in the graduate program.

Student impressions of the quality of the coursework LLM were confirmed by the Pearce Report in 1987, which held up the Monash program as a model that other universities should seek to emulate.[21] In particular, Monash was praised for the range and quality of postgraduate subjects, the relatively high

---

20 *Deputy Federal Commissioner of Taxation v Grollo & Anor* (1985) 85 ATC 4442.

21 Pearce, Campbell and Harding, *Australian Law Schools*, vol. 1 ch. 6.

number of full-time graduate students and the number of those students with scholarships.

As part of the Dawkins reforms, from 1988 universities were allowed to charge fees for postgraduate courses. Consequently, after some soul-searching, the faculty decided that all its graduate diploma courses would be full-fee paying from the start of 1989.[22] Fees were initially set at $400 per subject 'as a contribution towards the recovery of real costs', but the faculty long resisted the idea that the graduate program could be a profit-making operation to support the faculty's other activities.

In 1991 postgraduate enrolments were at a record level and teaching resources were stretched to the limit. The faculty considered imposing a quota but chose instead to raise entry standards. At the same time, in the face of rapidly increasing undergraduate student numbers and declining funding, resources were taken from the graduate program to shore up undergraduate teaching. In Bob Williams' view, the faculty was judged by the quality of its undergraduate teaching and this had to be maintained even at the expense of graduate teaching.[23] The range of subjects offered each year was cut back, less emphasis was given to developing new graduate subjects and fewer subjects were taught in the city. The inevitable result was a steady decline in student numbers.

Meanwhile the Melbourne law school was taking a very different path. The dean, Michael Crommelin, faced with the daunting task of reforming a law school that had been the subject of scathing criticism in the Pearce Report, argued that 'the only way we could acquire … an opportunity to do anything else, was by introducing a fee-paying programme'.[24] Fees were brought in for both the LLM by coursework and graduate diplomas, and the postgraduate program was heavily marketed to the profession. The new Melbourne postgraduate offerings were timed perfectly for the market, which at that time was craving specialist postgraduate education and, with the enormous advantage of a central location, the program soon became highly profitable.

By the mid-1990s, Monash's graduate diploma program had collapsed and coursework LLM numbers were also falling. In 1991 there were 162 coursework LLM and 113 diploma students; by 1994 coursework LLM numbers had fallen to 149 and there were only 22 remaining diploma

22 Faculty Board minutes, 6 April 1988.

23 Quoted in Marginson, *Monash: Remaking the University*, p. 237.

24 Quoted in Waugh, *First Principles*, pp. 246–7.

students. In that year the specialist graduate diplomas were disestablished, along with the two specialist masters' degrees in taxation. The diplomas were closed down primarily because of falling numbers, with the recognition there was 'no clear structure to any of the diplomas such as is to be found in the specialist graduate diplomas offered at the University of Melbourne', while the 'the recent departure of two experienced teachers [Krever and Reicher] has left us in a position where we cannot realistically mount the M Tax Law, M Tax Stud or Diploma in Taxation'.[25]

While the graduate diploma program was closed down, an important change was made to the coursework LLM in an attempt to revive its popularity. Since its inception the major problem with the coursework LLM had always been the thesis component. In addition to four subjects, students had to write a thesis of about 25,000 words, and a large number of students found this too big a challenge. Figures are difficult to compile, but less than half of all LLM students ever completed a thesis.[26] In addition, with growing undergraduate numbers, it was an increasing challenge to find supervisors for all the masters' theses. Consequently, the decision was made in 1993 to allow for a twelve unit LLM as an alternative to the existing eight units plus thesis.[27]

In 1994, clearly prompted by the growing strength of Melbourne's postgraduate program, the graduate studies committee reviewed the coursework LLM. It was easy to find weaknesses. There was 'little coherence in the subjects offered', 'little correlation between the Faculty's areas of research and teaching strength and the number and depth of subjects offered at the graduate level', 'relatively few members of academic staff involved at the graduate level', and 'doubts, particularly in more recent years' about the 'quality of some students admitted to the programme'.[28] There were glaring gaps in the faculty's postgraduate offerings in what should have been areas of strength, such as criminal law, evidence, family law, constitutional law and torts, as well as in admitted areas of weakness such as commercial law and taxation.

---

25 Sam Ricketson, chair of the graduate studies committee, Faculty Board minutes, 18 April 1994.

26 At Melbourne in the late 1980s the completion rate was only twelve per cent. See Waugh, *First Principles*, p. 246.

27 Faculty Board minutes, 21 July 1993.

28 'Discussion Paper on the LLM Coursework Programme', Faculty Board minutes, 20 July 1994.

The committee was 'unable to identify new areas into which the Faculty should move', with all the most promising areas of study already being taught at Melbourne. The review concluded that the faculty could differentiate itself from Melbourne by offering a high quality, academically rigorous program taught by full-time academics as against Melbourne's 'production line approach' taught largely by sessional staff.

High quality and academic rigour proved hard to sell. Numbers continued to fall, with only 90 new enrolments in 1997 against a target of 120. A major marketing problem was that, even though most subjects were taught at various premises in the city, the lack of a dedicated Monash law chambers in the city meant that most prospective graduate students believed that all subjects were taught at Clayton. Nonetheless, in the last years of Bob Williams' deanship the first moves were made towards reviving the postgraduate program. Much thought was put into revising the subjects offered, with tired and anachronistic subjects removed to be replaced by new and more relevant subjects like Electronic Banking; the Law of the Internet; Psychiatry, Psychology and the Law; and Native Title and Indigenous Land Rights. Further, the faculty belatedly sought to regain lost ground by reintroducing specialist masters' degrees and graduate diplomas. However, it would take many years to recover fully.

One of the most startling statistics the authors encountered in their research was a table of Monash PhD students enrolled by faculty in 1996:

Arts	336
Business and Economics	85
Computing	60
Education	152
Engineering	139
Law	**5**
Medicine	298
Science	226
Pharmacy	37

As this table shows, as late as 1996 the research culture symbolised by the PhD barely existed in the Monash law school, though it was much stronger at other law schools, particularly Sydney and UNSW. Between 1980 and 1998 there were only twenty-eight PhD completions in the law school. Significantly, twelve of these were before 1986, suggesting that interest in PhDs was actually declining. Further evidence for this is the fact that there were nine full-time PhD students in 1981 and 1983, a number that was not reached again before 1998. A PhD was not a prerequisite for a career as a legal academic nor was it valued by the large law firms, so the incentives to take on years of arduous research were weak.[29]

While the faculty found it difficult to persuade students to enrol for PhDs, it was even more difficult to guide them to completion. Accurate figures are hard to compile, but possibly only about one-third of students who began a PhD in law ever finished it. Many in the faculty believed that too many weak or poorly prepared candidates were admitted to the PhD with little realistic prospect of completion, and also that too many thesis proposals were poorly thought out and doomed to fail.[30] Dorothy Kovacs thought that 'some of the research in the 1990s was unrealistic with students starting off on empirically based PhD projects that could never be completed'. Many staff members were reluctant to take on PhD supervisions, and the absence of either a PhD coursework component or a research students' seminar program left many PhD students lacking in research skills and feeling isolated from other postgraduate students.

In 1998, at the end of the era of the two Bobs, postgraduate education could be seen as the area in which Monash had most clearly lost the superiority it had in 1980 over most other law schools. But equally it was the area in which the greatest opportunities existed for reforms and innovations that could be both financially and educationally valuable.

---

29 As late as 1995 the curriculum review committee report on the doctoral program explicitly stated that the PhD was only one of several satisfactory qualifications for an academic career in law.

30 See, for example, memorandum by Enid Campbell, 24 December 1992, Faculty Board minutes, 26 April 1993.

Chapter 18

An Eye on the Prize – Student Life in the 1980s and 1990s

The era 1980 to 1998 saw significant changes in the make-up of the student body and in the student experience of the Monash law school. The major generalisations are that the students became both more like those at the Melbourne law school and increasingly career-minded and vocationally focused. In the 1980s undergraduate student numbers were static – even falling in some years – and continually increasing demand meant that ever higher year twelve scores were required to get into the law school. Since 'academic performance tends to correlate with social background', as the faculty became more academically exclusive it inevitably tended to 'become more socially exclusive as well'.[1] The law school's students were increasingly from the private schools of Melbourne's eastern suburbs, with the proportion of government school students steadily falling. The trends of the 1980s were reinforced in the 1990s. Even though student numbers rose sharply, the 'cut-off score' continued to rise rapidly, leading to an ever-more exclusive student body. The trend was further strengthened by the introduction of HECS in 1989 and the admission of full-fee paying local students in 1996.

The trend towards social exclusivity was partially offset by increased racial diversification and the achievement of sexual equality (numerically and scholastically at least). There had always been a small number of overseas students, primarily from South-East Asia, but numbers rose as government policy changed to allow full-fee paying overseas students, although the appeal of law was never nearly as great as for medicine and commerce. In addition, there was a noticeable increase in the proportion of Australian students from non-Anglo-Celtic backgrounds, not so much as a result of deliberate policy but as the children of post-Second World War immigrants rose up the social ladder.

1 Marginson, *Monash: Remaking the University*, p. 39.

The steady rise in the proportion of female undergraduates was a reflection of many factors, few related to the policies or attitudes of the law school itself – primarily the changing position of women in society and the superior performance of girls in year twelve. The magic fifty per cent mark was not reached until 1992, although the growing academic superiority of female students was emphasised when seven out of eleven Supreme Court Prize winners during the 1980s were women.[2] It seems unlikely that the difficulties many women lawyers still faced later in their careers can be laid at the door of the Monash law school.

Less happy was the experience of Aboriginal students, though not for want of trying. The Monash Orientation Scheme for Aborigines (MOSA) was introduced in 1984 to offer Indigenous students a bridging program in preparation for university study. Those who completed the program successfully were guaranteed a place, initially in the faculties of law or arts.[3] The law faculty had eight Aboriginal students by 1987, eleven by 1993. However, few completed their degrees. In 1990 the exclusion committee reported that a significant proportion of the Aboriginal students had appeared before it because of unsatisfactory progress and they faced 'evident difficulties' with many aspects of their studies.[4] Figures are surprisingly hard to find, but it appears that even by 2013 there have been fewer than ten Indigenous graduates from the Monash law school.

The 1980s saw a large number of part-time law students, encouraged by the abolition of fees. They were from a variety of backgrounds and ages and did much to add diversity to an otherwise increasingly homogeneous undergraduate population. The largest single group of part-timers were clerks of courts who were taking the eleven compulsory subjects they needed to qualify to become magistrates as 'not for degree' students. Most years there were about fifteen clerks enrolled in the law faculty. Basil Fogarty was working at the Williamstown court when he began his 'NFD' course in 1978 and it would take him an hour to get to Monash after work in the evening for a fifty-minute lecture. On several occasions he had a catnap in the car when he arrived at Monash, only to wake up a couple of hours later with the lecture long finished.

---

2 They were Wendy Peter (1981), Mary Ferguson (1982), Glenys Fraser (1983), Ann Shorten (1985), Debra Mortimer (1986), Annette Rubenstein (1987), Kristine Hanscombe (1988). The 1986 prize was shared, hence the 11 winners in the decade.

3 *Monash Reporter*, March 1984, p. 1.

4 Faculty Board minutes, 5 April 1990.

He soon learnt which lecturers were worth making the effort to hear and which ones were a waste of time. Once he had completed his eleven 'NFD' subjects, Lawrie McCredie transferred him to the LLB, with exemption from doing the BJuris – so he did a straight LLB with only a few arts subjects. Fogarty found that McCredie was always sympathetic to part-timers and would make the rules to suit the circumstances of each student. He always went to the annual clerks of courts dinner, where he always finished his speech by saying, 'It's been a great evening – I don't know about the rest of you but I'm blind'. McCredie's secretary, Barbara Jones, was also highly supportive of the clerk of courts students – if there was a long queue of students outside her door and she saw one of the clerks, she would say, 'Oh, yes, you were waiting this morning – come to the front of the queue.'

There were only two criteria for Basil's choice of optional subjects: the timetable suited and he had heard on the grapevine that they were easy and passable. He soon worked out it was far better to take three easy half-year subjects than one big full-year subject like Taxation. Thus he did a half unit called the American Legal System – there were twenty questions on the exam and he recalls that the last one was 'If you've found the earlier questions too difficult, name the chief justice of the American Supreme Court and you'll pass.' Basil remembers there was a rule you had to finish a degree within ten years or you would start to lose credit for the early subjects. Many of the clerks took eight or nine years but Basil completed his in six by taking on a heavy load and doing summer school subjects every year, even though this meant he had no breaks at all in his studies.

From Foreign Aid to Foreign Trade: Full Fee Paying Overseas Students

Overseas students have always been part of the faculty, though the conditions under which they have come have changed frequently and dramatically. Under the Colombo Plan agreement of 1950, Australian universities provided free places for many students from South and South-East Asian countries. At the same time, a smaller number of private overseas students paid the same tuition fees as Australian students.[5] In 1979, the Fraser Liberal government imposed a substantial visa fee on private overseas students, a precursor to later decisions by the Hawke government that transformed

---

5 http://theconversation.edu.au/colombo-plan-an-initiative-that-brought-australia-and-asia-closer-3590.

education from foreign aid to foreign trade.[6] In the law school the rising number of overseas students became a matter of anxiety in the early 1980s because they provided no financial benefit to the faculty and, some argued, deprived Australian students of university places. Early in 1980, the faculty discussed imposing a sub-quota on overseas students. In that year, eleven per cent of all Monash students came from overseas, but the percentage was substantially less in law. At that time the faculty had only twelve overseas undergraduates and the faculty board resolved that it was opposed to any sub-quota.[7]

From the mid-1980s the number of fee-paying students, mostly from South-East Asia, grew substantially.[8] While some still argued for a limit, the faculty now benefited financially from overseas student fees and every dollar was welcomed in an era when budgets were under pressure. The total number of overseas students in the faculty was 152 in 1985 and 172 in 1986.[9]

Malaysia was the largest source of overseas students in the 1980s, because university places in Malaysia were reserved for ethnic Malays. Consequently many Chinese and Indian Malaysians sent their children overseas for higher education. Australian law courses were attractive to Malaysians because of a shared British common law heritage; until 1997 an Australian LLB was sufficient qualification to practise in Malaysia. When Stephen Gray was an undergraduate in the mid-1980s there was 'a big block of Malaysian students', who tended to sit down the front and work very hard.[10]

The increasing number of Malaysian students prompted the formation in 1982 of the Malaysian Law Students Association (MLSA). Its aims were to create and encourage 'active intellectual links' with Malaysian legal affairs and organise social activities for both Australian and Malaysian students. It held barbecues, visited courts, arranged talks and published a newsletter, *Nadi Kilau*. A particular emphasis of *Nadi Kilau* was the Malaysian legal system because, as 1982 president Kenny Yip wrote, the Monash course taught them nothing about the current legal system in their own country 'where most of us will be practising in the future'. Most articles in the journal

---

6 Grant Harman, 'New Directions in Internationalizing Higher Education: Australia's Development as an Exporter of Higher Education Services', *Higher Education Policy*, No. 17, 2004, p. 101; 'What Cost Full Fees?', pamphlet OSCAFF 1985–1986, MON 584/ 1997/02; Davison and Murphy, *University Unlimited*, p. 232.

7 Faculty Board minutes 31 March and 3 June 1980.

8 Ibid., 3 June 1980.

9 Total Enrolments, Law, University Statistics, 1986, p. 267.

10 Interview with Stephen Gray, 24 May 2012.

were in English, although some were in Malay.[11] The MLSA had nearly 100 members in 1983 and its social functions, especially when combined with food, attracted many non-Malaysians.

In 1993 a Malaysian student, Vino Krishnan, wrote of his experiences at Monash. His first choice had been to study in England, but he found out that it would take longer and be more expensive than Australia. These factors, together with the Australian climate, encouraged him to come to Monash. When he graduated he would only have to work as an articled clerk for nine months before being officially acknowledged as 'a fully-fledged lawyer'. Vino Krishnan reflected that while studying at Monash there was 'never a dull moment'.[12]

A smaller number of students in the 1980s came from Indonesia. Unlike the Malaysians, most Indonesian students were postgraduates. Zoe Pask, then the administrator of the graduate programs, dealt with the cultural concerns of the Indonesian students. One year, after Harry Reicher had taken the first class in a course he was teaching, several Indonesian students told Zoe that they couldn't stay in the course because Reicher was Jewish. As Muslims, they had been taught that a Jewish teacher would be prejudiced against them. Zoe assured them that they really had nothing to worry about, so they agreed to try it for a little longer. They came back to see her a short time later and told her she had been right![13]

Student Discipline and Complaints

In the early days of the law school a discipline committee was set up, but it was dissolved in 1969 having never had cause to meet. Over the next decade, complaints by or against students tended to be dealt with informally, often by Lawrie McCredie and Barbara Jones. However, in the 1980s three serious issues arose that revealed the need for more formal processes.

During the 1970s a significant number of female students were subjected to sexual harassment by a small number of male lecturers. The victims recall that they felt helpless and that there were no avenues for them to complain. The issue came to a head when a student publication warned female students against choosing a particular lecturer's subjects because he had a reputation as a 'sleaze'. Eventually the lecturer left the university, but this and other

---

11 *Nadi Kilau*, vol. 1, 1982, p. 2.

12 'A Malaysian Law Student in Australia', *Clayton's Law*, 1993, Vol. 5, No. 2, p. 15.

13 Email from Harry Reicher to authors, 19 March 2012.

issues in the late 1970s and early 1980s made it apparent that neither the faculty nor the university had any real avenues for dealing with issues of sexism and of sexual harassment. This was one reason why the law school liaison committee, which had fallen into abeyance, was resurrected in 1981 as a vehicle for airing student grievances, though it was to be another decade before effective grievance procedures were in place.[14]

Another issue arose in the early 1980s that also tested the faculty's procedures. In an era of hard marking and no fees, a far higher proportion of students failed subjects or sat for supplementary exams than today. One case of a supplementary exam became a *cause célèbre* and eerily foreshadowed a later and more serious crusade undertaken by the same student. In November 1982, Norman Rosenbaum failed Property I, the last subject he required for his LLB. He applied for a special examination on medical grounds but the progress committee chose to grant him a supplementary exam. He sat this in February 1983, but failed with a mark of forty-three per cent. Rosenbaum applied to the dean for another supplementary examination under Rule 9 of the faculty's supplementary and special examination rules. The dean rejected his application on the ground that neither the university examination regulations nor the faculty rules permitted a student to sit two supplementary examinations in a subject in the same year.

Rosenbaum refused to accept this ruling, querying the interpretation of the relevant statutes. In April 1983, the faculty board discussed the issue at great length and decided to set up an ad hoc committee consisting of David Allan, David Bailey, Sue Campbell, Marilyn Pittard and a student member, Michael Brugman.[15] After much deliberation, the committee decided the statute *was* ambiguous and that Rosenbaum should be allowed to sit another supplementary examination. The matter was then taken to the executive committee, which did not feel bound by the reasons and conclusions of the report or its recommendation that Rosenbaum be allowed a supplementary exam.

The faculty board debated the issue exhaustively and passionately at its October meeting, before finally resolving that Rosenbaum should be allowed a supplementary exam.[16] Fortunately for all concerned, he passed and graduated LLB in April 1984.[17] Rosenbaum went on to a successful career at

14 Faculty Board minutes, 6 August 1981.

15 Ibid., 19 July 1983.

16 Ibid., 17 October 1983; interview Marilyn Pittard 20 January 2012.

17 http://adm.monash.edu/records-archives/archives/cgi-alias/graduations/search-results.pl.

the bar, and became well-known for his passionate and ultimately successful fight to bring to justice those responsible for the death of his brother Yankel in New York in 1991. If those involved in the administration of justice in New York had been aware of Rosenbaum's fight for a supplementary exam at Monash University in 1983, they might have shown him greater respect when he took up his brother's cause.[18]

In the early 1980s, the law school liaison committee reported that the most common student grievances involved lecture and tutorial timetabling, congestion in classes, assessment methods, release of exam information, library facilities and research and social facilities for postgraduate students.[19] The committee was generally quite successful in resolving specific problems where only a small number of individuals were involved. Unfortunately, the committee advised, 'the resolution of issues requiring the involvement or understanding of large numbers of the staff and/or student body, or some financial outlay, were frustrated'. The path to the resolution of such student concerns was not altogether clear, as was shown by a controversy that arose in 1986.

In 1986, when the female to male student ratio was visibly changing, the *Counter Faculty Handbook* was again at the centre of a dispute. The *Handbook* included three critiques of Kumar Amarasekara's stream in Criminal Law. His teaching was commended, but two of the critics attacked his penchant for telling 'blue' jokes. To one reviewer, it was 'bad luck … if you happen to be female' because his explicit descriptions of all the sexual offences were 'repeated hundreds of times', while another wrote that 'Amarasekara's crude jokes and jovial manner were inappropriate, to put it mildly, when discussing rape'.[20]

In April 1986, the reformist executive of the LSS wrote to Louis Waller and the other two criminal law lecturers stating that it had 'received a number of complaints about lecturers' approaches to teaching sexual offences' in the Criminal Law course. They felt the subject was being taught in a way that trivialised the situation of victims and were anxious to ensure that 'this important area of criminal law' was discussed in a way that reflected the realities of situations which gave rise to sexual violence. They feared that the course was unlikely to produce lawyers sympathetic to most victims – or

---

18 The death of Yankel Rosenbaum, and Norman's fight for justice were the subject of a *Compass* documentary screened on ABC television in October 2011.

19 Faculty Board minutes 5 April 1982.

20 *Counter Faculty Handbook*, 1986, pp. 51–2.

news

LAW SCHOOL SEXISM SCANDAL!

At the start of 1986, a reformist group of students ran a campaign in the law faculty for control of the traditionally conservative Law Students Society. "Non Circum Coimus" (No Fucking Around") was elected to the five executive positions unopposed, and they proceeded to implement some of the concerns outlined in their election platform: encouraging students to take a critical approach to legal education, voicing student complaints to academics, and inviting speakers on law and society issues to Monash. Traditional LSS activities — an internal mooting competition and social functions — have also continued.

During their period of office, the LSS executive has received a number of student complaints about the teaching of sexual offences in the criminal law course. The complaints were twofold: students were dissatisfied with sexism (this ranged from academics using examples which trivialised the situation of the female victims to, in the past, one lecturer's propensity to tell lewd jokes) and also with the detachment with which academics treated the subject area.

On April 22nd, letters were sent to criminal law academics, outlining the complaints (as the executive had promised students they would) and expressing concern that the course equip its students to deal with clients on a human, as well as a legal, level. In retrospect, "Non Circum Coimus" believes letters were probably an improper vehicle for this kind of criticism — a personal approach may have worked better.

The response of three academics and many students to these actions has been quite vehement. Two lecturers treated the general letter as a personal attack and, in a meeting with LSS executive members, have asked for a statement from them to the effect that no students complained about their lecturing. Both have read the letters to their classes and asked students to bring complaints to them, not to the LSS. If it works, this will be a positive development. Another lecturer has told his classes that he has been trying to "clean up his act" by eliminating sexist humour (after complaints in previous years) and that the "attack" is unwarranted. In a letter to LSS executive members, this lecturer has indicated that he regards the letter to be merely a protest against humour in general and jokes about sex in particular. He has asked executive members to meet with him soon.

In response to this lecturer's protestations that such complaints could lead to the demise of his career, and out of a feeling that the complaints are either unfounded or dated, students have circulated three petitions (attracting, not counting duplicate signatures, about 100 names) criticising the LSS executive action. The LSS committee has also passed a motion expressing dissatisfaction with the executive's failure to consult with committee members before sending the letters (the executive concedes that this was a mistake) — although most committee members support the object of the letters. Opposition to the action is generally along the lines of majority-minority politics: students object to the LSS's name being used to back complaints which they say are not the views of most students: if most students are happy with subjects and teachers, they allege, there is no place for the LSS in taking up dissenting views.

The executive disagrees. Such a policy, they say, would lead them to do, effectively, nothing to challenge anything in the law faculty (and students are still making complaints about lecturers and subjects to them). Moreover, the "majority rules" view, taken logically, would mean that they would have to treat all complaints with less than fifty per cent support as wrong or illegitimate. (Complaints about anti-Semitic humour, to argue by analogy, are likely to fall into this category. So is student concern about lecturers leaving out important slabs of compulsory subjects — a complaint the LSS has recently been asked to deal with.)

There is some confusion within the law faculty as to the appropriate avenues for student complaints. LSS officers have been told that a revived staff-student liasion committee (a body which, despite student interest, never met last year) is the place for them, but initiative for calling a meeting of this committee seems to lie with the faculty, not the students. Functions of the faculty board are presently delegated in a way that leads to very little room for student participation — except on the library committee. The Dean, Professor Baxt, has asked LSS officers to bring complaints to him so that he can decide whether or not to act on them: in this particular case, the executive thought (unstrategically, perhaps) that a healthier approach was to go straight to the academics concerned.

The issues involved in this "dispute" are complex and sensitive, and are likely to give rise to controversy no matter how they are handled. The LSS executive has said it "does not intend to renege on its promise to voice student complaints. Nor will we disregard positive feedback about academics. The door remains open."

THE LATE LATE COLUMN

It's pretty interesting to see how the police have been behaving themselves in and around Sin City since the Drug Offensive booklet (it's hard to tell which is more offensive — the drugs or the booklet) made its way into letterboxes in and around Marvellous Melbourne. Already this paper has been inundated with reports from dubious sources about "mates" being shot by the police in and around St Kilda.

Heaps of these stories have been circulating. Last week, someone of quite a reliable nature and who holds a position that would put her well and truly in the know about these sorts of things (that's all I want to say about her credentials lest I cause some professional problem for her) told me that she had heard of two cases of the ultimate legal solution being applied.

According to my source, the local police were helping out the Big Brass set up a heroin deal in St Kilda. The police had been following their suspects for a long period of time, and with the aid of several props, set up an exchange. The suspects duly progressed to their rendezvous, where money was to be exchanged for illicit substances.

It's not altogether clear what happened next. It appears that the suspects were sprung in the act. One suspect made a move that one constable interpreted as a very suspicious and dangerous one, and duly shot the offending suspect through the head.

And there, dear readers, you have justice, St Kilda style, in the aftermath of the government's Drug Offensive.

Please don't accept this tract as a brief in favour of people who buy and sell drugs. Personally, I think that if drug use was decriminalised, then the nefarious drug-pusher would become something of an extinct species. Desperate people would have to move into other areas to support themselves at best, or, at worst, this country's businessmen would have to indulge in honest practices to sustain the lifestyles that they have become accustomed to.

Still, given the antipathy that most people seem to have for the suppliers of such substances, there should still be some degree of concern felt for the way in which the custodians of law and order in this city have also taken it upon themselves to dispense justice as well. With the passing of a bullet through the skull of any person in the aftermath of a crime, the police have taken it upon themselves to be enforcers, judge, jury and hangpersons.

It's indeed ironic that these incidents should come to light in the aftermath of Lionel Murphy's acquittal from charges of attempting to pervert the course of justice. After that trial in Sydney, where the jury found the High Court judge not guilty of the charges, the good Justice waxed lyrical on the courthouse steps about the values of the jury system.

For the two people who have been shot dead at the hands of the police, there was no recourse to a jury. Theirs was a justice reminiscent of vigilante law, where the gun rules supreme.

St Kilda has become a very dangerous place to be in the post-Drug Offensive climate. Suddenly all the good citizens of the city have been keyed up to accept the harsh "Punish the Offenders" line that the whole campaign has engendered without taking into consideration the many other reasons why people take drugs in a society such as this one.

There have been other incidents of excessive police force. Last week, one of the people who shares my house had her young sister over to stay for the weekend. A tall and mature girl, I guessed her age at about 17 or 18. It turned out she was only 15. She had just come back from one of her regular Saturday night haunts, the Locomotion disco at the old Seaview Ballroom, where there had been a police raid.

The police had raided the place in search of under-aged patrons such as herself. Some might say that the police are obliged to do these sorts of things. This may be so, but I found totally reprehensible the reports of the way the police went about the operation. Young kids were dragged out of the hotel quite violently, with some of them having their faces repeatedly slapped. There were other reports of violence perpetrated by the police against these under aged drinkers. Hardly a fair contest.

The Drug Offensive has created a peculiar climate in its wake. St Kilda is a very nervous town at the moment, where a false move could earn you a serious hassle with the police at best, or something far more permanent at worst.

LOT'S WIFE, Monday 5 May 1986 — 6

'Law School sexism scandal!' was highlighted in *Lot's Wife* in May 1986.
MU Archives

even offenders – if the classroom atmosphere was 'one of sarcasm and sexual innuendo'. Further, they emphasised that Criminal Law was by no means the only subject affected by sexism.[21]

Louis Waller was surprised and disappointed that the committee members had not come to see him about the matters raised in the letter and invited them to make an appointment. While Waller's response was one of surprise, the other academics, understandably, treated the letter as a personal attack. They asked the LSS for a statement to the effect that no students had complained about their lectures in particular. Bob Williams regarded the allegations made in the LSS letter as 'without any foundation whatsoever' and 'extremely serious'. Kumar Amarakesara insisted his students had not complained to him or to the LSS about his liking for 'blue jokes'.[22]

The action by the LSS polarised students. Three petitions were circulated criticizing the LSS executive's actions and supporting the criminal law lecturers, and a motion was passed expressing dissatisfaction with the executive's failure to consult committee members before sending the letters. Students objected to the LSS's name being used to back complaints which they said were not the views of most students. The executive disagreed: 'Such a policy… would lead them to do, effectively, nothing to challenge anything in the law faculty'.[23]

This episode revealed that, despite the existence of the law school liaison committee, confusion existed as to the appropriate avenues for student complaints. Jennifer Nielson, one of the instigators of the letter of complaint, maintains that 'People had made complaints before but there was no structure. … no procedure for complaints.' The law school liaison committee should have been the most appropriate place for such an issue to be aired, but it was only set up as a 'forum for students to present complaints about teaching, grading and administrative procedures'.[24] The faculty did not have a process to deal with issues of sexism, sexual harassment or discrimination.[25]

Some months later, when the furore had died down, the LSS executive wrote to Louis Waller:

---

21 LSS committee to Professor Louis Waller, 22 April 1986, MON 662, Louis Waller Law students' society file.

22 Kumar Amarakesara to Bob Baxt, 6 May 1986; Bob Williams to Tony Hynes, 23 April 1986, MON 662, MUA.

23 'Law School Sexism Scandal', *Lot's Wife*, 5 May 1986, p. 6.

24 *Student Handbook*, 1986, p. 18.

25 Davison and Murphy, *University Unlimited*, p. 158.

> In hindsight, we understand that the course of action we adopted may not have been the most appropriate. However, at that time, we had not been properly informed as to how to deal with such an issue, and there was no working, formal procedure for complaints within the faculty.

The Changing Face of the LSS

Taking a long view, the conservative coup of 1976 can be seen as marking the beginning of the modern face of the LSS. The path was not always smooth, with control of the society during the 1980s being contested between outward-looking social activists and inward-looking conservatives, interspersed by periods of inertia. By 1980 the energy of the conservative group which took control in 1976 waned, as the leaders graduated and the LSS once again fell into somnolence. It struck financial difficulties and in 1981 it was in debt and barely functioning.[26] Aware of its possible demise, in May 1981 a group of students stepped in and announced with a flourish that the LSS 'should aim to inject some form of relief into the seemingly endless academic lives of Monash law students'. This announcement, ignoring the financial problems faced by the society, appears to have lifted the spirits of the students and a reformation took place. A caretaker committee was formed, with Mark Fisher elected president. The immediate aim of the group was to meet the society's accumulated debts and continue trading. Confirmed in power by elections, the new committee re-introduced an important element of student life: the coffee service. It operated a twelve-hour service every weekday, with an extended service on Saturdays to allow part-time students to benefit. The annual ball was appropriately renamed 'the law liquidation ball' and turned a profit. *Oracle* had not been published in 1981, but an edition was planned for 1982. At the end of 1981, the president was able to report that the LSS's 'slight tax loss' had turned into a 'tax advantage' by making a small profit.[27]

The revival proved short-lived and the society had several more quiet years before the rise of the reformist 'legal action' group in the mid-1980s. The legal action group was in power at the time of the controversy over Kumar Amarakesara in 1986, taking a strong line against sexism. However, a strong reaction in the late 1980s from the increasingly conservative student

26 Monash University Annual Report 1981, p. 33.

27 Law Students' Society Report 1981.

body saw the legal action group lose control of the LSS. The society's new leadership not only built the society into the largest and wealthiest student society in the university but also developed a suite of new activities that saw the LSS become a service provider rather than an adjunct of student politics. As Richard Fox saw it, the LSS moved 'From an emphasis on social functions and a "let's get together and complain about the staff attitude", to become very consultative and responsible'. While students from the 1970s and 1980s might see this as rather sad, it was an accurate reflection of the changing nature of student life.

In 1991, when financial stringency forced a drastic reduction in tutorials, LSS president Madeline Garlick protested loudly, but without success. Responses to a questionnaire sent to all law students affirmed that students wanted weekly tutorials, so in 1993 the LSS began its own tutorial program. It quickly expanded to provide practical, problem-based tutorials conducted by senior students in parallel with what remained of the faculty's tutorial program. The LSS emphasised that, while it was happy to provide the service, it was wary of it becoming a substitute for faculty tutorials and wanted the faculty to re-introduce a full tutorial program.[28] This was not to be. As financial pressures forced the faculty to cut further, the LSS stepped into the gap and provided more and more educational services.

In 1994, the tutorial service employed ten final-year law students and articled clerks, who conducted thirty-three hours of tutorials per fortnight in contract, torts, property, criminal law, equity and trusts, and evidence. It was proposed to further expand the service to include tutorials in company law and tax. Attendance at tutorials varied from an average of fifteen to twenty students to peaks of forty students. The tutors were paid by the LSS.[29]

More than a decade before online lectures transformed university life, students were keen to record lectures on portable cassette recorders, the latest technology. This was not encouraged by the faculty, although some lecturers were happy for individuals to use their own tape recorders. The *Counter Faculty Handbook* critiques of law subjects noted whether particular lecturers allowed their lectures to be taped and if their lecturing styles adapted well to being taped. One reviewer censured Peter Ellinger for his habit of constantly pacing while lecturing 'which does not assist taping

---

28 Law Students' Society Report, 1995, p. 4.

29 *Counter Faculty Handbook*, 1994, p. 12; Faculty Board minutes, 28 October 1993.

and amplification'.[30] By 1992 the student demand for taped lectures was so great that the LSS decided to begin an organised service for taping lectures. Freehills was enlisted as a sponsor and in 1993 tapes were made of lectures in most compulsory subjects. Initially tapes had to be listened to in the Matheson library, but from 1994 they were available in the law library, though there were always concerns with the work required to administer the system and the pressures on space.[31]

In 1997, LSS President Andrew Hooper-Nguyen approached non-participating lecturers in an endeavour to 'expand the range of subjects and streams taped'. The law librarian, Nicholas Pengelley, was not happy with the increasing demands this service made on his staff. With simmering frustration and possibly displeasure, he wrote to Hooper-Nguyen: 'Two years back, after much discussion with [then LSS president] Joshua Frydenberg ...I agreed to allow the Library loans desk to be utilised for the provision of the LSS taped lecture service'. As he had predicted in 1994, demand for the tapes was now putting too much stress on loans desk staff. But that was not all that troubled him: 'Without any consultation with the Law Library' the LSS had doubled the number of taped lectures and this had placed even greater demands on library staff. Loans desk queues were now appreciably longer than in 1996 and the library staff 'have been abused and harassed by students angry that certain tapes are on loan'. Worse still, students complained that they had not been rewound, or, indeed, that 'there is only one copy of a given tape'.[32]

Presciently, Pengelley warned of the difficulty both students and the faculty would encounter a decade later when he wrote: 'it should be of some concern to the faculty that more and more students are placing reliance on the tapes'. Many students chose not to attend lectures because they had to work long hours while studying full-time and increasingly they chose to use the taped lecture service in preference to attending lectures. Despite the administrative challenge it presented to the library staff, the taped lecture service remained one of the LSS's most valuable education services until it was replaced by online lectures in the late 1990s and early 2000s.[33]

---

30 *Counter Faculty Handbook*, 1981, p. 70.

31 Faculty Board minutes, 30 July 1990.

32 This correspondence is in MON 662, 200/53/201, Louis Waller, Law students' society 1979–1989.

33 Andrew Hooper-Nguyen, 'Highlights of 1997', LSS President's Report 1997.

By the mid-1990s, the impact of the internet was being felt on campus. Turning the technology to positive use, and proud of its progressive move, in 1996 the LSS 'took the lead in the technology stakes' by setting up its own home page on the faculty's new web site. The home page gave students access to a number of academic references, careers information and links to company home pages as well as general information about the LSS.[34]

On Winning and Losing – Mooting in the 1980s and 1990s

For over three decades, participation in moot courts was compulsory. In 1984 the existing two moot court subjects were replaced with a new subject, 'Moot Court', normally to be taken in fourth year. Candidates enrolled in Moot Court were required to participate in one moot court as senior counsel, junior counsel or solicitor, presenting a jointly prepared outline of argument prior to the hearing and a thirty-minute oral argument. [35]

Peter Haug remembers his moot courts in the late 1970s with pleasure: 'It was a team of three – solicitor, junior counsel [same year level] and senior counsel [senior year]'. In the first moot he would have been either solicitor or junior counsel and stood in front of a senior judge; in the second moot he was a senior counsel. 'We wore suits and gowns too'.[36] Erol Chakir, on the other hand, found his moot court experience an ordeal. He was the instructing solicitor and the judge did not like his submissions and made him redo them. It was his first experience of a court-like situation.[37]

In general students seem to have valued the experience of mooting. Writing in *Clayton's Law* in 1994, Dale Renner proclaimed:

> If the learning of law only involved structured thinking, ability to reason, legal research skills, ability to work under time pressures, and the ability to express complex ideas in clear and simple way, then mooting would be the only subject in the curriculum.[38]

In addition to the compulsory mooting subject, in the 1980s the law school began to participate in national and international mooting competitions.

---

34 LSS Report 1996, Faculty Board minutes, 21 October 1996.

35 Faculty Board minutes, 28 March 1985.

36 Interview with Peter Haug, 14 June 2011.

37 Interview with Erol Chakir, 12 January 2012.

38 Dale Renner, 'Mooting Competition: Mental Decathlon', *Clayton's Law*, Vol. 6, No. 2, 1994 p. 18.

Successful in the 1985 international mooting competition.
Mooting team members, clockwise from top left: Alan Swanwick, Jonathan Slonim, Kate Schneeberger, John Jarrett, coach Harry Reicher, Jennifer Lalor, Andrew Hamlyn-Harris and Carmel Bianchi.
Photographer unknown, Monpix 823

A notable year was 1985, when the Monash team competed in the Philip C Jessup international law moot court competition, the world's premier moot court competition, with hundreds of law schools from up to 80 countries participating.

Harry Reicher coached the triumphant Monash team and recalls that preparation began when he was notified of the problem that would be the subject of the moot. He convened a meeting of interested students to assess their backgrounds and experience and determine who would bring the strongest qualifications to the campaign. In October 1984, thirteen students attended the meeting, which took place not long after the *Bodyline* television series on the 1932–33 Ashes series was broadcast. Echoing Douglas Jardine's advice to the English team, Harry finished his remarks in resounding fashion: 'We're not going to Washington to make friends. We're going to Washington to win!'[39] Preparation began immediately and continued right through the summer. Over the summer break the law building was virtually empty and the Jessup team was given special privileges, including access to the library twenty-four hours a day, seven

---

[39] Harry Reicher, correspondence with authors.

days a week. The rigorousness of the preparation, and the intensity of the atmosphere surrounding the Jessup campaign, meant that all the facilities made available were extremely well used.

In February 1985 the Australian regional finals were held at the Australian National University. Monash was successful, winning its way to the final in Washington in April 1985. The Monash team, consisting of Alan Swanwick, Jonathan Slonim, Kate Schneeburger, John Jarrett, Jennifer Lalor, Andrew Hamlyn-Harris and Carmel Bianchi won the memorials award, with Andrew Hamlyn-Harris and Alan Swanwick coming first and second in the oratory division.[40]

Toward the end of Bob Williams' deanship, the compulsory moot court subject was abolished, although some staff believed it could, and should, have been maintained.[41] Unlike other compulsory subjects in the law curriculum, Moot Court was not prescribed by the Council of Legal Education for admission to practice in Victoria. While the plumbers mourned the loss of the experience, the Pericleans were not disturbed and no opposition to the decision was expressed at the faculty board. However, just as the professional practice elective had provided a point of difference distinguishing Monash from other Australian law faculties, so too had the moot court experience. Again, as with tutorials, the LSS took up the challenge and began organising its own moot courts, although it could be argued that in relying on the LSS to provide the framework and mechanism for students to experience the moot court, the faculty abrogated its responsibility to its students.

From 1992 the LSS became both service provider and social club because lack of faculty funds demanded it. While it could be argued that adding mooting to its existing educational services was a natural progression, students and staff queried why fee-paying students had to be responsible for this aspect of their education. It appears the situation was accepted for what it was, and the LSS simply worked to the best of its ability to provide the necessary services. If the LSS committee hoped the faculty would reinstate mooting and tutorials, twenty years later the situation had not changed, even though the faculty's financial situation has greatly improved.

---

40 'Mastering the Moot', *Monash Reporter*, 3 April 1985, p. 4.

41 Interview with Guy Powles, Richard Fox, Susan Campbell, Bob Williams, 11 October 2010.

Students Behaving Badly

Allan York, the long-serving faculty manager, frequently had dealings with LSS presidents and other students. As time went on, his patience possibly declined and he became increasingly averse to untidiness and mess around the law building. One of his pet hates was bill-posting and he complained to LSS president Fiona Blackmore: 'The bill-posting activities of the Law Students' Society are turning the Law building into a slum'. York complained that he was 'continually removing posters and sticky tape' to 'preserve our asset for future waves of Law students'. Pointing out that there was very little money in the university for cleaning buildings and glass, painting walls or restoring woodwork, he fulminated: 'I wonder whether the Society has considered turning its energies to the raising of funds for the maintenance of the building and, in particular, the replacement of the flooring in the locker-rooms and the coffee-room.'[42]

The LSS regarded itself as 'the premier Law Students' Society in Australia', a claim not always in accord with the behaviour of its members. In 1993 the antics of students at the LSS 'Bottom of the Harbour Ball', held on the historic *Polly Woodside*, were reported in that notable journal of record, the Melbourne *Truth*. 'Law students cut up rough – sex and vomit at wild party', was the headline. According to *Polly Woodside* staff and bouncers, 'some of the behaviour was disgraceful'. The bars were said to be crazy all night: 'Every person attending was given a free shot glass when they arrived and free tequila and sambucca was distributed all night'. Worse still, full strength beer had to be rationed to stop the students from stealing it from under the bars and when it began to run out, they started drinking wine from the bottles! A couple was caught having sex behind the nearby Melbourne Maritime Museum. 'Our future judges and barristers don't behave any better than [at] a bucks' party in Brunswick', the paper declared.[43]

Enclosing the lurid report, the secretary of the Polly Woodside volunteers association, Jean Barry, wrote to the dean, Bob Williams. The Monash students had 'desecrated the ship and surrounding area by vomiting, urinating and leaving a trail of smashed glasses, cigarette butts and food scraps over the complex', she declared. What disciplinary action did he propose? Williams discovered that a substantial sum had been paid to ensure that 'an appropriate degree of organisation and control' would be maintained, but clearly something had gone wrong. He requested LSS

---

42 Allan York to Fiona Blackmore, 17 April 1989, MON 1096, MUA.

43 'Law Students Cut Up Rough – Sex and Vomit at Wild Party', *Truth*, 8 April 1993.

president Murray to contact the secretary and to make reparations for the damage to the site. How much damage the episode caused to the law faculty is harder to evaluate.

Eyes on the Prize

Through his school years at Mount Scopus, Josh Frydenberg was torn between his two ambitions of becoming a lawyer or a professional tennis player. The conflict was still not fully resolved when he came to Monash in 1991 (choosing Monash for its reputation and because many of his school friends were going there) and he took several years to settle into his law course. However, he became involved in the LSS and late in 1993 successfully stood for president against Brendan Darcy and Nivanka Fernando, with the slogan 'Let's make it a year of action'.[44]

Frydenberg came to the LSS presidency with big ideas. Student career prospects and student welfare were his major priorities. While the LSS already offered a range of services including Legibook, moot courts, tutorials and the taped lecture service, he felt that it should do more to prepare students to promote themselves and apply for jobs. The LSS already published a *Careers Directory*, and now it brought potential employers to Monash, with a 'careers fair'. The inaugural fair on 4 August 1994 attracted thirty-five legal employers, including large commercial firms, smaller suburban practices, patent attorneys, the Victorian bar, the attorney-general's department and companies employing in-house solicitors.[45] Bob Williams wrote to Josh, congratulating him on the 'outstanding success' of the careers' day and the publication *A Practical Guide: Careers for Law Students* which was produced for the day.[46] However, pleas to the faculty for a course and careers service were less successful, with the dean offering 'moral support' but no money.[47] Consequently, it was left to the LSS to develop its own services even further.

As articled clerkships became harder to find and the fight for places in large law firms grew more competitive, the LSS began to promote the faculty's graduates more aggressively. A survey had shown that of the 99 articled clerks taken on by the seven largest law firms in 1994, 32 were Monash graduates, 59 from Melbourne and 8 from other universities, even though

---

44 Interview with Joshua Frydenberg, 15 October 2012.

45 *Clayton's Law*, 1994, No. 2, p. 3.

46 8 August 1994, C R Williams to Joshua Frydenberg, Dean's Correspondence.

47 Luke Parsons to Professor Ian Chubb, Senior Deputy Vice-Chancellor, 15 August 1994.

Monash had approximately 40 per cent more graduates than Melbourne. The LSS ascribed this primarily to Melbourne's more generous marking and granting of honours degrees. Employers understandably equated the value of an honours degree at Monash with an honours degree at Melbourne, even though Monash gave far fewer of them. The LSS pushed successfully for the marking system to be brought into line with that of Melbourne, with a new scale of indicative marks being introduced in 1995.

Each year, the incoming LSS executive and committee came into office with a 'blank slate', with no systems or manuals to guide them. To overcome this, the 1994 committee developed a series of manuals instructing the latest incumbents on how to follow the systems. Another initiative in this era was a Monash law students' society lecture series featuring a galaxy of Australian legal stars, including the governor, Richard McGarvie, Justice Sally Brown, Ronald Sackville QC, Michael Rozenes QC, Malcolm Turnbull QC and Justice Michael Kirby. A request to the dean for financial assistance brought the reply, 'The series of lectures you have organised is quite outstanding. I congratulate you on your efforts. …I am prepared to provide $1,700 support for the lecture series as requested.[48]

A final achievement of the LSS in 1994 was a *Valedictory Yearbook*, something Bob Williams saw as a valuable contribution to the faculty. He bemoaned the fact that the practice of photographing the first year legal process class was not followed in the years following his own presence in that class in 1964, and reflected that 'thirty years later, sadly, [we are] unable to identify many of those students and have very few records of the events that occurred'. He concluded 'Thirty years from now, I am sure it will be treasured as a repository of information regarding old friends and the happenings of the most crucial formative period of persons' professional lives'.[49]

---

48 Williams to Frydenberg, 31 August 1994.

49 Dean's foreword to 1994 *Valedictory Yearbook*.

Chapter 19

The Clinical Program

A Transformative Experience

Its supporters have long held the clinical program up as the 'flagship' program of the faculty, and the most important point of difference between Monash and most other Australian law schools. On several occasions in the 1980s and 1990s, as financial stringency bit hard, the faculty bean counters sharpened their axes and threatened to cut down the flagpole. During the period of greatest financial restraint in the 1990s, when the faculty slashed the tutorial program and stopped running moot courts, the clinical program was another obvious target, but its supporters were able to mobilise sufficient support to ensure its survival. Again, in the mid-2000s, when the first review of the program was undertaken, its survival was ensured through support of the profession, politicians and community groups.

For a significant number of Monash law students, taking the professional practice elective proved to be an enlightening experience, where they suddenly saw the relevance of the rest of their law course to the practice of law. Jeff Giddings has vivid memories of the first time he served divorce documents. 'It was memorable having to front a guy who did not want to receive them, but you manage to muster the courage to do what you have to do. The clinical program was invaluable for that sort of training.' He also remembers a mum and dad couple, migrants from Germany, whose son had taken out a car loan. They had unwittingly been made guarantors and when the son defaulted on the loan, the finance company began to exert pressure. After a while the couple 'rather liked the idea of a wide-eyed, enthusiastic lad looking after them', although Jeff found it rather intimidating having people expecting him to deliver. This was a really memorable experience. He also vividly remembers the fun they had.[1]

---

1 Interview with Jeff Giddings, 18 October 2010.

The Legal Services and the Faculty

The three legal services – Springvale, Doveton and Monash-Oakleigh – had varied histories, structures, and relationships with the law school. By 1980 the Springvale Legal Service had an elected board independent of the university and was supported by professional staff including lawyers and social workers, with Simon Smith as co-ordinator. Alan Nicoll was employed full-time as an advocate as an interim measure, with fifty per cent of his salary funded by the Commonwealth Legal Aid Office, which also contributed towards the cost of social workers and interpreters. Funds also came from the Springvale city council and donations. The Springvale Legal Service was a strongly political organisation and there were continued tensions with the Monash law school arising from clashes between political and educational aims and objectives.[2] There were thirty-one students in each intake at Springvale.

The Doveton and District Legal Service, a community-based organisation with elected directors, was supported by local women volunteers who undertook the daytime administrative work. The community lawyer, Charles Aitken, was employed for three 4-hour sessions per week, and Guy Powles, Domenica Whelan and Elaine Canty (later a well-known ABC radio broadcaster) were the solicitor/tutors. The legal service worked closely with the Doveton-Hallam community health centre where it was located. Funding came from the Commonwealth, the health centre and the university. Seven students attended the Doveton centre.

The Monash Legal Service at that stage did not have a formal legal structure, being managed by the staff responsible for the clinical program. It was based in the former Marist College building in Normanby Road, with Carol Bartlett as solicitor and a university-funded secretary. Ten students enrolled each semester.

In 1980, a report by Guy Powles refocused the faculty on its twin objectives in running the clinical program – providing legal education to students and providing a public service reflecting the social needs of each community. He called for action to build a closer relationship and genuine understanding between the faculty and the three legal services, and this led to the establishment in July 1980 of a standing committee on professional practice.[3]

---

2 For a discussion of these conflicts and their resolution, see Giddings, *Promoting Justice Through Clinical Legal Education*, pp. 176–7.

3 Establishment of Standing Committee on Professional Practice to oversee matters related to the Professional Practice course, Faculty Board minutes 30 July 1980, Guy Powles memo to Professional Practice Review Committee, undated, 1980.

The close relationship and understanding were tested in the early 1980s by three major issues: part-time versus full-time staff, the appointment of Simon Smith to a continuing lectureship, and increasing financial stringency.

During the 1970s, supervision of students in the clinical program was in the hands of law school staff members and paid part-time supervisors, who were usually full-time solicitors. At Springvale, Simon Smith found both problematic – university staff because they would take their sessions but then took no responsibility for following up the issues that inevitably arose with clients, and paid part-timers because they increasingly referred cases from their SLS sessions to their friends' private practices. For Smith, the prime focus at Springvale had to be on service to the clients, and the existing staffing model was not ideal. Consequently, in 1981 Maureen Tehan was appointed as a second full-time lawyer, allowing greatly reduced use of part-timers and giving much greater continuity and attention to detail.[4]

Simon Smith's original appointment to the SLS had been as 'dean's assistant' and he felt that the clinical program would only gain legitimacy in the law school if he was given a proper academic appointment. Many in the law school resisted this on the grounds that the work was not genuinely academic and because Smith did not have a higher degree, but in 1982 Bob Baxt somewhat reluctantly offered him a lectureship. In spite of this success, there have been continuing issues ever since over the academic status of teaching staff in the clinical program.[5]

The expense of the clinical program and the lack of commitment to it on the part of a significant percentage of the staff made it an obvious target when there was talk of cutbacks.[6] The first financial crisis for the clinical program began in 1981 when the Monash Legal Service issued a press release revealing that 'unless the Faculty can find outside funds for the purpose, the course should be discontinued'. While it survived, pressure on the program meant that it was unable to take more than thirty-four students for the summer term. A grant in April 1982 of $10,000 from the Legal Aid Commission helped it continue but Monash's involvement with the Doveton clinic ceased in 1981. This decision was reached 'with hesitation

---

4 Giddings, *Promoting Justice through Clinical Legal Education*, pp. 176, 178.

5 Ibid., p. 179.

6 Interview with Richard Fox, Bob Williams, Sue Campbell and Guy Powles, 11 October 2010.

and disappointment', but without more external funding, the faculty could not continue its financial commitment to Doveton.[7]

Powles was concerned that the Monash Legal Service made little impact in its neighbourhood. Rather than just serving Monash students, Powles believed it was in the best interests of both the surrounding community and the law students that the service should be regarded as belonging to those people of the area who needed it.[8] He pursued his belief that the university must relate to areas far beyond its own boundaries, and argued that the service should seek to integrate itself with the social services of the City of Oakleigh.[9] This took place in March 1983. The newly named Monash-Oakleigh Legal Service (MOLS) shifted its focus to service more fully its various communities and relocated to 60 Beddoe Avenue, Clayton, within easy walking distance of the faculty.

The following year (1984), Sue Campbell became the co-ordinator of the clinical education program. Ranking with her namesake Enid as one of the dominant personalities of the Monash law school, Campbell was the daughter of a judge and educated at PLC, Lauriston and the University of Melbourne. After a period in private practice and teaching experience at the Leo Cussen Institute and Melbourne University, she was appointed to a lectureship at Monash in 1980. From the outset she threw a large part of her enormous energies into the clinical program, bringing all her qualities of dedication, tenacity, creativity and enthusiasm to motivate and enthuse colleagues and students. Those who dared question the value of the program knew they would face the full force of her scorn, her great powers of persuasion and her ability to mobilise support in high places. During his term as dean, clinical program staff felt that Bob Williams was 'benignly disengaged' from the clinics, being neither supportive nor opposed. However, while financial imperatives led him to axe tutorials and moot courts, they believed he hesitated to cut back or abolish the clinical program because he was intimidated by Sue Campbell, 'who had this way of looking at you that Bob in particular found thoroughly intimidating'.[10]

Sue Campbell was one of the faculty's outstanding teachers and she had a deep interest in curriculum development. Within the clinical program she

---

7 Report to faculty board by standing committee on professional practice, 5 August 1981.

8 Guy Powles to Allan J Nicoll, LACV, 21 September 1981. Guy Powles private papers.

9 Guy Powles paper 'Monash Legal Service Re-location and re-orientation proposals for a plan', 19 October 1982; Guy Powles to Ian Tate, Deputy Comptroller, Monash University, re: Monash Legal Service, 19 October 1982. Guy Powles private papers.

10 Interview with Adrian Evans, 3 April 2012.

was largely responsible for the instigation of a student appearance program that allowed students to represent legal service clients in court and to conduct court exercises with police prosecutors, and in the establishment of specialist clinics. She made many important contributions to the broader curriculum, designing the postgraduate diploma in legal practice, skills and ethics, and transforming the teaching of Legal Process. Her reputation as a leader in clinical legal education led to her unique appointment in 2000 as a professorial fellow in legal practice as well as to several invitations to advise other law schools looking to set up clinical programs. In 2007, her work was acknowledged with the award of an AM for 'Services to the law, particularly through the development of clinical legal education in Australia and community legal services in Victoria'. In typical Sue Campbell fashion she was self-deprecating and unassuming in her acceptance of acclaim from her peers for this achievement.

Adrian Evans, who worked closely with Sue Campbell for many years, wrote on her retirement that she had

> asserted the needs of the clinical program without fear in the face of numerous Deans (one even described her affectionately as a 'terror') and generally provided wise counsel to whoever knocked on her door. No shrinking violet, Sue Campbell has institutionalised the notion of the caring Monash teacher, someone who would take great pains to get a fair deal for a student in distress or difficulty, whilst simultaneously bending law school authority figures as the means to her noble ends. Fundamentally — as you would expect from a Judge's daughter — Sue is an advocate for whoever needs help.[11]

Such were the benefits to students of the clinical education program that a 1985 staff report affirmed that the faculty regarded its existence as 'vital for the training of those students who propose to pursue careers as legal practitioners', and as desirable for students generally in providing perspectives on the working of the legal system.[12] However, as Richard Fox found when assessing research undertaken in the faculty, academic staff who devoted their time to the clinical program were at risk of being disadvantaged. If their research productivity was low during their time in the

---

11 Adrian Evans, 'Au revoir Sue Campbell', *Springvale Monash Legal Service, Annual Report, 2003–4*, p. 17.

12 Full-time staff report 'Aims and Objectives of the Monash University Faculty of Law', 1985.

From left: Peter McCall (Mayor of Springvale), Kevin Westfold, Sue Campbell, Bob Baxt, Jim Kennan (attorney-general), and Simon Smith, cheque presentation at Springvale Legal Service, 1985.
Photographer unknown, Monpix 999

program it would reduce their prospects for promotion. Fox recommended making research an integral component of the clinical program and that clinical staff should attempt 'an annual piece of collective research associated with the work of the legal service'[13] From the late 1970s staff members had been publishing articles on the clinical program, but, until the publication of Sue Campbell's seminal work, 'Blueprint for a clinical program' in 1991,

13 'Research and the Clinical Legal Education Programme', Richard Fox to Bob Baxt, 30 July 1984, Guy Powles private papers.

these were more a record of the processes involved in establishing Monash's clinical program than collaborative research projects.[14] Later publications dealt with evaluations of clinical legal education, innovations in clinical legal education and practical legal skills.[15]

'An Essential Part of Every Victorian Solicitor's Library': The *Lawyers Practice Manual*

One of the most important initiatives to come out of the clinical program has been the *Lawyers Practice Manual (Victoria)*, first published in 1985. During the first decade of the clinical program, staff and practitioners at Springvale and Monash had produced practice guides and sets of sample documents for students covering questions not answered in statutes, reports or texts, but many of the finer points of legal practice were passed on by word of mouth. This could be 'hit-and-miss' and newcomers didn't necessarily have any structured sense of what they were doing.[16] The *Manual* was produced to fill this gap and came directly out of the experience of teaching students in the clinics. Sue Campbell, Guy Powles, Simon Smith and Maureen Tehan formed the first editorial committee and the *Lawyers Practice Manual* was created.

The *Practice Manual* was designed to show how lawyers should handle a variety of situations through a series of fictional stories on different issues written by one or more lawyer experienced in the particular field.[17] It emphasised the informal aspects of practice and each chapter included examples of completed documents. The first edition of the 'Green Book' was

---

14 Simon Smith, 'Clinical Legal Education – The Case of Springvale Legal Service', *Legal Service Bulletin*, 1974, pp. 49–53; Gerry Nash 'Skills Course or Clinic?' *Australian Law Journal*, Vol. 54, pp. 535–7; Carol C Bartlett, 'Towards Professional Competence – Clinical Legal Education', *Law Institute Journal*, 56, 1982, p. 121; Sue Campbell 'Blueprint for a Clinical Program', *Journal of Professional Legal Education*, vol. 9, no. 121, 1991.

15 See for example, Ross Hyams, Susan Campbell and Adrian Evans, *Practical Legal Skills*, Oxford University Press, South Melbourne, 1998, 2nd edition 2004 and 3rd edition 2007; Bronwyn Naylor, Ross Hyams, *Innovation in Clinical Legal Education: Educating Lawyers for the Future*, Alternative Law Journal, monograph, no. 1, 2007; and Ross Hyams, 'Multidisciplinary Clinical Legal Education: The Future of the Profession', *Alternative Law Journal*, June, 2012, vol. 37, no2.

16 'Practical Law Will No Longer Be Just Hit and Miss', review of *Lawyers Practice Manual (Victoria)* in *Monash Reporter*, 19 August 1985, p. 13.

17 Interview with Adrian Evans, 5 April 2012.

Copy of original brochure for the *Lawyers Practice Manual (Victoria)*.
Simon Simon Collection

published as a large loose-leaf volume, which could readily be updated, and cost $110 when first published in 1985.

Sue Campbell was leading joint editor of the *Practice Manual* from its inception. She predicted in 1985 that 'It will probably end up as an essential part of every Victorian solicitor's library' and, to a large extent, this has proved to be the case.[18] Although originally designed for students, it now attracts nearly 2,000 subscribers, with the royalties going to support the Springvale Legal Service.[19] The success of the *Lawyers Practice Manual* produced other benefits for the clinical program, not least the elevation of the clinical teachers' self-respect.[20] One of the arguments against the program

18 Interview in *Monash Reporter*, 19 August 1985, p. 13.

19 Interview with Sue Campbell, 5 November 2010.

20 Interview with Adrian Evans, 5 April 2012.

was that 'the clinicians did not recognise scholarship', but the production of the *Manual* proved that practitioners could think systematically and deeply about policy issues.[21] At the celebration held for the 25th anniversary of the *Lawyers Practice Manual* in November 2010, Guy Powles emphasised the major contribution made by Sue Campbell, who 'had her steady hand on the wheel of the good ship *LPM*, through rough seas and calm'.[22]

Since 2003 the *Lawyers Practice Manual (Victoria)* has been published in two formats, a loose-leaf book and an online version. Today, the manual's overall aim is to assist subscribers to gain practical insight quickly by providing a step-by-step guide with an overview of the law relevant to each practice area covered, supported by tools, such as practical hints, precedents, letters and standard forms. The manual is now well established as an integral tool for the legal fraternity in Victoria.

The Real World

By 1986 the clinical program had a team of full-time teachers, supervision had improved, and the seminar and tutorial programs were redesigned. Such was the reputation of the Springvale Legal Service that it was invited to conduct 'interviewing' seminars for organisations as diverse as Phillips Fox, the young lawyers and the Nunawading Legal Service. Its 'interpreting' seminar formed the basis of a Leo Cussen Institute video on working with interpreters.

The student reviewing the professional practice elective for the 1985 *Counter Faculty Handbook* clearly enjoyed the experience. Describing it as a 'must' and the 'best subject offered by the Law faculty', the reviewer saw the subject as an opportunity to gain 'some impression of what the real world' had to offer: 'You will get valuable experience in interviewing techniques, negotiation and mediation'. Accusations of marking according to political beliefs rather than effort and knowledge were refuted, for 'students are judged on their commitment to their clients and fellow workers'.[23]

A decade on, wishing she had discovered it sooner, a student reflected 'I finished my degree on a high note by completing Professional Practice elective at Monash Oakleigh Legal Service… the work at MOLS gave me a real sense of satisfaction'. Although she had experience in criminal

---

21 Ibid., 5 April 2012.

22 LPM Vic 25th birthday celebration, 30 November 2010, p. 3.

23 *Counter Faculty Handbook*, 1985, p. 53.

Springvale Legal Service Duty Beer Scheme Committee claimed compensation from CUB.

Clockwise from bottom left: George Georgiou, Bruce Webb, Stuart Baron, Jeff Giddings, Denise Woolerton, Michael Cosgrave (tutor) and Greg Crundall.

Photographer unknown, Monpix 1000

law, at MOLS she was exposed to family, property and contract law and 'it was great to be able to put some of that academic knowledge into practical application'.[24]

Students continued to gain from their practical experience and increasing legal knowledge. One group, which got together for a drink every Friday, turned their knowledge into profit. Jeff Giddings brought along a dozen bottles of Victoria Bitter to one of the 'Friday afternoon wind-downs', but they found that one bottle was only half full. After considering the matter, while consuming one of the full bottles, the group decided to take action. On behalf of 'the Springvale Legal Service Duty Beer Scheme Committee' they wrote a letter of complaint to Carlton & United Breweries. Displaying their vast legal knowledge by quoting *Donoghue v*

---

24 Anne Pattison, 'Reflections of a MOLS Student', *Monash Oakleigh Annual Report 2004–2005*, np.

Stevenson, they threatened CUB with legal action, alleging nervous shock and other effects from the find. Giddings delivered the letter and the defective bottle to CUB himself and shortly afterwards they received two dozen bottles in compensation.[25] CUB's public relations officer, William Turner, thought their letter of complaint, 'the funniest letter I have read in 14 years of beer'.[26]

In 1981 the Springvale service began an award for the most outrageous *faux pas* by a student, either uttered or observed, during a semester. It was named the Slade Trophy because when Simon Smith was unpacking a box of possessions, he found an old saucepan with Phil Slade's name on it. The annual student award was duly named the Slade Trophy.

But the Slade Trophy had a serious side. Simon Smith and Sue Campbell decided to make it a centrepiece of the celebration they held each year when students were invited to one of their homes. Rather than just having a social event where students and staff just 'stood around with a drink', they decided to make it a prize-giving night. Students were invited to bring a plate of food – no packets of biscuits were allowed – and they had to make an effort to participate in the celebration. It was a structured evening, where taped messages or telegrams from public luminaries – Gough Whitlam, Ron Barassi, Mary Delahunty, Bill Hayden – were read out to attendees. The attitude of the organisers was that there was 'no reason why the law can't be fun'. It was also a reminder to students that 'you might think we weren't listening but we were'.

Jeff Giddings remembers that some prize-winning student efforts were 'quite extraordinary':

> Simon Crawford won one semester – he ran out of time when he was preparing a will for a client and told him, 'you just sign at the bottom and I'll type it up'. Another Slade Trophy winner was the girl who visited a client in the Springvale Watchhouse and left him with a cigarette and a lighter – shortly afterwards the Springvale Watchhouse was burnt down.[27]

In 1986 the *Bulletin* noted that the presentation of 'this prestigious trophy' was the social highlight of the professional practice course. It even boasted that the Slade Trophy, then in its fifteenth year, was ranked 'alongside the

---

[25] Interview with Jeff Giddings, 18 October 2010.

[26] *Monash Reporter*, 3 April 1985, p. 4.

[27] Interview with Jeff Giddings, 18 October 2010.

Outgoing Slade Trophy winner Bill Sizeland with incoming winner Jim Mellas, c.1985.
Simon Smith Collection

University Medal and the Supreme Court Prize!'[28] Always held at the home of one of the staff, the Slade trophy was light relief and 'a fun party night'.[29]

In the mid-1980s the SLS experienced a major crisis arising from a critical staff shortage and increasingly inadequate premises. In 1984 Maureen Tehan left to work in Alice Springs and the following year community lawyer, Mary Anne Noone left for a clinical position at La Trobe University. It proved extremely difficult to fill the vacant positions and in April 1985 a public meeting of SLS supporters was told that the closure of the centre was a strong possibility. However, with Simon Smith shouldering an enormous workload, the SLS was able to keep going until the appointment of Tim McCoy in May 1986 alleviated the situation.[30] In announcing the appointment, Simon Smith said: 'Not only is Tim an experienced and talented lawyer but he has a proven record of commitment

---

28 SLS, press release no. 2, 12 February 1986.

29 Interview with Simon Smith, 5 April 2011 and Guy Powles, email to authors, 18 August 2013.

30 Giddings, *Promoting Justice Through Clinical Legal Education*, pp. 181–2.

to community involvement. We were beginning to wonder whether we could again find such a combination.' McCoy, then aged thirty, held degrees in commerce and law from Melbourne, where he also gained a double blue in rowing. Remembered with affection as 'a man of style, eccentricity and charm' who believed in kindness and food as two of the great civilising traits of humankind, he made a deep impact on the clinical program in the short time he was there.[31]

Along with most members of the faculty's left-wing legal action group, Jennifer Nielsen chose to take the professional practice elective, which she did at Springvale in 1986. In that year there were thirty-six in the faculty's honours program, and all the students doing the elective with her were honours students.[32] Springvale 'left a huge imprint' on Jennifer and her friends. She went on to articles with the Aboriginal Legal Service and also volunteered at the women's legal resources group where she stayed on after she went into practice.[33]

Each year the support given to the Springvale Legal Service by the Legal Aid Commission was acknowledged in a ceremonial cheque presentation. In 1988 Attorney-General Andrew McCutcheon presented a cheque for $50,000 on the day of the service's fifteenth birthday, and lawyer Susan Miller took advantage of the occasion to draw the attorney-general's attention to the pioneering work of the clinical program which she said 'brings a talented and enthusiastic staff and university resources to work for the local community and has a direct impact on improving the quality of education of the next generation of Victorian lawyers.'[34]

Poised for Change

In July 1987, Tim McCoy left Springvale to work at the Fitzroy Legal Service and was replaced by barrister Sue Miller. Soon after, community legal centres across Victoria were rocked when Tim McCoy died of an acute asthma attack aged only thirty-one. He is remembered for many things, including his watermelon earring, buttercup overalls and his fine facility with chocolate éclairs. He loved his clients and they loved him and travelled across the state to attend the community legal service he worked in. He was 'gentle and funny and fierce and fluent!' and the impact he made

---

31 Greenwood, *It Seemed Like a Good Idea at the Time*, pp. 63, 69.

32 Faculty Board minutes, 3 April 1986.

33 Interview with Jennifer Nielsen, 23 March 2012.

34 SLS press release no. 1, 19 February 1988.

on colleagues, clients and students is reflected in the large attendance at the annual Tim McCoy lecture and dinner which commemorates his contribution to community legal services in Victoria.[35]

In 1988, Simon Smith left Springvale after ten years to become the first insurance industry ombudsman and Adrian Evans took up the position of co-ordinator at Springvale. Evans had studied law because his father believed this would be good training for joining the family business. He completed law and commerce degrees at Melbourne, but then rebelled and refused to go into business with his father, though he agreed to do his articles. His articles year was with a small, now defunct, firm whose main area of practice was contested exhumations, dealing with people who had been buried in the wrong graves. After 'learning a lot about that area of the law but virtually nothing else', Evans spent a dismal year learning tax accounting at Price Waterhouse. It was not until 1976, when he went to La Trobe to work for the student legal service, that he felt he had found his niche. He also got a part-time job with the student union at Monash, which at that time ran the student legal service independently of the law school.

When the Monash-Oakleigh Legal Service took over the previously informal student legal service, Evans' job at Monash ceased, but he stayed at La Trobe for another ten years until he was appointed co-ordinator of the Springvale Legal Service. Simon Smith, 'the stalwart, the crusader', famous for his boundless energy, was always going to be a hard act to follow. In contrast, Adrian Evans was quickly described as 'cool, calm and authoritative, like the best cocktail'.[36] Evans saw Springvale as different and confronting for the students but also good for them. To him it represented the conscience of the law school, creating a sense of responsibility for social justice issues in the whole faculty. He feels that, if only for this reason, the clinical program was critical for Monash.[37]

Gradually Evans introduced changes to the clinical program at Springvale. Late in 1989 the clinical teachers began discussions with the police training academy in Glen Waverley, with a view to law students being able to take part in the advocacy exercises conducted at the academy for police recruits. The joint exercises commenced in 1990, giving Professional Practice students the opportunity for an additional and valuable educational experience.[38]

---

35 Greenwood, *It Seemed Like a Good Idea at the Time*, p. 73.

36 Ibid., p. 86.

37 Interview with Adrian Evans, 5 April 2012.

38 Faculty Board minutes 20 April 1990.

Adrian Evans was appointed Co-ordinator Springvale Legal Service when Simon Smith left in 1988.

Staff from left: Susanne Liden, Susan Miller and (standing) coordinator Adrian Evans, with Mr Julian Gardner director of Legal Aid at Legal Aid Commission of Victoria. Photographer Richard Crompton, Monpix 1004

In the 1990s a systematic integration of community development (or 'effecting desirable socio-legal change') into professional practice began. As Evans wrote in the annual report:

> It is understood to mean the process by which groups of clients are given the skills to articulate the reality (for their lives) of the consequences of their social and legal problems... [They] learn to reflect on what has happened to them... [and] begin to seek an active role in changing the conditions that lead to their individual problems.[39]

Good examples of the sort of work he had in mind were the family violence initiatives implemented in 1990. In January a family violence action group was established, in July the group initiated 'Wisewoman', a mutual support and self-help group for women victims of family violence, and in August

[39] Greenwood, *It Seemed Like a Good Idea at the Time*, p. 91.

it joined with the Westernport family violence network to initiate 'family violence awareness month'.[40]

In 1990, Roy Reekie came to Springvale as a casework lawyer. The son of Scottish immigrants, Roy Reekie was educated at Warrnambool High School before studying law at Monash, completing his LLB in 1987. His positive experience of the clinical program made him enthusiastic about working at Springvale. One memorable case began when he 'acquired' the Cambodian master of a refugee boat as a client. With Roy's background in maritime matters (based on crash courses in customs and imports and immigration law, as well as his Warrnambool upbringing), he took on this complex matter and 'achieved the desired result'. In the same year that Roy Reekie began at Springvale, Ross Hyams was appointed co-ordinator of Monash-Oakleigh Legal Service. Ross was a clinical alumnus from 1986 and had spent a few years in private practice but had been, as he described it 'severely bitten by the clinical bug'.[41]

In 1992, when Reekie took a six month sabbatical from Springvale, Melbourne Legal Aid Commission solicitor and author, Kerry Greenwood, worked as a locum and then stayed on as supervising solicitor for the Tuesday morning sessions. She later wrote *It Seemed Like a Good Idea at the Time: A History of the Springvale Legal Service 1973–1993*. An 'unconventional history' because 'the place is unconventional', she found the shape of the history was dictated 'by the nature of the Legal Service'. More than anything, Greenwood 'wanted to get across the revolutionary feel of the Legal Service' in the early days. An example was the Springvale morning tea, at which a politician or legal luminary seen as insufficiently co-operative was invited to morning tea, seated, and presented with tea, cake and a barrage of questions.

In 1998 the SLS celebrated twenty-five years at Osborne Avenue, Springvale. The milestone was marked with a distinctly multicultural celebration featuring Tanzanian music and food from around the world. More than 150 people, including faculty staff, students, former volunteers and local community members, attended the celebration where John Phillips CJ cut the birthday cake.[42] At MOLS, Guy Powles and Ross Hyams sought to improve the service by seeking a larger, better designed and equipped premises at the same address. The university was persuaded to undertake a complete re-modelling of the premises and a purpose-designed legal service

40 'Timeline: 1971–1993', in ibid., pp. 133–4.

41 Interview with Ross Hyams, 25 September 2013.

42 'Quarter of a Ton Legal Event', *Monash Memo*, Issue 21, 23 September 1998, p. 3.

was built to accommodate, as well, community and family law assistance programs and a tutorial room for students. The present building in Beddoe Avenue was opened in 1998, again by John Phillips.

In April 1999, Sue Campbell and Adrian Evans secured funding of $100,000 per year for three years for the establishment of a self-help clinic for people in contested family law proceedings.[43] The Monash family law assistance program (FLAP), located within the Monash-Oakleigh Legal Service, was officially launched in April 2000 by federal attorney-general Daryl Williams. Within a short time FLAP was praised as an 'innovative and holistic family law assistance program' that was bringing significant benefits to the Family Court.[44] FLAP has since evolved into a program consisting of 100 students and volunteers per year, assisting approximately 1800 clients per year, and with about 250 active cases at any time. It also runs a weekly duty lawyer service at the Dandenong Federal Circuit Court, seeing 25 clients every week, who otherwise would have no access to legal advice. Much of this success is due to the tireless work of its principal solicitor, Malcolm Bennett, who has run the program continuously since 2000.

In 2000 postgraduate students for the first time were able to experience the clinical program, with the establishment of the postgraduate diploma in legal practice, skills and ethics. The new diploma was designed to satisfy the post-degree practical training requirements for admission to legal practice for those looking for an alternative to articles. All students participated in the clinical program by attending clinics and advising clients. The postgraduate diploma was phased out in 2007, but a separate postgraduate professional practice session was introduced in 2012 at Monash-Oakleigh Legal Service, which has proved very popular amongst postgraduates eager for practical experience.

In late 1999 the Springvale Legal Service was re-named to more accurately reflect Monash's commitment and involvement, becoming the Springvale Monash Legal Service (SMLS). By 2000, when Ross Hyams became co-ordinator, the service had thirteen full and part-time staff, twenty law students on regular rotation and approximately eighty volunteers. Prior to his appointment to Springvale, Ross Hyams had been manager of the Monash-Oakleigh Legal Service for ten years. He was the principal author of *Practical Legal Skills* (OUP) and an editor of the family law section of

43 Faculty Board minutes 21 April 1999.

44 *Monash Memo*, 3 May 2000.

the *Lawyers Practice Manual (Victoria).* At the same time as Hyams came to Springvale, Fay Gertner, who had been acting co-ordinator there, moved to MOLS.

Many students were apprehensive prior to commencing the professional practice elective, either at SMLS or MOLS. In February, students in the first semester intake asked 'Will we remember the law we are supposed to already know? What will we say to clients? Will they smell our fear and ask to speak to a real lawyer?' By April, either 'SMLS has taken over our lives' or 'they wouldn't have chosen this subject if they'd known'. By May they 'are much more confident with the clients' and beginning to make their own assessments of their legal problems; they are amazed that they really know some law. Attitudes to clients range from, 'they've been given the run around and really need our help' to 'how the hell did they get themselves into this mess?' By June they are 'old hands'. Success has bolstered their confidence, and in July when the changeover occurs, they acknowledge 'I'm going to miss this [and] … this subject should be compulsory'.[45]

Paul Mishura is typical of many students who regard Professional Practice as 'the best Monash experience' and in his opinion 'it's what puts Monash above Melbourne'. Paul was at Springvale and found it 'emulated practice as closely as possible and was very realistic'. For Paul, Professional Practice confirmed that he'd made the right choice in his course and career, though he realised that for others it confirmed that they'd made the wrong choice. There was a bit of luck involved. One girl in his class saw only some really bad cases and nasty people – it was literally the luck of the draw who you got. In contrast, Paul's experiences were very positive and encouraging. A highlight was a dispute over rented residential premises that went to VCAT. He felt at one stage that the case was 'going to pieces before my eyes', when the landlord pointed out that the 'rotten window frames' alleged by Paul's clients were in fact steel. However, Paul saw that the landlord (a solicitor) was digging himself into a hole over his own failures to act within the law and so he was able to sit back while his client's position improved. In the end the case was settled with both parties walking away and bearing their own costs. Paul recalls that

> We were also supposed to have found a lawyer to sit in and give us feedback. I naively gave my feedback form to the presiding VCAT member and she provided amazing feedback. When I took it back to

[45] Julie Haylett, Professional Practice Student, *Springvale Monash Legal Service Annual Report 1999–2000*, p. 14.

> Springvale they were blown away, for no-one had ever received feedback from a VCAT member before (probably entirely because we were not supposed to ask them), so it was a real first, and just good luck on my part.

While he found many subjects like Constitutional Law remote from real life, 'Professional Practice is the law in action'.[46]

To encourage those students enthused by the clinical program, in 1995 Adrian Evans established a new clinical unit, Advanced Professional Practice, to allow students to specialise in a specific area of socio-legal service. The unit provides a range of specialist placement clinics embedded in partner legal organisations. In 2013 there were eight specialist clinics: the joint sexual assault clinic, in conjunction with the South-East Centre Against Sexual Assault at Springvale Monash Legal Service; the human rights clinic, in conjunction with the Castan Centre for Human Rights, at Holding Redlich, involving litigation with human rights dimensions; the commercial law clinic, in conjunction with Moores Legal, involving commercial legal work for 'not-for-profit' organisations; the family violence clinic at Springvale Monash Legal Service, assisting victims of family violence; the migration clinic, working with South Eastern Migration Service on refugee and migration matters; the employment law clinic at Jobwatch; the Monash/Ashurst corporate governance and responsibility clinic; and the Victoria Legal Aid strategic advocacy clinic.

Faculty Review of the Clinical Program

Supporters of the clinical program were understandably apprehensive when Arie Freiberg became dean in early 2004. In his earlier stint at Monash, Freiberg had been a vocal opponent of the clinical program, as not fitting his vision of what a university should do. Their fears were calmed to some extent when Freiberg visited Springvale and Oakleigh centres and appeared to listen to Adrian Evans and others passionately arguing that the clinical program was a (if not *the*) vital distinguishing feature of the Monash law school. Nonetheless, there were still deep concerns when a review of the clinical program was held in 2006 – the first formal review of the clinical program since its introduction thirty-one years before.

The champions of the clinical program worked effectively to mobilise support. Fifty-three written submissions were made to the review committee,

---

46 Interview with Paul Mishura, 2 July 2012.

which consisted of Elizabeth Boros and Jennifer Beaton from Monash law school, Serge Sztrajt of Victorian Legal Aid and Jeff Giddings, now of Griffith University. The panel met over two days and one evening and toured both the Monash-Oakleigh Legal Service and Springvale Monash Legal Service, speaking to directors, solicitors, staff and students.

There was great relief on the part of the program's staff, students and supporters when the panel reported that its overwhelming impression of the program was that it was 'a transformative experience for students' and one of the most valuable elements of the educational experience at Monash.[47] While it was argued in many of the submissions that the clinical program was a 'flagship' of the faculty, perhaps surprisingly the existence of the program did not appear to be the reason students chose to study law at Monash. Rather, students took the unit because they had heard about it from other students. Alarmingly, employers did not differentiate between the Monash and the Deakin programs; and there was limited knowledge of the clinical program within the wider faculty. The panel recommended measures to increase awareness of the uniqueness and benefits of the program among school students, first year students, potential employers and the faculty.[48] This resulted in an expansion of the first year 'court report' assessment task to include the ability to observe, participate and report on the work of the legal services, thus familiarising students with the clinical program at the commencement of their law studies. Student placements into the legal services have also become available as part of the research assignment requirements of other 'mainstream' law units.

Reflecting a growing trend in legal practice, Monash-Oakleigh Legal Service introduced a multidisciplinary clinic in 2010. The Faculties of Law, Business and Economics, and Medicine joined together to place law, finance, and social work students in teams, in which the students from the three disciplines began seeing legal service clients all at the same time. In doing so, clients who agree to participate are interviewed by the team in order to have their issues addressed holistically and be provided with an expanded service. The popularity of this approach to legal education and client service has seen this program grow to two sessions per week and has also included social work students working in the FLAP program for family law clients. It has also lead to strong and dynamic teaching and research collaborations between the law, finance and social work supervisors.

---

47 Review of the Undergraduate Clinical Legal Education Program, December 2006, p. 3.

48 Ibid., pp. 1–15, Response to the Review, pp. 6–7.

In recent years, clinical staff have increasingly viewed the clinical program as not only a centre for innovative practical legal education, but as a focus for 'applied research'. As a result, Ross Hyams and Adrian Evans, both long serving clinical supervisors, have published a number of articles and spoken at international conferences on the pedagogical value of clinical legal education in diverse areas such as ethics, multidisciplinary lawyering, emotional intelligence, reflective journaling, assessment and therapeutic jurisprudence. Clinical legal education has proved to be a rich source of empirical research as it has matured and become more sophisticated.

In 2015 Monash celebrates forty years of clinical legal education in the form of a professional practice elective. It has consistently been taken by about one quarter of students in the fourth or fifth years of their studies. The majority of students who take the elective finish it with the belief that it should be a compulsory subject. The staff are passionate about the program and the benefits it provides to students and to society. Although funding cuts during the 1980s and 1990s saw the viability of the clinical program questioned by the faculty and the university, it has survived and remains a major point of difference between Monash and most other law schools.

PART FOUR

THE MONASH LAW SCHOOL IN THE 21ST CENTURY

Chapter 20

Parker's Band and a Whole New Songbook

Since the original appointment of David Derham in 1963, succeeding deans of the Monash law school had all been internal appointments from among the ranks of the faculty's professors. Bob Williams was the ultimate internal appointment, having been one of the faculty's original students and then joining the staff immediately upon his return from Oxford. The faculty, therefore, had no idea what to expect when the selection committee announced in October 1998 that the new dean would be Stephen Parker, a British born and educated professor at Griffith University in Queensland – not just an outsider, but an unknown outsider.

Those who were curious about their new dean could find out that he had an LLB from Newcastle-upon-Tyne and a PhD from Cardiff and that he had taught and practised in England before coming to a senior lectureship at the ANU in 1987. In 1994 he was the second professor appointed to the new law school at Griffith University, where he had an interesting five years as that law school had a far more troubled childhood than Monash had experienced three decades before. Parker's own teaching and research interests were in family law and law and sociology and, among many others, he was the co-author of the popular texts *Law in Context* and *Family Law in Context*.

When he met the selection committee, Parker did not hold back in his critique of the state of the Monash law school and presented a blueprint for radical reform. In his view, the faculty had become overly focused on doctrinal, black letter law and had largely lost sight of its radical past. It had appointed too many of its own graduates and become highly suspicious of the outside world. It had become too limited in its approaches to the law, with, for example, no teaching or research on law and economics or law and sociology. The members of the selection panel were impressed that Parker did not wait to be asked about the controversies at Griffith, but raised them himself.

Professor Stephen Parker singing to his own tune.
Photographer Greg Ford, Monpix 8318

When Parker arrived in early 1999, staff members found him charming and a good communicator, full of energy and bursting with ideas. He rode his bike to work from his home in Beaumaris, played the guitar and cheerily dressed up as Santa Claus for the Christmas party. Jeff Goldsworthy regards him as 'incredibly clever, one of the smartest people I've known'. Many of the staff welcomed his approach as a breath of fresh air after a decade of conservatism and retrenchment. 'I'd never met anyone like him before,' Elizabeth Lanyon recalls, 'as a strategist he was absolutely on the money'.

Those who felt threatened by the changes Parker introduced reacted with passive resistance rather than open opposition, and he did not stay long enough for serious opposition to develop. Symbolically, the strongest focus of discontent was the refit for the staff library for which the dean brought in interior decorators who, among many other changes of questionable taste, rearranged the books by colour. Peter Balmford refused to enter the room again, while HP Lee thought it looked more like a bordello than a staff library. But while the old guard focused on cosmetic changes, many more fundamental changes were rapidly implemented.

When Parker arrived at Monash, his first impression of the law school was that it was a 'sad, dismal place' with no sense of optimism. He felt that the design of the building was increasingly inimical to a spirit of collegiality as increasing numbers closed their doors, leaving a cold feeling of endless, lifeless corridors. Like those on the previous curriculum review, he felt that the faculty had developed too much of a 'silo mentality', where each group from the criminal lawyers to the community legal services was more concerned with protecting its own turf than with the overall good of the faculty.

Bob Williams' careful husbandry had left the faculty's finances in a healthy state, with several nest eggs that had been hidden away for a rainy day. The Monash law school foundation had raised over $2 million, although Parker recalls there was a problem because the donor law firms were 'starting to beat down the door saying they'd given money and nothing had been done with it'. Parker assured them he would make sure it was well used. Further, the Howard government's decision to allow universities to admit full-fee paying local students promised to be a bonanza for the law faculty, as the insatiable demand for legal education meant that it could effortlessly fill as many places as it was allowed to offer. For the first time since the mid-1970s the faculty was 'awash with money' and Parker set about spending it.

Whereas Bob Williams had an aversion to the changes of the Dawkins era, Parker was completely in tune with them. The requirements to find new sources of income, boost research performance, and internationalise came instinctively to him, and he was also in tune with the need for more effective management structures to cope with the increasing bureaucratisation of university life. Parker argued that:

> It has become clear that a high quality legal education cannot be delivered by relying on government funded places. The amount that comes to the Faculty of Law from [government] funded students is insufficient to offer high quality teaching of the traditional kind, let alone innovative clinical and skills-based subjects or small group

> discussion. We must increasingly attract and retain fee-paying students; and this means staying responsive to conditions of the market and the reasonable needs of those who come to us.[1]

Student fees were the most obvious source of new income, particularly as government policy was increasingly moving towards a full 'user pays' system of tertiary education. During the 1990s the faculty had already opened itself up to fee paying international students, both postgraduate and undergraduate, and these had helped sustain the faculty's finances through some difficult years. However, the Asian financial crisis of 1997–98 had led to a sharp decline in international enrolments, and the decision of the Malaysian authorities to insist that Monash graduates pass further exams before they could practise led to a collapse in the number of Malaysian undergraduates. The faculty board was told in April 1999 that 'the bottom seems to have fallen out of the Undergraduate international market [with] only 4 commencing students compared with 15–20 in previous years'. Again, while the faculty attempted to tap into a market for postgraduate legal education for international students, this market was always small, and the weakness of the Monash postgraduate program in the 1990s made it hard to sell. In 1999 there were only fifteen fee paying international postgraduate students.

Consequently, a major goal during Stephen Parker's deanship was to increase the number of full fee paying local students, both undergraduate and postgraduate. In 1999 only six per cent of LLB students were local fee-payers, but this percentage was set to increase rapidly with 131 fee-payers in the first year cohort of 457. In that year the VCE cut-off mark for HECS students was 98.5, while for fee-payers it was 93.5. The potential of fee paying undergraduates was seen by 2002 when the 284 full fee-paying undergraduate students provided almost one quarter of the faculty's income. In the circumstances of the early 2000s, income from full-fee paying local students was money for jam – demand for the Monash LLB appeared unlimited and fee paying student numbers were limited only by the government policy that they should make up no more than twenty-five per cent of students and the ability of the faculty to teach them.

Earning money from postgraduate education was more of a challenge, primarily because Melbourne had built up such a strong lead during the 1990s, particularly with its wide range of specialist diplomas and the introduction

---

1 Stephen Parker, Introduction to 'The Law School for a Changing World: Faculty of Law Operational Plan 2000–2002', p. 4.

of a juris doctor (JD) course.[2] Elizabeth Lanyon recalls that there had been some talk that Monash should abandon its postgraduate coursework program altogether, but in the last year of Bob Williams' deanship the decision had been made to develop specialist masters' degrees and revive graduate diplomas. Stephen Parker decided to compete directly with Melbourne by rapidly expanding the range of masters' and graduate diploma courses on offer, developing a postgraduate course leading to admission and establishing city premises as a base for the postgraduate program. A critical first step was to move the LLM by coursework program from a HECS funded basis to a fee paying basis (with the resulting freed up HECS places being available to support a hoped-for increase in higher degree by research students). Then, over three frantic years the rest of the structure was put in place. New courses were developed, approved and introduced, and large numbers of new subjects were offered to make them both viable and attractive. By 2004, the faculty was offering twelve specialist masters' degrees, six for non-law graduates and six for law graduates, six specialist graduate diplomas, two postgraduate certificates and a postgraduate professional practice course. While many of these duplicated existing courses at Melbourne, an effort was made to develop unique specialisations. For example, Melissa de Zwart and Dimity Kingsford-Smith built up a masters' course in internet and electronic law that was well ahead of any other Australian university. An Australian first, the subject Law of the Internet was, appropriately, taught only online. At the same time, the requirements for masters' degrees had to be eased to match those of Melbourne, which had reduced its requirements in the early 1990s – few students would opt for an arduous Monash degree when a Melbourne qualification could be gained with less effort. Consequently the masters by coursework was reduced from twelve units (or eight units plus thesis) to eight units (or four units plus thesis). Academic purists argued that this was a 'dumbing down' and that the degree was no longer a real masters, but realists pointed out that neither was Melbourne's and there was no future in offering a degree that attracted a negligible number of students.

A completely new area that the faculty sought to enter was practical legal training, designed primarily to satisfy the post-degree practical training requirements for admission to legal practice for those looking

---

2 For the growth of the Melbourne postgraduate coursework program in the 1990s, see Waugh, *First Principles*, pp. 247–50. The JD was introduced at Melbourne in 1998 as the first postgraduate course to offer entry to legal practice. The American name was controversially adopted, although the course was essentially a fee paying LLB and carried no right to use the title 'doctor'.

for an alternative to articles. In October 1999 the faculty announced the introduction of a diploma in legal practice, skills and ethics to begin the following year. 'In introducing this Postgraduate diploma, the Law Faculty will establish for Monash University a radically new dimension in its role as a provider of legal education and training in Victoria,' it claimed.[3] By 2003 a 'flexible' online version of the diploma designed for articled clerks had been developed by Len Webster, with the intention of offering it to the major national law firms for pre-admission training.

The faculty also explored ways to compete with the Melbourne JD. The concept of a postgraduate fee paying course leading to admission was obviously attractive, but the graduate studies committee could not bring itself to use the odd and misleading JD title for a course that was essentially a fast-tracked LLB. Consequently, the name initially chosen was master of laws (legal practice), although in almost every respect the degree was an open copy of the Melbourne JD, with the addition of the required teaching of practical skills and professional ethics to qualify for practice.[4] The new course was launched in 2001 and initially limited to twenty-four students, with Cherie Burke, the student recruitment officer, reporting 'that the response and high calibre of applicant for the LLM (LP) was so impressive and overwhelming that a second intake of students is due for August of this year'.[5]

In 2003 the decision was made to introduce a JD as 'an alternative pathway to a legal qualification'. As if to emphasise the anomaly of the name, this was to be the same course as the LLM (legal practice) but without the units comprising the postgraduate diploma in legal practice, skills and ethics. It was in fact explicitly described as 'an early exit point from the LLM (LP)'.[6]

A vital factor for the success of a relaunched graduate program was the establishment of a new presence in the city. As Melbourne's traffic coagulated and people felt (rightly or wrongly) increasingly time poor, few prospective postgraduate students were willing to drive to Clayton when attractive options were available in the CBD. For years, the postgraduate program had been divided between Clayton and various premises around the city, but surveys showed that most prospective students believed that all subjects were taught at Clayton. The only way to overcome this perception was to acquire prominent city premises and advertise widely that all postgraduate

3 Faculty Board minutes, 18 October 1999.

4 Ibid., 19 July 2000.

5 Ibid., 11 April 2001.

6 Ibid., 21 October 2003.

courses were only taught there. In early 2002 the faculty took a lease on the Equity Chambers at 472 Bourke Street, ideally located next door to the Law Institute. Elizabeth Lanyon, as associate dean of graduate studies, oversaw the leasing and fitting out of the new chambers, with the objective of 'making it look like a postgraduate space rather than an undergraduate space'. Lanyon feels that it helped create a different culture just by looking different from a building designed for undergraduates. The city chambers were expensive to set up and operate but were essential if the law school was to mount an effective and competitive postgraduate program.

By 2004 the postgraduate program was humming along nicely. It had not yet caught up with Melbourne but was attracting healthy numbers and was proving to be increasingly profitable. Expressed in equivalent full time student numbers, the postgraduate coursework program had 74 EFTSU in 2000 and 222 in 2003, by which time postgraduate fees made up ten per cent of the faculty's income. Any voices expressing regret at the perceived diminution of academic quality of the LLM were muted at most.

In his early statements to the faculty, Stephen Parker emphasised the increasing primacy of research in the new university environment. Since the late 1960s, Monash had been in the forefront of law schools for its research, but this lead faded as other schools reacted more quickly to the new paradigm. Although Monash maintained its good publications record, many academics had not adjusted to the bureaucratic decision that only research published in particular journals, or books of a particular type, would be counted when assessing research. Consequently, although the overall number of publications continued to rise steadily in the late 1990s (from 57 in 1997 to 70 in 1998 to 79 in 1999) Monash's performance by the official measures steadily fell in comparison with its rivals. Further, the new world order placed great emphasis on winning research grants (even though they are largely irrelevant for legal research except as an inefficient means of buying time), and, again, Monash law school adapted more slowly to this necessity than other law schools.

The reaction of some academics was to query the rules. The faculty board was told in July 2003 that by the official measurements Monash's performance was mediocre compared to other law schools and other Monash faculties. In defence it was claimed that 'the basis of comparison remains a weighted set of criteria that may be appropriate for other disciplines, but is not well suited to law'.[7] Several months later the faculty's research committee reported

---

7 Ibid., 28 July 2003.

that, 'the current formula applied by the University is disadvantageous to legal methods of research', and a decision was made to review the criteria.[8] However, the reality was that there was not the slightest chance of changing the rules. The law school had to learn to play by the new rules or give up its claim to elite status. Stephen Parker was fully aware of this, though in retrospect he thinks he was too gentle in encouraging the faculty to adapt to the new realities.

Many measures were taken during Parker's deanship to boost research performance, though they were in the nature of long-term solutions rather than immediate fixes. Increasing efforts were put into attracting research funding and winning Australian Research Council (ARC) grants, including financial incentives for those whose applications survived the first cull and seminars to assist applicants. As the number of higher degree by research (HDR) students was a vital element in the new system of measuring research performance, the faculty set about recruiting PhD and LLM by research students. Parker felt that when he arrived, many Monash staff were more like practitioners who liked to teach than scholars of the modern kind, and there was an urgent need to build up a critical mass of scholars. In October 1999 he told the faculty board that 'Increasingly it is anticipated that career legal academics will possess a doctorate' and from this time it was anticipated that all new staff members would be enrolled for doctorates if they did not already have one.[9] The number of HDR enrolments doubled in Parker's first year and by 2003 there were thirty-six PhD students (nine international) and three LLM by major thesis. While the increase in staff with PhDs was clearly essential, there was a danger, however, particularly with international students, that students would be fast tracked into PhDs with no realistic chance of completing a major research project. It was not a coincidence that in 2004 the faculty felt obliged to raise the English language requirement for international HDR students.[10]

A major part of Stephen Parker's push to boost research was the establishment of new centres with the intention that they become dynamic research hubs. The first to come to fruition was the Castan Centre for Human Rights established in July 2000. The growing strength of human rights law at Monash in the 1990s made it an obvious area to focus on and soon after Parker's arrival at Monash Sarah Joseph and Julie Debeljak presented him

---

8 Ibid., 21 October 2003.

9 Ibid., 18 October 1999.

10 Ibid., 22 July 2004.

with a proposal for a human rights law centre. Parker was enthusiastic and preliminary work was well under way at the time of the death of prominent human rights lawyer and former faculty board member, Ron Castan, in October 1999. The decision to name the new centre for him was met with widespread approval.

For the position of director of the Castan Centre, Stephen Parker head-hunted David Kinley, a former colleague at the ANU in the early 1990s. Born in Belfast and educated at Sheffield and Cambridge, Kinley taught constitutional law and a new elective on human rights at the ANU before moving to the Australian Law Reform Commission. He then worked as a consultant for the Human Rights Commission, while also teaching at UNSW, and was looking to return to academia full time when Parker asked him to apply for the position of director of the proposed Castan Centre. Being slightly cynical, Kinley commends Parker for seeing that a centre for human rights law was a great move since nobody would say they oppose human rights. The Castan Centre was established with a wide range of objectives: research, attracting higher degree students, expanding human rights electives and providing national and international human rights consultancies.[11] David Kinley believed that the emphasis should be on law rather than on multidisciplinary work, in contrast to the existing (but almost dormant) Australian human rights centre at UNSW. There was a solid core of people in the faculty teaching and researching in human rights and related areas, notably Sarah Joseph, Julie Debeljak and Melissa Castan (Ron Castan's daughter), and the centre encouraged many more to become involved.

The Castan Centre rapidly built up a strong public profile, starting a successful lecture series featuring people like Phillip Alston, Aden Ridgeway, Alexander Downer, Kevin Rudd and Cherie Booth; holding an annual conference (which is now the only annual human rights conference in Australia); publishing a regular newsletter; offering a visiting fellowship and much more. The centre soon began to attract project funding, but this quickly led to controversy. The minister for foreign affairs in the Howard government, Alexander Downer, approached the centre asking it to work on a major project engaging with the military junta in Burma. It was a difficult decision to agree to participate, as many NGOs were leaving Burma and boycotting the regime, but Stephen Parker strongly supported participation on the grounds that the elected government of Australia had invited them to engage with the dictatorship to try to get the message through to the generals

11 Ibid., 19 April 2000; interview with David Kinley, 24 February 2012.

about the importance of human rights and the need to respect the rulings of international bodies such as the International Labour Organisation. Castan Centre staff visited Burma many times in the course of the project and David Kinley thinks their work contributed greatly to the gradual liberalisation of the Burmese regime.

Before the establishment of the Castan Centre, the faculty offered only one undergraduate and one postgraduate unit with a human rights orientation, but by 2004 the number had risen to twenty postgraduate and undergraduate units. The expansion of teaching fostered the growth of research, as shown by the development of a pioneering course on Human Rights and the Global Economy, which complemented ARC grants which were won in this field. The establishment of the centre galvanised research and teaching in the whole broad field of human rights. Students could see that the centre had real momentum and they were drawn to it for PhD research. The existence of the centre also encouraged many in the faculty to give their work a human rights element. After David Kinley's return to Sydney in 2004, the Castan Centre continued to grow strongly under the leadership of Sarah Joseph, with human rights law now firmly established as one of Monash's greatest strengths.

Another innovative centre set up in the Parker era was the Centre for the Study of Privatisation and Public Accountability. Its origins lay in a research grant application submitted by Bronwyn Naylor, Moira Paterson and Pam O'Connor in 1999 to study the then highly controversial subject of privatisation. This soon led to the realisation that the whole area of privatisation and public accountability was 'under-researched' and there was a real need for greater understanding of 'the wide-ranging changes in the relationship between government, citizens and the private sector which have occurred over recent years'.[12] This fitted neatly with Stephen Parker's aims to boost research, develop more multidisciplinary work and encourage empirical work, and a grant of $50,000 from the Monash law school foundation provided the seed money to establish the new centre.

From the outset the proposed centre aspired to be multidisciplinary, with contributions from economics, politics, management and other disciplines as well as law. However, it was somewhat of a surprise when a non-lawyer was appointed as its director. Graeme Hodge was a Monash graduate in engineering science, who had played French horn in the Melbourne Symphony Orchestra for a year before returning to university to complete a masters in engineering and then an MBA. During his MBA he saw that

---

12 Marcia Neave, presentation to Faculty Board, Faculty Board minutes, 19 April 2000.

economists knew much about how to measure the performance of firms, but less about governments, and he began to research ways to measure the performance of governments. While teaching management and economics at RMIT, he completed a PhD thesis on a detailed statistical survey of the successes and failures of privatisation based on hundreds of studies and reviews from around the world. This was published in 2000 as *Privatization: An International Review of Performance*, being eloquently described by a reviewer as 'masterful' and 'a superb book'.[13]

Looking back on the establishment of the Centre for the Study of Privatisation and Public Accountability, Graeme Hodge comments that 'It is always a tough gig for a centre that relies on winning grants – it means there are continual crises. The central challenge is to raise money and to do this you have to stay visible and relevant and get out and sell the centre's services.' With this sort of pressure, there was no time for a leisurely ramping up of the centre's activities. Its first annual report shows a busy research program was already in place, with the greatest emphasis being on the privatisation of the electricity industry. Several major grant applications had been submitted and already some significant consultancies and training programs had begun, including six major international executive training programs on subjects such as 'accountability in public sector management' for Indonesian and Thai government officials.[14] In addition to Graeme Hodge, the centre employed Valarie Sands, another non-lawyer with Monash degrees in psychology and statistics and a masters in public policy and management, and Diana Bowman, who was qualified in law and science. Many law school staff became involved in the work of the centre, notably Marcia Neave, Susan Kneebone, Bronwyn Naylor, Pam O'Connor, Judd Epstein, Rowena Cantley-Smith and Moira Paterson.

An important element in Stephen Parker's plans for reviving the law school was to rebuild the pre-eminence in commercial law which had faded in the late 1980s and never fully recovered. Two key steps in this strategy were the recruitment in 2000 of Elizabeth Boros and Dimity Kingsford-Smith. Boros came to fill the Sir Keith Aickin chair of company law on the departure of Sam Ricketson, and Kingsford-Smith was appointed as another professor in the commercial law area, with particular expertise in

---

13 Nicholas Henry, 'Is Privatisation Passé: The Case for Competition and the Emergence of Intersectoral Administration', *Public Administration Review*, vol. 62, no. 3, May/June 2002, pp. 374–5.

14 Centre for the Study of Privatisation and Public Accountability, 'Report for Year 1: 2001', Faculty Board minutes, 23 April 2002.

the law of the digital economy. With strong encouragement from the dean, the two new professors proposed the establishment of a Centre for Law in the Digital Economy. At the height of the dot-com boom, the potential of the digital economy seemed limitless and the possible legal complexities had barely been considered, so the areas in which the new centre could operate were seen as very wide.

The centre was formally set up in 2001, with Dimity Kingsford-Smith and Elizabeth Boros as joint directors and thirteen more staff members associated, including Olujoke Akindemowo, Melissa de Zwart and Elizabeth Lanyon. The centre developed three postgraduate courses and ten postgraduate units, ran an active seminar program and conducted consulting and training activities, and its members were active researchers. However, the collapse of the dot-com boom and a severe downturn in the information technology industry made it difficult to attract external funding and the centre's ARC grant applications were unsuccessful. Further, what had been innovative in 1999 was becoming mainstream by 2004 and consequently, when Dimity Kingsford-Smith returned to Sydney in 2005, the centre was closed.[15]

One of Stephen Parker's aims was to engage more closely with the judiciary and the courts as he felt this had been lacking in the past due to Monash's remote location and because no Monash graduates had become judges until Nahum Mushin's appointment to the Family Court in 1990. During the 1990s and early 2000s many more Monash graduates were appointed to various courts, notably Ray Finkelstein, Ross Sundberg and Mordy Bromberg to the Federal Court, Marilyn Warren, Mark Weinberg and Lex Lasry to the Supreme Court, Kevin Bell, Murray Kellam and Stuart Morris to VCAT, Michael Rozenes, Tony Howard and Felicity Hampel to the County Court and Diana Bryant to the Family Court. Parker encouraged judges and former judges to become involved in the faculty's teaching and research. The most prominent example of this was the appointment of George Hampel as full-time professor of advocacy and trial practice in September 2000 after his retirement from the Supreme Court.

In 2001 Hampel led the establishment of an 'international institute [or academy] of forensic studies' with the aim of promoting research and teaching on the functioning and processes of courts and tribunals. The proposal envisaged the academy as 'a new area of research strength

---

15 'Proposal to Establish a Centre for Law in the Digital Economy', Faculty Board minutes, 11 April 2001; 'Report of the Review of the Centre for Law in the Digital Economy', Faculty Board minutes, 7 April 2005.

in forensic studies in its broadest sense [which] will provide a base from which many facets of forensic studies can be researched such as the rules Australia-wide and internationally relating to expert evidence, the ethical and legal issues relating to advocacy and approaches to decision-making.'[16] The academy tapped into one of the great strengths of the faculty, with Bernadette McSherry and Jonathon Clough joining Hampel as principal researchers and Bob Williams, Richard Fox, Sue McNicol and others being heavily involved. The institute held a highly popular inaugural conference at Prato, Italy in July 2002 attended by 128 delegates, ran successful seminars and workshops and developed a profitable graduate certificate course in forensic studies for accountants, which became its primary source of income. George Hampel was also involved in teaching various trial practice and advocacy subjects at undergraduate level. However, a second conference at Prato attracted only thirty-one delegates and the institute's research aspirations were not achieved – a 2005 review noted that it had generated no research income and 'no research work has been completed'.[17] It continued as a centre providing teaching and consultancy services, under the new name of the Monash forensic studies program.

When Monash University embarked on its massive expansion in the early 1990s, its ambitions always went far beyond taking over a few colleges of advanced education. While all Australian universities began to look overseas for students, Monash's leaders wanted to spread the Monash brand around the world in a style reminiscent of John Elliot's grandiose plans in the late 1980s to 'Fosterise the world'. Monash campuses were set up at Sunway in Malaysia, Prato in Italy and near Johannesburg in South Africa. Under Bob Williams' cautious leadership, the law faculty trod warily around these ventures, although in the early 1990s it did begin teaching legal process and contracts to Malaysian students who could then come to Australia to complete their degrees.[18] Stephen Parker, however, took on 'internationalisation' as a central plank in his program for the law school. In his 'operational plan' for 2000–2002, internationalisation was placed at the head of his aims and he wrote 'the overall direction of the Law School is strongly towards internationalisation. Our aim to be "the Law School

16 'Proposal for an International Academy of Forensic Studies', Faculty Board minutes, 11 April 2001.

17 'International Institute of Forensic Studies, Report of Review Panel', Faculty Board minutes, 7 April 2005.

18 Faculty Board minutes, 22 October 1990.

for a changing world", emphasises "world" as well as "changing".'[19] Twenty-six separate actions were listed as part of the internationalisation strategy, including measures designed to attract more overseas students; developing a full LLB course at Sunway; building links with overseas law schools, notably Kings College, London, the Oxford Institute of Legal Practice, and the Washington College of Law; developing a presence at the new Monash campus in South Africa; encouraging students to spend at least one semester overseas and giving more support to international mooting. In the early years of Stephen Parker's deanship nearly all of these were at least attempted, though some were inevitably stillborn.

One venture that took a great deal of time, thought and money before it eventually failed was the Centre for Law and Reconstruction in Southern Africa, set up in 2002 as a joint venture of Monash South Africa and the law school. The centre was established with high aims:

> The purpose of the Centre is to establish and maintain a specialist capacity that will make a significant contribution to the reconstruction and development of Southern Africa by empowering leaders and managers (in business and government) though the provision of information, capacity-building support and expertise in law, justice and governance.[20]

An eminent researcher in the field of law and development, Professor Theo Scheepers, was appointed director of the centre. The centre was intended to carry out research and provide training and short courses, but there were no plans to teach Monash law courses in Africa.

In retrospect it is not altogether surprising that the centre failed to live up to the high aspirations of its foundation, with few of its initial targets in terms of teaching, research or income being met. A review in 2004 showed that it had little prospect of achieving financial self-sufficiency and eventually the decision was made to close it in 2005.

Far more successful, though not before some rocky moments, has been the faculty's involvement with the campus at Prato. Stephen Parker was in charge of the university's European programs and in 2002 he announced that 'we will position ourselves as the Australian university which has the closest ties with Europe'.[21] The Prato campus near Florence became central

---

19 'The Law School for a Changing World' Faculty of Law Operational Plan, 2000–2002, p. 11.

20 'Proposal to Establish a Centre for Law and Reconstruction in Southern Africa', Faculty Board minutes, 1 August 2002.

21 Quoted in Davison and Murphy, *University Unlimited*, p. 273.

to this aim. The brainchild of history professor Bill Kent, Prato became a reality in 2000 thanks to the financial support of the Grollo family. The law school's commitment to Prato was encouraged by Judd Epstein, who had studied in Florence in 1967, loved Italy and took on the development of law teaching at Prato with great energy and enthusiasm. Originally law had not been part of the plans for Prato, but with Stephen Parker's support Epstein arranged for seven undergraduate units to be offered there in 2002, four with a strong international or comparative component and three that were normally taught at Clayton. Epstein expected about thirty-five students to enrol, but they ended up with seventy-six. He did much of the teaching himself and enlisted friends from the University of Florence to assist.

In the early years, Epstein ran Prato in a free and easy way or, as he puts it 'in a way that did not necessarily conform to the accepted protocols at Clayton' and the students uniformly had a good time. One student who greatly enjoyed his semester at Prato was surprised they just did Australian law subjects in English – the only differences were that he thought the subjects were much easier than in Australia and everyone passed! Judd Epstein reflects that the small classes at Prato and the lack of the usual distractions such as part-time work provided an excellent learning environment, with close to 100 per cent attendance and much closer student–teacher relationships than at Clayton. The subject offerings were determined by the desire to have a mix of subjects in international or comparative law with some basic Australian law subjects to ensure that students would not be disadvantaged by attending Prato.[22] There was no doubt that studying at Prato expanded students' horizons. In 2010 Richard Fox set a complicated exam problem for a Prato unit and a student came up with a brilliant opening sentence comparing the problem to an Italian chocolate cake 'multi-layered and every so often you hit an olive, which makes you rethink a few basic principles'.

In 2000, the faculty adopted a major curriculum reform when the compulsory and quasi-compulsory undergraduate subjects were semesterised, a proposal that had been made and rejected several times in the previous decade. The strongest opposition to the change came from the constitutional and administrative law teachers, who felt, understandably, that their subjects were undervalued by being reduced to single semester units. When Marcia Neave, who designed the revised curriculum, was asked whether the semesterised core subjects would be approved by the Council of Legal Education, she pointed out that there would be no problem as

22 Email from Judd Epstein to authors, 29 August 2013.

'nearly all other law schools in Australia have already semesterised core law subjects', incidentally indicating the extent to which Monash had ceased to be an innovator in legal education in the 1990s. The big advantage in semesterisation was that the reduction of some of the core subjects, notably Administrative Law, Constitutional Law and Corporations Law, to single-semester subjects opened up more optional subjects, but Stephen Parker recalls that he and Marcia Neave were unable to push through their plans to also have more theory and context inserted in the curriculum.[23]

Parker was a strong proponent of the modern enthusiasm for subjecting academic leaders (including himself) to scrutiny and review, and late in 2002 the first external academic review of the faculty was held, chaired by Ian Pyman. In retrospect it was remarkable that the faculty had been in existence for nearly forty years before being subjected to external review, as reviews had become commonplace in most universities in the 1980s. Overall the review was highly complimentary:

> All the best aspects of the Monash Law School must be celebrated. The Faculty has sustained a reputation for quality and innovation for nearly four decades. It has a Dean who is not apprehensive of change and who has been able to inspire the commitment of the faculty's leadership team. There is a distinguished group of scholars and teachers among its academic staff. The academic program is intellectually stimulating, varied and relevant at both graduate and undergraduate levels.
>
> The Law School is a leader in certain areas of teaching and research, such as ethical practice, justice and human rights. The well known clinical programs ... are strongly supported by students, community groups and the legal profession. Students report a high level of satisfaction with the Law course ... The quality of the Faculty's Library services is often mentioned by students and staff.
>
> A survey conducted in 2002 of 32 law firms confirmed the status of Monash Law graduates as highly regarded, with a "uniformly positive impression of the rigour and practicality of the Monash Law degree".[24]

Among the challenges faced by the faculty, the review panel believed there was 'a degree of reluctance by some academic staff to accept the reality of the new research environment', larger class sizes caused by reduced funding made it difficult to maintain quality teaching, and 'heavy staff workloads

23 Faculty Board minutes, 16 October 2000.

24 'Academic Review 2002', Faculty Board minutes, 28 July 2003.

may have an adverse impact on the collegiality of academic staff.' The panel thought the law building looked and felt 'tired' and its design worked against the development of a sense of community among the staff and would be 'daunting' for many students. On the curriculum, the panel argued that there were 'worrying deficiencies', pointing to the lack of legal history, legal philosophy and critical legal theory, and the continued shortage of options in the commercial area. Concern was expressed that there was a strong trend back towards exams as the only form of assessment, with students choosing not to do optional essays and staff not encouraging them. The panel quoted one former student: 'We were taught legal research skills in Legal Process but never having had to use them again, I doubt many students remember them.' On internationalisation, the panel felt that the faculty's objectives and strategy had not been adequately communicated and there was 'a need to consider … how its focus on internationalisation will translate into the undergraduate and postgraduate curricula.'

Although the faculty leadership disagreed with some of the findings, overall it accepted them and set about adopting the recommendations.[25] However, before the impact of any changes could be seen, Stephen Parker was called to higher duties in rather unusual circumstances. Many in the faculty had the feeling that the deanship was only a stepping-stone in Parker's inevitable rise to a vice-chancellorship and it was no surprise that he took an active part in wider university affairs. He was in general agreement with the strategies of vice-chancellor David Robinson and supported him in his attempts to force the Faculties of Arts and Science to get in step with the rest of the university. Robinson in turn supported Parker's reforms in the law school and was happy not to interfere. However, in June 2002 the situation suddenly changed when allegations of plagiarism were made in *The Times Higher Education Supplement* relating to Robinson's publications dating back to the 1980s, and further cases were soon revealed. The chancellor, the university council and most of the deans initially supported Robinson, but Parker believed that the vice-chancellor had to go. 'I could not see as the dean of law that we could possibly countenance [Robinson's actions]', Parker says, 'If the law faculty wasn't the university's conscience, then where was it.'[26] This was reinforced at a local level when the usual stern words to students on the evils of plagiarism were met with roars of laughter.

---

25 'Faculty Response to Final Report of the Faculty Review', Faculty Board minutes, 28 July 2003.

26 Interview with Stephen Parker, quoted in Davison and Murphy, *University Unlimited*, p. 290.

Parker was initially concerned that his strong stand against Robinson might end his Monash career, but, when further instances of plagiarism were discovered, Robinson was forced to resign, and Parker suddenly found himself at the centre of university affairs. Many believed that he would be the ideal replacement for Robinson as vice-chancellor. While the selection committee eventually decided to bring in Richard Larkins from Melbourne, Parker was appointed deputy vice-chancellor, and in October 2003 stood down as dean of the law school.

In his inimitable style, HP Lee summed up the Parker era at Monash:

> From his appointment as Dean in 1999 to the day of his resignation … we have witnessed a massive upheaval in or a transformation of the Faculty – it all depends on your perspective. Even if there does exist a chorus of divergent opinions regarding his legacy, there is no division of views regarding his fervent commitment to usher the Faculty into the reality of a rapidly changing tertiary environment. One could aptly proclaim that he was a Dean who fitted the times.
>
> … when he arrived on the doorsteps of this Law School he came armed with an ambitious vision for this institution and a broad new broom. The vigorous sweeping by the broom in the first year of his Deanship would have even made Harry Potter dizzy and broomsick.
>
> For a number of us, it was the first time we were exposed to a broad array of the armoury of the modern day Dean. We became familiar with brain-storming sessions at Faculty retreats in comfortable locales, the use of a facilitator at retreats, with notions of bonding and with rolling operational plans …
>
> Given his verve and vigour, his ability and creativity, his pleasant manner of speech and conduct, it was clear to many of us that he was destined for a higher calling. His elevation to the position of Deputy Vice-Chancellor of Monash University is a neat illustration of *res ipsa loquitur.*[27]

In 2007 Parker was appointed vice-chancellor of the University of Canberra, where he has transformed a struggling old college of advanced education into a vibrant and competitive university.

---

27 H P Lee, 'Minute of Appreciation: Professor Stephen Parker', Faculty Board minutes, 30 March 2004.

Chapter 21

'Always Learning' Meets 'Always Earning'

The Pragmatic Incrementalism of Arie Freiberg – and Beyond

In the 1970s and 1980s one of the most identifiable groups among the law school staff was the group of younger lecturers, radical in their politics but conservative in their ideas of what a university should stand for. They had major misgivings about Bob Baxt's strong push into commercial law and fund-raising entrepreneurialism but chafed at what they felt to be the inertia that followed Baxt's departure, and all left the faculty in the early 1990s. Prominent among them was criminologist Arie Freiberg. In the late 1980s Freiberg was an outspoken critic of the 'big vision' the university adopted after the Dawkins' reforms. When the vice-chancellor addressed a meeting of the law school staff he famously asked whether the continual pressure to generate income meant that the university motto should be changed from 'Always Learning' to 'Always Earning'. In 1991 Freiberg joined the exodus from Monash to become the foundation professor of criminology at Melbourne.

When he left Monash, Freiberg felt that he had left the law far behind, as criminology at Melbourne is in the Faculty of Arts. He became heavily involved in interdisciplinary research and later in administration as head of department and later dean of arts. He had not thought at all about returning to law until Richard Fox, who had found him his first job as a tutor at Monash many years before, contacted him to say that the deanship was vacant at Monash law school. Freiberg was concerned whether his former colleagues would accept him as dean after twelve years away, but Fox 'assured him that people had forgotten what he was like'. His term as dean of arts at Melbourne was nearing an end and Monash appeared an exciting challenge. He was encouraged to apply by the new Monash vice-chancellor, Richard Larkins, with whom he had worked at Melbourne, and he was appointed dean from the start of 2004.

After a succession of internal appointments and one dramatic external appointment, Arie Freiberg's appointment had elements of both, as his fifteen years in the faculty made him a Monash person, while his twelve years away gave him something of the perspective and attitudes of an outsider and an objective view of the faculty's strengths and weaknesses. In his own words, what Monash had chosen as its new dean was a 'monomaniacal academic, whose hobby was work and whose idea of a good time on a holiday was to visit law courts'. He also had an impish sense of fun, and jokes, good and bad, peppered all his meetings. He told an early staff meeting that the door to his room would always be open, but he might not be there.

Freiberg's impression on his return was that Stephen Parker had energised the faculty but there were many reforms still needed and many challenges ahead (most of which had been foreshadowed by Parker in his final report as dean).[1] Chief among these was the weakness in research, where Monash had faded from a leading position in the 1980s to being well behind Melbourne and other universities in the early 2000s.[2] The budget was in deficit and growing deficits were projected. Faculty governance needed reform, there was a need for stronger staff appraisal and he questioned whether the law school should be running practical legal training courses.

In contrast to his predecessor, Arie Freiberg had an antipathy to five year plans, operational plans, mission statements, and the paraphernalia of modern managerialism, although he did show a propensity for reviews. Parker's motto, 'a Law School for a changing world' was quietly dropped. Freiberg avoided dramatic changes and grand gestures, while gradually steering the faculty in the direction he wanted.

Another contrast with his predecessor was Freiberg's insistence on budget discipline. Stephen Parker had felt he had to take risks to revive and revitalise the faculty, but the new regime insisted that the bottom line had to be taken into account. An operational deficit of $1.9 million was reduced over three years, with surpluses being achieved every year from 2006. Some felt that Freiberg took penny pinching too far – when a moth flew over the table at a dinner, one wag exclaimed, 'Look, Arie's opened his wallet'.

One of Arie Freiberg's early priorities was to restructure the faculty's governance structures. Under Bob Baxt and Bob Williams the dean had

1 Faculty Board minutes, 21 October 2003.

2 The measurement of research is a subject fraught with difficulty but almost any measure would show that Monash was ranked lower in research in the early 2000s than in the 1980s.

Arie Freiberg with Faculty of Law manager Janet White (back, left), Stephen Davey, Professor Richard Larkins and Law Chambers facility manager Lynette Dean in the expanded Law Chambers.
Photographer Greg Ford, Monpix 7540

borne the load of administration with the aid of a tiny administrative staff and relatively little input from academics. This began to change under Stephen Parker with a rapid expansion in the numbers of administrative staff and delegation of more responsibilities to senior academics. Arie Freiberg changed the structure introduced by Parker by ending a division between planning and operations on the executive committee, removing administrative staff from the executive committee and introducing a

Presenting the Academics Thinking Song at the 40th anniversary celebrations.
Left to right: Graeme Hodge, Jeff Goldsworthy, Greg Taylor, Elspeth McNeil and Jeff Waincymer. For full text of the song see appendix, p. 349.
Graeme Hodge Collection

form of 'cabinet government', with the academics giving policy leadership and the administrative staff carrying out the policies. Academics were allocated 'portfolios' – there are now twenty-one of them – in an attempt to spread the ever-increasing burden of administration. As a response to the insatiable demands on the faculty made by the university and government bureaucracies, this is probably as good a model as any, though some junior staff have felt that responsibility has been delegated too far down the food chain, while long-serving academics look back nostalgically on the days when Bob Williams did all the work and shielded them from the demands of the outside world.

The fortieth anniversary of the foundation of the Monash law school was celebrated in 2004, with the main theme of the celebrations being the success of the alumni in the profession. Much pride was taken in the fact that that the chief justice, chief judge of the County Court, chief magistrate, president of the Children's Court, president of VCAT, the coroner and the solicitor general were all Monash graduates. A celebratory dinner, attended by hundreds of alumni, was entertained by one of the faculty's most famous graduates, Campbell McComas, who sadly died soon afterwards. 2004 was also a year of reviews with the new dean setting up reviews of all the faculty's centres, faculty governance, practical legal training and the Prato program. The reports of the reviews and the implementation of their recommendations largely set the tone for the early years of Freiberg's deanship.

One area that was not reviewed within the faculty was research, as the new dean had a clear view of what needed to be done, although a submission was made to a university-wide review.[3] This submission outlined many of the barriers in the way of improved research performance, primarily the many demands placed upon academics' time and the unsuitability of applying funding formulae designed for the sciences to legal research. The reality was, however, that there was little that could be done to break down these barriers and ways had to be found to boost research in spite of them. The main method used was simply to demand that staff be active researchers. The message was spelt out loud and clear that the faculty was going to have a research active staff, and those who were not research active were moved on. Minimum publishing requirements were laid down and it was, for the first time, made virtually a precondition of appointment that new staff members have PhDs. Stories are told of non-publishing academics telling the dean when pressured to produce that quality was more important than quantity, only to be told firmly that the quality of zero is still zero.

Coincidentally, the faculty recorded much improved research results in 2004, boosted by the publication of four authored books and over eighty refereed journal articles. Given the lag between the completion of research and its publication, this was clearly the result of measures taken under Stephen Parker, although the continued steady improvement reflected the efficacy of Freiberg's efforts to ingrain a research culture more deeply.[4]

The reviews of the faculty's research centres resulted in some major changes. The Centre for Law and Reconstruction in Southern Africa was closed when the review confirmed that it was poorly run, losing money and had little prospect of recovery.[5] The Centre for Law and the Digital Economy was closed because Dimity Kingsford-Smith had decided to return to Sydney, the centre had been unable to raise funds to support its

3 'Submission to Research and Management Review', Faculty Board minutes, 26 October 2004.

4 Faculty Board minutes, 25 October 2005.

5 'Review of Centre for Law and Reconstruction in Africa', Faculty Board minutes, 7 April 2005.

research, and its work was becoming increasingly mainstream and no longer justified a specialist centre.[6]

The Centre for the Study of Privatisation and Public Accountability received a glowing report from its review, which said that it 'significantly boosted the faculty's research performance in terms of publications, higher degree enrolments and research grants and consultancies, as well as assisting the Faculty's media profile'.[7] However, it was noted that 'if the work of the Centre was to continue, a different business model would be required' and it was recommended that it be merged with a new Centre for Regulatory Studies then in the process of establishment. The privatisation centre's director, Graeme Hodge, became director of the new centre, and it was able to draw many more members of the faculty into its work, including Pam O'Connor, Bronwyn Naylor, David Lindsay, Karinne Ludlow and Arie Freiberg. Freiberg's book, *The Tools of Regulation*, a product of the centre's research, showed the multidisciplinary nature of the subject, as it analysed the wide variety of tools available for changing behaviour in a desired direction including economics, government regulation, contracts, grants, performance measures, regulation by process design, and the law, which he saw as the last tool of the regulator.

The review of the Castan Centre was entirely positive and the centre was retained. Under the leadership of Professor Sarah Joseph it has steadily expanded its activities and is widely recognised as Australia's leading human rights law centre. As a result, Monash Law has run a masters degree since 2007 dedicated to the study of human rights law, with consistently good enrolments. The number of human rights electives at both undergraduate and postgraduate level has steadily increased, with large numbers of staff, including eminent visitors, involved in teaching. The centre's research output and the impact of its research have greatly expanded. Similarly its resources have grown and its income now comes from a wide and sustainable base, with donations making an important contribution. The centre now runs about ten to twelve major events each year, attracting an average of 100+ attendees, and with many garnering media attention. A highlight was a lecture by Julian Assange in May 2010, shortly before Wikileaks became a global phenomenon. The centre has also taken social media seriously so it is now a key means of showcasing its work and building up its profile. The centre's

6 'Review of Centre for Law in the Digital Economy', Faculty Board minutes, 7 April 2005.

7 Review of Centre for the Study of Privatisation and Public Accountability, Faculty Board minutes, 7 April 2005.

Aboriginal graduates Mick Dodson and his daughter Inala Cooper, with Patrick Dodson.
Greg Ford Photography

highly competitive internship program offers some of the most sought-after university-based internships in the country, and gives opportunities for students to work abroad with human rights related organisations.[8]

The masters course in human rights law has attracted students from a wide variety of backgrounds. An outstanding recent student has been Inala Cooper, whose father Mick Dodson was the faculty's first Aboriginal graduate. After graduating with a degree in Arts, Drama & Contemporary Dance from Deakin in 1998, Cooper enrolled in a Bachelor of Education at Deakin in 1999. She soon found this was not for her, and moved to a Diploma of Arts at Swinburne. After graduation she worked as a performance artist and then in retail until 2006 when she was accepted into the graduate program of the Department of Human Services. At DHS she worked in the secretariat of the Indigenous Housing Unit and then for the ministerial taskforce for Indigenous Affairs, chaired by the attorney-general Rob Hulls. In 2009, through her work at DHS and a

8 'Report of the Review of the Castan Centre for Human Rights Law', Faculty Board Minutes, 7 April 2005; interview with Sarah Joseph and Marius Smith, 8 August 2005.

chance meeting with Monash vice-chancellor Ed Byrne, she attended the 'Closing the Gap in Education? – Improving Outcomes in Southern World Societies' conference at Monash's South African campus where her father was giving a paper focusing on education.

When the Indigenous Advisory Council was set up at Monash in 2010, Inala was engaged part-time as a policy adviser. In that year she attended the UN Permanent Forum on Indigenous Issues in New York as an assistant to Mick Dodson, who was there in his final year as an expert member for Australia on Indigenous issues. At the end of 2010, when deputy vice-chancellor (education) Adam Shoemaker asked Inala what he could do to keep her at Monash she said she wanted to do a Masters degree but she couldn't afford it. She applied for and was awarded an Indigenous staff development scholarship which allowed her to work in the Indigenous unit and study part-time for two years. She found her masters in human rights law by coursework to be a fantastic experience. She was closely connected with the Castan Centre, (having known Ron Castan in her younger days), and had a strong sense of trust and respect for Castan and the Centre. After completing her masters degree she became a full-time executive officer at the Indigenous Advisory Council.[9]

The result of the review process in 2004–5 left the faculty with only two active centres, and in later years the establishment of new centres, such as the Australian Centre for Justice Innovation, became an important part of the research strategy.

The review of the Prato program found that it 'is an important part of the Faculty's and University's international strategy', particularly as the faculty did not teach at the Malaysian campus and was cutting its links with South Africa. Past administrative corner-cutting was forgiven, though stricter guidelines were laid down for the future.[10] The Prato program grew rapidly – the 2008 program for instance attracted 100 students from Monash, 17 from Osgoode Hall, 11 from University of Paris, 11 from Arizona State, 3 from the Georgian American University and 1 from Tel Aviv University, with lecturers from Monash, Mallesons, the Florence Bar, University of Florence, Osgoode Hall, Arizona State, Georgian American University and the Washington College of Law. The success of Prato encouraged the development of a similar program at the Monash Sunway campus in Malaysia, with the first subjects being taught in 2010.

---

9 Interview with Inala Cooper, 20 September 2013.

10 'Review of the Prato Program' Report, Faculty Board minutes, 7 April 2005.

Arie Freiberg was doubtful about the faculty's move into practical legal training with courses like the postgraduate diploma in legal practice, skills and ethics. He felt these were not core faculty activities, that they diverted resources from more important activities, and was concerned that the staff involved in them tended not to be research active. In 2006 a review was held into the postgraduate coursework program and the panel endorsed Freiberg's view, saying it 'did not think that the provision of practical legal training was the direction that a law school in a research intensive Group of Eight university should take'.[11] The program was soon ended, with the last vestige, a training program for articled clerks at Minter Ellison, finishing at the end of 2008.

The defenders of the clinical program felt understandably nervous when Arie Freiberg became dean, as he had been among the program's opponents in the 1970s and 1980s. As with postgraduate practical training in the early 2000s, he saw it as a distraction from his idealistic model of university education. However, when he came back to Monash he came to see the strength of the arguments of the program's advocates – that it is a vital distinguishing feature of the Monash law school. He held a review of the clinical program which was largely positive, although it did recommend some changes to make the program less of a financial drain.[12]

If demand is any indication, the Monash LLB program was increasingly highly regarded, with the required entry score rising every year, and the differential between Monash and Melbourne steadily declining. With seemingly insatiable demand from would-be students, it would be easy for the faculty to become complacent, and this has prompted regular reviews to avoid hubris and maintain the quality of the degree. In 2004–5, for example, the faculty held a major review of the LLB, looking at the quality of the undergraduate experience rather than the curriculum. The general conclusion was that 'the Faculty has advanced and effective processes, procedures and mechanisms for achieving most of its objectives', but also found that 'a lack of resources inhibits the Faculty from fully achieving some of its stated objectives in relation to issues such as alternative assessment'. While the committee found there was a generally high level of overall satisfaction among LLB students, 'some students are concerned about issues such as a lack of feedback from and interaction with teachers,

---

11 'Review of Postgraduate Coursework', Faculty Board minutes, 4 April 2007.

12 'Report of Review of Undergraduate Clinical Legal Education Program', Faculty Board minutes, 4 April 2007.

a lack of development of some graduate skills and an insufficient sense that they are part of a learning community'.[13]

A central issue has always been class sizes, which are primarily a function of the staff:student ratio. The golden era of the 1960s and 1970s when the law school enjoyed a ratio of 1:14 or better seemed long gone by the early 2000s when the ratio was stuck at 1:23 or worse. Attempts were made to teach some of the early year units in small groups, although this could only be done at the cost of having even larger classes for other units. Socratic teaching, staff-student interaction and the possibility of staff members knowing students as individuals rather than as part of an amorphous mass all diminish as class sizes increase.

For a large cohort of undergraduates in the early 2000s, their years in the law school were dominated by an unrelenting focus on getting articles with one of the major law firms. The free and easy attitude of the 1960s and early 1970s, when there were more jobs than law graduates, had long since gone, but it was only after the emergence of large national firms in the late 1980s that the procedure for obtaining articles ceased to be a mixture of luck, contacts and persistence and became a more formal process requiring constant effort from at least the beginning of the third year of a student's law course.

By the early 2000s, possibly one quarter of students spent their undergraduate years focused on obtaining articles with a big firm. The essentials were to get good results, build an impressive CV replete with achievements in a wide range of activities, participate in such things as exchange programs, international mooting competitions and the Law Students' Society, and impress potential employers during summer clerkships. For these students the whole summer clerkship and articles process was 'huge from third year and was the most consuming thing among their group of friends'. Zoe Bateman was in Mannix College so she knew some people who 'weren't into the clerkship/articles process,' but 'most of the people who spent all their time in the law school building were the ones who were going to make it'. There were a lot of people she and her friends had 'never seen who turned up and sat the exams, and many others dropped out'. The clinical program 'just wasn't on the radar of those who were looking to get articles with the big commercial firms', and they 'were totally focused on what to do to get jobs with the big firms'. Zoe, for instance, volunteered with the Public Interest Law Clearing House, a pro bono referral service supported

13 'Report of LLB Review Committee', Faculty Board minutes, 25 October 2005.

by all the big firms, partly because she had heard good things about it, but also because she thought strategically it would be better to volunteer there rather than at Springvale.[14]

Monash had an excellent record of getting its students into the top-tier law firms. For those who were prepared to work hard and jump through the hoops, the success rate was very high. Ross Schloeffel remembers that he and his friends organised six tables of ten at the LSS ball in their final year. Of those sixty students, fifty-eight got articles at top firms.

An alternative pathway into the top law firms, as well as an illustration of the varieties of pathways to the law school, was shown by Sandra Draganich. After working as research manager for the Royal Australian Institute of Architects, Sandra moved to Minter Ellison in 2001 as a research assistant. Soon after, she began her law studies at Monash, where an unbroken sequence of outstanding results culminated in the 2004 Supreme Court Prize. She was an editor of the *Monash University Law Review* in 2003 and co-authored with Bob Williams an influential article on the 'Admissibility of Propensity Evidence in Paedophilia Cases'.[15] Admitted to practice in 2005, Sandra remained at Minter Ellison where she was a highly regarded lawyer until her tragically early death in April 2013.

However, for every student who was fully engaged with the law school, whether in the single-minded pursuit of good articles, motivated by the experience of the clinical program, or possibly even excited by the intellectual challenge of studying the law, there were probably two who experienced university simply as a 'degree factory'. For many, perhaps the majority, of students in the early 2000s, university was a radically different experience to that of earlier generations of students. The increased financial pressures on students made the old image of students spending their university days on campus with coffee, cannabis and conversation redundant, as part-time work became almost universal. For many years it was university policy that students working more than eight hours a week could only enrol part-time, but now many full-time students work twenty hours a week or even more. The introduction of taped lectures and then of online lectures has led to a dramatic falling-off in attendance. Many lecturers estimate that no more than twenty-five per cent of students regularly attend lectures. University for many students is now a physically remote, part-time and online experience.

---

14 Interview with Zoe Bateman, Ross Schloeffel, Ben O'Hoy and Andrew Meagher, 21 May 2012.

15 *Deakin Law Review*, vol. 11, no. 1, 2006.

One of the aspirations of the law school has been to increase the diversity of the student population. The faculty's 'operational plan' for 2005–7 stated that 'One of the key values in the plan was "diversity"', and the faculty aimed 'to achieve a staff and student profile that broadly reflects the diversity of our society as a whole'.[16] Although many measures have been taken in pursuit of this aim, such as scholarships for rural, disadvantaged and Indigenous students, these have had little impact in countering strong forces acting to decrease diversity. Massive federal funding for private schools at the expense of government schools, the preference of parents to send children to private schools and the creaming off of the brightest children through private school scholarship schemes, combined with the ever-rising cut-off score required for entry to law school, have made the undergraduate student body increasingly clone-like, with the vast majority of students coming from private schools in Melbourne's eastern suburbs.

Between 1997 and 2008, fees from full-fee paying Australian undergraduates made an important contribution to the faculty's income, peaking in 2008 at over $6 million out of a total income of $32 million. However, the Labor Party always maintained its opposition to full-fee paying places, arguing that they bias the education system even more strongly in favour of the wealthy, effectively allowing them to buy degrees for their children, and the Rudd Labor government (surprisingly!) kept its election promise to abolish them. While this had no discernible impact on the social make-up of the undergraduate body, it forced the faculty to place even more emphasis on the postgraduate program to maintain its financial position.

In late 2006 the postgraduate coursework program was scrutinised by an external review panel, which recommended a 'substantial expansion of the JD program', while insisting that it required 'improved quality control, particularly in terms of its materials, assessment and rules'.[17] The review also recommended 'a substantial expansion and strengthening of the LLM program', with more electives and, again, improved quality control. Examining the JD, the panel found that students enjoyed the small class sizes, flexible timetable and range of different learning styles, but there was some concern with variable teaching quality among the sessional practitioner teachers. There was also concern that some teachers appeared

---

16 Faculty Board minutes, 22 July 2004.

17 'Review of Postgraduate Coursework: Report of the External Review Panel', Faculty Board minutes, 4 April 2007

to assess JD students more gently than LLB students and that there was no provision for prizes or honours in the JD.

The number of students in the JD program increased from 36 EFTSL in 2002 to 116 in 2008 and then exploded to 599 in 2012. The number of students in the LLM by coursework program also grew rapidly. The two programs became one of the faculty's main sources of revenue. In 2005 revenue from the programs was $3.5 million and by 2012 it reached $11.6 million – over twenty-five per cent of the faculty's income. The income from postgraduate education is critical for supporting other areas of the faculty's activities, especially the expansion of research. Arie Freiberg points out that without this income, and with the phasing out of full-fee paying undergraduate students, it was likely that both academic and administrative staff numbers would have had to be substantially reduced.

There is intense competition for postgraduate students, most directly with Melbourne, but increasingly also with the new law schools as they expand their postgraduate programs. This competition has somewhat perverse implications for the quality of the programs. On the one hand it is vital that they are perceived to be of high quality, but on the other it is detrimental if they are seen as more difficult than competing programs. It is a fine balancing act to get this right, as was shown in the 1990s when Monash's LLM program, while unquestionably of higher quality than Melbourne's, was also significantly more challenging, and this led to a collapse in enrolments.

The opening of the city chambers at 472 Bourke Street in 2002 was a vital step in reviving the Monash postgraduate program. In October 2004 the university agreed to fund the fitting out of another floor of the building, enabling the further expansion of city-based postgraduate courses. In 2008 the faculty was told that there were to be substantial building works in and around the Bourke Street building and the opportunity was taken to lease premises at 555 Lonsdale Street, which were both closer to the heart of the legal precinct and substantially larger than the Bourke Street premises. The move was made in June 2011 and has proved highly successful, with the premises becoming not only the location for the graduate programs, but also a popular venue for lectures, seminars and conferences run by the faculty, the university and external bodies.

However, the smooth progress of the city buildings was in stark contrast to the uncertainty and indecision surrounding the future of the law building at Clayton. Soon after the fourth floor was added in 1993, talk began about the need for a major refurbishment of the building. In October 2002 the dean said, 'The building clearly needs to be modernised, but we want that modernisation to be driven by educational principles; in particular, how we think that law teaching at Monash should take place in the future.'[18]

These adverse comments prompted the faculty to allocate $3.5 million to spend on the building in 2005–6. However, before the money was spent, the possibility arose of moving to a new building as part of a planned development of the 'western precinct' of the Caulfield campus, rather than renovating the Clayton building. Early in 2006 a master planning committee was set up to consider the two options, with the promise that 'staff and students will be involved at all stages of the planning process'.

On 4 April 2007, Arie Freiberg gave a presentation to the faculty board on the alternatives, which was followed by 'by extensive but inconclusive discussion'. Caulfield was favoured for its location and its excellent public transport, and some liked the smaller campus. The proponents of Clayton queried timetabling and transport issues for double degree students, the lack of campus life at Caulfield and possible problems if the law library was at Caulfield with the Matheson library at Clayton. The promise of a completely new building at Caulfield as opposed to a refurbished building at Clayton was an argument that convinced many. With Melbourne law school having recently moved into a glamourous new building close to the city, some believed it was vital for Monash to be able to match this.

Discussions continued through 2007 and finally on 20 March 2008 a staff meeting resolved by a narrow majority to move to Caulfield. Architects Bligh Voller Nield prepared a concept design for a building which promised an environment of exciting modernity in sharp contrast to the genteel shabbiness of Clayton. Early in 2009 the plans for the building were approved by the Glen Eira City Council, but world events then intervened to derail the scheme. In April the dean reported that:

> The University is still awaiting advice from the developers of the Western Precinct, Equiset, as to whether the whole development will proceed. The prolonged uncertainty about the status of the development is primarily due to the global financial crisis and the difficulties of sourcing finance. However, funding for the law building itself, which is only one component of the development, has been committed by the University.[19]

---

18 Faculty Board minutes, 15 October 2002.

19 Ibid., 1 April 2009.

When advice did come from Equiset (a subsidiary of the Grollo group) it was to the effect that the financial crisis had made it impossible to secure finance. The university then terminated its development agreement with Equiset. Subsequent attempts to move the project along have all failed and, at the time of writing, the whole question of the future physical location of the law school is uncertain, with the choice still being between Caulfield and Clayton, but with the new possibility of building on one of the car parks at Clayton.

The Freiberg era saw the final passing of the old academic lifestyle. Worsening staff:student ratios, the greatly increased use of casual staff for teaching, the need to publish often and in top journals, the incessant pressure to win research grants and the greatly increased administrative workload have transformed academia. The last of the non-publishers were eased out in the early years of Freiberg's deanship and now it is impossible to make a career as a legal academic without both a PhD and a substantial publication record.

Almost without exception today's academic staff lament the decline in collegiality in the faculty over recent years, with most pointing to the end of the tradition of morning and afternoon tea as the symbol of this decline. Increased pressure of work, the development of technology that both enables people to work from home and means that physical access to the library is no longer essential, and the requirement for many to teach at the city chambers have all contributed to make the law school a much quieter place than in earlier years.

In October 1998 there were eight new appointments to continuing lectureships in the law school. All of them were women. The number of women on the academic staff had been gradually increasing since the 1960s, but 1998 saw the achievement of numerical equality and the percentage of women on the academic staff has remained at slightly over fifty per cent ever since. Equality at senior levels has been harder to achieve. In 1998, following the retirement of Enid Campbell, Marcia Neave was left as the only female professor and early the following year the faculty's 'affirmative action working group' reported that its 'main focus ... over the past two years has been on career development in order to encourage women to apply for more senior positions'.[20] The next fourteen years saw this barrier largely overcome, with nine out of nineteen professorial appointments, along with a majority of appointments to associate professor, being women.

---

20 Ibid., 21 April 1999.

The success in overcoming barriers to gender equality in the law school has had one unintended consequence. As the dean's report to the faculty board noted in October 2006:

> Because of the gender balance requirement on University Committees, and the relatively high proportion of women at senior levels in the faculty compared with the wider University, female Law academics are frequently called upon to participate on Committees, resulting in high demands on senior academic women from the Law School. The overworking of women on University Committees equates to less time for research and other duties.[21]

The rapid growth in the number of professors – a direct reflection of the faculty's increased ability to fund them – led to the gradual abandonment of the tradition of naming chairs after eminent legal figures. The names had never done more than deliver a certain gravitas to the title of the holder as they carried with them neither endowments nor obligations, but they seem to have disappeared almost by accident as their holders retired and new professors were not given the titles. As of 2012, the only remaining holder of a chair named for a distinguished judge is HP Lee, the Sir John Latham professor.

One new named chair, however, was established in the early 2000s. Following the retirement of Louis Waller in 2001, the faculty honoured his contribution over thirty-five years with the establishment of the Louis Waller chair and a large-scale fundraising effort raised sufficient capital to endow the chair. Soon after Arie Freiberg's arrival it was decided that the establishment of the chair should be a central plank of the strategy to boost research, with the holder to be associate dean (research) with a specific brief to improve research performance and give research leadership. The first holder of the Louis Waller chair was Bernadette McSherry and, on her appointment in 2008 to a federation fellowship, she was followed by Bryan Horrigan, a Queensland Rhodes Scholar, who came to Monash from Griffith University. Both fulfilled the original vision for the chair by maintaining high quality research in their own fields and promoting a research culture throughout the faculty.

Another important facet in the push to improve research performance has been the establishment of new research centres and groups. Bernadette McSherry and Bryan Horrigan have led the way in this with the formation

---

21 Ibid., 26 October 2006.

of the Centre for the Advancement of Law and Mental Health (CALMH) and the commercial law group respectively, with another new centre being the Australian Centre for Justice Innovation (ACJI) headed by Tania Sourdin. Until her departure in 2013 to become foundation director of the Institute for Social Equity at the University of Melbourne, Bernadette McSherry was one of the most highly regarded researchers in the law school. Her interest in mental health and the law – together with her extraordinary success in gaining research grants – led in 2011 to the establishment of CALMH to promote research into the intersections between law, policy and mental health issues. With McSherry as director and Penny Weller and Ian Freckleton as deputy directors, the centre soon attracted a significant number of PhD students and developed an ambitious research program.

Set up under the leadership of UNSW graduate Tania Sourdin, the ACJI is a joint initiative between the law school and the Australasian Institute for Judicial Administration. Its main focus is on non-adversarial justice research and practice, including facilitative, advisory and adjudicative forms of dispute resolution. In 2013 it was engaged on several major projects covering issues ranging from pre-action protocols and restorative justice conferencing to self-represented litigants and timeliness.

Since the departure of Bob Baxt and the closure of the Centre for Commercial Law, commercial law had been something of a backwater at Monash, in spite of its ever-increasing importance in the wider economy. An important step in rebuilding the faculty's strength in this area was the appointment of Stephen Barkoczy in 2006. Barkoczy had studied Arts/ Law at Monash beginning in 1981, choosing Monash over Melbourne in part at least because Monash has more tennis courts. Back in the 1980s Monash was the 'life be in it' university and for many students the sporting facilities were a big attraction. Barkoczy spent a lot of time on the tennis courts and was actively involved with the Monash Ski Club where he was president for a year. In his Arts course he majored in languages, studying Indonesian and Malay. After commencing his legal career working for two small firms, he came back to Monash to teach tax in the Faculty of Business and Economics while studying a master of taxation law taught by Harry Reicher, Jeff Waincymer, Rick Krever and Tony Pagone. He went on to complete a PhD thesis on tax and venture capital law in 2002. In 2006 he came back to the law school where he has built up a reputation as an outstanding teacher and a prodigious researcher. His teaching has been recognised with the dean's Award for Teaching Excellence, the vice-chancellor's Award for Teaching Excellence and an Australian Learning and Teaching Council Award for Teaching Excellence in Law. In 2008, he received the Prime Minister's Award for Australian University Teacher of the Year. During 1991 and 1992, Barkoczy was national tax director of the accounting firm Pannell Kerr Forster and from 1998 to 2010 he was a consultant with Blake Dawson (now Ashurst). In 2011, he was appointed by the federal government to the venture capital committee of Innovation Australia.

Another critical appointment in the commercial area was Bryan Horrigan, who came as the Louis Waller professor and associate dean, research, in 2008. Bryan Horrigan worked to raise the profile of commercial law, leading in 2010 to the formation of the Commercial Law Group. By 2013 there were about thirty faculty members actively engaged in a broad range of commercial research and teaching. Horrigan completed an Arts/Law course at the University of Queensland before winning a Rhodes scholarship. He was awarded a DPhil from Oxford in 1983 for his thesis on 'Limits of Judicial Reasoning with particular reference to decisions of the Australian High Court to overrule its previous decisions'. His supervisor was John Finnis, the highly distinguished professor of law and legal philosophy at Oxford, who has had an abiding influence on Horrigan's career.

Returning to Australia, Horrigan planned to go the bar, but circumstances led to him working with leading Brisbane firm Feez Ruthning (now part of Allens Linklaters). He also began teaching in the masters program at QUT. Although he continued to work as a consultant until his appointment as dean, increasingly his interest was in academia. He taught at QUT, University of Canberra and Macquarie University before coming to Monash in 2008, and at various times was director of the National Centre for Corporate Law and Policy Research, deputy director of the National Institute for Governance, and foundation co-director of the Centre for Comparative Law, History, and Governance. Horrigan's main areas of teaching and research are in in public and corporate law and governance from Australian, transnational, and cross-disciplinary perspectives. As a consultant he advised on issues ranging from contractual good faith and unconscionable business conduct to corporate social responsibility and rights-based scrutiny of legislation, and he published widely on these issues. He also served on the expert panels of several significant government inquiries, notably one that resulted in major reforms to the franchising code of conduct and the *Trade Practices Act* (now the *Competition and Consumer Act*) that came into effect in 2012.

The Freiberg years saw a steady increase in the number of higher degree by research students, with enrolments rising from fifty-one in 2004 to almost 100 in 2012. The majority of these have been studying for PhDs or the new doctor of juridical science (SJD), with few opting to undertake an LLM by major thesis. The SJD is a professional doctorate program that combines coursework units with a 50,000 word thesis. It was first proposed in 1992 and eventually introduced in 2002, with numbers gradually increasing each year.

The enormous effort put into the promotion of research in the Freiberg years showed signs of paying off by 2008 with the faculty being ranked second in the 'composite performance index' of the group of eight universities, a measure which ranked performance in relation to the number of higher degree by research students, research income and publications. While the various rankings lists have fluctuated over the years since, Monash law school's performance has been consistently at the top end of the scale, culminating in the achievement of the highest possible ranking in the 2012 Excellence in Research for Australia report. There is no doubt, however, that this achievement has been at the expense of increasing staff discontent with the bureaucratic requirements of modern research. As Richard Fox puts it, 'How a lawyer does research is very different from the way the government imagines it is done' and the whole system of basing research around a structure designed for the sciences has led to 'a real sense of oppression among the staff from the demands made by the university'. Further, the pressure to research is continually growing and this makes it hard not to sacrifice teaching.

During Freiberg's term as dean, the faculty's gross revenue almost quadrupled from about $11 million in 2003 to about $40 million in 2011, though the central university administration now takes about twenty-five per cent of that amount. From significant deficits in his early years, by the early 2010s the faculty was running a substantial surplus (nearly $5 million in 2011). Only about thirty per cent of the faculty's income now comes from the federal government, with student fees providing well over fifty per cent and the balance coming from other sources such as research grants and consultancy fees. During this time student numbers (EFTSL) increased from about 1700 to about 1950, but staff numbers have remained static at about 70 full-time equivalents. The number of undergraduates peaked at 1622 in 2009, but with the abolition of fee paying local places, it has since fallen to less than 1500.

In 2012 Arie Freiberg notched up a unique achievement, becoming the first dean of the Monash law school to officially retire while dean. Previous deans had been promoted to higher office (Derham and Parker), left academia (Nash and Baxt) or stepped down, with varying degrees of enthusiasm or persuasion, to continue as professors in the faculty (Waller, Campbell, Allan and Williams). Freiberg was the first to survive in office long enough to earn his gold watch. Although the university and the faculty would have been happy to see him continue as dean, he chose to step down primarily to spend more time on research and, as he said in his message to his colleagues, he 'wanted to spend more time with his footnotes'. He continues to chair the Victorian Sentencing Advisory Council.

Arie Freiberg was fortunate in his era. While the general perception is that times are tough in Australia's universities, the reality is that the current system strongly favours those disciplines able to generate fee income from overseas and postgraduate students. While law does not quite enjoy the rivers of gold that have flowed to the leading accounting schools, there is a consistently heavy demand from students for law degrees from the group of eight universities and Monash has been skilfully positioned to take advantage of this demand. As fee income soared following the establishment of the JD and the opening of the city premises, so the financial worries that bedevilled Bob Baxt and Bob Williams gradually faded. While Freiberg always carefully guarded the faculty's finances, the fact that the faculty's income was steadily rising gave him far more freedom than his immediate predecessors. As the demands of government bureaucracy and the university administration steadily grew, Freiberg was more aware than most academics that there is no better shelter from these pressures than a solid financial foundation.

Freiberg's nine years as dean saw no great crises or controversies, with the only divisive issue being the proposed move to Caulfield. Most staff members were kept too busy with the pressures to publish, win research grants and achieve good student assessments to engage in plotting or politicking. While many grumbled at increasing workloads, few blamed the dean. Similarly modern students are kept far too busy with part-time work and social media for disruptive agitations or even pranks. They caused no problems for the dean. Arie Freiberg did not see himself as a 'grand vision person' but as 'a pragmatic incrementalist offering safe, effective and financially responsible management and implementing gradual change'. Within these terms, his deanship was undoubtedly successful. By almost any measure he left the faculty in good shape.

* * *

Arie Freiberg's successor, Bryan Horrigan, cheery of face and secure of trousers, had previously held the Louis Waller chair and was associate dean, research. Horrigan inherited a faculty that was performing well by almost any measure: the finances sound, student demand for its courses high, research performance excellent and reputation glowing. His message to the Monash law school community early in 2013 was one of celebration of 'the outstanding work and personal successes of … student, staff and alumni members of our community' and the 'scholarly, professional and public impact of our members'. After two decades of rapid and radical change, the faculty had reached a position where it would be easy to sit back, relax and indulge in well-earned self-congratulation. Taking over the deanship in this environment presented Horrigan with significantly different challenges from most of his predecessors. Whereas they could win plaudits for tackling large and obvious problems, for Horrigan, nothing but continued success and upward progress will be considered adequate. He is rather in the position of a new coach of a successful football club, for whom anything less than a premiership will be considered a failure. His greatest challenge is to ensure that the faculty avoids the dangers of hubris and complacency. In his view there are many issues the faculty still needs to address, but it will be a major test of leadership to maintain the pace of change without risking losing some of the gains of recent years.

Within six weeks of Bryan Horrigan taking office two important moves were made to maintain the faculty's strengths in the basic academic roles of teaching and research. Firstly, the faculty agreed to implement the recommendations of a major curriculum review. The key features of this include a new approach to the fundamental skills and knowledge to be taught in first year, a new course framework exposing all students to public and private law and civil and criminal law, a far greater emphasis on research and the introduction of a compulsory commercial law unit. In Horrigan's view it is imperative to equip students to succeed in the best law firms, if that is where they want to make their careers, and for this an early introduction to commercial law is a great advantage. He believes it is vital to give more emphasis in the curriculum to mooting, debating and advocacy skills, and plans to give more support to the LSS mooting competitions and to students participating in international mooting competitions.

Appointed Dean in 2013, Bryan Horrigan inherited a faculty that was performing well by almost any measure.
Law Faculty website

The second early initiative was the introduction of a new research standards framework designed to maintain the outstanding research performance that resulted in the faculty receiving the highest possible score in the 2012 ERA report. Horrigan believes that research must be adequately supported and that the faculty needs to ensure that it produces the research that is needed, especially in its core areas. In his view, the faculty has expertise across far wider fields than is generally known and is looking to share this more widely by encouraging deeper engagement with all branches of the legal profession. Examples of this in 2013 included seminars on important areas of national economic regulation run by the faculty's commercial law group in collaboration with the 600 members of the Federal Court's commercial bar and the hosting of an Innovation Australia venture capital meeting to display the faculty's venture capital and innovation law capacity.

Research performance is crucial in the modern tertiary education environment, primarily because it is a central component of the various rankings which have become critical in attracting students. The faculty suffered a major blow in 2013 with the departure of one of its leading researchers, Bernadette McSherry, to Melbourne. Following this, the decision was made to abandon her research area of mental health law and consolidate and diversify the faculty's research focus in the broad thematic areas of human rights law, commercial and regulatory studies, justice system innovation, public law and governance and clinical legal education. An early success has been the achievement of the faculty's largest ARC discovery grant for a project on the design of venture capital programs to enhance the commercialisation of Australian research.

As the legal profession becomes increasingly global, Bryan Horrigan sees a strong need for the faculty to embrace internationalisation. He emphasises that two of the faculty's six campuses are overseas – at Prato and Kuala Lumpur – and he believes that it is important to develop links with the profession on a global scale and to build meaningful relationships with first class law schools around the world. A concrete example of this policy was the signing late in 2013 of an agreement with Oxford University that will enable early entry for Monash JD students to undertake the prestigious Bachelor of Civil Laws or Masters in Law and Finance. JD students who are accepted into either of these courses will begin studies at Oxford in the final semester of the JD degree, and in a year of postgraduate study earn credit to complete their JDs as well as qualify for their Oxford degree.

History does not provide a crystal ball for the future and it is impossible to foretell the future of legal education or the role and position of Monash law school. Such has been the pace of change in the last two decades that it is almost impossible to guess what the law school might be like in fifty years' time. In the immediate future, competition from the myriad new law schools will inevitably continue to grow and the rapid growth of online learning options adds a whole new element of uncertainty. Monash law school is at a high point as it celebrates its fiftieth anniversary, but it will require continual innovation, reinvention and flexibility if it is to maintain that position until its centenary and beyond.

Chapter 23

Of Judges, Silks and Severed Heads

On 16 January 2013, those who keep in touch with current events from the pages of that notable journal of record, *Perth Now*, read with interest that 'An underworld figure whose head recently washed up on a beach once claimed to have studied law at Monash with former federal treasurer Peter Costello.' The story continued:

> A long-time member of the seamier side of the racing industry in Victoria and WA, Stephen Cookson was convicted in WA in 2000 on one count of being in possession of a quantity of heroin with intent to sell or supply. He unsuccessfully appealed that conviction all the way to the High Court, where the former law student chose to represent himself.
>
> In 2005, Cookson was fined $5000 for improper conduct by WA racing authorities, namely assaulting a former horse owner Peter Graham, breaking his nose. That fine was also appealed unsuccessfully.
>
> A self-appointed "equine consultant", Cookson had been due to appear in WA's District Court this Friday on a charge of possession of methylamphetamine with intent to sell or supply …
>
> Those who knew him said he was extremely intelligent but highly volatile, well known in racing circles in his adopted state of WA and was a huge gambler.
>
> Melbourne barrister David O'Doherty, who'd acted for Cookson previously, said he was highly intelligent and well-read. Mr O'Doherty said Cookson boasted of being a member of Mensa. While he did not know if this was true, Cookson was clearly intelligent enough to qualify.
>
> Mr O'Doherty said he was a tough client to help and often did not help himself. His lost teeth, requiring attention from a dental technician,

> were another stumbling block. "He had a plate done so he could smile at the jury," Mr O'Doherty said.

Fifty years after the first law students arrived at Monash in March 1964, former students are spread far and wide through Australian society and around the world, though fortunately most not as widely dispersed as Mr Cookson. While some have served time in gaol or high political office, relatively few, it is believed, have been dismembered. There are now about 14,000 law school graduates and possibly the same number again who, like Mr Cookson, enrolled in law courses they never completed. Naturally the faculty is proud of the many alumni who have scaled the heights, primarily, of course, in the law, but also in politics, business, the arts, community service and many other fields. Many have been mentioned in this book and more are listed on Wikipedia for those who enjoy perusing these things.[1] Of those who perhaps just missed out on being classified as notable, probably about half have carved out careers in the law, while others have used the skills and qualifications gained at Monash to pursue many different roles, ranging from radio personality to spy.

If a staff member or student from 1969 (when the faculty was ensconced in its new building) were to be transported in time to the law school of today, what would be familiar and what would be surprising? The law building is fundamentally the same, in spite of its general shabbiness, the addition of the fourth floor and the recent demolition of the ramp and rebuilding of the main staircase, though the increasing redundancy of the library as the 'living heart of the law school' would bemuse the time traveller. Both staff and students would be surprised by the sleepiness of the campus and the lack of interest in politics. Even more surprising would be the impact of new technologies on everything from reading cases and listening to lectures to communications between staff and students and the dummy-like dependency today's students appear to have on their mobile devices. The bus service is better than it was, but only the most optimistic would have hoped that Monash might have its own train line. Demands by both students and staff have resulted in a shuttle bus service between all campuses, easing the burden of driving between campuses. Parking is still a central part of the Monash experience, though the radicals of 1969 would be appalled at the passive acceptance of hefty parking fees. The core curriculum would be comfortingly familiar, though the students of 1969 would be envious of today's range of options, the low

---

1 http://en.wikipedia.org/wiki/Monash_University_Faculty_of_Law#Notable_alumni.

fail rate and the way honours grades are handed out like lollies at a children's party. On the other hand, today's students might argue persuasively that on average they probably study just as hard even though the large majority have part-time jobs and they almost all have a significantly greater burden of fees.

It is chastening to reflect on David Derham's scathing critique of the worst form of legal education current in the early 1960s, which was characterised by 'Little or no teacher/student contact, little or no supervised work by the students, little or no student work concerned with original materials, and, for the majority of students, a strong temptation to satisfy all requirements by cramming potted information in short periods before examinations.'[2] A central part of his vision for the Monash law school was to ensure that it gave more than this basic conveyor-belt education. Until about 1990, the faculty's excellent staff:student ratio allowed it to come close to realising Derham's aspirations. Since that time, however, there has been an almost complete return to the kind of undergraduate legal education that Derham abhorred, 'fairly simple and very cheap' but with 'very little else to recommend it'. Ever-increasing student numbers and lower funding per student have led to larger classes, the abandonment of Socratic teaching, a reduction in assessed written work and a return to exams as the primary form of assessment. The changes have met with no opposition from students. On the contrary, they have provided much of the impetus for them. The competition between law schools to attract students and the evaluation of teaching by student popularity polls means that students are now in a far more powerful position than ever before. The vast majority of students will always choose shorter and easier over longer and harder. Student evaluation inevitably encourages 'spoon feeding' and 'dumbing-down', because students will praise lecturers who mark easily and present information in a way that can easily be regurgitated in exams.

However, the time traveller would be much more enamoured with the JD course and the way it is taught. David Derham believed that law should ideally be a postgraduate course (hence the establishment of the BJuris/LLB course as the closest achievable in the 1960s), and he would surely be delighted by the JD course, with its mature students, small, seminar-style classes and access to a wide range of electives from the masters program, though he would be astonished by the scale of fees and the faculty's reliance on them.

---

2 Derham, 'Legal Education in Australia', pp. 55–6.

The students of 1969 would probably look favourably on the development of the clinical program. Its close links with the community legal service movement would appeal to the more radical students of the late 1960s, while many others would appreciate the taste of real-life legal practice it provides. About 4000 of the 14,000 Monash law graduates have experienced the clinical program and for many of them it is the major feature that distinguishes Monash from other law schools.

The visitor from 1969 would be comforted by seeing the familiar and barely altered face of Louis Waller around the law school, though it is many years since he lectured in a gown or terrified first year students with his probing questioning. Whereas in 1969 Waller was one of only four professors, now the name plates on almost every third door indicates a professor lurks within. An even bigger change than the proliferation of professors has been the feminisation of the academic workforce and the growing number of women in senior roles, though Enid Campbell remains the only female dean. The growth in the faculty's non-academic staff would also surprise the time traveller from 1969. Allan York and a handful of secretaries handled the administration and typing in 1969, while now there is a bevy of marketing, finance, communications, human resources, library, IT and other professional staff. In spite of this, the administrative load for academic staff has greatly increased, as the business demands of the central university administration and the government have risen rapaciously.

For the staff members of 1969, one of the greatest changes they would observe would be the transformation of research. In 1969 only a small proportion of legal academics were research active. Few had PhDs and most published sporadically, if ever. Today it is rare for a new appointment not to have a PhD and those who do not publish regularly in top journals are quickly moved on. In 1969, the faculty's research report noted that 12 staff members (out of 40 full-time academic staff) had been responsible for the production of 4 books and 20 articles. The most recent research report notes 9 authored books, 7 edited books and compilations, 38 book chapters and 100 refereed journal articles, along with numerous reports, notes, book reviews and the like, with almost all full-time staff making at least one contribution. Perhaps even more startling than the exponential growth in the number of publications has been the expansion in the range of subjects that have become legitimate topics of legal research. The academic of 1969 would have stared with blank incomprehension at titles such as *Code Wars: 10 Years of P2P Software Litigation*, *Mabo in the Courts: Islander Tradition to Native Title*, 'Moving towards a sustainable, low carbon-intensive energy future', 'A transformative perspective on public-private partnerships', and 'It makes no sense: adoption by same-sex couples in Australia'.[3] From the earliest years, Monash academics were pioneers in many new areas of legal research, beginning with Elizabeth Eggleston's studies of Aboriginals and the law in the late 1960s. In the 1970s there was the work of Jim Lahore on intellectual property, Bob Baxt on trade practices and Peter Hanks and Terry Carney on poverty and social security law. Later there were Louis Waller's work on the legal ramifications of in vitro fertilisation, Henry Finlay's pioneering studies of the legal implications of changing sex, Neville Turner's work on sport and the law, Peter Heffey's highly influential article on the duty of care of schools and teachers, Christie Weeramantry's ground-breaking publications on the illegality of nuclear weapons, and Kumar Amaresakara's intensely personal writing on euthanasia. Since 2000 there has been the work on human rights of David Kinley, Sarah Joseph, Julie Debeljak, Melissa Castan and other members of the Castan Centre, Bernadette McSherry on mental health and the law, Susan Kneebone on migration, refugees and human trafficking, and Melissa de Zwart, Graham Hodge, Christine Parker and others on privatisation and regulation, none of which were considered as legitimate or even possible topics of legal research in the 1960s.

In 1969 university rankings were unknown and, given that there was no real competition between universities, unnecessary. The only comparator of any interest was with Melbourne, the *alma mater* of half the staff, and the preferred university to which most of the students would have gone if they could. Today rankings are regarded as being of critical importance and Monash is still basking in the glow of being declared the thirteenth best law school in the world in one survey (admittedly one which appears to ignore all European universities), but it is only reluctantly that the faculty's website

3 Rebecca Giblin, *Code Wars: 10 Year of P2P Software Litigation,* Edward Elgar Publishing, 1st ed, 2011; Bryan Keon-Cohen, *Mabo in the Courts: Islander Tradition to Native Title: A Memoir,* Australian Scholarly Publishing, 1st ed, 2011; Rowena Cantley-Smith, 'Moving Towards a Sustainable, Low Carbon-Intensive Energy Future: Key Challenges and Responses' in Lillian Wylie and Pascaline Winand (eds), *Energy and the Environmental Challenge: Lessons From the European Union and Australia,* Peter Lang, 2011, pp. 393–406; Carsten Greve and Graeme Hodge, 'A Transformative Perspective on Public-Private Partnerships' in Tom Christensen and Per Laegreid (eds), *The Ashgate Research Companion to New Public Management,* Ashgate, 2011, pp. 265–277; Adiva Sifris and Paula Gerber, 'It Makes No Sense: Adoption by Same-Sex Couples in Australia' in Victor Marsh (ed), *Speak Now: Australian Perspectives on Same-Sex Marriage,* Clouds of Magellan, 2011, pp. 211–221.

admits that Melbourne is ranked (an equally dubious) fifth.[4] Bob Williams, the most thoroughly committed Monash person in the history of the law school, believes that the existence of the Melbourne law school has been 'the decisive feature in the history of Monash law'. From its formation, Monash had a battle to gain firstly acceptance and later prestige from the legal profession. The faculty's research is compared with universities around the world, but the comparisons that matter are entirely with Melbourne. Until the changes brought about by the 'Melbourne model', probably the most closely scrutinised numbers in the Monash law school were the relative entry scores and first preferences for Monash and Melbourne. When Elizabeth Lanyon came to Monash from private practice, she found that Monash was always looking over its shoulder at what Melbourne was doing – even though Monash was far ahead of Melbourne at that time – and this continued while Melbourne caught up and passed Monash again during the 1990s.

One of the most significant features of the Monash law school has been the persistence of the culture that was established and maintained by Louis Waller and Enid Campbell, David Derham's most significant appointments. Waller and Campbell both remained at Monash for the rest of their long careers and grew to be larger than life figures who had a profound impact on succeeding generations of academics and students. While Waller and Campbell both served short terms as dean, their influence came from their powerful intellects, strong personalities and memorable teaching rather than any formal positions of authority. Other long-serving academics who joined the staff in the late 1960s and early 1970s and largely shared Waller and Campbell's approach to the law included Francis Trindade, HP Lee, Richard Fox, and, most notably, Bob Williams. The law school they shaped was characterised by the centrality of criminal law, with constitutional, administrative and international law as major strengths, and the marginalisation of commercial law. The pervasiveness of the culture was shown by the failure of Bob Baxt's attempts to boost commercial law in the 1980s. Baxt was, with the possible exception of Stephen Parker, the most dynamic and innovative dean in the faculty's history, but all his vigour proved ineffective against the passive resistance of those who did not believe that commercial law was real law, combined with the difficulty of recruiting commercial lawyers.

---

4 http://www.topuniversities.com/university-rankings/university-subject-rankings/2013/law-and-legal-studies, accessed 15 June 2013.

The Monash law school culture has also been shaped by its isolation and distance from the city, which has led to an inevitable detachment both from the profession and the business world. If anything, this tendency has strengthened over time as increasing traffic has made the journey from the city to Clayton ever more unpleasant. Again, in the 1980s Bob Baxt worked energetically to build bridges to business and the profession, but the 1990s saw a rapid reversion to isolation. Whether the city premises will help overcome this is still an open question.

On the other hand, Monash's isolation from the profession and business has aided the cause of Pericles against the plumber. With typically Australian lack of vision, the profession and business almost always call for the law school to produce graduates with all the practical skills required to be productive from their first working day. The Periclean aims of teaching students to think and to understand the theoretical, philosophical and historical underpinnings of the law are widely derided by those who see themselves as being in the 'real world'. The law school's ability to resist this pressure and maintain a balance between Pericles and the plumber is shown by the large number of contextual, theoretical and philosophical units available as options. The plumbers are left shaking their heads over subjects such as Legal Philosophy; Lawyers, Literature and Cinema; Law, Gender and Feminism; and Comparative European Legal Systems. Would suburban solicitors look to employ graduates who had taken Great Books of the Common Law? This subject was described in the 2013 handbook:

> This unit begins with a detailed discussion of several well-known cases from the common law of Contract. The goal is to notice the gaps between the rules and the ultimate decisions. The course continues with a discussion of Max Weber's classical statement of how legal questions are decided in the civil law and his suggestion that adjudication in the common law is irrational. The unit then attempts to respond to Weber's challenge by focusing on the classical discussion of this question by some of the great theorists of the common law, together with contemporary writers who contribute to the same discussion. Students will read and discuss chapters by several writers, including Blackstone, Holmes, Maitland, Cardozo, Llewellyn, Hart and Sachs, Gilmore, Posner, Unger, Frug, Williams, and Fisher. Emphasis will be on discussion, both the discussion among the theorists themselves and our own discussion with the competing traditions that we discover in the reading.

The balance in the continuing battle between Pericles and the plumber has also been tilted in favour of Pericles by the pressure on the faculty since the late 1990s to boost its research output. The increasing need to research and publish has led to a marked resurgence of the academy away from the profession, with academics increasingly focused on producing research for publication in academic journals. The faculty's recent research reports reveal a steady increase in the proportion of publications that could be broadly categorised as 'Periclean'. As academics generally enjoy teaching in their areas of research, this has been a strong contributing factor in the increasing number of Periclean subjects on offer.

Internationalisation also favours Pericles. Around the world the leading law schools are not jurisdiction specific – students do not come out of Harvard qualified to practise in the Commonwealth of Massachusetts or anywhere else. As the market for legal education becomes increasingly global, there is awareness that international students will be attracted by a reputation for high quality teaching and research (as measured in world rankings) rather than the promise that a degree would meet the requirement to practise in Victoria. While it is hard to foresee that the Monash law school might cease to design its curriculum around the requirements of the Council of Legal Education, the idea does not seem as absurd in 2014 as even ten years earlier.

It is hazardous to predict the future of legal education or of the Monash law school, but for the foreseeable future there is a certain comfort in the knowledge that every March another cohort of fresh-faced new students will eagerly file into the lecture theatres (or perhaps more likely, listen online) to hear the initial utterings of the lecturers in their first law subjects. These first words will range from the traditional 'Um' to eloquent paeans of praise to the majesty of the law. Perhaps it will be expecting too much for any future lecturer to top Louis Waller's startling sentence with which he introduced generations of students to the study of criminal law, 'Imagine, if you will, that I am Queen Victoria'.

The Academic's Thinking Song (aka the Monty Python Philosophers' Drinking Song)

Now,
Louie Waller was a bloody fine scholar, who was
very very able
David Derham didn't keep a harem, but the
Law School wears his label
Robert Baxt was never never lax, Timid
or un – com – fort able, and
Gerry Nash was hardly ever rash, he was
funny and so stable…, (there's)

Nothing Williams couldn't teach 'bout
Evidence and Crime
And He's done so here for such a
bloody long time! (Bom bom) The

Ladies Campbell they would never ramble, But they'd
easily kill a bloke with a puff of smoke
Fox they say would work away On a
hundred thousand footnotes every day
Prof Pittard laboured oh so hard with
Morris in the air, and
Mc-Credie and Jones heard the student groans, but were
scrupulously fair! …Peter

Hanks he sold his soul when he signed
Onto that bar roll
A hairy little fella who tended to be droll!

Jim Lahore was rarely a bore, he
talked until his throat was sore
HP Lee's never tried to flee, since he
came here from a-cross the sea
Marcia Neave, well she just went on leave, she's
now the stuff of fable, and
Judd Epstine was very fond of wine, he could
drink you under the table. (Our)

Brian Dwyer's been a tryer since
property be - gan, and
Yetty Bryant's hardly been a
flash in the faculty pan!

F. Trindad is a really good sport, when it
comes to teaching personal torts
Our Beth Gaze spends all of her days
Helping straights as well as all the gays
Sue McNicol was never ever fickle, Neville
Turner loved the Bard
Heffey doesn't rhyme but given now the time, it
shouldn't prove too hard.….Those

Seventies saw Peter Balmf'd,
David Allen Thrive!
Bloody lucky now, so glad we did survive!

Ian Gray, we	all did say he'd
Make Chief Magis	-trate one day,
Young Ms Tate, she	never did wait, top
speed to Solicitor	General's gate,
Judge Rozenes, yeah	we concur, your
Court's a real big	stir, with their
public private	partnership ya
finance is a	blur! ... Stephen
Parker came to	us with all his
internation'l	style, whilst
Christy, Wicky	and Guy Poles dreamt
of some far flung	Isle!
Mar – i - lyn	(of Warren kind), Chief
Justice she did	quickly find,
Stuart M-o-rris	happy with the horrors of the
VCAT system;	planning blind
Arie F. he	is tone deaf so his
rhymes to us did	send, but with his
mate Jon Faine	inter-viewed again, they
drive us	round the bend! and
Yes the Law School's really been a	
	bloody good 'ol place
Forty short years, And we	don't forget a face!
Forty short years, And we	don't forget a face! **Ooi!!!**

Academic's Thinking Song.

To celebrate the 40th anniversary of the Faculty, Arie Freiberg created the initial version of 'the Academic's Thinking Song' based on the Monty Python sketch of the 'Philosopher's Drinking Song'. Graeme Hodge then extended it to include some of the Faculty's famous graduates (Ian Gray, Pamela Tate, Michael Rozenes, Marilyn Warren, Stuart Morris, Jon Faine) as well as other faculty academics including Stephen Parker, Peter Balmford, Susan Campbell, David Allen, Marcia Neave and Arie Freiberg himself.

Bibliography

Archival and Other Unpublished Sources

Matheson, Sir Louis. Draft manuscript of autobiography, *Still Learning*, Rare Books Collection, Matheson Library

Monash University, Faculty of Law, Advisory Board Minutes, 1963–1965

Monash University, Faculty of Law, Faculty Board Minutes, 1965–2013

Monash University Archives

MON 1 Administration Correspondence Files, alpha-numeric

MON 8 David Derham Personnel File

MON 662 Peter Louis Waller subject files

MON 806 Faculty of Law Dean's subject correspondence files

MON 974 Administration Correspondence Files, annual single number

MON 1096 Faculty of Law, Faculty Office subject files

University of Melbourne Archives

1968.0027, Derham, David Plumley, Sir (1920–1985), 1951–1964

Williams, Bob. 'Some Reflections on Monash', notes to the authors, 10 November 2011

Monash University and Monash Law School Publications

Clayton's Law

Counter-Faculty Handbooks

In Gremio Legis

Law Matters

Lot's Wife

Monash Memo

Monash Reporter

Monash University Calendar

Monash University Gazette

Monash University Law Review

Nadi Kilau (journal of the Malaysian Law Students Association)

Pobble

Snark

Books and Articles

Anderson, Tom, *The Objectives of Legal Education in Victoria: Rhetoric, Restraint and Reality. A Study of Melbourne and Monash University Law Schools*, Melbourne University Student Union, Melbourne, 1990.

Aubin, Tracey, *Peter Costello: A Biography*, Harper Collins, Sydney, 1999.

Ayres, Philip (ed.), David Derham, *Talks on Universities, History and the Law*, Oryx Publishing, Melbourne, 2009.

Balmford, Peter, 'The Foundation of the Monash Law School', *Monash University Law Review*, vol. 15, nos 3 and 4, 1989.

Bartlett, Carol C, 'Towards Professional Competence – Clinical Legal Education', *Law*

Institute Journal, vol. 56, no. 2, March 1982.

Bird, Greta, 'Race, Ethnicity, Class and Gender: Integral Issues for a Law Curriculum?', *Crosscultural Communication and Professional Education*, 1990.

Bird, G, Campbell, S, Barbaryannis, M, Smith, H, 'Preparing Lawyers for a Multi-Cultural Society', *Journal of Professional Legal Education*, 1986.

Blaze, Douglas A, 'Déjà Vu All Over Again: Reflections on Fifty years of Clinical Education', *Tennessee Law Review*, Vol. 65, 1997.

Campbell, Sue, 'Blueprint for a Clinical Program', *Journal of Professional Legal Education*, vol. 9, no. 121, 1991.

Carney, Shaun, *Peter Costello: The New Liberal*, Allen & Unwin, Sydney, 2001.

Committee on Australian Universities, *Report of the Committee on Australian Universities*, (Keith Murray, Chairman), Government Printer, Canberra, 1957.

Costello, Peter, and Coleman, Peter, *The Costello Memoirs: The Age of Prosperity*, Melbourne University Publishing, Melbourne, 2008.

Cowen, Zelman, *A Public Life: The Memoirs of Zelman Cowen*, Miegunyah Press, Melbourne, 2006.

Cowen, Zelman, 'Selection Processes in the Law School 1963', *Law Institute Journal*, May 1963.

Cownie, Fiona (ed.), *The Law School – Global Issues, Local Questions*, Ashgate, Brookfield, 1999.

Cownie, Fiona, *Legal Academics: Culture and Identities*, Hart Publishing, Oxford and Portland, Oregon, 2004.

Davis, Richard, *100 Years: A Centenary History of the Faculty of Law, University of Tasmania, 1893–1993*, University of Tasmania, Hobart, 1993.

Davison, Graeme, and Murphy, Kate, *University Unlimited: The Monash Story*, Allen & Unwin, Sydney, 2012.

Derham, D P, 'Beginning a Law School at Monash', *Monash University Gazette*, vol. III, no. 1, September 1966.

[Derham, Sir David], 'A Conversation with David Derham', in two parts, *Law Institute Journal*, December 1982 and February 1983.

Derham, David P, 'Legal Education', *New Zealand Universities Law Review*, vol. 2, 1966–67.

Derham, D P, 'Legal Education and Training for Practice', *Law Institute Journal*, December 1966

Derham, David, 'Legal Education in Australia', *The Australian University*, vol. 1, no. 1, August 1963.

Derham, D P, 'Legal Education in Victoria', *Australian Bar Gazette*, vol. 1, no. 4, December 1964.

Derham, D P, 'Problems of University Selection; the Story of a Quota', *Ormond Papers*, vol. I, no. 3, 1967.

Derham, David P, 'A Venture as yet Unproved', *Melbourne Studies in Education*, 1963.

Dixon, Marion, *Thirty Up: The Story of the UNSW Law School 1971–2001*, UNSW Law School, Australia, 2001.

Farouque, Farah, and Freund, Peter, 'Champion of Family Laws, a Survivor of Tyranny', obituary of Henry Finlay in the *Age*, 6 August 2005.

Farrar, John, 'Professor David Allan, AM', *Bond Law Review*, vol. 15, no. 2, 2003.

Frank, Jerome, 'Why Not a Clinical Lawyer-School', *University of Pennsylvania Law Review*, vol. 81, no. 8, June 1933.

Freiberg, Arie, 'Deaning Down-Under', *University of Toledo Law Review*, vol. 38, 2007.

Giddings, Jeff, *Promoting Justice through Clinical Legal Education*, Justice Press, Melbourne, 2013.

Goldsmith, Andrew, 'Standing at the Crossroads: Law Schools, Universities, Markets and the Future of Legal Scholarship' in Fiona Cownie (ed.), *The Law School – Global Issues, Local Questions*, Ashgate, Brookfield, 1999.

Goldsmith, Andrew, 'Heroes or Technicians? The Moral Capacities of Tomorrow's Lawyers', *Journal of Professional Legal Education*, 1996.

Griswold, Erwin, N, 'Observations on Legal Education in Australia', *Journal of Legal Education*, vol. 5, 1952.

Hanks, Peter, 'Elizabeth Eggleston', *Oracle*, 1977, p. 72.

Hanks, Peter, 'A New Law Curriculum', *Law Institute Journal*, vol. 45, no. 11, November 1971.

Harman, Grant, 'New Directions in Internationalizing Higher Education: Australia's Development as an Exporter of Higher Education Services', *Higher Education Policy*, No. 17, 2004.

Hyams, Ross, 'Multidisciplinary Clinical Legal Education: The Future of the Profession', *Alternative Law Journal*, June, 2012, vol. 37, no. 2.

Greening, Hulbert A, 'Presidential Address', *Law Institute Journal*, April 1962.

Greenwood, Kerry, *It Seemed Like a Good Idea at the Time: A History of the Springvale Legal Service 1973–1993*, Faculty of Law, Monash University, 1994.

Hiscock, Reginald, 'David Allan, 1928–2006', *Bond University Law Review*, vol. 18, no. 1, June 2006.

Lacey, Nicola, *A Life of HLA Hart: The Nightmare and the Noble Dream*, Oxford University Press, Oxford, 2004.

Laird, Cathy, 'Legal Education: Theory or Practice?', *Law Institute Journal*, November 1996

Lawson, F H, *The Oxford Law School, 1850–1965*, Oxford University Press, Oxford, 1968.

MacCrate, Robert, 'Educating a Changing Profession: From Clinic to Continuum', *Tennessee Law Review*, Vol. 64, No. 4, 1997.

Mackinolty, John and Judy, *A Century Down Town: Sydney University Law School's First Hundred Years*, Sydney, 1991.

Marginson, Simon, *Monash: Remaking the University*, Allen and Unwin, Sydney, 2000.

Martin, Sir Leslie, *Tertiary Education in Australia: Report of the Committee on the Future of Tertiary Education in Australia*, 2 vols, Commonwealth Government Printer, Canberra, 1965.

Matheson, Sir Louis, *Still Learning*, Macmillan, Melbourne, 1980.

McInnis, Craig, and Marginson, Simon, *Australian Law Schools after the 1987 Pearce Report*, AGPS, Canberra, 1994.

Nash, Gerard, 'Clinical Education in Australia – The Monash Experience', *Council on Legal Education for Professional Responsibility, Inc.*, vol. XII, no. 1, October 1979.

Nash, Gerard, 'Skills Course or Clinic?', *The Australian Law Journal*, Vol. 54, September 1980.

Naylor, Bronwyn and Hyams, Ross, Innovation in Clinical Legal Education: Educating Lawyers for the Future, *Alternative Law Journal*, monograph, no. 1, 2007.

New, Victor, 'Clinical Legal Education at Monash', *Law Institute Journal*, vol. 51, no. 8, August 1977.

Noone, Mary Anne, 'Australian Community Legal Centres – The University Connection', Jeremy Cooper and Louise G Trubek (eds), *Educating for Justice: Social Values and Legal Education*, Ashgate Dartmouth, Aldershot, 1997.

O'Keefe, Kevin, *Paddy's Road: Life Stories of Patrick Dodson*, Aboriginal Studies Press, Canberra, 2003.

Parker, C, and Goldsmith, A, 'Failed Sociologists in the Market Place: Law Schools in Australia', *Journal of Law and Society*, 1998.

Pearce, Dennis, Campbell, Enid, and Harding, Don, *Australian Law Schools: A Discipline*

Assessment for the Commonwealth Tertiary Education Commission, 3 vols, AGPS, Canberra, 1987.

Rankin, Penny, 'Forty Years On: A Legal Review', *Monash Magazine*, no. 20, spring/summer 2007.

Smith, Simon, 'Clinical Legal Education – The Case of Springvale Legal Service', *Legal Service Bulletin*, 1974.

Summers, Kevin 'Looking for Mr Right', written August 1999, http://www.assistnet.info/kev/reith0899.htm, accessed 24 June 2013.

Tompkins, Pauline, 'Australian Higher Education and the Murray Report', *Journal of Higher Education*, vol. 29, no. 7, October 1958.

Tomsen, Stephen, 'Professionalism and State Engagement: Lawyers and Legal Aid Policy in Australia in the 1970s and 1980s', *Australia and New Zealand Journal of Sociology*, Vol. 28, No. 3, November 1992.

Trumble, Peter, 'The Council of Legal Education Course', *Law Institute Journal*, March 1963.

Twining, W L, 'Pericles and the Plumber', *Law Quarterly Review*, vol. 83, no. 3, July 1967.

Wallace, Jude and Fiocco, John, 'Recent Criticisms of Formalism in Legal Theory and Legal Education', *Adelaide Law Review*, vol. 7, no. 3, 1980.

Waller, P L, 'The Monash Law School', *Australian Bar Gazette*, no. 1, December 1966.

Waugh, John, *First Principles: The Melbourne Law School, 1857–2007*, Miegunyah Press, Melbourne, 2007.

Websdale-Morrissey, Di, *Blind Optimism: The Life of Lawrie McCredie*, Arcadia, an imprint of Australian Scholarly Publishing, North Melbourne, 2013.

Weeks, Phillipa, 'Elizabeth Moulton Eggleston', *Australian Dictionary of Biography*, vol. 14, Melbourne University Press, Melbourne, 1996, p. 84.

Weeramantry, C G, *Towards One World: The Memoirs of Judge Weeramantry*, vol. 1, 'The Sri Lankan Years', [nd] vol. II, 'The Australian Years', 2012, Weeramantry International Centre for Peace Education and Research, Colombo.

Williams, C R, 'Monash Law School in the 1990s', *Law Institute Journal*, vol. 64, 1990.

Interviews

2010

Richard Fox, Guy Powles, Robert Williams, Susan Campbell, 11 October
Jeff Giddings, 18 October
Susan Campbell, 5 November
Alan York, 6 November
Jenny Beaton, 12 November

2011

Mark Aronson, 21 February
Damian Barry, 23 March
Denis Liner, 23 March
Nahum Mushin, 23 March
Dianne O'Neill, Susan Maunder, Jan Jay, 23 March
James Kimpton, 28 March
Richard Fox, 4 April
Simon Smith, 5 April

Stephen Stern, 12 April
Tony Pagone, 3 May
David Denton, 2 June
Susan Kneebone, 7 June
Peter Haug, 14 June
Sir Zelman Cowen, 17 June
Bob Baxt, 22 June
Louis Waller, 11 July
Lyn White, 14 July
Adrian Evans, 2 and 23 August
Richard Fox, 27 September
H P Lee, 28 September
Gerry Nash, 3 October
Lawrie McCredie, 5 October
Christie Weeramantry, 10 October
Francis Trindade, 20 October
Ruth Thomas, 21 October
Barbara Jones, 26 October
Graham Hodge, 8 November
Honours Lunch: Ruth Thomas, James Kimpton, Chris Chenoweth, Bob Williams, 9 November
Arie Freiberg, 24 November
Stephen Parker, 13 December
Mary Hiscock, 13 December

2012

Adam Kempton 10 January
Basil Fogarty, 11 January
Erol Chakir, 12 January
Sarah Murray, 15 January
Marilyn Pittard, 20 January
Greg Carne 21 January
Bronwyn Naylor, 25 January and 9 February
Bryan Keon-Cohen, 12 February
Judd Epstein, 15 February
Jack Fajgenbaum, 22 February
Terry Carney, 23 February
David Kilney, 24 February
Mal McComas, 27 February
Ron McCallum, 28 February
Dorothy Kovacs, 2 March
Sue McNicol, 7 March
Julian Burnside, 7 March
Jon Faine, 7 March
Pam O'Connor, 13 March
Yuri Grbich, 21 March
Jennifer Nielsen, 23 March
Adrian Evans, 3 April
Don Greig, 21 April
Peter Bartlett, 26 April

Stephen Barkosczy, 1 May
Jack Hammond, 2 May
Jan Whitehead, 10 May
Marcia Neave, 11 May
Deborah Glass 12 May
Ray Finkelstein, 13 May
Bebe Loff, Julia Pullen, Bronwyn Naylor, 20 May
Andrew Meagher, Ross Schloefell, Zoe Bateman, Ben O'Hoy, 20 May
Mark Birrell, 22 May
Victor Purton, 22 May
Stephen Gray, 24 May
Amanda George, 9 June
Marilyn Pittard, 13 June
Jude Wallace, 15 June
Graeme Golden, 25 June
Elizabeth Lanyon, 26 June
Paul Mishura, 2 July
Sam Ricketson, 11 July
Janice Luck, 11 July
Tom May, 11 July
Anne Lahore, 17 July
Pat Kilbride, 8 August
Felicity Hampel, 8 August
Marilyn Warren, 9 August
David Rush, 16 August
Guy Powles, 20 August
Peter Hanks, 22 August
Guy Powles, 19 September
Mark Davison, 16 October
John Duns, 16 October
Richard Fox , 30 October
Maeve McDonnagh, 15 November
Dru Marsh, 29 November

2013

Mick Dodson, 9 January
Tony Howard, 6 February
Bryan Horrigan, 14 March
Jeffrey Goldsworthy 24 May
Carol Bartlett, 14 August
Inala Cooper, 20 September

Index

Note: *p* indicate photographs; *n* indicates note